1971 India–Pakistan War

50 Years Later

Editors

Sujan Chinoy
Bipin Bakshi
Vivek Chadha

MANOHAR PARRIKAR INSTITUTE FOR DEFENCE STUDIES AND ANALYSES
मनोहर पर्रिकर रक्षा अध्ययन एवं विश्लेषण संस्थान

PENTAGON PRESS LLP

First published in 2022 by

PENTAGON PRESS LLP
206, Peacock Lane, Shahpur Jat
New Delhi-110049, India
Contact: 011-64706243

Typeset in AGaramond, 11 Point
Printed by Aegean Offset Printers, Greater Noida, U.P.

ISBN: 978-93-90095-69-8 (HB)

www.pentagonpress.in

Contents

Preface

Fifty years ago, India fought for a just and humanitarian cause, and defeated a state that was responsible for the reprehensible genocide of innocent Bengalis in the erstwhile East Pakistan. The 1971 India–Pakistan War not only led to a stunning and comprehensive victory for India and for the people of East Pakistan, with highest standards of military professionalism and timely strategic decisions, it also saw the birth of a new nation—Bangladesh. The war represents one of the most significant events of the 20th century. It changed national boundaries and this was achieved over a span of mere 13 days after the commencement of hostilities on the part of Pakistan on the 3rd of December 1971.

The 1971 India–Pakistan War had far-reaching strategic implications for India, Bangladesh and Pakistan. It gave a chance to India and Bangladesh to work together for the upliftment and betterment of the lives of millions. The war paved the way for the fullest realisation of the aspirations of the people of Bangladesh who had until then been suppressed and denied equitable resources. The laudatory progress of Bangladesh since then in every sphere of socio-economic activity, as indicated by its human development index, is a clear reflection of this reality.

Wars are neither planned nor executed in isolation. The 1971 Indo-Pak War can be viewed from a number of perspectives—military, diplomatic, geopolitical, strategic, bilateral and even anecdotal to converge some of these areas of study. This edited book, comprising 17 chapters, is an attempt at presenting the military aspects of the war in great detail, while also touching upon other aspects that had a profound impact on the war.

From the military perspective, this book highlights the role of each major constituent of the conflict. This includes detailed narratives describing actions of the armed forces as well as the Mukti Bahini. The impact of the special operations in support of the main military effort has also been covered well.

It is hoped that this book would be a suitable source for those who wish to explore the military aspects of the 1971 Indo-Pak War in detail. For those who already have an in-depth understanding of the war, it provides fresh perspectives and rekindles interest in a momentous chapter in the history of the sub-continent.

I would like to compliment the contributors and also my co-editors for their painstaking efforts for coordinating and putting together this book. It is an apt commemoration marking 50 years of India's historic victory in the 1971 Indo-Pak War.

Sujan Chinoy
Director General, MP-IDSA

Acknowledgements

This edited book was planned and executed on the basis of a joint project which was initially released as a Special Issue of the *Journal of Defence Studies* (JDS), and subsequently with additional chapters in its present form as a book. The editors would like to thank the JDS Advisory Board and JDS Editorial Committee for their support and guidance during the project planning and execution stage.

Amb Sujan Chinoy, *Editor, Journal of Defence Studies*
Maj Gen (Dr) Bipin Bakshi (Retd), *Managing Editor, Journal of Defence Studies*
Adm Arun Prakash (Retd), Editorial Advisory Board member
ACM B.S. Dhanoa (Retd), Editorial Advisory Board member
Lt Gen S.K. Saini (Retd), Editorial Advisory Board member
Dr Rajan Katoch, Editorial Advisory Board member
Dr V.K. Saraswat, Editorial Advisory Board member
Shri Sanjay Mitra, Editorial Advisory Board member
Dr Sanjay Badri-Maharaj, Editorial Committee member
Dr Laxman Behera, Editorial Committee member
Col Vivek Chadha (Retd), Editorial Committee member
Gp Capt Ajey Lele (Retd), Editorial Committee member
Dr Anit Mukherjee, Editorial Committee member
Cmde Abhay K. Singh (Retd), Editorial Committee member

The editors would also like to thank the contributing authors for their hard work and timely effort for bringing out this publication. A special thanks to Ms Madhavi Ratnaparkhi, Associate Editor of JDS, who remained closely involved with the project from its inception. The team also acknowledges the efforts of Pentagon Press, especially Shri Rajan Arya, who has delivered a high-quality project.

List of Contributors

Col Guru Saday Batabyal, Retd, PhD, FRHistS, has 43 years of cross-functional experience in the Indian Army, United Nations, Industry and Academia. He is the author of many articles, book chapters and a book titled *Politico-Military Strategy of Bangladesh Liberation War, 1971*.

Lt Gen (Dr) J.S. Cheema, PVSM, AVSM, VSM, Retd, superannuated from the Indian Army in November 2017 as the Deputy Chief of the Army Staff. Post retirement, he did his doctorate in Defence and National Security Studies and is now the Vice-Chancellor of Maharaja Bhupinder Singh Punjab Sports University, Patiala.

Ms Dorothy Deb is a PhD candidate at Centre for International Politics, Organization and Disarmament, School of International Studies, Jawaharlal Nehru University, New Delhi.

Amb Shamsher M. Chowdhury, Bir Bikram, graduated as a Regular Commissioned Officer in 1969 from the Pakistan Military Academy and took active part in the Bangladesh War of Liberation in 1971. For his bravery and contribution in the battlefield, the Government of Bangladesh conferred upon him the gallantry award Bir Bikram. As a Foreign Service Officer, he has served in Bangladesh Embassies and High Commissions in various countries. He was the Foreign Secretary of Bangladesh from 2001 to 2005.

Maj Gen P.K. Chakravorty, Retd is a Senior Fellow (Veteran) at the Centre for Land Warfare Studies (CLAWS), New Delhi.

Col Vijay Yeshvant Gidh, Retd, has served as an instructor in National Security Guard (NSG) Training Centre, Manesar; Brigade Major of Jelepla Brigade; United Nations Peacekeeping Mission in Angola; Commanding Officer of 14 Punjab (Nabha Akal); and Centre Commandant, The Punjab Regimental Centre, Ramgarh Cantonment, Jharkhand.

Air Marshal Diptendu Choudhury, Retd is former Commandant of National Defence College.

Air Vice Marshal Rajesh Isser, Retd is an IAF veteran with combat experience in Kargil War, DR Congo (UNPK), Siachen Glacier and IPKF (Sri Lanka). He is a Distinguished Fellow at Centre for Air Power Studies.

Cmde Srikant B. Kesnur, VSM, Retd, is a navy historian, author and a maritime studies professional. Prior to his retirement on 30 June 2022, he was the Director, Maritime Warfare Centre, Mumbai and the Officer-in-Charge, Naval History Project. He has been Lead Author/Chief Editor of 11 books/ monographs for the Navy. He holds a Ph.D. from Mumbai University apart from five other postgraduate degrees in Sciences and Social Sciences.

Capt M. Doraibabu, NM (Gallantry) is a serving officer and is currently the Officer-in-Charge, Naval History Project authoring the forthcoming history volume of the Indian Navy for the decade 2011–2021. He has been the author of one book and Executive Editor/ lead member of six other books/ publications. He contributes regularly to defence think tanks and in-house journals. He holds an M.Phil. and two other postgraduate degrees in Defence and Strategic Studies and Telecommunications.

Cdr Ashish Kale, Retd, an alumnus of the 56th Naval Academy Course was commissioned into the Executive Branch of the Indian Navy on 1 July 1999. A recipient of the CNS Silver Medal, the officer held various Fleet & Staff appointments including the Command of a Ship, Training Commander of Indian Naval Academy and Training Coordinator/ Instructor at INS Dronacharya. He underwent the Joint Defence Staff College Course at the Ecole de Guerre, Paris wherein he received a Masters Degree from PSL University, Paris in April 2011. He also holds two other postgraduate degrees. The officer retired from Naval service on 31 October 2021.

Dr Somita Chakraborty is former Research Scholar, School of Social Science, Indira Gandhi National Open University (IGNOU). She completed Ph.D. on a theme focusing on India's diplomatic strategy to secure the sea lanes through the South China Sea.

Lt Gen Vinod Bhatia, Retd, is former Director General Military Operations (DGMO) and former Director, Centre for Joint Warfare Studies (CENJOWS).

Mr Sandeep Unnithan is Editor, News9 Plus, India's first OTT video news magazine.

Dr Saroj Bishoyi is a Strategic Affairs Analyst with main research focus on USA, India–US Relations and Indo-Pacific. He received his Ph.D. degree from the School of International Studies, Jawaharlal Nehru University, New Delhi, and was ICSSR Doctoral Fellow. He has over 12 years of post-Ph.D. research experience and has published several articles in leading journals, edited books, think tank websites, magazines and newspapers.

Dr Smruti S. Pattanaik is a Research Fellow at Manohar Parrikar Institute for Defence Studies and Analyses (MP-IDSA), New Delhi. Her area of specialisation is South Asia.

Dr Ashok K. Behuria is a Senior Fellow and Coordinator of the South Asia Centre at Manohar Parrikar Institute for Defence Studies and Analyses (MP-IDSA), New Delhi. A close observer of South Asia politics, he has been awarded the K. Subrahmanyam Award for excellence in strategic studies in 2009. He has written extensively on the regional security environment, internal political dynamics in Pakistan, conflict resolution, and the neighbourhood in research journals, news magazines in India and abroad.

Ms Karnika Jain is a Ph.D. Research Scholar at Centre for South Asian Studies, Jawaharlal Nehru University, New Delhi, former Fellow, Ryoichi Sasakawa Young Leaders Fellowship Programme (Sylff) at the Nippon Foundation and former Fellow at Institute of South Asian Studies of Sichuan University.

Ms Shruti Pandalai is an Associate Fellow at Manohar Parrikar Institute for Defence Studies and Analyses (MP-IDSA), New Delhi. Her research uses Strategic Narratives as inter-disciplinary lens to unpack the understanding of India's Foreign and Security Policy.

Introduction

Bipin Bakshi and Vivek Chadha

Five decades may not be a long time in a nation's history. It is however, long enough to take a dispassionate and objective look at events that change the path of history. The 1971 India–Pakistan War, along with the incidents that preceded it and followed its culmination, is perhaps one of the most important ones for the future of the Indian subcontinent.

It is not often that political objectives and military strategy are able to contribute in a way that assists in achieving the desired end state of a war. It is even rarer for such an end state to be achieved in a short time frame, wherein, war was still guided by the means and tools of the industrial era. The achievement is further magnified by the fact that the victorious Indian armed forces had suffered an embarrassing defeat in 1962 against China, less than a decade prior to the epochal events of 1971. Just like the Indian armed forces, the Mukti Bahini too literally rose from the ashes of a genocide, unleashed in East Pakistan by the Pakistani Army commencing on 25 March 1971, through a ruthless crackdown.

It is therefore no surprise that the combined impact created by the resolute people of Bangladesh and the professional approach of the Indian state, successfully converted a catastrophe of epic proportions into a victory of the people, won through their stoic resolve and the professionalism of the armed forces.

There have been a number of books, memoirs and articles over the years that have documented first person and academic accounts of events that marked this period of history. Not surprisingly, most were written during the period succeeding the war and after the birth of Bangladesh. This book is an attempt to evaluate events with the benefit of a five-decade time lapse. In doing so, the focus remains firmly on the military aspects of the war, accompanied by a brief account of political events, diplomacy, influence of major powers, public perception and the role of Mukti Bahini.

This project was initiated after a series of discussions in the Military Centre at the Manohar Parrikar Institute for Defence Studies and Analyses. It was meant to coincide with the 50th Anniversary of the 1971 Indo-Pak war. The first leg of the project was designed around a special issue of the *Journal of Defence Studies*. Most articles featuring in the book found a place in this special issue. However, it was simultaneously felt that a book on a similar theme can reach a distinct readership, given additional channels of distribution. Accordingly, it was planned as a follow up to the special issue. We had also hoped for additional contributions making their way, by the time the book went into publication, which is indeed the case.

The publication of this book coincides with the culmination of a year-long period during which a number of events were held to mark the momentous occasion.

Keeping the scope of the endeavour, which was a retrospective assessment of military issues associated with the 1971 Indo-Pak war, an attempt was simultaneously made to see these events through the advantage afforded by five decades of introspection. This also provided a simultaneous opportunity to contextualise events to present-day realities. The papers that form a part of this edited volume, have been threaded together keeping these objectives in perspective.

The book can broadly be divided into three core themes. The first provides a politico-military backdrop to events that led to the war. This includes a chapter titled "Politics in Pakistan and the Bangladesh Liberation War, 1971" by Col Guru Saday Batabyal. The chapter highlights the failure of the ruling elite from West Pakistan to take on board the cultural, economic and political aspirations of their East Pakistani partners. This led to a growing divide, which culminated in mass protests after the Pakistani Army decided to subvert the electoral results which would have brought Sheikh Mujibur Rahman into power, as the Prime Minister of Pakistan. Even as the author traverses the socio-political journey of Pakistan post-independence, he also explores the roots of cultural distinctiveness of an artificially created country. This narrative reinforces the fragility of a religion-based construct that Pakistan had attempted to employ for its creation. Fifty years after the 1971 war and the creation of Pakistan, the limitations of this unifying factor and its obvious contradictions are yet again coming to the fore. The resentment against domination by the Pakistani Punjab over the rest of the country, is all too obvious to ignore. This is not only reflected in the hierarchy that governs

Pakistan, but also its most powerful institution—the Pakistan Army. Batabyal highlights how the attempt at providing a newly created Pakistan a unifying identity was taken up by removing Bengali language from currency notes, postal stamps and government forms. Instead, Urdu was thrust upon the people as the state language, despite it being spoken by only 2.5 per cent of the population in East Pakistan and 7 per cent in West Pakistan.

The absence of a grassroot narrative that could bind Pakistan organically, can be seen over the years through the adoption of religious practices and military iconography that had little to do with Pakistan's historical realities. The naming of Pakistani missiles as Ghauri, Ghaznavi and Abdali are illustrative of a deep-rooted insecurity that continues to fuel competition with India.

The chapter by Lt Gen J.S. Cheema titled "India's Politico-Military Strategy for the 1971 India–Pakistan War", provides a backdrop to the politico-military strategy adopted by India. The author provides insights into the political thought process in India, diplomatic initiatives undertaken, handling of the refugee crisis, employment of Mukti Bahini and the military strategy, as it unfolded over a period of time.

The third chapter "Language, Culture and the Creation of Bangladesh" by Ms Dorothy Deb gives a background to the war and focuses primarily on the role of language and culture in the creation of Bangladesh. Deb reinforces the vicious cycle created by the dismissive attitude adopted by the Pakistani elite towards Bengali language and culture, which in turn fuelled the demand for autonomy and eventually led to the secession of the eastern half of the country.

The fourth chapter is unique in many ways. It has been written by a Bengali officer of the Pakistan armed forces as a first-person account of the crackdown that took place in East Pakistan. He describes a series of incidents that took place immediately thereafter, including the resistance put up by him and his colleagues against the violence that had been unleashed against the people. He goes on to further describe his captivity, the torture he underwent and his story of survival. Amb. Shamsher M. Chowdhury, the author of the chapter "1971, the War as I Saw It", subsequently became a diplomat, though he continues to carry the residual impact of injuries sustained through torture during those eventful years. This chapter also acts as a bridge between events preceding the war and military actions that followed the dark shadow of atrocities in East Pakistan.

These four chapters are followed by a specific focus on military issues. This has been attempted through individual chapters describing the military strategy on land, at sea and in the air. In addition, there is special emphasis on special forces operations, role of Mukti Bahini and employment of helicopters.

The first chapter by Maj Gen P.K. Chakravorty titled "Land Warfare in the Eastern Theatre: 1971 Indo-Pak War", provides a comprehensive understanding of the strategy, objectives and progress of battle over the course of the war.

This is followed by the only battle account in the book by Col Vijay Yeshvant Gidh, covering "The Battle of Garibpur". This chapter describes in detail the exploits of 14 Punjab (Nabha Akal) on 21–22 November 1971, a few days prior to the official declaration of war between the two countries.

The focus of most of the books on 1971 war has remained on the conduct of the war effort on land. A concerted attempt has been made to provide a balanced perspective through equally detailed chapters describing air and naval operations. Air Marshal Diptendu Choudhury, in his chapter "Eagle Unleashed: IAF Strategy and Operations", gives a detailed account of the air operations during the war. The chapter covers both theatres and details the impact of air operations on ground forces as also strategic targeting, including the bombing of Dacca. This action undoubtedly led to the early surrender of Pakistani forces, breaking the will of the Pakistani leadership to continue with the fight.

If the contribution of the air force is relatively less known during the 1971 war, the specific role of helicopters is even lesser so. The chapter "Sagat and Helicopters: True Pillars of Victory" by Air Vice Marshal Rajesh Isser, provides an in-depth perspective of the contribution made by helicopters in shaping the victory in the Eastern Theatre. In doing so, he also focuses on the dynamism and initiative of Lt Gen Sagat Singh, who displayed the foresight and initiative to exploit helicopters, one of the most flexible military assets during the war.

There is a reason why the Indian Navy is often referred to as the "Silent Service". Their role during the 1971 Indo-Pak war often tends to get neglected as a result. After the decision to keep the navy out of the 1965 war, 1971 provided the service an opportunity to make their presence felt as part of the wider military and national effort. The impact that the navy created not only made up for years of neglect, but also showcased the dynamism and influence that could be created on the open seas as also against shore-based targets. A comprehensive chapter by Cmde Srikant B. Kesnur, Capt M. Doraibabu and Cdr Ashish Kale titled "Operational Aspects of the 1971 War in the Maritime Domain", documents these accomplishments in detail.

A closely interlinked aspect to the naval operations during the 1971 war, was the need to protect the sea lanes, given the potential vulnerability of merchant ships. The chapter, "The Protection of Sea Lines of Communication during 1971 War" by Dr Somita Chakraborty, explores the importance of this aspect and the specific accomplishments during the war.

Special Forces operations traditionally play a crucial part in major wars. However, given the nature of such endeavours, very often, these tend to get buried under classified sections of military history. This volume dedicates two chapters to this vital aspect of military operations. Lt Gen Vinod Bhatia in his chapter "Planning and Impact of Special Operations during the 1971 Indo-Pak War", presents a detailed description of major special forces operations. This not only includes the airdrop at Tangail but also the raid on a gun position in West Pakistan, covering both theatres of war.

The second chapter by Mr Sandeep Unnithan, "The Mukti Bahini: Three Dimensional Guerillas", provides a backdrop for special forces operations and guerilla warfare as a prelude to the creation of the Mukti Bahini. He gives a brief description of how the Mukti Bahini was created and the impact made by this three-dimensional force, with its own land, air and naval arm.

One of the most important external actors that influenced the course of the 1971 Indo-Pak war was the United States of America. The US was clearly sympathetic to the Pakistani cause during this period of history. It not only attempted to diplomatically influence events, but also made a military endeavour to coerce India, through the often-quoted entry of the Seventh Fleet into the Bay of Bengal. Dr Saroj Bishoyi, in his chapter "Role of the United States in the 1971 War: Implications for India–US Relations", analyses the impact of the US in detail during this period.

The impact of information and media is often seen as a more recent phenomenon. However, even as the tools of information warfare as we know it today have changed, the role of media in shaping opinions has remained similar. Dr Smruti S. Pattanaik in her chapter, "Shaping the World Opinion: Media, War Reporting and Radio Broadcasting", discusses the role of media reporting and how it shaped opinions around the world.

The last section of the book includes three chapters, which provide a more retrospective look at events that transpired during the period. Dr Ashok Behuria in his chapter, "Did Pakistan Learn from its Bangladesh Experience?" deals with the trajectory of demands that led to the war in 1971 and assesses the lessons that Pakistan may or may not have learnt from its debacle.

Ms Karnika Jain, in her chapter, "Mistakes on Repeat Mode: Pakistan's Civil–Military Debacle", discusses the tensions between civil and military institutions in Pakistan and its impact on events that led to the 1971 war. Further, the author analyses more current secessionist challenges and the possibility of history repeating itself.

The last chapter by Ms Shruti Pandalai, "50 Years After 1971: State Narratives, People and Politics in the Subcontinent", discusses the narratives that have emerged from the countries, impacted by the events of 1971. It also provides a more contemporary perspective of these events to take a more objective view of what transpired five decades back.

This book, despite being a retrospective project, is not the culmination of scholarship on this important subject. It is merely an attempt at continuing the process of evaluating the past to derive lessons for the future. We also hope to reach the younger generations, who may not have lived those momentous times, but are provided access to one of the most important chapters in sub-continental history.

SECTION I

Politico-Military Backdrop

1

Politics in Pakistan and the Bangladesh Liberation War, 1971

Guru Saday Batabyal

Human history is replete with examples that prove politics and war are intertwined. According to Clausewitz, war is not merely a political act but also a real political instrument.[1] A Harvard professor, commenting on decolonised Asia and Africa, wrote: 'They are not yet nations in being but only nations in hope.'[2] State formation in Pakistan took a wrong trajectory after its inception and the persistent denial of the principle of equal rights and self-determination to the people of East Pakistan, defying the much-promised democratic norms, was the root cause of the problem. Continuous dissentions caused societal frictions, which took the shape of conflicts.

> Political and constitutional history of Pakistan, and the social, cultural, racial and economic equations between her two erstwhile wings...reveal the startling paradox of a dependent people in a technically independent country. This is what Sheikh Mujibur Rahman meant by his familiar Bengali phrase *swadhin desher paradhin nagarik* (Dependent people of an independent country).[3]

Political scientists, while theorising causes of war, have mostly ignored domestic political variables.[4] The 1971 Bangladesh Liberation War is a classic example of how domestic political variables added much significance to the cause of war. Continuously denying a rightful place to the political leadership of East Pakistan resulted in political alienation of Bengalis. In addition, economic deprivations and cultural conflict caused by the imposition of Urdu triggered a movement that culminated in a war of liberation.

Political decisions, therefore, need careful consideration because they have repercussions. This is what happened with Pakistan in December 1971: wrong politics since its creation, interwoven with the internal conflicts between its two wings, concluding with India's intervention, led to its cessation. There is a need to understand how politics in Pakistan forced East Pakistan to reach the stage of seeking liberation that ended with the birth of Bangladesh, which altered the geography of South Asia and ushered in a new political order for India in the region.

Divisive politics had begun with the Bengali Muslims even before the creation of Pakistan, but for the sake of brevity, this paper covers the period after decolonisation of the Indian subcontinent, with a brief prelude to politics leading to the Partition of India. The topic under discussion is being dealt with in various sections, such as the landmark political events in Pakistan leading to the Liberation War, India's political compulsions and the Cold War geopolitics during the war in 1971.

Politics, Partition of India and Its Fallout

The nexus between politics and religion had led to much mistrust between the religious communities in India, specially in the last 150 years of British rule. Though there had been occasional rifts between Hindus and Muslims, it was the British rulers that added fuel to the fire with their *divide et impera* policy. In the early stages of his political career, Jinnah exhibited no religious bias. In fact, after the conclusion of Lucknow Pact in 1916, Sarojini Naidu hailed him as the apostle of Hindu–Muslim unity. However, in 1920–21, Jinnah was ridiculed by the Congress leaders for criticising their support to Khilafat movement and for questioning Gandhi and the Congress for mixing religion with politics. Fearing marginalisation, Jinnah commenced to rechart his path.

> Jinnah's ultimate embrace of what he once called 'the communal fringe' was a political response to his marginalization within the Congress, and the decimation of the Muslim League in the 1937 elections to the state legislature. He was hell-bent on the creation of Pakistan as a Muslim country....[5]

It remains a puzzle if the two-nation theory was Jinnah's core belief or his political manoeuvre to ensure an edge in the power-sharing game. As a shrewd politician and a pragmatic person, he publicly took a hard stand demanding a separate

Muslim state, but 'Privately Jinnah reassured his sceptical colleagues that Partition was only a bargaining chip: the British could not hand over power to Nehru as long as Hindus and Muslims did not even agree on whether they were one nation or two.'[6]

Jinnah's reciprocal hatred for Nehru, dislike for Gandhi and Mountbatten and above all, obsession for power made him a changed man by 1946. Although the Lahore Resolution of March 1940 had introduced the idea of a separate homeland for Muslims, it was only in 1946 that there was official endorsement of the concept of a single state of Pakistan. Further, the idea of an undivided Bengal received a death knell when the Bengal Legislative Assembly voted for Pakistan on 20 June 1946. Jinnah, the sole spokesperson for the Muslims of Indian subcontinent, sold the dream of Pakistan to people of the common faith of 'Islam'.[7] Historian Ayesha Jalal observed:

> The term Pakistan was put forth as the panacea for all problems facing Muslims. Its meaning was kept deliberately vague so that it could mean all things to all people. Upper crust thought, the new state will give them great opportunity to occupy powerful positions and the lower strata of the society thought, their miseries will be alleviated: Pakistan will be a land of honey and milk.[8]

The geographical separation of thousand miles between East and West Pakistan, including their diverse culture, was thought to be no barrier because it was assumed that 'commonality of faith' will be sufficient to hold the nation together. When the common Bengali Muslims voted overwhelmingly for the Muslim League in 1946, they were not voting for Pakistan but for a life free from *zamindari* rule and famines. As the zamindars were mostly Hindus, many saw it as expression of Muslim Bengalis to separate from their Hindu brethren.

From June 1946 onwards, the political climate became so charged that no single individual could have stopped the Partition, but collectively they could have displayed the wisdom to withdraw from the maddening game. Jinnah and Nehru became the main players; and Jinnah became more aggressive because he lost trust in Nehru and Congress. On 16 August 1946, the Muslim League called for a 'Direct Action Day', with Jinnah proclaiming that they shall have 'either a divided India or a destroyed India'. The violence unleashed that day set in train a series of events that made the Partition of India unavoidable. The riots started in Calcutta, but soon spread to the Bengal countryside. Then, Bihar and the United Provinces erupted and finally, and most savagely, the Punjab.[9]

In March 1947, when India was reeling under communal violence and a political slugfest regarding the partition of the country, Admiral Mountbatten replaced Field Marshal Lord Wavell as the Viceroy of India. Lord Mountbatten decided to accelerate independence of India and transfer the power earlier than the original time frame of June 1948. Hearing this, many top leaders, irrespective of political affiliations, got intoxicated with power politics, so much so that kingship became more important to them than the kingdom. Even Gandhiji could not stop the mad race for power, or maybe his relevance at that juncture had lessened. Jinnah, Nehru and all top-rung leaders failed miserably to anticipate the tribulations of the Partition, which was executed through a most violent process: a retributive genocide and a holocaust of religion, where more than 2 million people were killed, more than 75,000 women raped and 14 million people were displaced—a tragic fallout of the execution of an insufficiently imagined political decision.

The economic and social linkages established since many centuries in undivided India were abruptly severed, which had a telling effect during state making. British scholar Yasmin Khan judges that the Partition 'stands testament to the follies of empire, which ruptured community evolution, distorted historical trajectories and forced violent state formation from societies that would otherwise have taken different—and unknowable—paths.'[10] The Partition of India was the biggest man-made cataclysm, which had an enduring impact. In retrospect, many top leaders then displayed 'self-delusion on a heroic scale'.

Politics and Journey of Pakistan (1947–71)

Jalal writes: 'General perception about the statehood in the contemporary South Asia has been the "success" of democracy in India and its "failure" in Pakistan...Interestingly, after gaining independence, South Asia, despite inheriting a common British colonial legacy led to contrasting patterns of political development.'[11] Moot question, therefore, is: why India and Pakistan took a different trajectory despite Jinnah's promise to make Pakistan an exemplary democratic and secular state? He had stated in his very first address to the Constituent Assembly on 11 August 1947: 'you may belong to any religion or caste or creed—that has nothing to do with the business of state. We are starting with this fundamental principle that we are all citizens and equal citizens of one state.'[12]

However, ironically, he himself deviated from what he envisioned. Immediately after the creation of Pakistan, East Bengal (renamed East Pakistan in 1955) got its first jolt when popular mass leader, Hussain Shaheed Suhrawardy, was excluded from a senior ministerial position at the centre, as also the post of chief minister of East Bengal, due to political machinations of Liaquat Ali Khan, Jinnah's trusted lieutenant. Instead, his chosen person was Sir Khawaja Nazimuddin; and he too was undemocratically replaced within a short span by Governor-General Ghulam Muhammad, a West Pakistani. The episode brought many East Bengal parties together to form the United Front, which expressed its dissent through a 'twenty-point agenda', including autonomy of the province in line with the Lahore Resolution of 1940. In the years that followed, Bengali politicians were rarely given important portfolios. In fact, Pakistan failed to hold regular election and most importantly, it did not have a constitution which could give it legal and functional directions. Stephen Cohen commented:

> Most of the key power players in Pakistan respected democracy and wished Pakistan to be a democratic but they were not willing to make it so. These included the army, which admired democracy in the abstract but found it troubling in practice, civilian bureaucrats, who tended to equate democracy with civilian governments in which they played a major role; and the left which advocated democracy in theory but also had authoritarian inclinations. In fact, many groups in Pakistan lacked a nominal commitment to democratic forms, let alone substance.[13]

During the first 24 years after becoming an independent state, Pakistan made constitutions twice, once in 1956 and second time in 1962. The frequent political instability and domestic disorder in the initial years culminated into military rule. On 7 October 1958, all political parties were abolished and provincial governments were dismissed by the President of Pakistan, Major General Iskander Mirza. He also promulgated martial law and installed the Pakistan Army Chief, General Ayub Khan, as the Chief Martial Law Administrator. Three weeks later, Mirza was sent to exile in London and Ayub Khan became the supremo of Pakistan. Ayub tried to bring in a new vision for Pakistan. He ruled Pakistan through an established civil–military coalition, where military played the dominant role of principal partner. Punjabi-dominated army always considered the Bengalis an inferior community *vis-à-vis* the so-called martial races, like Punjabis and Pathans. Cohen opined that in the dominant west wing, the idea of Pakistan pertained to a martial people defending its Punjabi stronghold. Bengal and Bengalis only figured as an investment opportunity or source of foreign exchange.[14]

Despite Jinnah's promise of equal treatment for all in 1947, in the same year it was proposed that Urdu be the sole state language, which would also be used in media and in schools. Urdu was perceived as the more Islamic language which would help to integrate the newly born nation. As a result, Pakistan Public Service Commission removed Bengali language from the list of approved subjects. Bengali was also removed from currency notes, postal stamps and government forms. This decision was vehemently resented as only 2.5 per cent population in East Bengal and 7 per cent in West Pakistan spoke Urdu. It led to a language agitation, which was further inflamed due to Jinnah's speech at Dhaka on 22 March 1948, where he declared that the state language of Pakistan is going to be 'Urdu and no other language'.[15] This was a big blow to the Bengali Muslims and the agitation on the language issue continued for a number of years. It brought all political parties in East Bengal onto a common platform: '1952 language movement created myths, symbols and slogans that consolidated the vernacular elite.'[16]

Language movement is critically important because politics in East Bengal changed then onwards. It demonstrated how brutal the Pakistani leadership and army could be in repressing fellow citizens living in East Bengal. It also sowed the seeds of sub-regionalism: a new political initiative for 'an autonomy of the region that the delta had last experienced in pre-Mughal times'.[17] Jinnah's Pakistan looked rather illusive to the Bengali Muslims. The growing politics of regionalism and clash of identity had a huge future ramification. The West Pakistanis perceived themselves to be racially superior and looked down upon the Bengalis as a non-martial race. The Bengalis were seen as not only socially inferior but also lesser Muslims because they did not adhere to many cultural practices that North Indian Muslims considered properly Islamic. Further, it was felt that Bengalis had been and were still under considerable Hindu cultural and linguistic influence.

In 1966, Sheikh Mujibur Rahman, leader of the Awami League, adopted a six-point programme for reconfiguration of the Pakistani federation. This led to the so-called 1968 Agartala Conspiracy Case, where Sheikh Mujib, some serving and retired army personnel and senior government officials were arrested and charged with sedition. The mass protest that followed, however, compelled the Pakistan government to withdraw the case.[18] The Agartala Conspiracy Case raised the political stature of Sheikh Mujib, catapulting him as the spokesman of the Bengalis. On his release from prison, thousands gathered to greet Sheikh Mujib and he was honoured as 'Bangabandhu', that is, friend of Bengal. On 24 February 1969, Bangabandhu flew to Rawalpindi to argue the case for the six-point programme.[19]

The landslide victory of Awami League in the 1970 elections, in which it gained absolute majority in East Pakistan, raised the hopes of Bengali people for parity. It led to frantic parleys to form government at the centre, but these negotiations, which carried on till March 1971, were a camouflage. Concurrently, troops and military equipment from West were being secretly moved to east to once and for all sort out the problem of Bengali nationalism. The plan was to arrest the top leaders; decapitate Awami League; de-arm and demobilise Bengali police and men of East Bengal Rifles; and eliminate intellectuals, students and front-line people challenging the government's authority. As the negotiations reached a dead end, Yahya Khan ordered his commanders to launch 'Operation Searchlight', a military operation that led to brutal killings.

Politics of Economic Development

Since the beginning, Pakistan generated unfair economic policies which facilitated economic domination over East Pakistan by the central government in West Pakistan. All key individuals in resource allocation were always West Pakistanis. Political cleavages arising out of ethnic disunion became glaringly visible, along with the regional economic disparities, which made Pakistan further volatile and unstable. In fact, before the national elections in December 1970, Sheikh Mujib said:

> ...to the appalling record of economic disparity it is seen that during the last 20 years, out of the total revenue expenditure of the Government, only about Rs. 1,500 crores (that is only one fifth of the total) was spent in Bengal, as against over Rs. 5000 crores in West Pakistan. Of the total development expenditure during the same period, Rs. 3,060 crores (that is only one third of the total) was spent in Bengal, as against over Rs. 6000 crores in West Pakistan...Bengalis account for barely 15 percent in Central Government services and less than 10 percent in the defence service...The price of essential commodities has been 50 to 100 percent higher in Bengal than in the West Pakistan...Total economic impact of such discrimination is that the economy of Bengal is today in a state of imminent collapse. Near famine conditions are prevailing in most of the villages.[20]

General impact of the politics of economy has been a considerable transfer of resources;[21] and economic exploitation and denial of political rights are of the essence of every race-oriented colonial administration. Scenario in Bengal fitted into what Abraham Lincoln said:

> Turn it in whatever way you will—whether it came from the mouth of a king or from the mouth of men of one race as a reason for enslaving the men of another race, it is the same old serpent that says: 'You work and I eat, you toil and I enjoy the fruits of it.'[22]

Also, Mao Tse Tung wrote, 'A potential revolutionary situation exists in any country where the government consistently fails in its obligation to ensure at least a minimally decent standard of life for the great majority of its citizens.'[23]

Besides cultural invasion, economic deprivation and the constant denial of fair share in political space, especially when the mandate of 1970 elections was dishonoured, made the Bengalis of East Pakistan realise that they would not get a fair deal from Islamabad and hence, they revolted.

India's Problems and Politics

The events in Bangladesh at midnight of 25 March 1971, and in the months that followed, came as a rude shock to India, as it did to millions all over the world. Under the circumstances, India could not remain a mute spectator without severe damage to its own economy. Also, it had to get involved in the internal affairs of Pakistan as the problem had crossed the international boundary and reached India. The situation was assessed by New Delhi based on realpolitik.

India realised that a long-drawn civil war in East Pakistan may trigger a left-leaning pro-communist movement, overshadowing Awami League, a pro-India party. The Indian leadership also felt that the Maoist-inspired guerrilla movement in East Pakistan may join hands with the ongoing Naxalite movement in West Bengal and the surrounding region in eastern India. Thus, deserting Mujibur Rahman and Awami League would not have been beneficial at all; on the contrary, supporting him and his political agenda benefited India and the Bengali refugees, who were mostly Hindus. From a strategic point of view, 'Bengali uprising provided India with the "opportunity of the century"...to break up Pakistan and thus eliminate the threat of a two-front war in any future confrontation.'[24]

On 30 March 1971, Prime Minister of India, Indira Gandhi, moved a resolution in both houses of the Parliament, condemning the happenings in East Pakistan and outlining the approach of the government. On 3 April, she promised support, including an office in Calcutta, to Mujib's nominee for prime minister of the provisional government. Indira Gandhi did not want to provoke a war by recognising Bangladesh as an independent country; however, she did start considering the military option as many political leaders and strategists put pressure on her for an immediate military intervention to throw out the marauding Pakistani Army from East Pakistan. India's initial strategy was to covertly sponsor a Bengali guerrilla insurgency within East Pakistan, as evident in the secret letter by D.P. Dhar to P.N. Haksar: 'War—open declared war—fortunately in my opinion, in the present case is not the only alternative. We have to use the Bengali human material and the Bengali terrain to launch a comprehensive war of liberation.'[25]

Indira Gandhi and her administration, while handling domestic pressure on the East Pakistan crisis, showed remarkable amount of patience and maturity to arrive at a well-charted course of action. In addition, while supporting the freedom movement in Bangladesh, India had to factor the dangerous fallout it could have on the north-eastern states and in Tamil Nadu, which often demanded separation because of distinct ethno-linguistic and cultural identity. New Delhi also had to take note of the idea of Greater Bengal, which surfaced often. It was, thus, a great dilemma for the central leadership. After a tour of the refugee camps, on 24 May, Indira Gandhi debated in the Parliament:

> Conditions must be created to stop any further influx of refugees and to ensure their early return under credible guarantees for their safety and wellbeing...unless this happens, there can be no lasting stability or peace on the subcontinent. We have pleaded with other power to recognize this. If the world does not take heed, we shall be constrained to take all measures as may be necessary to ensure our own security and the preservation and development of the structure of our social and economic life.[26]

On 15 June 1971, during the budget session, Pranab Mukherjee initiated a discussion on the floor of Rajya Sabha (Upper House) that India should accord diplomatic recognition to the Bangladesh's government-in-exile in Mujibnagar. He said:

> I am talking of a political solution which means categorically recognising the Sovereign Democratic Government of Bangladesh. Political solution means giving material help to the Sovereign Government of Bangladesh. I remind the House of many instances in world history where intervention on similar ground had taken place.[27]

Moreover, by July–August 1971, 90 per cent of the refugees, who were mostly Hindus, were concentrated in the border districts of West Bengal which had large Muslim populations. Consequently, it was felt that if India did not act quickly to ensure their return, there was danger of serious communal strife. Also, India could not indefinitely bear the economic cost of such a big refugee population.

The failure of the international community to prevent 'history's biggest and cruellest migration' and violation of human rights resulted in a most formidable threat to peace in South Asia. When peace was threatened in Rhodesia, United Nations (UN) acted promptly, but nothing was done in the Indian subcontinent even after the consummation of an unprecedented tragedy.

India's Political Decisions

1. East Pakistan crisis is a political problem and can only be resolved by a political process through the acceptance of the election mandate of the general elections in Pakistan. To start the process, Mujibur Rahman must be released immediately and the government must work with him.
2. Pakistan should immediately stop military operations in East Pakistan and troops should return to the barracks.
3. The international community should pressurise through bilateral, diplomatic and UN channels and impress upon Pakistan to resolve the crisis in East Pakistan by peaceful means. The UN must adopt immediate and adequate relief measures to assist refugees in India and ensure their early return home.
4. Domestic public opinion should be built up within the country for the probable extension of formal and active support to the liberation struggle of East Pakistan. Simultaneously, a well-planned diplomatic initiative should be undertaken to sensitise the world about the plight of the Bangladeshis and India's compulsions.

Though election result demanded that Mujibur Rahman be invited to form the government but Bhutto with only 80 seats in West Pakistan demanded parity, thus ignoring the first principle of democracy, that is, "rule of majority". Under the pressure Yahya indefinitely postponed the session of the Pakistan National Assembly scheduled to be held from 3 March 1971. On 7 March at Dhaka Racecourse Maidan, Mujibur Rahman at a massive public rally appealed to all Bengalis to unite and called for the struggle of liberation. He also called for total non-cooperation with the national government. He summed up his historical speech in a bold voice stating, "'We have given blood, we will give more blood"'. From 7–25 March, there were two governments: the *de jure* government led by Gen Yahya Khan and the *de facto* government by Mujibur Rahman. Gen Yahya along with Bhutto travelled to Dhaka to break the deadlock. And simultaneously secretly transported troops and equipment from West to East building military might therein the name of discussion between 16–24 March 1971. Pakistan also did not have a constitution. Under these circumstances no meaningful political strategy for the war was formulated by the leaders beset with military mindset. Only policy direction in the struggle for liberation was 'keep India away' because India was seen as the core problem. It was true that Awami League had India's support; but Pakistan's historical obsession with India blurred its vision so much that she failed to see the internal problem and widening the gap between the two wings. And Pakistan opted for a military solution to a political problem.[28]

Cold War Geopolitics in South Asia

The superpowers, namely, the United States (US) and the Soviet Union, did not show much interest in the Indian subcontinent till the end of the British rule and a few years thereafter. Subsequently, the Cold War imbroglio and the interest and influence of superpowers in South Asia made them party to the Bangladesh Liberation War and Indo-Pakistan War of 1971. In addition, the actions and influence of China, the United Kingdom (UK), other countries of Europe, Africa, the Islamic countries and the neighbouring countries during the conflict, including their involvement either directly or through their voice in the UN, had implications on the political strategy of the warring factions. Interestingly, the US, China and the Islamic countries were more supportive of Pakistan's cry for stopping disintegration than the cry of millions of terror-stricken East Pakistanis and hence, they closed their eyes to the gross violation of human rights by the Pakistani military and its supporters.

Pakistan's search for security status and identity coincided with the US' search for an ally in South Asia to buttress its global strategic objective. In 1954, Pakistan became a member of military pacts—Central Treaty Organization (CENTO) and Southeast Asia Treaty Organization (SEATO)—sponsored by the US. As a result, Pakistan offered the Peshawar Air Base, adjacent to Soviet Union territory, for operation of the US military spy planes.

International Media Response and India's Final Political Option

Interestingly, as opposed to many official views, international media and various luminaries took pro-Bangladesh stand and forecast the separation from Pakistan at the beginning of the civil war. They also condemned Pakistan's action, the US and UN inaction and Yahya's obstinacy in not talking to Mujibur Rahman. Further, they lent support to India's legitimate involvement to get over the refugee problem. A few examples are cited next.[29]

On the brutality of Pakistan Army in East Pakistan, *Time* magazine of US wrote as early as 5 April 1971: 'Even if President Agha Mohammed Yahya Khan is prepared to accept casualties of a geometrically greater magnitude, the outcome is likely to be the final breakup of East and West Pakistan and the painful birth of a new nation named Bangladesh.'[30] *The New Statesman*, London, commented on 16 April 1971: 'If blood is the price of a people's right to independence, Bangladesh has overpaid.'[31] *Newsweek*, on 2 August 1971, wrote: 'Pakistan died in March...says a Karachi editor... There can never be one nation in the future, only two enemies.'[32] A former British minister, who was also member of the parliamentary delegation that visited East and West Pakistan, wrote:

> This downward spiral can only be reversed by political solution acceptable to the people of East Pakistan. In practice this must mean a political solution acceptable to Sheikh Mujibur Rahman and the Awami League...Yahya Khan must either accept this or continue with his policy of suppression—a policy which is bound to fail sooner or later...That the United States should line up with China in supplying armed forces of Pakistan at the moment is some thing that defies any rational explanation...There should be the most explicit condemnation from the governments and parliaments and influential commentators from all kind...it must be made clear that the world identify themselves with the aspirations of the people of Bangladesh, and that are united in demanding shift in policy by the government of West Pakistan.[33]

International Official Response

National interest is the core of foreign policy framework in any country. During Bangladesh crisis of 1971, the US and China supported Pakistan, as did the Islamic nations, ignoring the cries of brothers of same faith in East Pakistan because they did not want dismemberment of an Islamic country, as such many of them were already allied with both US and Pakistan. European and African nations too supported Pakistan—many genuinely and a few not to antagonise big brother, the US. Then many African nations were facing internal problems related to the demands of independence similar to Bangladesh, hence not to add fuel to the fire in their domestic troubles they sided with Pakistan. Amongst the neighbouring countries, except for Bhutan, none outrightly supported Bangladesh or India. The Union of Soviet Socialist Republics (USSR) and the communist bloc supported Bangladesh and India.

From the moment it came into being, Pakistan thought of the US as its primary source of military and diplomatic support against India. When the civil war broke out in East Pakistan, India was getting closer to Soviet Union and Nixon had tilted more towards the military-ruled Pakistan. To protect Pakistan during the Liberation War, the US gave economic aid for relief of refugees. Further, it urged India not to use the military option and advised Pakistan to settle disputes with East Pakistan. Yahya, on Nixon's request, facilitated rapprochement between the US and China. Thus, when the war ultimately occurred, Nixon administration resorted to 'gun boat diplomacy' by deploying *USS Enterprise* in the Bay of Bengal.

Nixon wrongly presumed that the Liberation War was a fallout of the Cold War. He failed to visualise that it was a fundamental development in the subcontinental affairs and its resolution was to be found from within rather than through the influence of external powers.

Indo-USSR Friendship Treaty, signed on 9 August 1971, was a game changer as it ensured a balance of power between the two superpowers who were getting close to two regional states of South Asia. This treaty also helped to check the physical participation of China. Most importantly, USSR's viewpoint during the debate and use of veto power thrice during voting in the Security Council allowed India and the Mukti Bahini some time to conclude the swift military operation in East Pakistan, resulting in victory.

Interestingly there were a few unexpected developments during the preparatory period of 1971 Indo-Pakistan War. Anwar Sadat of Egypt, whom India supported during Arab–Israel War of 1967, and condemned Israel for attacking, supported Pakistan on the basis of Muslim brotherhood while Israel with whom India did not have any diplomatic relations secretly helped India with arms and ammunition.

From the analysis of the official response of international bodies, it can be deduced that there were divergent views regarding the 1971 South Asia crisis. By far, there was a consensus that the influx of millions of East Pakistani refugees was an unbearable burden for India—both from an economic point of view and due to the threat of imbalance in social harmony. However, there was no uniform view on creating requisite conditions for the refugees to return home. On the question of self-determination of the people of Bangladesh, two trends were discernible: (i) it was an internal matter of Pakistan and there was no requirement for the international community even to discuss it; and (ii) it was not a matter solely within the domestic jurisdiction of Pakistan, and the situation called for a political solution.

India's Quest for Peace Fails: Opts for Military Intervention

After Indira Gandhi's exhaustive final phase of foreign tours in quest of peace, preceded by the tours of other Indian leaders—like Jayaprakash Narayan, Atal Bihari Vajpayee, Yunis Khan, Siddhartha Shankar Ray and Pranab Mukherjee—to many countries across the globe to garner support, the conclusion drawn was that India has to fight it out alone, though it could bank on the USSR's support in the UN.

After exhausting all diplomatic options for an amicable political solution to the crisis in East Bengal, which could have paved the path for the installation of

Awami League government as mandated in the election along with return of 10 million refugees and above all saved Bangladesh from further genocide, rape and wonton destruction India opted to exercise 'the military option' as an instrument for achieving its national objective. It was a classic case of humanitarian intervention. The primary objective was the capture of maximum territory in East Pakistan so that Bangladesh government-in-exile could be relocated at the earliest to their soil, and refugees could also return. In the meanwhile, through various inputs, it was assessed that China was unlikely to participate in the proposed war physically. Indian Armed Forces were all set for a war from 4 December 1971. However, Pakistan commenced an all-out two-front war against India with a pre-emptive air strike on 3 December 1971. This action of Pakistan made it the aggressor who officially started the war.

Once the war broke out, the US made a last-ditch attempt to save its client state Pakistan from disintegration and thwart Bangladesh's liberation. It made frantic efforts to impress upon the Soviet Union to not oppose their move in the UN, in addition to pressurising India for a ceasefire. Simultaneously, the US urged Iran and other Islamic countries, like Turkey, Jordan and Saudi Arabia, to supply weapons to Pakistan. Washington also thought of drawing the Chinese into this imbroglio to scare the Indians. However, India could not be stopped from participating in the war.

UN and Bangladesh Liberation War

The division of a state into two separate states has been a permissible mode of implementing self-determination according to the will of the people. For example, Singapore separated from the Federation of Malaysia. Quincy Right has observed: 'There is no rule of international law forbidding revolutions within a state, and the United Nations Charter favours self-determination of the people.'[34]

Bangladesh Liberation War was fought when the Cold War was at its peak. Amongst the five permanent members of the UN Security Council, the US and China supported Pakistan, while Soviet Union supported the cause of Bangladesh. The UK and France, though sympathetic to Bangladesh's liberation struggle, abstained from voting to avoid direct collision with the US. Throughout the liberation struggle, Pakistan Army committed all forms of human rights violations. The UN could not effectively stop this because it can be effective only if the five permanent members of the Security Council act together. As evident, the UN Security Council was a divided house. Even the UN General Assembly did not take up the issues related to East Pakistan to ameliorate the subjugation and sufferings of millions of people there. Subrata Roy Chowdhury wrote: 'It had never occurred to anybody that a repetition of the atrocities of Nazi Germany was possible under the regime of the United Nations Charter...A persistent denial of the principle of equal rights and self-determination was the root cause of the problem....'[35]

The political and constitutional history of Pakistan before the civil war commenced in East Pakistan amply demonstrates the denial of autonomous status, which was the spirit behind the formation of Pakistan, inherent in the text of Lahore Resolution. An objective analysis with a historical perspective infers that in 24 years since the creation of Pakistan, East Pakistan was transformed into a colony. The struggle for self-determination reached its crescendo during the civil war, which should have prompted the UN and its members to intervene to deliver justice due to the people of Bangladesh.

A peaceful political solution recognising the right of people of Bangladesh to govern themselves was the only way out of the crisis. However, UN did not push Pakistan for a political solution to resolve the Bangladesh crisis, which was a great failure in preventive diplomacy. It could not also invoke Chapter VII for enforcing peace in Bangladesh as the Security Council was a divided house. This inaction of the UN became a big question mark on the credibility of the august organisation. On 27 December 1971, *Time* magazine stated: 'Islamabad was the principal looser in the outcome of war. But there were two others as well. One was the UN and the other was Washington, who appeared wholeheartedly committed to the Pakistan dictator.'[36]

Conclusion

The break-up of Pakistan happened because, as a nation, it could not integrate its two wings socially, economically and politically. The disintegration commenced with the denial of thousand years of deep-rooted cultural traditions of Bengal. Forceful imposition of Perso-Arabian culture and denial of the rightful place of Bengali language triggered the conflict between the two wings of Pakistan, which grew manifold with the passage of time. Economic deprivation and political alienation added fuel to the fire. The Pakistani establishment failed to realise that to the Bengalis, a common religious identity that was shared with other Pakistanis had never meant that they were to be denied their own cultural traditions. 'Most Bengalis, initially, did not see any contradictions in being a Bengali, a Muslim and a Pakistani all at the same time. The contradiction was to be perceived with other Pakistanis.'[37]

By the end of 1970, Pakistan had witnessed two ineffective and feeble constitutions, one military coup and two martial law administrators. Pakistan had turned into a praetorian state, derailing the much-dreamt democracy of its founder father, Muhammad Ali Jinnah. In a praetorian state, the military, instead of fighting and winning international wars, maintains its influence in the domestic political system, controlling decisions or supporting some particular political faction to maintain its own interests.[38] In 1971, the Pakistan Army politically supported Bhutto and influenced every decision of the government. As observed by Samuel Huntington: 'authoritarianism may do well in the short term but experience clearly has shown that only democracy produces good government over the long haul.'[39]

Senator Edward Kennedy characterised Pakistan Army's inhuman brutality in Bangladesh as the 'greatest human tragedy in modern times'.[40] Between 1948 and 1967, the total number of Arab refugees from Israel amounted to 13,50,000; in Laos, 7,00,000 were displaced; in Vietnam, displaced people numbered 6 million during the longest war in America's history; and in 1971 war, about 10 million refugees from Bangladesh took shelter in India.[41] India was passionately concerned about the events unfolding in East Pakistan. The plight of millions of Bengalis who took refuge in India stirred the hearts of the people. The unbearable economic strain and socio-political and psychological factors due to the East Pakistan crisis made India's involvement in the liberation struggle inescapable. The point to be understood is that India's support to the liberation struggle was not an orchestrated pre-planned move, but a politico-strategic response befitting the situation. Since the beginning of the East Pakistan crisis, 'Mrs. Indira Gandhi believed and made it amply clear through various statements that there must be a political, rather than military, solution to Pakistan's problem in its eastern province and that the great powers had a special responsibility to help see such a solution through.'[42]

In the Bangladesh Liberation War, the political aim of the Government of India was to enable 10 million refugees to return safely to Bangladesh and to ensure the security of India's border. Along with this, Indian strategists felt that the creation of a new friendly neighbouring nation would be in India's strategic interest, as it would cut Pakistan to size, reducing its potential and stature. India, all through this period, had to bear tremendous pressure from the US and posturing from China. Well aware of the perils of getting involved in a major conflict with Pakistan and its supporters, India ensured support of the USSR by signing a Friendship Treaty on 9 August 1971.

For Indian Prime Minister Indira Gandhi, it was not an easy task to manage internal and external politics during the nine months of the war. Friendship treaty with the USSR was a master stroke, which ensured external support during the most crucial period of the war through its veto power in the UN Security Council. Regarding political hurdles within the country, Pranab Mukherjee observed, 'Mrs. Indira Gandhi proved as adept and adaptable dealing with the recalcitrant elements in both her own party and the opposition.'[43] There was pressure on her to prolong the military operation in the western theatre to liberate Pakistan-occupied Kashmir. Militarily, it may have been achievable; but Indira Gandhi showed political maturity to conform to her original war aim, and also to prove to the world that India was not out to Balkanise Pakistan as many, specially the US, thought so. India unilaterally declared ceasefire before the Security Council could pass a resolution to this effect and pulled its troops out of Bangladesh, amply proving its claim that it was fighting the war primarily as a humanitarian intervention and not a conquest. Though India's intervention was criticised by many governments who were supporting Pakistan, including a section of people—specially international legal experts—who viewed India's action as violation of international law and defiance of just war theory, many political scientists pointed out that Bangladesh was 'a paradigmatic case of a justified humanitarian intervention'.[44]

The *Time* magazine, capturing the grim realities after the war ended, stated:

> In the aftermath of the Pakistani army's rampage last March, a special team of inspectors from the World Bank observed that some cities looked 'like the morning after a nuclear attack.' Since then, the destruction has only been magnified. An estimated 6,000,000 homes have been destroyed, and nearly 1,400,000 farm families have been left without tools or animals to work in their lands. Transportation and communications systems are totally disrupted. Roads are damaged, bridges out and inland waterways blocked. The rape of the country continued right up until the Pakistani army surrendered a month ago. In the last days of the war, West Pakistani-owned businesses—which included nearly every commercial enterprise in the country—remitted virtually all their funds to the West. Pakistan International Airlines left exactly 117 rupees ($16) in its account at the port city of Chittagong. The army also destroyed bank notes and coins, so that many areas now suffer from a severe shortage of ready cash. Private cars were picked up off the streets or confiscated from auto dealers and shipped to the West before the ports were closed.[45]

In the midst of Cold War geopolitics and Sino-US reproachment, such a massacre could happen because of the deafening silence of big powers, like US and China, and many who gave overriding importance to Pakistan's territorial integrity than the sufferings of majority of its people. Bangladesh Liberation War is, thus, a classic example of an intra-state conflict that grew to become an inter-regional conflict and ended as a global conflict—a result of the Cold War geopolitics. Garry Bass captures the East Pakistan crisis of 1971 in these words:

> With hundreds of thousands of people killed in Pakistan's crackdown, these atrocities were far bloodier than Bosnia and, by some accounts, on approximately the same scale as Rwanda. Untold thousands died in squalid refugee camps as ten million Bengalis fled into neighbouring India in one of the largest refugee flows in history. The crisis ignited a major regional war between India and Pakistan...And it brought the United States, the Soviet Union, and China into crisis brinksmanship that could have ignited a military clash among superpowers—possibly even a nuclear confrontation.[46]

The root of cessation of Pakistan can be traced to the very idea of Pakistan which was created on Jinnah's two-nation theory. The Partition of India happened to suit the political aims of many leaders. Since religion was used as a vehicle to reach their objectives, artificially constructed Pakistan had to break someday. Had Pakistan remained politically correct, been fair and treated all citizens equally, as promised by Jinnah at the beginning of its journey, and come out with a political solution rather than going to war, the country would not have been dismembered. Unfortunately, the leadership was fixated in seeing all problems as India's handiwork. On 16 December 1971, Bangladesh rose on the ashes of Pakistan, forever burying Jinnah's two-nation theory in the deep sea of Bay of Bengal.

The military strategy of India was tailored to meet the government's political objectives. Through humanitarian intervention of 1971, India, ably supported by the Mukti Bahini, deftly executed the Liberation War. Three million Bengalis sacrificed their lives at the altar of freedom to get their sovereign, democratic Republic of Bangladesh. India achieved its politico-strategic objectives while carrying out her 'responsibility to protect', an international norm which came into vogue many years later in 2005, after being endorsed by the member states of UN.

While concluding, I would like to draw attention to a salient observation of a study group on World War II, as it is also applicable for the Bangladesh Liberation War:

> No amount of operational virtuosity...redeem fundamentals flaws in political judgment. Whether policy shaped strategy or strategic imperatives drove policy was irrelevant. Miscalculations in both led to defeat, and any combination of politico-strategic error had disastrous results...*Mistakes in operations and tactics can be corrected, but political and strategic mistakes live forever.*[47]

Thus, as war and politics are deeply interlinked, moral responsibility for the end result that charts the course of history of a nation squarely rests on its leaders, whose political decisions and actions lead to better or worst outcomes. Cessation of Pakistan through the traumatic birth of Bangladesh after a nine-month war is a testimony of political *hara-kiri* on the part of Pakistan.

NOTES

1. Carl von Clausewitz, *On War: On the Nature of War*, Dummlers Howard/Paret version No. 1, 1984, p. 20; Carl von Clausewitz Quotes, BrainyQuote.com, BrainyMedia Inc, 2021, available at https://www.brainyquote.com/quotes/carl_von_clausewitz_403393, accessed on 3 November 2021.
2. Rupert Emerson, *From Empire to Nation: The Rise to Self-assertion of Asian and African Peoples*, Cambridge: Harvard University Press, 1967, p. 94.
3. Subrata Roy Chowdhury, *The Genesis of Bangladesh*, Calcutta: Asia Publishing House, 1972, p. vii.
4. Jack S. Levy, 'Domestic Politics and War', *Journal of Interdisciplinary History*, Vol. XVIII, No. 4, Spring 1988, pp. 653–73.
5. Rohit Prasad, 'The Contrasting Game Theories of Gandhi and Jinnah', *Mint*, 4 June 2018, available at https://www.livemint.com/Opinion/TqmeVu0fCwQZlGlqvFbhwL/The-contrasting-game-theories-of-Gandhi-and-Jinnah.html, accessed on 2 November 2021.
6. Moon Pendel, *Divide and Quit*, US: Oxford University Press, 1998, p. 21.
7. Guru Saday Batabyal, *Politico-Military Strategy of the Liberation of Bangladesh, 1971*, London: Routledge, 2020, p. 7.
8. Ayesha Jalal, *The Sole Spokesman: Jinnah, the Muslim League and the Demand for Pakistan*, Cambridge: Cambridge University Press, 1985, quoted in Ibid., p. 7.
9. Ramachandra Guha, 'Divided or Destroyed—Remembering Direct Action Day', *The Telegraph*, 23 August 2014, available at https://www.telegraphindia.com/opinion/divided-or-destroyed-remembering-direct-action-day/cid/157755, accessed on 7 November 2021.
10. Yasmin Khan, quoted in William Dalrymple, *Great Divide*, available at https://www.newyorker.com/magazine/2015/06/29/the-great-divide-books-dalrymple, accessed on 21 January 2020.
11. Ayesha Jalal, *Democracy and Authoritarianism in South Asia: A Comparative and Historical Perspective*, New York: Cambridge University Press, 1995, p. 1.
12. Muhammad Ali Jinnah, 'Presidential Address to the Constituent Assembly of Pakistan', 11 August 1947, available at www.pakistani.org/pakistan/legislation/constituent_add_11th August1947.html, accessed on 8 August 2014.
13. Stephen Phillip Cohen, *The Idea of Pakistan*, Washington, DC: The Brookings Institution, 2004, pp. 15–34.
14. Ibid.
15. Philip Oldenburg, 'A Place Insufficiently Imagined: Language, Belief and the Pakistan Crisis', *The Journal of Asian Studies*, Vol. 44, No. 4, August 1985, pp. 711–33.
16. Rounaq Jahan, *Pakistan: Failure in National Integration*, New York: Columbia University Press, 1972, p. 44.
17. Willem van Schendel, *A History of Bangladesh*, Cambridge: Cambridge University Press, 2009, p. 114.

18. Archer Blood, *The Cruel Birth of Bangladesh: Memoirs of an American Diplomat*, Dhaka: The University Press, 2002, p. 50.
19. Syed Badrul Ahsan, 'The Agartala Case as it Transformed History', *Dhaka Tribune*, 18 June 2020.
20. J. Lee Auspitz, Stephen A. Marglin and Gaustav F. Papenek, 'History of Economic and Political Dominion of East Pakistan', in *Bangladesh Documents*, New Delhi: Ministry of External Affairs, September 1971, pp. 5–9.
21. Ibid.
22. Abraham Lincoln, 'Chicago Speech', 10 July 1858, quoted in Roy Chowdhury, *The Genesis of Bangladesh*, n. 3, p. 19.
23. Mao Tse Tung, *On Guerrilla Warfare*, translated by Samuel Griffith, Champaign: University of Illinois Press, 2000.
24. Mohammed Ayoob, 'Explaining 1971', *The Hindu*, 15 March 2018, available at https://www.thehindu.com/opinion/op-ed/explaining-1971/article23247097.ece, accessed on 2 November 2021.
25. 'Letter from D.P. Dhar, Ambassador to the Soviet Union, India, to P.N. Haksar, Principal Secretary to the Prime Minister, India (1971)', Nehru Memorial Museum and Library, Teen Murti Bhavan, Delhi, India, P.N. Haksar Papers, III Instalment, quoted in Garry J. Bass, 'Indian Way of Humanitarian Intervention', *Yale Journal of International Law*, Vol. 40, No. 2, 2015, available at https://digitalcommons.law.yale.edu/yjil/vol40/iss2/2, accessed on 2 November 2021.
26. Lok Sabha Debates, 24 May 1971, p. 187.
27. Pranab Mukherjee, *The Dramatic Decade: The Indira Gandhi Years*, New Delhi: Rupa, 2014, p. 43.
28. Ibid., pp. 33–42.
29. International newspapers and magazines cited in Roy Chowdhury, *The Genesis of Bangladesh*, n. 3, pp. 248–50.
30. Ibid.
31. Ibid.
32. Ibid.
33. *The Sunday Times*, 11 July 1971, quoted in Ibid.
34. Quincy Wright, 'Intervention on Invitation', *American Journal of International Law*, Vol. 53, 1959, pp. 119–21, cited in Roy Chowdhury, *The Genesis of Bangladesh*, n. 3, p. 199.
35. Roy Chowdhury, *The Genesis of Bangladesh*, n. 3, p. vii.
36. 'India: Easy Victory, Uneasy Peace', *Time*, 27 December 1971, available at http://content.time.com/time/subscriber/article/0,33009,905593-4,00.html, accessed on 7 November 2021.
37. Ayesha Jalal, *Self and Sovereignty: Individual and Community in South Asian Islam since 1850*, Oxford: Routledge, 2005, p. 570.
38. This definition of praetorian state is attributed to Daniel. R. Headrick, professor of history and social science at Roosevelt University.
39. Samuel P. Huntington, 'Democracy for the Long Haul', *Journal of Democracy*, Vol. 7, No. 2, April 1996, p. 6.
40. Senator Kenney's remark published in *The Statesman*, Calcutta, 15 August 1971, to be read in conjunction with Quincy Right, *The Middle East Crisis (1970)*.64. No.4. AJIL, pp. 71, 82, cited in Roy Chowdhury, *The Genesis in Bangladesh*, n. 3, p. 223.
41. Roy Chowdhury, *The Genesis of Bangladesh*, n. 3, p. 223.
42. J.N. Dixit, *Across Borders: Fifty Years of India's Foreign Policy*, New Delhi: Sangam Book Limited,

1998, p. 105, cited in Batabyal, *Politico-Military Strategy of Bangladesh Liberation War*, n. 7, p. 85.

43. Mukherjee, *The Dramatic Decade*, n. 27, p. 43.
44. Michal Walzer, *Just and Unjust Wars: A Moral Argument with Historical Illustrations*, 1977, pp. 90, 101–08, cited in Bass, 'Indian Way of Humanitarian Intervention', n. 25, p. 229.
45. Cited in 'Bangabandhu's Fight to Eradicate Poverty', *The Asian Age*, Dhaka, 11 May 2021.
46. Bass, 'The Indian Way of Humanitarian Intervention', n. 25.
47. Williamson Murray, Mac Gregor Knox and Alvin Bernstein (eds), *The Making of Strategy: Rulers, States and War*, Cambridge: Cambridge University Press, 1994, p. 3. Cited in Batabyal, *Politico-Military Strategy of Bangladesh Liberation War*, n. 7, p. 251.

2

India's Politico-Military Strategy for the 1971 India–Pakistan War

J.S. Cheema

The simmering discontent between East and West Pakistan reached a climax in the beginning of 1971. The West Pakistan-dominated military government denied the legislated right to the East Pakistani political party, Awami League, to form a government after it had won an absolute majority in the National Assembly elections held in December 1970. The failure of political negotiations between the military Government of West Pakistan, under General Yahya Khan, and Awami Party leader, Sheikh Mujibur Rahman, led to large-scale protests, often turning violent. The Pakistan Army, overwhelmingly drawn from the West, launched a ruthless military crackdown, 'Operation Searchlight', on 25 March 1971, to suppress the people of East Pakistan. Predictably, the people retaliated against the military operation leading to an open rebellion. The brutality of the army operation led to a large-scale exodus of refugees, including thousands of former East Pakistani regular soldiers and paramilitary troops, into India. The earlier political demand for autonomy of East Pakistan turned into a secessionist movement. The leaders of the Awami League, who managed to escape the carnage and reach India, proclaimed the 'independence of Bangladesh' and formed a 'Provisional Government of Bangladesh' (PGB) in exile on 17 April at Mujib Nagar near Calcutta (Kolkata).

The continuous refugee deluge precipitated an enormous economic and security crisis in India. There was a nationwide uproar by the politicians—cutting across party lines, particularly from the affected states—the media and the public against the atrocities perpetrated by the Pakistan Army against the hapless populace of East Pakistan. The people demanded recognition of Bangladesh's government-in-exile and immediate military intervention to liberate East Pakistan from the clutches of Pakistan. Despite the public outcry, widespread sympathy for the Bengalis, and the demand for recognition and application of force in April 1971, the Indian government acted cautiously.

This paper examines the macro perspective of the evolution of policy formulation and the resultant armed forces' strategy to achieve the political objective. The paper comprises three main sections. The first section traces the evolution of India's politico-diplomatic strategy, starting from formulating the political objective and the various means to achieve the same. The constraints of achieving the desired outcome through diplomacy, indirect military support, and recurring economic cost and other political developments increased India's propensity to exercise the last resort, that is, the military option. The second section discusses India's war-fighting military strategy on the eastern, western, and northern fronts, with East Pakistan as the centre of gravity. The gradual escalation of sub-conventional military activities in East Pakistan provoked Pakistan to carry out pre-emptive air strikes on Indian airfields on 3 December 1971, marking the commencement of the 1971 India–Pakistan War. A quick military campaign led to the capitulation of the Pakistan Army and the liberation of Bangladesh. The third section critically analyses India's politico-diplomatic and military strategy in the backdrop of geopolitics playing out between the superpowers beyond the battlefield, followed by the conclusion. The paper does not examine the military's operational and tactical-level execution unless to derive a specific point.

The research and analysis of India's politico-diplomatic–military strategy sheds light on its political resolve, robust military capability, and deliberate decision-making process to transform a humungous human crisis into a significant strategic success without succumbing to the intense international pressure.

India's Politico-Diplomatic Strategy

The refugee influx presented a significant challenge to the government. The initial response of the Indian government to the military action in East Pakistan was circumspect; it wanted neither to arouse greater hostility in Pakistan against India nor to encourage demands for immediate action from political groups in India.[1] India granted asylum to the Awami League political leaders and other cadres. Still, it did not recognise the PGB. The Army Chief, General (Gen) SHFJ Manekshaw, advised against military intervention due to the likely Chinese threat, the impending monsoons, and the considerable time required for building logistics. Despite reservations by a few Cabinet ministers, the government accepted the Chief's advice to plan a military intervention with adequate preparations for assured success. Also, India would have found it difficult internationally to justify military action without exploring diplomacy and other options. However, domestically, the decision did not cut much ice with the public and the intelligentsia. K. Subrahmanyam, a strategic analyst, stated: 'the breakup of Pakistan is in our interest, and we have an opportunity the like of which will never come again' and suggested, 'intervention on a decisive scale sooner than later is to be preferred'.[2]

Formulation of Political Objective and Strategy

By the end of April, it was not only the continuous unabated refugee deluge but also the changing demographic composition that became worrisome for India. The change in demographic composition, from 20 per cent to 80 per cent Bengali Hindu refugees by the end of April 1971, made India apprehensive of their non-return even after a political settlement. Further, India feared the destabilising influence of refugees on its fragile socio-economic-cum-security structure in the north-eastern states and the re-ignition of insurgency extremist movement by Bengali radicals in West Bengal and neighbouring states. It constituted an 'indirect aggression' to the country's core values of integrity and unity. India concluded that Pakistan was trying to solve its internal problems by cutting down the size of its population and changing the communal composition through an organised and selective programme of eviction.[3] The Indian Prime Minister (PM) stated in the Parliament on 24 May 1971:

> what was claimed to be an internal problem of Pakistan has also become an internal problem for India; Pakistan cannot be allowed to seek a solution of its political or other problems at the expense of India and on Indian soil. If the world does not take heed, we shall be constrained to take all measures as may be necessary to ensure our security.[4]

This was a significant statement that reflected the Indian government's policy.

The policy focuses on three main issues: 'the end to be achieved, the way it is to be achieved, and the means allocated to achieve the desired end.'[5] The strategy is the bridge that connects the means with the ends. India strategised to orchestrate the refugee crisis by a deft exploration of available means to achieve a strategic objective. It devised the following politico-diplomatic–military strategy:

- *Political*: Seek the transfer of power to the moderate Awami League leadership in East Pakistan that would create conducive conditions for the return of the refugees.
- *Diplomacy*: Mobilise international support for a political solution in East Pakistan that should lead to a moderate Awami League-led government.
- *Indirect military support*: Provide calibrated indirect military support to the Mukti Bahini to compel Pakistan to seek a political settlement and wear down the Pakistan Army.
- *Direct military support*: If all the above proved unsuccessful, be prepared to escalate to direct military intervention as a last resort at an appropriate time. War, after all, is an act of policy to attain a political purpose.

Diplomacy

Though belonging to two different realms, diplomacy and military are considered two sides of the same coin. Diplomacy is the first line of engagement to avert a war, and the military is the last resort to wage it. India put in a sustained diplomatic effort to highlight to the world community the human tragedy unfolding in East Pakistan, urging it to restrain Pakistan from its repression policy. The PM, ministers, and diplomats visited the United States (US), the Union of Soviet Socialist Republics (USSR), Britain, France, Germany, Canada, the Islamic world, and the United Nations (UN) to pressurise Pakistan to negotiate a political settlement. It could not, however, elicit support from the US, which mattered the most. India also rejected the UN proposal of deploying observers on the border to monitor the refugees, which hardened its stance against India and made the world believe Pakistan's accusations of India instigating the rebellion in East Pakistan. The possibility of international pressure against Pakistan further receded.

India revisited the friendship treaty with the USSR, under negotiation for nearly six years, and signed the Treaty of Peace, Friendship, and Cooperation in New Delhi on 9 August 1971. The treaty, with regards to China, stipulated: 'In the event of either party being subjected to an attack or a threat thereof, the parties shall immediately enter into mutual consultations in order to remove such threat and to take appropriate, effective measures to ensure peace and security of their countries'.[6] Concerning Pakistan, it stipulated both sides 'to abstain from providing assistance to any third party that engages in armed conflict with the other party'.[7]

Thus, the world, on the whole, showed sympathy for India, but considered the evolving siuation to be an internal matter, which encouraged Pakistan to continue its repression policy. The treaty, however, assured India of the USSR support in the war.

Indirect Military Support

Indian planners were aware that armed intervention in April–May 1971 would evoke hostile reactions worldwide, with its efforts to garner sympathy and support for Bangladesh being drowned in the Indo-Pak conflict.[8] India, therefore, planned a guerrilla campaign to harass the Pakistani forces and compel them to seek a political solution. The Indian Army trained, armed, and guided the Mukti Bahini, organising it into brigades and battalions. It included the East Pakistan regular troops who had deserted the Pakistan Army. It planned that the Mukti Bahini would have an initial strength of 20,000 personnel, gradually enlarged to 1,00,000.[9] This would enable India to slowly upscale the scope of guerrilla activities in a planned manner.

Meanwhile, the Mukti Bahini leaders were disenchanted as they felt that India was not doing enough as it had neither recognised the PGB nor intervened militarily. They did not consider Pakistan strong enough to counter India militarily due to the geographical constraint of maintaining its forces in East Pakistan and concerns of Indian retaliation in the West.[10]

Preparations for Direct Military Intervention

Indian Armed Forces concurrently began deliberate preparations and training for the impending contingency of going to war. The armed forces built up the reserves, raised/relocated additional formations/units, and undertook forward dumping of ammunition and supply stocks. The Indian Army raised 2 Corps Headquarters (HQ) and relocated the formations employed in counter-insurgency for operations in East Pakistan. It enjoyed a distinct quantitative advantage over the Pakistan Army in the eastern theatre, with Mukti Bahini as the force multiplier. It was near parity on the western front, though Pakistan claimed its technological superiority in its armoured fleet. The Indian Air Force (IAF) and the Indian Navy enjoyed a qualitative and quantitative advantage over their Pakistani counterparts. Having 350 and 160 combat aircraft in the western and eastern theatres,[11] the Indian Air Force was a potent force. The Indian Navy had an aircraft carrier, besides cruisers, frigates, and destroyers. Having been left out in the 1965 war with Pakistan, it was eagerly waiting for its first operations. The relative military capability of India and Pakistan is given in Table 1.

Table 1. Relative Military Capability of India and Pakistan[12]

Formations/Units	*Western Theatre*		*Eastern Theatre*	
Army	India	Pakistan	India	Pakistan
Infantry/Mountain Divisions	13	10	11	4
Armoured Divisions + Independent Armed Brigades	1+4	2+3	2 Regiments + 2 Squadrons	1 + 1
Parachute Brigades	1		1	
Mukti Bahini/East Pakistan Civil Armed Force			1,06,844	25,000
Air Force				
Combat Aircraft	350	254	160	19
Navy				
Aircraft Carrier	-	-	1	-
Submarines	2	3	1	1
Cruisers/Destroyers/Frigates	16	6	5	-

A Committee, comprising of the secretaries of defence, home, finance, external affairs, and others, was set up to take executive decisions dealing with the war preparations.[13] The Pakistan Army had augmented its troop levels in East Pakistan from 14,000 to 60,000 (about four infantry divisions and 25,000 paramilitary forces).[14] India, on its part, suitably calibrated its military preparations in the light of its public declarations of seeking a political solution through diplomacy. Gen Yahya Khan, on the contrary, built up the war phobia. He stated in August 1971: 'war with India is very near, and Pakistan would not be alone in case of war.'[15]

Political Developments

The Pakistan government published a white paper on 5 August 1971 blaming the Awami League for the crisis. It ordered an in-camera trial of Sheikh Mujibur Rahman for treason and disqualified 79 of 160 Awami League members in the National Assembly, charging 30 of them with treason. It also published the district-wise tally of refugees in late August 1971, putting the total figure at just over 2 million, closely resembling the number of Muslims among the Bengali refugees.[16] The development convinced India of the unlikelihood of the emergence of any political solution and reinforced its apprehension of the Pakistani government not allowing the Hindus to return to their homes.

Economic Constraint and Cost–Benefit Ratio

As mentioned earlier, the continuous influx of refugees posed a substantial economic burden on India. Up to the end of July 1971, 7.23 million refugees had taken shelter in India. By 15 December 1971, the estimated figure was 10 million. The approximate cost of maintaining the refugees was Rs 525 crores, while the external aid received was a meagre Rs 112.5 crore.[17] The estimated cost of the war was around Rs 500 crore.[18] An economic assessment in July 1971 underlined that India was not immediately vulnerable on account of foreign exchange reserves until March 1972, even if international aid was adversely affected by the suspension of existing commitments if India opted for war.[19] Thus, as an aid recipient, though India was susceptible, the size of the debt made the creditors vulnerable to our reactions.[20] The one-time cost of the war was cheaper than the recurring cost of maintaining the refugees. The cost-benefit analysis, therefore, favoured the war.

By the end of August 1971, the aforementioned developments catalysed a strategic shift in India's approach. It increased its propensity for the military option, yet it projected itself amenable to a political solution to establish a conducive environment for the return of refugees.

India's Military Strategy

India calibrated the war-avoidance and war-fighting strategies through a judicious blend of sub-conventional and conventional operations, respectively, with a decisive shift of focus towards the latter. Diplomacy continued to explicitly impress the international community to pressure Pakistan for a political solution. It implicitly aimed to expose the inability of the world community to evolve an acceptable political settlement, enabling it to exercise the best possible option.

War-fighting Strategy: Conventional Operations

Pakistan strategised to mount a major offensive to capture maximum territory in the West to offset the likely losses in the East. It planned a defensive posture on the eastern front and firmly held the cities and garrisons located along the major roads. It hoped that world pressure, particularly from the US, would prevent India from launching an offensive in East Pakistan. It further believed that China would militarily intervene, and the UN might effect an early ceasefire. India's military strategy envisaged a 'Defensive along the Northern borders, an Offensive–

Defensive in the West and a Swift Offensive in the East.'[21] The following were the military objectives:[22]

- *Northern borders*: To defend territorial integrity against likely Chinese offensive by deploying adequate forces in a defensive position.
- *Western theatre*: To prevent Pakistan from capturing any Indian territory of consequence in Jammu and Kashmir (J&K), Punjab, Rajasthan or Gujarat by adopting a holding strategy, with plans to execute limited offensive operations.
- *Eastern theatre*: To assist the Mukti Bahini in liberating a part of East Pakistan, enabling the refugees' return to live under their government.

India maintained the defensive deployment of four divisions along the northern borders against China: 17 and 27 Mountain Divisions remained deployed in Sikkim, with 2 and 5 Mountain Divisions in Arunachal Pradesh. The 6 Mountain Division less a brigade was relocated from the Uttar Pradesh–Tibet border in central sector to be kept as a reserve in 33 Corps zone for any contingency requirements against China.

The terrain of East Pakistan, now Bangladesh, was interspersed with numerous rivers and nullahs. Three rivers, the Ganges, the Brahmaputra and the Meghna, bifurcated it into four distinct sectors: western, north-western, northern and south-eastern. The land strategy envisioned capturing maximum territory bordering the Brahmputra and the Meghna river lines and setting up a 'provisional Bangladesh government', with Khulna and Chittagong being the principal objectives.[23] Subsequently, it envisioned the liberation of the whole of East Pakistan.[24] The eastern theatre planned a multi-pronged offensive to achieve a quick victory as follows (see Map 1):

- *Western sector*: 2 Corps with 4 Mountain Division and 9 Infantry Division to capture Jessore, Jhenida and secure Khulna and Faridpur.
- *North-Western sector*: 33 Corps with 20 Mountain Division and two independent brigade groups to capture Bogra/Rangpur.
- *Northern sector*: 101 Communications Zone with a mountain brigade and a sector to capture Jamalpur and Mymensingh and secure Tangail with airborne forces.
- *South-eastern sector*: 4 Corps with 8, 23, and 57 Mountain Divisions planned to capture Meghna Bulge between Chandpur and Ashuganj, Sylhet, Daudkandi–Mynamati, and Chittagong.

- Dacca was to be captured by any formation after defeating the enemy in detail.[25]
- The IAF aimed to achieve total air superiority in the East and support the army and navy operations, besides attacking the enemy's strategic targets. It had considerably enhanced its transport fleet in the East to accelerate operations.
- The Indian Navy deployed the aircraft carrier, *INS Vikrant*, in the East to secure a complete blockade of the East Pakistan coasts and Chittagong and Khulna Ports.

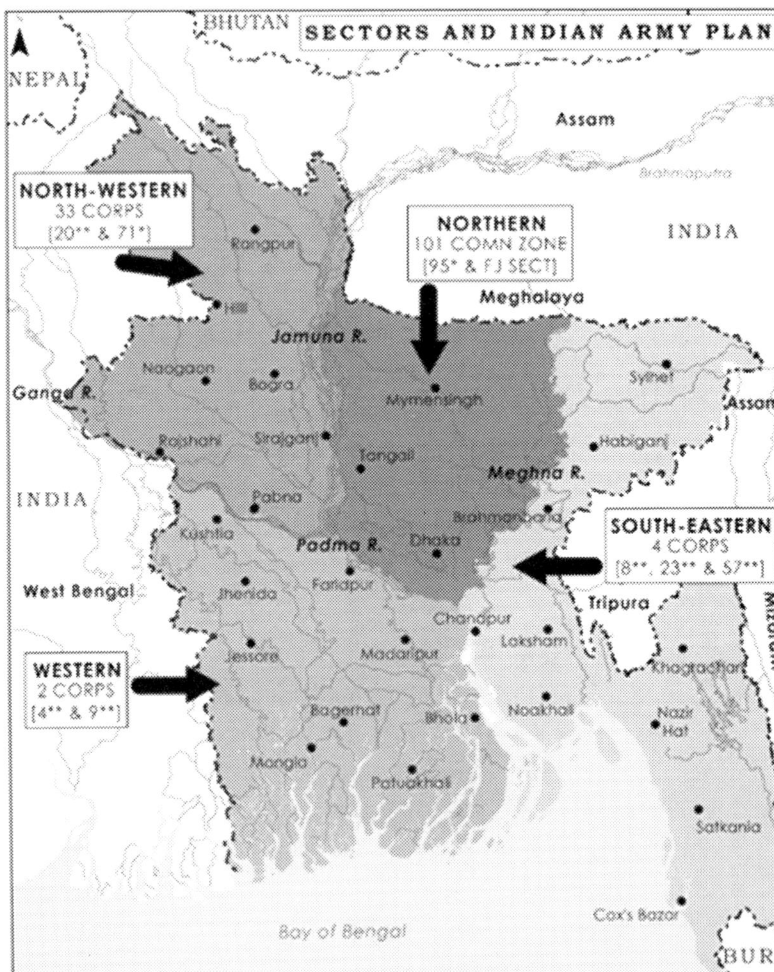

Map 1. Map Showing the Sectors and the Indian Army Plan

Pakistan, in turn, had deployed a division in each sector to deny ingress to the Indian Army in the east.

The western theatre adopted a holding strategy with plans to execute limited offensive operations. Western Command's 15 and 11 Corps deployed 10 divisions to defend J&K and Punjab and conduct limited offensive operations. The strike 1 Corps, with three infantry divisions, was tasked to protect the sensitive Samba–Pathankot area and launch the main offensive in Shakargarh sector after Pakistan's likely attack. The 1 Armoured Division was the Army HQ reserve positioned near Ferozepur to execute the offensive after discerning Pakistan's intentions. The Southern Command held the desertic Rajasthan sector with two divisions. It planned minor offensive operations in Jaisalmer and Barmer sectors to capture territory. The Pakistan Army deployed three corps (1, 2 and 4) on the western front, with 10 infantry divisions, two armoured divisions, and three independent armoured brigades.

India tentatively decided to execute its military strategy at the end of November or early December, should no political solution emerge until then. The mountain passes along the northern borders would get snow-covered, minimising possible Chinese attack. This time, however, coincided with the session of the UN General Assembly. India presumed that the USSR veto power would forestall or delay any action by the UN Security Council against India.

Escalation: Sub-conventional Operations

The Army aimed to secure maximum area in the shortest possible time, due to the imminent international pressure. Air Chief Marshal P.C. Lal observed: 'caution dictated that the military people commanding the East should work to limited objectives, but go about achieving them as rapidly as possible.'[26] Therefore, the Army HQ envisaged escalating the sub-conventional military operations in East Pakistan with a sophisticated combination of employing the regular troops along the international border to draw the Pakistan Army away from the interior and tasking Mukti Bahini to establish its control in the interior. Commando troops were stealthily embedded to fight alongside Mukti Bahini within East Pakistan territory.[27] Appreciating that India would capture limited areas close to the border to carve out liberated zones to establish a puppet Bangladesh government and recognise the same internationally, the Pakistan Army moved out in strength away from Dacca to build robust defences around significant areas and towns.[28] A Pakistani Commanding Officer confirmed the same: ' our intelligence evaluators appear to have concluded that India would attempt to secure a small chunk of

East Pakistan where the Bangladesh Government would be installed; we modified our plans to adopt a forward defensive posture.'[29]

The denuding of the hinterland interior enabled the Mukti Bahini to dominate the geographical space. Irked by intensified activities in the East, Pakistan concurrently mobilised in the West to deter India from the war in the east. India refrained from moving any forces to the western border to avoid any provocation to Pakistan to start a war, yet it was worried about the Pakistani attack. India was in a dilemma: moving troops in anticipation of an attack could create a misunderstanding; if not done, it would seriously jeopardize the western front's defense.[30] India carried out war preparations in a progressive manner after ascertaining Pakistani moves. The Pakistan Army was battle-ready by mid-October, while the Indian Army attained a minimum operational readiness by mid-November.[31]

From the second week of October 1971, India further exacerbated its operations within East Pakistan, leading to a sharp increase in their scale and intensity. The Pakistani and Indian forces were engaged in air and tank battles between 19 and 22 November.[32] Indian troops, after 21 November 1971, began to position themselves within East Pakistan to improve their defensive posture and secure suitable launch pads for subsequent offensive operations.[33] The tactical conflict between the two sides was in full force by end November. It was a matter of time as to who would convert the ongoing conflict into war.

The Pakistan Army considered attacking India in the western theatre on 22 November; however, President Yahya restrained from it, hoping the UN Security Council would intervene in Pakistan's favour. He made the last-ditch attempt to install a civilian government in Dacca,[34] but it did not work. The Indian PM, in the last week of November 1971, accorded approval to launch a full-scale offensive in East Pakistan on 4 December 1971.[35] The Pakistani President, too, had decided, on 30 November 1971, to launch an invasion on the western front on 2 December 1971, but postponed it by a day. Finally, Pakistan launched pre-emptive airstrikes on 3 December 1971, at 5.45 p.m., on several Indian airfields in the western sector.[36] The Indian PM declared hostilities on Pakistan and decided to recognise Bangladesh. The Indian Armed Forces launched attacks on 4 December 1971, concurrently in the western and eastern theatres.[37]

The War and the Victory

The Indian Army's multi-pronged offensive into East Pakistan made rapid progress. It captured Jessore, Jhenida, Jamalpur, Mymensingh, the Daudkandi–Chandpur area, and the eastern bank of the Meghna River by 10 December. The IAF neutralised the Pakistani Air Force effectively and achieved total air superiority by 7 December, paving the way for uninterrupted close air support and heliborne/airborne operations. It then shifted a few fighter squadrons to the West. The Indian Navy sunk the Pakistani Navy submarine, *Ghazi*, outside Visakhapatnam harbour and established a naval blockade to prevent any Pakistani build-up in the region. However, the sinking of the *Ghazi* is still shrouded in mystery. It remains unclear whether it was sunk or was it a suicidal foray into a mined area.[38] Nevertheless, it provided the necessary freedom of action to *INS Vikrant* in the Bay of Bengal.

To exploit the rapidly deteriorating situation, the Indian Army modified its plans. India pulled out two brigades from the Chinese border on 8 December.[39] It also airdropped a parachute battalion at Tangail on 11 December. The advancing 4 Corps, employing a combination of helicopters and river crafts, built up almost a division-sized strength across the Meghna River by 12 December. As the US Seventh Fleet entered the Bay of Bengal on 13 December 1971, India carried out intensive bombings on naval assets to render them unusable. The IAF launched a successful airstrike at the governor's house on 14 December, causing a huge psychological blow to Pakistan. The planned amphibious operation with a brigade of the Army at Cox's Bazaar on 14–15 December night was unsuccessful. By the morning of 16 December, the Army had encircled Dacca with nearly five brigades. Four infantry battalions and an independent armoured squadron entered the city by the afternoon.

All of this intensified psychological pressure on the Pakistan Army to surrender. On the other hand, the Pakistan government desperately sought an UN-sponsored ceasefire as a face-saving mechanism to avoid the ignominy of surrender. Time was of utmost essence. Poland submitted a resolution to the UN Security Council for discussion on 15 December. It asked India and Pakistan to accept an immediate ceasefire; withdraw forces from each other's territory; renounce claims to any occupied territories; and transfer power in East Pakistan to the representatives elected in December 1970 elections. A ceasefire, followed by troops' withdrawal before the capture of Dacca, would have deprived India of Pakistani forces' surrender and substantially curtailed its capacity to ensure the smooth accomplishment of Bangladesh's liberation—the desired end state. The resolution failed due to Bhutto's ulterior motive,[40] leaving Pakistan Army with no option but to surrender on 16 December 1971. India announced a unilateral ceasefire on the western front, which Pakistan accepted, ending the 14-day war on 17 December 1971.

The western theatre saw intensified operations all along the front: 15 Corps captured Turtok, vital posts in Kargil, a significant portion of the Lipa Valley in Kashmir and the Chicken's Neck area in the Jammu region. The Pakistan Army, as appreciated, launched offensives in Punch and Chhamb sub-sectors. The Indian Army defended Punch resolutely but suffered a significant reverse in Chhamb. The 11 Corps captured Jassar Enclave and Sehjra Bulge, but lost Kasowal Enclave. It also suffered a reversal in the Ferozepur and Fazilka sub-sectors.

The strike 1 Corps launched the main offensive in the Shakargarh sector on 5 December, when the likely Pakistani offensive did not materialise. It achieved limited success, failing to exploit the battle opportunities. The Southern Command captured Parbat Ali overlooking the Naya–Chor defences in the Barmer sub-sector. It tenaciously defended the Longewala post in the Jaisalmer sub-sector, with the air force playing a significant role. However, it could not successfully pursue Rahim Yar Khan, despite Pakistan troops being in total disarray. The Army did not issue orders to execute any offensive to the reserve 1 Armoured Division. The Indian Navy conducted a well-planned missile attack on Karachi harbour, causing substantial damage.

India, thus, achieved a decisive victory over Pakistan, securing the surrender of nearly 93,000 Pakistani soldiers and capturing 16,282 square kilometres of territory against the loss of 375 square kilometers on the western front.[41]

Analysis of India's Strategy

The paradigm of war typically follows the sequence: confrontation–crisis–conflict–war–resolution. The 1971 India–Pakistan War too generally unfolded in this pattern. India's decision to resolve the unprecedented refugee crisis evolved progressively, with the military replacing the politico-diplomatic strategy in a phased manner. An extensive diplomatic campaign followed the formulation of a political objective. Support to the indigenous liberation movement was progressively escalated to the conflict stage, finally leading to war in December 1971.

Political Objective

The PM's informal decision-making body, comprising a small informal core group of experienced and trusted bureaucrats, functioned very efficiently, exercising general authority.[42] It relegated the formal apex body, Parliamentary Affairs Committee (PAC), to a traditional structure without authority and power.

India formulated a clear-cut political objective and asserted to the world that it would not accept any 'peaceful solution' that did not ensure the return of refugees. Mr K. Subrahmanyam called the PM's discreet and the first official threat to the possible use of force to achieve the political objective as 'a shift from the diplomacy of persuasion to the threat of force to avoid a compulsive drift into a war later on.'[43] The return of refugees to their native place after displacement triggered by military genocide was also a humanitarian and just cause: 'Just war should be dictated by a right intention, for an injury received, not for territorial conquests or any secular or religious crusades.'[44] The massive refugee deluge constituted an 'indirect aggression,' threatening India's vital national interest of socio-cultural identity.

Military Intervention and Recognition of PGB

Before formulating the political objective and exploring other alternatives, India's decision not to exercise the military option, and recognise the Bangladesh government-in-exile, was eminently correct and necessary to shape the world opinion, in April–May, in its favour. Recognition would have been premature and drawn flak internationally. Going to war without exploring diplomacy and engagement with the international community would have led to collective world isolation, as most countries considered the uprising an internal affair of Pakistan. The PM believed that India should 'tread the path with a great deal of circumspection, and not allow feelings to get the better of us.'[45] She was apprehensive of being accused of adopting double standards in recognising PGB and applying force in East Pakistan while maintaining that J&K was an internal matter that brooked no interference. It also fitted very well with the military requirements of training, equipping, strategic positioning of forces, and calibrating the indigenous freedom movement of Bangladesh. It enabled India to project its military intervention, to support a Muslim-led East Pakistan liberation movement rather than another Indo-Pakistani conflict. The trained Mukti Bahini acted as a force multiplier during the war. Though India ruled out the military option in April–May 1971 on politico-diplomatic–military considerations, the narrative built over the years ascribed 'military consideration' being the dominant reason.

Diplomatic Strategy

Indian diplomacy succeeded in projecting the unfolding crisis in East Pakistan, but the international community viewed it from its national interests. The US' interest in building a long-term relationship with China, assisted by Pakistan, dictated its policy. Richard Nixon, the US President, and Secretary of State Henry

Kissinger believed that 'if they allowed India to humiliate Pakistan, their reputation in the eyes of China would suffer irreparable damage'.[46] The US, therefore, decided to buy time and deter India from military intervention, at least until Nixon's trip to Beijing.[47] India, in turn, was justified in rejecting the UN proposal of deploying observers on the borders to monitor the refugees. The UN plan merely focused on the consequence without addressing the root cause of the political problem. India rightly apprehended that UN observers' deployment would label the ongoing crisis as an Indo-Pakistan dispute and divert attention from Pakistan's military oppression and fundamental issue of the return of refugees.

Several analysts and political observers believed that the Indo-Soviet treaty achieved deterrence against China and set the stage for India's decision for military intervention, which is not the correct inference. The US Secretary of State, Henry Kissinger, stated, 'the Soviet Union had seized a strategic opportunity ' by assuring India of its continued support and providing a hedge against Chinese intervention in support of Pakistan.[48]

China was perhaps the first country that saw the writing on the wall of Bangladesh's inevitable secession as early as April 1971 and accordingly calibrated its policy regarding India and Pakistan. Concerned about the developing strategic cooperation between Russia and India, China did not want to push India further close to the Soviet Union.[49] It also intended to keep Bangladesh from becoming an independent nation by using its influence to counter India and Russia. Overtly, China assured Pakistan of support against any Indian military adventure and supplied it with military hardware to equip two new divisions.[50] Secretly, it conveyed its disapproval of the military crackdown and urged Pakistan to seek a political solution.[51] By July 1971, the Indian government had copies of letters in which the Chinese government had explicitly stated that its military force would not intervene in another Indo-Pakistan war.[52] The September 1971 coup attempt by Mao's designated successor, Lin Bao, supported by some air force and army elements, led to the grounding of the air force for some time. It further reinforced India's appreciation of China's unlikelihood to intervene militarily.

India appreciated that both the US and China would support Pakistan in any UN resolution on Bangladesh; therefore, the USSR veto was crucial to counter the same. The treaty assured USSR support in the UN and strove to neutralise the growing US–Pakistan–China relationship. It also pre-empted USSR military assistance to Pakistan. The treaty envisaged support only if the country was subjected to aggression by another country. India, therefore, assiduously orchestrated its military strategy to provoke Pakistan to attack first and then, retaliated in defence.

The unwillingness and inability of the international community to influence Pakistan for a political settlement in East Pakistan exposed its limitations to address an unparalleled human tragedy. This response suited India's objectives and made it easy for India to determine the course of action in its national interest. The more international pressure proved ineffective, the closer Indian thinking moved to the only alternative, namely, war, and the more India thought of war, the more it alienated official thinking in other countries.[53] Its shift to a proactive strategy from September onwards was most timely and prudent. By calibrating the escalation from September onwards to peak by the end of November, with military intervention in December, India achieved military superiority against Pakistan through deft use of terrain, timing, and force generation. It could also exploit geography and weather as deterrence against likely Chinese threat along the northern borders.

Impact of Indirect Military Support

The synchronised intensified activities, as part of the well-planned escalation matrix along the borders and harassing actions in the interior, forced the Pakistan Army into a decision dilemma about India's likely strategic objective. Would India capture limited areas close to the border to carve out liberated zones to establish a puppet Bangladesh government and recognise the same internationally or launch a full-fledged military offensive to capture the whole of Bangladesh? India succeeded brilliantly in creating an impression of capturing key areas close to the border to install a puppet Bangladesh government and achieved strategic deception, causing a psychological dislocation in Pakistan's political and military leadership. Pakistan relocated from the interior near Dacca to significant towns closer to the border, enabling the Mukti Bahini to dominate the critical geographical mass.

Indian Army's occupation of East Pakistan territory since 21 November provoked Pakistan to initiate the war and it fell into India's strategic ploy. The Pakistani officers were greatly incensed with their leadership for not reacting to the Indian occupation of its territory. They felt strongly about declaring war on India as a matter of pride, prudence, and necessity.[54] Adding fuel to the fire, Bhutto warned President Yahya that if he did not react forcefully to India's aggression, he would be lynched by the people.[55] Yahya ordered pre-emptive airstrikes on 3 December 1971. D.P. Dhar, a member of PM's core group, welcoming the Pakistani strikes, succinctly remarked, '*The fool has done exactly what one had expected.*'[56] India earned a fig leaf for not being seen as an aggressor, though some analysts believed India started the war in November 1971. Richard

Sisson and Leo Rose observed that the war began on 21 November, when Indian military units occupied East Pakistan territory in more realistic terms.[57] However, this observation is incorrect. Before 3 December, there were routine tactical-level engagements between the two armies, with air force employed only once. However, Sisson and Rose's observation that India's decision was based on expectations that did not materialise is correct. 'The escalating threat of war narrowed expectations of peacefully arranged outcomes; indeed, the field of expectation became so narrow that it excluded the contemplation of alternatives.'[58]

War-fighting Military Strategy

Considering East Pakistan to be the centre of gravity where the war was to be won or lost, the overall Indian military strategy was eminently logical, sound and prudent. A quick offensive in East Pakistan was imperative to achieve a decisive victory before the international community could intervene. With a strategy precisely opposite to India's, Pakistan had planned to defend East Pakistan by exploiting its armour superiority in the West, hoping to compel India to withdraw forces from the East, enabling the international community to intervene. However, Pakistan could not aggressively pursue its offensive plans in the West. In East Pakistan, the strength of the Pakistan Army, in conjunction with the terrain's defence potential, was adequate to contest the Indian offensive and buy time for international intervention. India's superior strategy outmanoeuvred Pakistan Army, who lost the will to fight aggressively. A critical analysis of India's military strategy is given next.

Eastern Theatre: Dacca Not a Military Objective

The Indian Army did not earmark Dacca—the capital and geopolitical centre of power of East Pakistan—a military objective, not even a contingency task. The Army left it to be considered during the operations as and when the opportunity came up.[59] The planners appreciated its capture as an ambitious proposition, considering crossing one of the three rivers—the Padma, the Jamuna, or the Meghna—a tall order in the face of enemy opposition to an attack on Dacca. Major General K.K. Singh, the Director of Military Operations, felt that 'the Indian Army with its inherent inhibitions against anything unorthodox and a more speedy type of manoeuvre was ill-suited for attempting the capture of Dacca.'[60] The Army Chief, overruling Eastern Command's proposal to keep Dacca as the final objective in August 1971, felt that by capturing Khulna and Chittagong, Dacca would automatically fall and hence, there was no need to take it.[61] However, both Khulna and Chittagong did not fall until 16 December—the day the Pakistani forces surrendered. Hard-fought tactical battles between the two armies convinced India to bypass fortified positions, and accordingly, it carried out some modifications in the operational plans.

The Indian Army, learning from the 1965 war experience, factored in the likely international pressure for a ceasefire. It appreciated that its military's rapid progress would lead to the eventual collapse of the Pakistani resistance, rendering Dacca untenable before a ceasefire. Apprehending that an early ceasefire might end the war without capturing the entire country, it opted to secure maximum territory. Thus, the task assigned to Eastern Command was 'limited to occupying the major portion of Bangladesh instead of the entire country'.[62] India, however, did not expand its strategic aim to secure Dacca even after achieving significant success in the first week of the war. Instead, it needlessly captured some tactical objectives that did not contribute to the strategic aim of a swift offensive to occupy vast territory. The advance to Khulna after the fall of Jessore; the capture of Hilli, Jhenida, Rangpur; and the attack on Mynamati are examples. The Indian Army justified fighting attrition battles for these tactical objectives to have substantial territory in its control before any UN-sponsored ceasefire. Gen K.V. Krishna Rao, former Army Chief, rightly lamented: 'If forces employed on these strategically unimportant and infructuous missions could be utilized for developing thrust towards Dacca, perhaps its capture would have been further speeded up, and the number of casualties reduced.'[63] There is merit in this observation. The campaign could have been executed more expeditiously if Dacca had been kept as a strategic military objective, with complementary thrust lines developed along the western, northern and south-eastern sectors.

In the final analysis, the manoeuvre executed by crossing the mighty Meghna River posed a significant threat to Dacca, which made the Pakistani position militarily untenable. Lieutenant General (Lt Gen) Sagat Singh's boldness to achieve a brilliant manoeuvre, transporting more than a division-size force by helicopters and river crafts across the Meghna River, made the crucial difference. However, the same boldness and ability to execute manoeuvre operations were missing in other senior commanders. The 2 Corps lost an opportunity to reach Dacca first due to inflexibility to exploit initial success after the early capture of Jessore. Even 33 Corps failed to optimise its full combat potential and remained engaged in tactical battles that did not contribute strategically to the overall campaign. Despite India having credible intelligence about Chinese non-military intervention and the Indo-Soviet treaty's deterrence, it remained unduly worried about the Chinese threat. The Army did not employ 6 Mountain Division barring a brigade from supplementing any offensive and pulled out forces from the Chinese border only on 8 December 1971.

The Meghna River's crossing demonstrated the highest degree of close coordination between the Army and the air force. Lt Gen Sagat Singh and Group Captain Chandan Singh meticulously planned and brilliantly executed the heliborne lift of almost three brigades in over 350 sorties. The synergy assumed greater significance as it was not pre-planned but optimally exploited the Pakistan Army's rapid collapse. The pressure exerted by the Indian Navy on Chittagong and Cox's Bazaar, including interdiction of Pakistani shipping, added to Pakistan's psychological pressure to surrender. Mukti Bahini played a valuable role in providing intelligence and harassing Pakistani forces by raiding isolated/lightly held posts and static installations; however, they could not undertake independent operations.

Western Theatre: Cautious Approach

The Western theatre, adhering to its strategy to hold ground, considerably succeeded in thwarting Pakistani designs and capturing significant territory. India took a considerable risk in deploying its defensive formations quite late to avoid provoking any Pakistani offensive. Had Pakistan mounted a surprise attack, the situation would have become precarious for the Army. The Western Army Commander, Lt Gen K.P. Candeth, remarked, 'Until the third week of October, the Western border was virtually open and, had Yahya Khan attacked before the middle of October 1971, he would have certainly succeeded in overrunning a large part of Punjab.'[64] The decision not to launch the 1 Corps offensive until Pakistan mounted its offensive led to the loss of initiative and surprise but ensured the Pathankot corridor's security. Excessive caution in its employment limited its potential and could not secure Zaffarwal or Shakargarh. In the Chhamb sector, the field commander's obsession with offensive operations led to the neglect of defensive preparations despite impending enemy attack inputs. The defensive plans were also faulty. The main defences were sited well in-depth, with only covering troops operating forward. It overlooked the implications of the loss of territory in a short war. Pakistan's inability to successfully pursue the offensive after securing a foothold across the Munawar Tawi River saved the day for India. Unfortunately, the corps did not attempt to muster the available forces to exploit denuding of the area by Pakistani troops and remained content to keep the defensive line resting on Munawar Tawi River. Inactivity is inexcusable in the context of short wars.[65]

In Rajasthan, the Barmer sector's offensive achieved significant success and set the stage for further exploitation, but the lack of adequate logistic support inhibited it. After successfully thwarting the Pakistani attack on Longewala, the Jaisalmer sector's operations exhibited extreme caution and failed to pursue the retreating enemy. The 1 Armoured Division remained unemployed throughout the war, catering to a Pakistani threat that did not materialise. Nor did it pose any threat to Pakistan, despite its offensive in Shakargarh and Rajasthan, drawing in additional Pakistan forces. India did not visualise how to employ its offensive forces should Pakistan fail to launch its attacks. Arjun Subramaniam commented aptly, 'The anticipated mother of all battles between the two armored divisions remained in the realm of fiction.'[66] Gen Krishna Rao was correct in asserting that India could have made substantial gains in the Western theatre if the strategy could have been executed more vigorously.[67] Indian Army failed to employ its total resources optimally and allowed the opportunities to slip by.

War Termination

As India's offensive made rapid progress in East Pakistan, the US despatched its Seventh Fleet to the Bay of Bengal on 13 December 1971. India, apprehending the US aim to deter it from liberating Bangladesh, bombed the Chittagong naval port to render it unusable and claimed to remain undeterred. However, the US aim of dispatching the Seventh Fleet was different. Realising the inevitability of Bangladesh's independence, the US invented an intelligence input about India's plans to partition West Pakistan and even created the bogey of a global conflict to rope in the USSR. It asserted that the fleet prevented India from dismembering West Pakistan after the liberation of Bangladesh. Henry Kissinger wrote, 'by using diplomatic signals, and behind the scenes pressures, we (implying the USSR) had been able to save west Pakistan from the imminent threat of Indian aggression and domination.'[68]

With East Pakistan as its centre of gravity, India had strategised to conduct holding and limited offensive operations in West Pakistan. Even after the Pakistani forces' surrender and pressure from some political leaders, the Indian government did not alter its pre-war strategy. It considered the political advantages of international prestige and goodwill accruing from a unilateral ceasefire of far greater significance than inflicting additional attrition and capturing crucial territory. As the loss of East Pakistan had become a reality, the US dispatched the Seventh Fleet to exhibit explicit support to Pakistan and an implicit resolve to China and the Soviet Union. Subrahmanyam commented: 'The story of an Indian plan to launch an offensive in West Pakistan was invented to justify the sending of Enterprise mission; this kind of disinformation is standard practice in intelligence operations.'[69]

Conclusion

In 1971, India comprehensively achieved its political objective through a decisive military victory. The establishment of lasting peace after the war is an essential ingredient of the paradigm of war, but it has rarely happened. If we go by the Clausewitzian dictum that the object of war is not victory but enduring peace, most wars would fall short of the standards.[70] The 1971 Indo-Pakistan War partially exemplifies the same. India comprehensively attained the national interest of maintaining its socio-cultural identity. 'India had not only won a decisive military victory but had seemingly exorcised the specter of the "two-nation" theory that had haunted the subcontinent since 1947.'[71] The creation of friendly Bangladesh on the eastern borders has significantly denied external support to the lingering insurgencies in the North-East.

However, the political gains should provide the victor enough bargaining leverages to extract concessions from the vanquished to establish enduring peace by resolving lingering issues. India did not dictate terms to Pakistan on the Kashmir issue in the Shimla Agreement despite its leverages. The inception of proxy war in J&K in the late 1980s made this conviction grow stronger. The Treaty of Versailles that imposed humiliating conditions on Germany after its defeat in World War I, leading to the rise of Nazism and World War II, perhaps influenced Indian decision-makers not to inflict further humiliation on Pakistan by imposing a solution to the Kashmir problem. It was a noble and well-meaning intention. India possibly miscalculated that strengthening the civilian democracy in Pakistan would resolve the Kashmir issue amicably. However, the unfolding of the crisis under intense international pressure signified India's steely political resolve, robust military capability, tremendous synergy exhibited by all the organs of the government and immense public support for a national cause spearheaded by a well-oiled apex decision-making apparatus.

India orchestrated the refugee crisis by a deft calibration of politico-diplomatic–military strategy. It took a deliberate decision to intervene after exhausting other alternatives, which proved eminently right militarily. Some historians and scholars, even in hindsight, favoured early intervention. S. Raghavan commented, 'Had such an intervention been successfully undertaken, it would have mitigated the brutalities visited upon the Bengalis, and the incalculable loss of life and violation of human dignity.'[72] A military campaign conducted at the time and place of India's choosing was necessary for assured success. A stalemate would have resulted in an UN-sponsored ceasefire, with India failing to achieve its political objective. India formulated a workable, clear political objective of the return of refugees, asserting to the world that it would not accept any 'peaceful solution' that did not ensure their return, and then steadfastly pursued it. India calibrated military and diplomacy very effectively. Seeing the unwillingness and inability of the international community to nudge Pakistan to a political solution, India affected a timely strategic shift in its approach and assiduously calibrated the military support to Bangladesh's indigenous freedom struggle, ostensibly signaling its deference to a political settlement.

Its well-planned escalation matrix provoked Pakistan to initiate the war for which India had prepared diligently. Just war theorists rightly alluded to India's application of force for a humanitarian cause. 'Indian involvement was a better case of humanitarian intervention not because of the singularity and purity of the government's motives but because its various motives converged on a single course of action that was also the course of action called by the Bengalis.'[73] India did not prosecute military operations in West Pakistan after the Pakistan Army's surrender in the East and thus could not create long-term strategic deterrence on any futuristic Pakistani misadventure. It overlooked the Clausewitzian theory of suppressing the will of the enemy: 'If our opponent is to be made to comply with our will, we must place him in a situation which is even more oppressive to him than the sacrifice which we demand.'[74]

On balance, the 1971 India–Pakistan War was India's triumphant moment. India achieved a decisive politico-military victory, creating a new state of Bangladesh by splitting its arch-rival Pakistan. It was one of the shortest wars in world history but had profound global ramifications. The Shimla Accord signed between the two warring sides in July 1972 did not usher in enduring peace; yet, it has been a touchstone of India's foreign policy ever since, framing its bilateral interaction with Pakistan. Sisson and Rose summed up aptly: 'There was strong and consistent control in democratic India during the Bangladesh crisis, but relatively weak and inconsistent control in authoritarian Pakistan; democratic India was the hard state; authoritarian Pakistan the soft.'[75]

NOTES

1. Richard Sisson and Leo E. Rose, *War and Secession: Pakistan, India, and the Creation of Bangladesh*, Berkeley: University of California Press, 1990, p. 141.
2. 'Bangladesh and Our Policy Options by K. Subramanyam', Subject File No. 276 (III

Instalment), P.N. Haksar Papers, Nehru Memorial Museum and Libray (NMML), New Delhi.

3. 'Haksar to Sikri, 13 May 1971', Subject File No. 166 (III Instalment), Haksar Papers, NMML.
4. Lok Sabha Debate, 'PM's Statement in Lok Sabha, 24 May 1971', p. 187.
5. Rupert Smith, *The Utility of Force: The Art of War in the Modern World*, New York:Vintage Books, 2008, p. 262.
6. S.N. Prasad and U.P. Thapliyal, *The India–Pakistan War of 1971: A History*, Dehradun: Natraj, 2014, p. 467.
7. Ibid.
8. 'Haksar's Note to Indira Gandhi on Meeting with Opposition Leaders on 07 May 1971', Subject File No. 227, Haskar Papers, NMML.
9. Srinath Raghavan, *1971: A Global History of the Creation of Bangladesh*, Ranikhet: Permanent Black, 2013, p. 73, quoting Prasad and Thapliyal, *The India–Pakistan War of 1971: A History*, n. 6, pp. 173–74.
10. Raghavan, *1971: A Global History of the Creation of Bangladesh,* n. 9, pp. 210–12.
11. Prasad and Thapliyal, *The India–Pakistan War of 1971,* n. 6, pp. 109, 207, 354; K.V. Krishna Rao, *Prepare or Perish: A Study of National Security*, New Delhi: Lancer, 1991, p. 157; Major General Lachhman Singh Lehl, PVSM,VrC (Retired), *Victory in Bangladesh*, Dehradun: Natraj Publishers, 1981, p. 33; Colonel John Gill, *An Atlas of the 1971 Indo-Pak War: The Creation of Bangladesh*, Department of Defence, Near East South Asia Centre for Strategic Studies, 2003, pp. 69–90.
12. Prasad and Thapliyal, *The India–Pakistan War of 1971*, n. 6, pp. 109, 207, 354; K.V. Krishna Rao, *Prepare or Perish*, n. 11, p. 157; Major General Lachhman Singh Lehl, *Victory in Bangladesh*, n. 11, p. 33; Colonel John Gill, *An Atlas of the 1971 Indo-Pak War*, n. 11, pp. 69–90.
13. Sukhwant Singh, *India's Wars since Independence*, New Delhi: Lancer, 2009, p. 48.
14. Prasad and Thapliyal, *The India–Pakistan War of 1971*, n. 6, p. 14. Also see Krishna Rao, *Prepare or Perish*, n. 11, p. 157.
15. Krishna Rao, *Prepare or Perish*, n. 11, p. 158.
16. Raghavan, *1971: A Global History of the Creation of Bangladesh*, n. 9, p. 209. Also see 'Agha Shahi to U Thant, September 2, 1971', S-0863- 0001-02, UNSG U Thant Fonds, UN Archives, New York. Fonds are the records of U. Thant, UN Secretary-General, relating to his responsibilities as chief administrative officer of the Secretariat and as chief coordinator of the legislative, political, socio-economic and military bodies of the UN.
17. Raghavan, *1971: A Global History of the Creation of Bangladesh*, n. 9, pp. 206–07.
18. K. Subrahmanyam, *Bangladesh and India's Security*, Dehradun: Palit and Dutt Publishers, 1972, p. 106.
19. 'Note on "Economy under Conditions of Crisis" by Mr. PN Dhar, Economist and Secretary to the PM, July 21, 1971', Subject No. File 260 (III Instalment), Haksar Papers, NMML, quoted in Raghavan, *1971: A Global History of the Creation of Bangladesh*, n. 9, p. 207.
20. Ibid.
21. Krishna Rao, *Prepare or Perish*, n. 11, p. 170; and Prasad and Thapliyal, *The India–Pakistan War of 1971*, n. 6, pp. 105–06.
22. Prasad and Thapliyal, *The India–Pakistan War of 1971*, n. 6, p. 105.
23. J.F.R. Jacob, *An Odyssey in War and Peace*, New Delhi: Roli Books, 2011, pp.79–80. Also see Raghavan, *1971: A Global History of the Creation of Bangladesh*, n. 9, p. 238.
24. Krishna Rao, *Prepare or Perish*, n. 11, p. 171.
25. Singh, *India's Wars since Independence*, n. 13, p. 59.
26. P.C. Lal, *My Years with the IAF*, New Delhi: Lancer International, 1986, pp. 171–72.
27. Raghavan, *1971: A Global History of the Creation of Bangladesh*, n. 9, p. 213.
28. Ibid., p. 222.
29. Hakeem Arshad Qureshi, *The 1971 Indo-Pak War: A Soldier's Narrative*, Karachi: Oxford, 2013.

30. Krishna Rao, *Prepare or Perish*, n. 11, p. 208.
31. Ibid.
32. Prasad and Thapliyal, *The India–Pakistan War of 1971*, n. 6, pp. 88–89; and Raghavan, *1971: A Global History of the Creation of Bangladesh*, n. 9, p. 232.
33. Sisson and Rose, *War and Secession*, n. 1, p. 213.
34. Raghavan, *1971: A Global History of the Creation of Bangladesh*, n. 9, p. 232. Also see Gul Hassan Khan, *Memoirs of Lt Gen Gul Hassan Khan*, Karachi: Oxford University Press, 1993, p. 322.
35. Raghavan, *1971: A Global History of the Creation of Bangladesh*, n. 9, p. 232, quoting personal interview with P.N. Dhar, 24 November 2009. Also see Katherine Frank, *Indira: The Life of Indira Gandhi*, London: HarperCollins, 2001, p. 338; Depinder Singh, *Field Marshal Sam Manekshaw, MC: Soldiering with Dignity*, Dehradun: Natraj, 2002, p. 157; and S. Muthiah, *Born to Dare: The Life of Lt Gen Inderjit Singh Gill*, New Delhi: Penguin, 2008, p. 186.
36. Raghavan, *1971: A Global History of the Creation of Bangladesh*, n. 9, pp. 233–34. Also see Shuja Nawaz, *Crossed Swords: Pakistan, its Army, and the Wars Within*, Karachi: Oxford University Press, 2008, p. 295; Hasan Zaheer, *Separation of East Pakistan: The Rise and Realisation of Bengali Muslim Nationalism*, Dhaka: University Press, 2001, p. 360; and Aboobaker Osman Mitha, *Unlikely Beginnings: A Soldiers' Life*, Oxford: Oxford University Press, 2003, p. 353.
37. Raghavan, *1971: A Global History of the Creation of Bangladesh*, n. 9, p. 234.
38. Arjun Subramaniam, *India's Wars: A Military History, 1947–1971*, Noida: HarperCollins, 2016, p. 378.
39. Jacob, *An Odyssey in War and Peace*, n. 23, p. 84.
40. Bhutto had calculated that only an ignominious surrender of the Pakistan Army would lead to his political ascendancy; and he was proven right in this regard. On 20 December 1971, five days after the resolution was submitted, he took over as President and Chief Martial Law Administrator of Pakistan. The previous day, when President Yahya, seeing an opportunity to avoid surrender, rang up Bhutto in New York to ask him to accept the Polish resolution, the latter pretended not to hear despite repeated calls and admonished even the operator, who intervened to state that the telephone connection was good. See Raghavan, *1971: A Global History of the Creation of Bangladesh*, n. 9, p. 261, quoting 1614th Meeting of the UN Security Council, 14–15 December 1971, S/PV.1614, UN Archives, New York. While speaking in the Security Council, Bhutto censured the UN for not acting on time, tore up a copy of the resolution and walked out of the session. No further discussion took place, and the resolution was dead.
41. Prasad and Thapliyal, *The India–Pakistan War of 1971*, n. 6, pp. 415, 416, 428, 438.
42. The core group was comprised of: P.N. Haksar, Principal Secretary to the PM; P.N. Dhar, Secretary in PM's Office; D.P. Dhar, former Ambassador to the USSR and Chairman of the Policy Planning Committee; R.N. Kao, Director of the Research and Analysis Wing (R&AW); T.N. Kaul, the Foreign Secretary; and some other administrative secretaries, like G. Ramchandra, M. Malhotra, Sharada Prasad and B.N. Tandon. At the Cabinet level, Swaran Singh, the Foreign Minister, Jagjivan Ram, the Defence Minister, and Y.B. Chavan, the Finance Minister, were the principal advisors. Mr Haksar and D.P. Dhar were close advisors and confidants of the PM. See Sisson and Rose, *War and Secession*, n. 1, p. 138; and J.N. Dixit, *India–Pakistan in War and Peace*, New Delhi: Books Today, 2002, p. 181.
43. Subrahmanyam, *Bangladesh and India's Security*, n. 18, p. 227.
44. David Fisher, *The Just War Tradition*, Palgrave Macmillan, 1985, p. 23.
45. Raghavan, *1971: A Global History of the Creation of Bangladesh*, n. 9, p. 60.
46. Ibid, p. 227.
47. Ibid.
48. Raghavan, *1971: A Global History of the Creation of Bangladesh*, n. 9, p. 108, quoting Henry

Kissinger, *The White House Years,* London: George Weidenfield & Nicholson, 1979, pp. 866–67.

49. Ibid., pp. 192–93.
50. Gen Yahya Khan's interview in *Newsweek*, 8 November 1971, quoted in Prasad and Thapliyal, *The India–Pakistan War of 1971*, n. 6, 2014, p. 75.
51. Raghavan, *1971: A Global History of the Creation of Bangladesh*, n. 9, p. 188; and Sisson and Rose, *War and Secession*, n. 1, p. 203. Also see 'Zhou to Yahya, April 11', in J.A. Naik, *India, Russia, China and Bangladesh*, New Delhi: S. Chand, 1972, p. 138, and *Pakistan Times*, 13 April 1971, for the text of Zhou En-lai's letter as circulated by the Pakistani government.
52. Sisson and Rose, *War and Secession*, n. 1, p. 203. The source of this information includes one former official of the Pakistan Foreign Service who provided copies of the Sino-Pakistani correspondence to Indian intelligence services at the home of a well-known Indian journalist in New Delhi.
53. Pran Chopra, *India's Second Liberation*, Delhi: Vikas, 1973, p. 81.
54. Sisson and Rose, *War and Secession*, n. 1, p. 228.
55. Ibid., p. 230, quoting interviews in Pakistan and the US, 1979.
56. J.N. Dixit, *Liberation and Beyond: Indo-Bangladesh Relations*, New Delhi: Konark Press, 1999, p. 89, quoted in Raghavan, *1971: A Global History of the Creation of Bangladesh*, n. 9, p. 234.
57. Sisson and Rose, *War and Secession*, n. 1, p. 214.
58. Ibid, p. 280.
59. Singh, *India's Wars since Independence*, n. 13, p. 79.
60. Raghavan, *1971: A Global History of the Creation of Bangladesh*, n. 9, p. 236.
61. Jacob, *An Odyssey in War and Peace*, n. 23, p. 80.
62. Raghavan, *1971: A Global History of the Creation of Bangladesh*, n. 9, p 236, quoting Singh, *India's Wars since Independence*, n. 13, pp. 68–69, 72, 90–91.
63. Krishna Rao, *Prepare or Perish*, n. 11, p. 200.
64. K.P. Candeth; *The Western Front: Indo-Pakistan War 1971*, Dehradun: The English Book Depot, 1997, p. 12.
65. Singh, *India's Wars since Independence*, n. 13, p. 256.
66. Subramaniam, *India's Wars: A Military History*, n. 38, p. 418.
67. Krishna Rao, *Prepare or Perish*, n. 11, p. 244.
68. Richard Nixon, *The Memoirs of Richard Nixon*, New York: Grosset & Dunlap, 1978, p. 530, quoted in Raghavan, *1971: A Global History of the Creation of Bangladesh*, n. 9, p. 262.
69. K Subramanyam with Artur Monterio, *Shedding Shibboleths India's Evolving Strategic Outlook*, Delhi: Wordsmiths, 2005, p. 330.
70. V.R. Raghavan, 'Wars Old and New: Structural Changes', adapted from the Field Marshal Memorial Lecture delivered on Infantry Day, 27 October 2015, published in *USI Journal*, Vol. CLXV, No. 602, October–December 2015, p. 463.
71. Raghavan, *1971: A Global History of the Creation of Bangladesh*, n. 9, p. 265.
72. Ibid., p. 272.
73. Michael Walzer, *Just and Unjust Wars: A Moral Argument with Historical Illustrations*, New York: Basic Books, 1977, p. 147.
74. Lennart Souchon, Military Strategy Magazine, *Strategy in the 21st Century: The Continuing Relevance of Carl von Clausewitz*, Tel Aviv, Israel: The IJ Infinity Group, December 2020, available at https://dokumen.pub/strategy-in-the-21st-century-the-continuing-relevance-of-carl-von-clausewitz-1st-ed-9783030460273-9783030460280.html, accessed on 14 August 2021.
75. Sisson and Rose, *War and Secession*, n. 1, p. 277.

3

Language, Culture and the Creation of Bangladesh

Dorothy Deb

In 1947, India and Pakistan became two independent nations, born of a violent partition. Pakistan was a geographical oddity as the two provinces of the nation remained separated by almost 2,000 kilometres of the Indian landmass. The two provinces were topographically varied, culturally unfamiliar and linguistically different from each other. The only linking factors between these provinces were Islam and the memory of British colonialism. Soon after attaining independence, the difference between the two provinces began to cloud the strength of the common linking factors. West Pakistan was the administrative seat of the nation and all major bureaucratic and military institutions were based out of it. Also, most of the administrative and military positions in Pakistan were held by the West Pakistani elites (mostly Punjabis and Sindhis). As a result, there was a greater concentration of effort and energy into the issues of the western province; and the eastern province was treated like a satellite unit. While a major chunk of revenue and resources for Pakistan came from the eastern province, it was not given priority in the developmental expenditure. In addition, East Pakistan was under-represented in the government and the military. This disparity gave rise to a sentiment among the population of East Pakistan that they had moved from the colonial rule of the British to the colonial rule of West Pakistan.

East Pakistan was largely homogeneous in its ethno-linguistic character, with the majority population identifying as Bengali and speaking the Bangla language. In terms of population too, they formed the single-largest community in Pakistan. Thus, to feel adequately represented, the Bengali population demanded that Bangla be recognised as one of the national languages of Pakistan. However, the Pakistani administration was averse to adopting Bangla as a national language. They believed that Pakistan should have one national language for the sake of maintaining unity in the nation, and that language must be Urdu. As mentioned earlier, Pakistan was a geographical oddity with multiple contending cultural identities and hence, the Pakistani administration was trying to develop the national identity based on a common language and culture that spoke closely to their religious identity. Therefore, they mandated that the media and educational institutions must exclusively use Urdu. This was unacceptable for the Bengali population in East Bengal and to sections of the Sindhi and Punjabi population in West Pakistan, who did not have a cultural affinity to Urdu. Mass protests erupted in Dhaka on 8 December 1947, in opposition to imposition of Urdu, giving birth to the first major rift between the two provinces of Pakistan in the form of the Language Movement or the 'Bhasha Andolon'.

The Bhasha Andolon gave a new life to Bengali nationalism that had existed in the pre-1947 phase in the Bengal province of the Indian subcontinent. This Bengali nationalism had somewhat been subverted to the demands for a separate country for Muslims, but it had never disappeared from the lexicon of the Bengali people. Thus, Bengali nationalism was not a new concept that had developed out of the Liberation War. Ideological visions for a united Bengal had been in place right from 1905, when Bengal was partitioned for the first time. In 1947, when the communal division of the subcontinent became evident, some public intellectuals and political figures called for an undivided, independent Bengal to emerge. It was H.S. Suhrawardy and Sarat Chandra Bose who presented the proposal for an independent, undivided Bengal in April 1947.[1] The proposal was rejected by the Muslim League and the Hindu Mahasabha, citing heightened religious polarisation in Bengal.[2] However, the idea of an independent Bengal had continued to lurk under the surface, even after the Partition. Thus, when the Bengali identity was being marginalised and targeted, Bengali nationalism resurfaced as a political agenda. It was an accessible concept and an effective tool to mobilise people.[3] The population of East Pakistan had come to recognise language and culture as a major collectivising force that could amplify their demands to the Pakistani government. The same language and culture would go on to be the basis of an independent Bangladesh decades later.

This paper aims to revisit the journey of Bengali nationalism from its nascent state in the Bhasha Andolon to its virile state in the 'Mukti Juddho' (Liberation War). The paper undertakes a historical analysis of the period between the 'Bhasha Andolan' and the eventful 1971 Bangladesh Liberation War. There has been an explication of the major political developments that led to the independence of Bangladesh, where language and culture were major propellants. While the political disenchantment and the prolonged denial of rights finally led to the calls for independence; we enquire into the role of language and culture in the political disenchantment and the denial of rights.

As we step into the 50th year of the Bangladesh Liberation War, it would be useful to revisit one of the core components that fuelled the calls for an independent Bangladesh. The paper has been divided into different sections, which trace language and culture as a source of othering, oppression and solidarity. The next section tries to analyse how the cultural differences between the two provinces of Pakistan became evident and manifested themselves into calls for the autonomy of East Pakistan. The following section looks into how language and culture became the cause of oppression and led to a military crackdown on the people of East Pakistan. The penultimate section traces the global networks of solidarity, built on language and culture that helped sustain the Liberation War. The concluding section sums up three distinct impacts of language and culture and how they gradually solidified the demands for independence.

Language and Culture as a Source of Othering

It was with the Bhasha Andolon that, for the first time, the Bengali population of East Pakistan asserted their linguistic and cultural identity in conjunction with their Pakistani identity. In 1947, when the state language of Pakistan was being deliberated upon, a one nation, one language policy became the popular choice of the West Pakistani elites, with Urdu being the language of choice. The Pakistani leadership believed that Urdu would reassert the Muslim identity of the nation and bind the provinces together in a singular national identity. Urdu was hardly spoken in East Pakistan, the people of the Eastern province had little affinity to the language. Thus, the exclusive use of Urdu as a medium of education and in official communication was discriminatory towards the Bengali-speaking majority community of East Pakistan. The Bengali population saw this forced imposition of Urdu as a negation of their linguistic identity. As a result, protests erupted on 8 December 1947 in Dhaka, with the people demanding recognition of Bangla as a national language.[4]

The Bhasha Andolon was sustained for over four years. In this period, leaders of East Pakistan organised several rallies, meetings and called for strikes in opposition to the language policy. The motion to include Bangla as a national language was introduced by Dhirendranath Dutta in the Constituent Assembly on 23 February 1948, but was opposed by Prime Minister Liaquat Ali Khan.[5] As time passed, the population of East Pakistan started to grow more restive due to the recurring denial of their demand. In 1949, when the Awami League was formed, the people of East Pakistan found renewed hope in the representation of their interests, giving the Language Movement a fresh life. The Awami League, under Maulana Bhasani, devised a new protest itinerary in 1952. On 21 February 1952, protest demonstrations and hartals (strikes) were called for in defiance of Section 144. Protesting students from the Dhaka Medical College were met with a baton charge by the police. They grew agitated and the police opened fire at them, killing three students and a nine-year-old boy and injuring several protesters.[6]

The police repression made the protesters more resolute in their demands. It also forced the administration to gradually discard their 'one state language' stance. The East Bengal Legislative Assembly adopted a resolution recommending Bangla as a state language in 1952; and on 7 May 1954, the Constituent Assembly finally recognised Bangla as a state language along with Urdu.[7] Thus, the Language Movement, first, laid bare the colonial attitude that the Pakistani administration had towards the eastern province. Second, it was the first non-communal movement that East Pakistan had seen since the Partition, forging bonds of solidarity based on ethno-linguistic identity rather than religious identity. Third, it brought Awami League forward as an important voice of the people of East Pakistan. These three reasons were going to increase the already stark differences between the two provinces.

The Bengali language was the mode of access to religion in Bengal. The Muslim masses who had no knowledge of Arabic had to access their religion through fables and folklore in Bangla, as the Qur'an had not been translated to the Bengali language in the sixteenth century when Islam travelled towards eastern undivided India. The masses in Bengal would access all social, political and religious information through Bengali language. Even when Urdu and Persian became the official languages of choice for Muslim elites in India in the eighteenth and nineteenth centuries, they could not replace Bangla among the masses. The vacuum that was left in Bangla literature by the lack of patronage from Muslim literati was filled by Hindus. Thus, the imagery and worldview created in the Bangla language community was an amalgamation of Hindu and Muslim sensibilities.[8] The masses in East Pakistan were informed by this unique cultural–linguistic sensibility that was rooted in the Bangla language. This stood in sharp contrast with the cultural sensibility of West Pakistan, which was more rooted in Islamic religiosity.

Owing to the vast cultural differences, the West Pakistani elites had a stigmatised perception of Bengalis. They believed that the Bengali population was religiously frivolous and martially incapable—a stigma that was deepened in the wake of the Bhasha Andolon. They also considered the Bengali masses to be irritants to the efficient governance of Pakistan. Further, there was clear disparity in the allocation of developmental funds allotted to the two provinces, as also a disparity in terms of representation in key administrative and military positions. East Pakistan had a recurring feeling of being deprived of resources and opportunities, with much of this deprivation linked to the cultural differences that existed between the two provinces.[9] The East Pakistani population was also indifferent to the major causes that West Pakistan was focusing on, primarily the Kashmir issue and the militant anti-India sentiment.[10] This attitude added to West Pakistan's stigma against their Bengali brethren. In addition, the ethnic traditions of East Pakistan were unwelcome in West Pakistan, for instance, the Bengali women dressed in saris and donned a bindi irrespective of their religious identity. This was seen as an undermining of Islamic traditions by a section of West Pakistani elites. The cultural differences between the two provinces were thus visible in the everyday realities of the population, like food habits, clothing and language. These realities gave birth to stereotypes, which led to stigma, which finally boiled down to a sense of detachment.

The differential treatment of East Pakistan by the Pakistani government soon became a political issue and propelled the calls for greater autonomy of East Pakistan. The people realised that unless they are adequately represented in a democratic government, the colonial treatment of the Bengali people would not stop. In 1966, the Awami League, sensing the strong demand for autonomy of East Pakistan, came up with a six-point programme to strengthen Pakistan's federal structure. The six-point programme and the calls for greater autonomy stemmed from a secularised Bengali nationalism that the Awami League subscribed to: it was a composite of Bengali culture, language, folklore, mores and the general Bengali environment, from which Bengalis could receive inspiration and be motivated to strive for the uplift of the society.[11]

The six-point programme called for: a genuine federal constitution; restricting powers of the federal government to defence and foreign affairs; two separate currencies for the two provinces; devolving fiscal policies to the federal units;

separate foreign exchange earnings of each wing; and a separate militia for the defence of the east wing.[12] The programme represented the lack of faith that was simmering in East Pakistan against the Pakistani government, as well as East Pakistan's desire to have a greater say in its own administration and defence. These six points went on to become the main election agenda of the Awami League and the root of the final breakdown of relations between the two wings.

The general elections in Pakistan in 1970 exposed the cultural differences that manifested themselves into partisan voting patterns. The Awami League, under Sheikh Mujibur Rahman, was contesting the elections, riding the wave of populist sentiment that sought greater autonomy for East Pakistan. Awami League's supporter base involved the significant Bengali Hindu minority, progressives and leftists. The influence of these groups increased the realms of secularism within Bengali nationalism in East Pakistan and attuned it to a unique cultural sensibility that was contesting the dominant West Pakistani influence on the nation. Meanwhile, in the western province, the Pakistan People's Party (PPP), under Zulfikar Ali Bhutto, was contesting the election to consolidate and retain the supremacy of Punjabis and Sindhis over the military and administrative units of Pakistan, and the cultural narrative of the nation. A third entity, the military government of Yahya Khan, was hoping to retain power and prominence even after the general elections. Wanting to maintain his status quo position as the President of Pakistan, it was in Yahya Khan's interest that there was no great shuffling in the power dynamics of Pakistan. The military administration thus covertly supported Bhutto in the hope that the Awami League would be unable to secure a majority mandate in the elections. A senior officer visiting Dhaka in December 1970 assured his colleagues that they would not 'allow those black bastards to rule over us'.[13]

In the run-up to the elections, East Pakistan had to face two major natural disasters. In July 1970, floods caused large-scale damage to life and property and in November 1970, tropical cyclone Bhola hit the province. The cyclone was the worst natural calamity that the eastern province had seen in decades. Rural Bengal was razed to the ground, crop fields were submerged, dead bodies were piled up along the coast, cattle were washed away and a large number of people were left homeless. The death toll was close to 2,30,000 people. The government's response to the crisis was languid and lackadaisical. President Yahya Khan took an aerial survey of the affected areas on his way back from China; and no other West Pakistani leader paid a visit to the affected areas.[14] Also, the government's relief efforts were inconsistent and sparse. The international community was much more proactive in the delivery of aid to the affected areas and the affected people.[15] Mujibur Rahman categorised the government's response as 'criminal negligence', reasserting that East Pakistan was being treated as a colony and a market.[16] Thus, the people of East Pakistan felt ignored and alienated by their government, strengthening the demands for autonomy. This feeling of alienation, coupled with the undercurrents of Bengali nationalism, became the major determinant of East Pakistan's voting pattern in the general elections of 1970.

On 8 December 1970, the election results were declared. These results were as polarised as the cultural milieu of Pakistan. The Awami League secured 160 seats out of the 162 in East Pakistan, giving them the absolute majority to form the government in Pakistan. The single-largest party that emerged victorious in West Pakistan was the PPP; the Awami League failed to secure any seats in the western province. The results were contrary to the military government's expectations as Yahya Khan had hoped that the elections would lead to a hung parliament, which would finally call for fresh elections.[17] However, the Awami League's landslide victory gave them a legitimate claim to form the government and design a constitution. The military government feared that the six-point programme would now turn into reality and the military's position would be greatly reduced in the administration of the country. Also, Bhutto wanted to play a greater role in the government and constitution formation in Pakistan; he did not want to play a subsidiary role to the Awami League in the National Assembly. As a result, the military government and the PPP forged a secret alliance to prevent the Awami League from forming a government in Pakistan.[18]

The military administration delayed the formation of the National Assembly, constantly coercing Mujibur Rahman to come to a consensus with Bhutto on the six-point programme.[19] However, no such consensus was reached as the PPP was vehemently opposed to greater autonomy for East Pakistan. Further, the military administration covertly coaxed the smaller parties in West Pakistan to avoid the National Assembly.[20] On 15 February 1971, Bhutto's PPP declared that they would not be attending the National Assembly. The major reason cited for the boycott was the Awami League's insistence on the six-point programme.

In the meantime, the legitimately elected Awami League and its supporters in East Pakistan were growing impatient. The military government's colonial mindset was becoming evident to them as they were being denied constitutional justice. Public meetings and rallies were being carried out day and night in East Pakistan to register their protest against the delay in convening the National Assembly. Seeing a surge in public unrest, Mujib had to restore the faith of his constituency. He declared: 'No power on earth could subjugate the Bangalees anymore' and 'we will die but we will not surrender'.[21] The process of othering was now complete: the two provinces stood in opposition to one another on social, cultural and political fronts.

Language and Culture as a Source of Oppression

The military government in West Pakistan had no intention of peacefully transferring power to the Awami League. While negotiations for the National Assembly continued, the army was asked to continuously increase its presence in East Pakistan. The plans for a military crackdown had been set in motion as early as 20 February 1971. Yahya Khan was simultaneously trying to build a political consensus against Mujibur Rahman and the Awami League, citing their separatist tendencies.[22] On 1 March 1971, the National Assembly was postponed sine die. This caused massive outrage in East Pakistan as the Bengali population felt betrayed. The more radical sections of the Awami League and the student community in East Pakistan now began demanding a unilateral declaration of independence. However, Mujibur Rahman was cautious not to make any such declarations he believed could invite violent confrontations with the army.[23] Simultaneously, he did not want to exhibit complacency at the postponement of the National Assembly, so he called for a six-day protest demonstration which included strikes, rallies and public meetings. When Mujib addressed the crowd of supporters on 7 March 1971, he raised his fist in the air and declared: 'Our struggle this time is a struggle for independence.'[24]

The people of East Pakistan began a non-cooperation movement against the Pakistani government, in the form of non-payment of taxes and withdrawal from government services. The student community in Dhaka formed the Central Students Action Committee of Independent Bangladesh and chose Tagore's 'Sonar Bangla' as their national anthem. On 7 March, the government imposed curfew in Dhaka, but the protesters broke the curfew and continued with the demonstrations.[25] This led to the army opening fire at the protesters, killing 172 people—a repeat of the repression that had taken place during the Bhasha Andolon. Contrary to the army's expectations, the Bengali population did not bow down to the martial law and became more resolute in their demand for independence. The demonstrations represented an overwhelming sense of Bengali nationalism and Bengali pride embodied in the calls for independence. The cultural identity that had been a source of discrimination was now being reclaimed and reasserted for not just equality but also independence.

Several rounds of negotiations were held between 15 and 24 March, but all of them were unsuccessful. The military government was trying to coax the Awami League to settle the constitutional matters with the PPP. Initially, the Awami League was pressing for the repeal of the martial law and a quick transfer of power to the civilian government in the provinces. Yahya Khan, however, was averse to repealing the martial law, stating that it would create a legal vacuum and make the transfer of power to the civilian government more difficult. On 16 March 1971, Yahya Khan, flustered with the direction of the negotiations, told General Tikka Khan: 'The bastard (Mujib) is not behaving. You get ready.'[26] The approach of the military government was clear: either the Awami League surrenders to its terms or there would be a military crackdown.

Unaware of the plans of a military crackdown, the Awami League continued working on the draft constitution. On 24 March, members of the Awami League sought to meet the West Pakistani officials to finalise the draft constitution, but their request was denied. With the plans for a military crackdown already underway, Yahya Khan had given up on the idea of a peaceful settlement. On 25 March, Yahya Khan finally met the military officials in Dhaka and gave them the green signal for a military operation that was to begin that night. He simultaneously gave orders that all West Pakistani delegates must leave Dhaka the next morning. At 11:30 p.m. on 25 March 1971, Operation Searchlight began. All doors for constitutional justice were shut for East Pakistan, but the war for the liberation of Bangladesh had just begun.

The military crackdown was brutal and was targeted specifically towards the Bengali-speaking population. The worst affected by the crackdown were the Bengali Hindus who had stayed back in East Pakistan after the Partition. The Pakistani government conveniently pinned the responsibility of the unrest on the Hindus, considering them as agents of India. Students who came out on the streets to protest were shot at, houses were looted and the Bangladesh flags were torn down and burnt. On 26 March, Yahya Khan addressed the nation, blaming the Awami League for attacking the solidarity and integrity of Pakistan, and promised that such a crime would not go unpunished. Mujibur Rahman was arrested and sent to West Pakistan and the Awami League was banned.[27]

The military crackdown had one intention only: to rid East Pakistan of any and every secessionist tendency. In trying to achieve the same, the army went on a murderous rampage, killing men, women and children. Anyone that the army suspected to be a Hindu or a rebel was shot at sight. Villages were burned down or pillaged to 'cleanse' them of rebels. As Anthony Mascarenhas puts it in his narrative-altering article of 1971: 'This is Genocide conducted with amazing casualness.'[28] Indeed, genocide it was—a targeted killing of Bengalis in East Pakistan. The Pakistan Army used cultural markers, such as language and attire, to target and murder Bengalis. Earlier, the same language and culture had been used to stigmatise Bengali-speaking population. This stigma led to a denial of constitutional justice and finally, resulted in the inhuman repression of the population in East Pakistan by the Pakistan Army.

The oppression of the population of East Pakistan had begun long before 1971 and any and every demand for equal treatment was met with police brutality or military repression. The rightfully elected Awami League was symbolic of the aspirations of the Bengali population. Thus, when the Awami League was denied its place in the National Assembly and ultimately banned by the Pakistani government, the Bengali population perceived it as an obliteration of their aspirations, leaving no reason for them to believe in the constitutional processes of Pakistan and continue to live as second-class citizens in their own country. The secularised explications of Bengali culture had been a major eyesore for the Pakistani government. They believed that the calls for autonomy stemmed from the growing allegiance to secular values that were propelled by the Hindus in East Pakistan. Thus, the oppression was targeted towards the secularised Bengali nationalism and all its adherents, especially non-Muslims.

Language and Culture as a Source of Solidarity

While language and culture became a source of othering between the two provinces of Pakistan, they also led to the development of various networks of solidarity within and outside of East Pakistan. The Bengali-speaking population, particularly in India and in the West, were drawn to the cause of Bangladesh. The oppression that the population of East Pakistan was facing at the hands of the Pakistan Army became a cause for rallying and seeking international intervention. The Bengali diaspora led campaigns across the world to develop awareness about the Liberation War, and also to materialise networks of aid and assistance.

On 26 March, when Operation Searchlight was set in motion, Bengali officers mutinied against the Pakistani military. They refused to take up arms against their language brethren. The erstwhile officers joined the Bangladesh Liberation Army to rally for the cause of independence.[29] As the crackdown intensified and more people were killed, the Bengali diaspora community refused to pay remittances to the Pakistani government as a sign of protest. This led to a fall in Pakistan's remittance income to one-third. The diaspora community in the United

Kingdom (UK) and the United States (US) organised themselves and began producing news reports and public documents to increase awareness. They also organised lectures and teach-ins to promote the cause of Bangladesh. The diaspora in the US tried to reach out to sympathetic senators and congressmen to lobby for Bangladesh, and also to pressurise the US to restrain Pakistan from brutality. The efforts of the Bengali community were successful in capturing the attention of several activists and humanitarian organisations.[30] Action Bangladesh was started by a group of young internationalists and activists in Britain who started protesting against the Pakistan Army's atrocities in East Pakistan. Organisations such as Oxfam, Pugwash and Commission of Churches also took up the cause of increasing the outreach of Bangladeshi voices.[31] The humanitarian organisations tried to use their own networks to convince various governments and international organisations to press on Pakistan to refrain from further violence. The efforts of these organisations and the diaspora community led to a paltry but steady flow of aid to the Bangladesh Liberation Army and the refugees who had fled East Pakistan.

On the other hand, the Indian states bordering East Pakistan also faced an indirect impact of the crisis in East Pakistan. The persecuted Bengali population in East Pakistan started fleeing to West Bengal, Tripura and Assam for sanctuary. These states saw an inflow of close to 10 million refugees,[32] leading to severe pressure on the resources. The Bengali population in India was aggrieved by the treatment being meted out to their language brethren. Regional newspapers, while reporting the crisis in East Pakistan, blamed the Pakistani government for their vindictive approach towards the Bengalis. Student groups in Bengal carried out protests condemning the brutalities of the Pakistani Army, while simultaneously urging the Indian government to intervene in the crisis. Bound by the same language, familial ties and shared cultural history, the Bengalis on the Indian side of the border were naturally drawn to the cause of an independent Bangladesh. The idea of the 'desh', which had so far represented a place of belonging, now had a chance of real existence. Bangla 'desh', or the land of the Bengali people, was an idea that had existed even in the pre-independence era; and it had captured the imagination of the linguistic community beyond religious identities. The Bangladesh Liberation War gave fresh hope to that idea and drew support from Bengalis across the world. The Awami League was also careful to tread the secular line, so that they could retain their broad support base. Indeed, Awami League's secular politics helped in drawing sympathies from India. The Indian administration was much more sympathetic to a moderate Mujibur Rahman, as opposed to a hardliner like Bhutto, during the Pakistani elections of 1970. Thus, the idea of persecution of Bengalis created an important bond of solidarity that, ultimately, led to the materialisation of the dream of an independent Bangladesh.

During the war, the heart-wrenching sights of refugee camps in West Bengal, with widespread poverty, disease and hopelessness, became a talking point across the world. These sights had a great impact on another Bengali hailing from West Bengal, Pandit Ravi Shankar. Some of Ravi Shankar's own distant relatives had to flee East Pakistan in the face of the crisis, and his sympathies were with Bangladesh. He, therefore, decided to raise funds to help the refugees. Ravi Shankar recorded several Bengali songs with the Apple Records and donated the proceeds to refugee relief.[33] In addition, he organised 'The Concert for Bangladesh' with George Harrison in New York's Maddison Square Garden to raise funds for relief operations. The concert, attended by the greats of Western music, including Bob Dylan, John Lennon and Eric Clapton, was a huge success. It was able to raise close to 2,50,000 dollars.[34] The funds, funnelled through the United Nations Children's Fund (UNICEF), were used for refugee relief. The concert was instrumental in bringing about greater awareness regarding Bangladesh. It was also instrumental in inspiring several other artists across the world to express their solidarity with Bangladesh. An oppressed cultural identity had made its way into popular culture and gained wide acceptance within the international civil society. Be it Joan Baez, or Allen Ginsberg, or John Lennon or Sunil Gangopadhyay, all were connected in solidarity towards Bangladesh.

Bangladesh was, thus, able to make its place in the minds of the international civil society. The allegiance to the Bangla language and the Bengali culture had propelled Bengali people across the world to support the liberation movement. The Bangladeshi government-in-exile, based out of Kolkata, became the nerve centre for the coordination of efforts towards the independence movement, and all networks of solidarity fed into the efforts of this government-in-exile. 'Joy Bangla' (All hail Bengal), the slogan for the Liberation War, became the common call for the Bengali community across the world.

Conclusion

It was language that lay at the core of the creation of Bangladesh. Starting from the Bhasha Andolon to the Liberation War, the larger aim remained the same: to reassert the ethno-linguistic identity of the majority population of East Pakistan. However, the calls for complete independence came about gradually, after a prolonged denial of recognition, respect and rights. The mobilising power of ethno-linguistic identities became a blind spot for the Pakistan government. In their effort to subjugate the cultural dissenters, they further alienated their own citizens, giving rise to a self-fulfilling prophecy that the Bengalis were trying to break up Pakistan.

In the nation-building process of Pakistan, the Bengali language and culture could not find a place in the imagination of the West Pakistani elites. As a result, the much-needed bonds of fraternity and horizontal solidarity that make a nation were absent between the two provinces of Pakistan. On the other hand, the continued negation of the Bengali identity, and the recurring and compounding oppression on the people, gave rise to strong bonds of comradeship among the people of East Pakistan. Thus, when the Pakistani national identity was contested by the Bengali national identity in East Pakistan in 1971, the latter emerged victorious.

Since 1947, East Pakistan had been looking for constitutional justice, in the form of representation and opportunities; and when it was denied the said justice, grievances simmered. The Pakistani government did not recognise these grievances emerging out of the eastern province. In an attempt to unify the nation, the Government of Pakistan tried to raze the ethno-linguistic identity of the people in East Pakistan. The oppression, which had begun in the form of neglect, increasingly took the shape of obliteration. As the oppression of the Bengali identity increased, the demands for independence hardened. None of the initial demands of East Pakistani people were targeted against the unity of Pakistan; they simply sought greater representation! However, the Pakistani government's repeated denial of resources and representation led to demands for autonomy within a federal structure. The Pakistani government mistook these demands as secessionist tendencies and led a targeted attack on the Bengali population, so that they were coerced into subverting their Bengali identity to the Pakistani identity. Owing to this recurring increase in invalidation of the Bengali identity, the Bengali population felt that any compromise they made on demands for autonomy would only validate the government's oppressive tendencies, leading to further marginalisation of their identity. Thus, when the West Pakistani elites finally gave up on negotiations on 25 March 1971 and the army began Operation Searchlight, the masses and leaders of East Pakistan saw no other option but to struggle for complete independence. The calls for complete independence were a direct result of the military junta's inability to treat East Pakistan at par with West Pakistan, as also its inability to deal with dissent through pacific means. Be it the Bhasha Andolon, the students' movements or the protests against the postponement of the National Assembly, the Pakistani government resorted to the use of force on every occasion. This attitude further convinced the Bengali people that they were second-class citizens in their nation.

The Bangladesh Liberation War was supported by multiple networks, including diaspora community, humanitarian organisations, international civil society and the Indian government. The diaspora community was the most rooted in the crisis and had the highest allegiance to an independent Bangladesh. They raised awareness for Bangladesh and garnered sympathy for the persecuted Bengali people. In the war, the diaspora community was linked to the actual crisis by familial and cultural links. Their innate relationship to the Bangla language and the Bengali culture propelled their strong response. Language and culture have an immense binding force, that can evoke loyalties beyond political and geographical borders. The 'Mukti Juddho' exhibited the loyalties of the Bengali people across the world towards their language brethren.

Language and culture do not possess the brute force of arms, hence they cannot determine the outcome of a war independently. Yet, language and culture were the propellants behind the Liberation War: the source of differences, the source of solidarity and the source of constant motivation for the Mukti Bahini. If we look back at the popular slogans of the Liberation War, we find a common thread of loyalty to the Bangla language and the Bengali people. 'Joy Bangla', the official slogan of the Liberation War, expresses allegiance to an independent Bangladesh, which subverts the religious nationalism of 1947 to the ethno-linguistic nationalism. It also called for glory to the Bengali identity that had been marginalised and persecuted in Pakistan. 'Bir Bangali Astro Dhoro, Bangladesh Swadin Koro' (Brave Bengalis take up arms for the liberation of Bangladesh) was a call to the Bengali people, urging them to pick up arms for the cause of Bangladesh. The slogan was used to signify the responsibility that all Bengali people had towards their language community and was also a push-back against the stereotype that Bengalis are meek and non-martial. A third slogan, 'Amar Desh, Tomar Desh, Bangladesh, Bangladesh' (We owe our allegiances to our country Bangladesh), gained popularity amongst Bangla-speaking people across the world. It invoked the sentimental connotations of a 'desh' or a country, which represented a sense of belonging. People in West Bengal were particularly drawn to this slogan and felt united with the larger language community in the struggle for an independent Bangladesh. The Liberation War created a sociality among the Bengali people, built on language, oppression and a common hatred for the Pakistani military junta.

On revisiting the war 50 years later, I have tried to go back to the root of differences and analyse the role of language and culture in the creation of Bangladesh. To sum up, the creation of Bangladesh had as much to do with the cultural aspirations of the Bengali people as it had to do with the cultural suppression by the military junta. The successive governments in Pakistan had never made a real effort at understanding and accommodating the people of East Pakistan in the process of nation building, and this had long-term effects on the psyche of the people. There was never any fair cultural exchange between the two provinces that could bind them together beyond religion. As mentioned earlier, the popular sentiment among the Bengali people was that they had replaced one colonial rule for another. In addition, the Pakistan government was unable to deal with dissent tactfully. Be it the Bhasha Andolon or the protests following the general elections, the government's response was violent suppression, which became an important cause of the rift between the government and the people of East Pakistan. Also, the narrow partisan interests of the military government and the PPP led to an unfair denial of the Awami League's electoral victory. A smooth transition of power to the civilian government could have halted the violent break-up of Pakistan. At the core of government's inability to pacify East Pakistan was cultural othering that had taken deep root in the two provinces. This othering gave way to oppression, and prolonged oppression resulted in secession.

The Bangladesh Liberation War of 1971 is an important learning experience for all nations with diverse cultural identities. National identities are a powerful and contested space, usually inhabited by a dominant community. However, if the dominant community is unable to recognise the various contesting currents and sedate them at a nascent stage, the dominant community may lose its control over the discourse of national identity.

NOTES

1. Craig Baxter, *Bangladesh: From a Nation to a State*, New York: Routledge, 2019, p. 56.
2. Ibid.
3. Ishtiaq Hossain and Mahmud Hasan Khan, 'The Rift within an Imagined Community: Understanding Nationalism(s) in Bangladesh', *Asian Journal of Social Science*, Vol. 34, No. 2, 2006, pp. 324–39.
4. Bashir Al Helal, 'Language Movement', in Sirajul Islam and Ahmed A. Jamal (eds), *Banglapedia: National Encyclopedia of Bangladesh*, 2nd edition, Dhaka: Asiatic Society of Bangladesh, 2012.
5. Ibid.
6. 'Dhaka Medical College Hostel Prangone Chatro Shomabesher Upor Policer Guliborshon: Bishwabidyalayer Tinjon Chatroshoho Char Bekti Nihoto O Shotero Bekti Ahoto' (Police repression on student's gathering in Dhaka Medical Hostel campus), *The Azad* (Bengali), 22 February 1952.
7. Bashir Al Helal, *Bhasha Andoloner Itihas* (History of the Language Movement), Dhaka: Agamee Prakashani, 2003.

8. Zillur R. Khan, 'Islam and Bengali Nationalism', *Asian Survey*, Vol. 25, No. 8, 1985, pp. 834–51.
9. Khawaja Alqama, *Bengali Elite Perceptions of Pakistan*, Karachi: Royal Book Co., 1997, pp. 264–85.
10. Archer Blood, *The Cruel Birth of Bangladesh: Memoirs of an American Diplomat*, Dhaka: University Press, 2005, pp. 31–32.
11. Based on the interview with Sheikh Mujibur Rahman by Zillur R. Khan on 17 July 1973 in Zillur R. Khan, 'Islam and Bengali Nationalism', *Asian Survey*, Vol. 25, No. 8, 1985, pp. 834–51.
12. Richard Sisson and Leo Rose, *War and Secession: Pakistan, India, and the Creation of Bangladesh*, Berkeley: University of California Press, 1990, pp. 19–20.
13. Siddiq Salik, *Witness to Surrender*, Dhaka: University Press, 1997, p. 29.
14. Herbert Feldman, *The End and the Beginning: Pakistan 1969–1971*, Karachi: Oxford University Press, 1975, p. 92.
15. Blood, *The Cruel Birth of Bangladesh: Memoirs of an American Diplomat*, n. 10, p. 97.
16. Ibid., pp. 217–22. Also see Srinath Raghavan, *1971: A Global History of the Creation of Bangladesh*, Cambridge, MA: Harvard University Press, 2013, p. 33.
17. A.R. Siddiqi, *East Pakistan: The Endgame—An Onlooker's Journal, 1969–1971*, Karachi: Oxford University Press, 2004, p. 43.
18. Sisson and Rose, *War and Secession: Pakistan, India, and the Creation of Bangladesh*, n. 12, pp. 57–58.
19. Raghavan, *1971: A Global History of the Creation of Bangladesh*, n. 16, p. 38.
20. Abdul Rehman, *East Pakistan: The Endgame: The Onlooker's Journal*, Karachi: Oxford University Press Pakistan, p. 57.
21. Mujib's statements in *Dawn* (Karachi), 20 February 1971; *Pakistan Times* (Lahore), 25 February 1971; *Dawn* (Karachi), 1 March 1971.
22. Shuja Nawaz, *Crossed Swords: Pakistan, its Army, and the Wars within*, Karachi: Oxford University Press, 2008, pp. 264–66.
23. Kamal Hossain's testimony in *Bangladesher Shadhinata Juddho: Dalil Patro* (Bangladesh Liberation War: Documents and Papers), Dhaka: Ministry of Information, Government of People's Republic of Bangladesh, 1985, pp. 256–58.
24. Sheikh Mujibur Rahman's speech in *Dawn* (Karachi), 8 March 1971; and *Pakistan Times* (Lahore), 8 March 1971.
25. Raghavan, *1971: A Global History of the Creation of Bangladesh*, n. 16, p. 43.
26. Salik, *Witness to Surrender*, n. 13, pp. 62–63.
27. *Dawn* (Karachi), 27 March 1971; and *Pakistan Times* (Lahore), 27 March 1971.
28. A. Mascarenhas, 'Genocide', *Sunday Times* (London), 13 June 1971, available at https://www.thedailystar.net/supplements/victory-day-special-2017/genocide-1505440
29. M. Rafiqul Islam, *A Tale of Millions: Bangladesh Liberation War, 1971*, Dhaka: Ananya, 2005.
30. S.N. Prasad, *The India–Pakistan War of 1971*, New Delhi: Ministry of Defence, 1992, p. 101.
31. Raghavan, *1971: A Global History of the Creation of Bangladesh*, n. 16, pp. 139–49.
32. UNHCR, 'The State of The World's Refugees 2000: Fifty Years of Humanitarian Action', Geneva, 2000.
33. Ravi Shankar, *Raga Mala: An Autobiography*, New York: Welcome Rain, 1999, pp. 217–18.
34. Raghavan, *1971: A Global History of the Creation of Bangladesh*, n. 16, pp. 144–45.

SECTION II

Military Issues

4

1971, the War as I Saw It

Shamsher M. Chowdhury

I joined the Pakistan Military Academy in Kakul, Abbottabad, as a cadet in November 1967 and passed out from there as a Regular Commissioned Officer in October 1969. My first posting as a Second Lieutenant (2Lt) was in 1st East Bengal Regiment, a highly regarded and decorated infantry battalion, popularly known as the Senior Tigers. At that time, the unit was located in Jessore (now Joshor) in the then East Pakistan. My stay in this unit was, however, relatively short-lived as I was transferred to Chittagong (now Chottogram) in August 1970 to help raise the 8th East Bengal Regiment as a Lieutenant (Lt). It has always been a matter of great pride and joy for any Bengali army officer to serve in the East Bengal Regiment and those days, it was more so. For me, the added prize was having the opportunity to start my career with the eldest member of the Tiger family and move on to help raise the youngest.

Changing Political Scenario in Pakistan

As such, 1969 was an eventful year, if not a defining one, for Pakistan. Indeed, in Pakistan's little over two decades of existence until then, the country had seen its share of eventful years. Just seven months before my commissioning from the Pakistan Military Academy, the government of President Ayub Khan was overthrown in a bloodless military coup and was replaced by another military government under General (Gen) Agha Mohammad Yahya Khan, Commander-in-Chief (CNC) of the Pakistan Army. The year also marked the beginning of the end of a united Pakistan.

Before stepping down, Ayub Khan was forced to withdraw the sedition case against Sheikh Mujib and other co-accused. Sheikh Mujibur Rahman walked free from prison on 22 February. The following day he was given a tumultuous welcome in Dhaka and was seen as a hero by all sections of the people in East Pakistan. Addressing a massive rally in Dhaka the same day, he announced his continued commitment to, and struggle for, securing the legitimate rights of the people. This was when Mujib was given the title of 'Bangabandhu' (friend of the Bengal).

The collective disquiet against Pakistan's ruling class found its most clear manifestation at the general elections held on 7 December 1970 and on 17 January 1971, in which the Awami League (AL), under the charismatic leadership of Bangabandhu Sheikh Mujib, won 160 of the 162 seats allotted for East Pakistan and all the seven seats reserved for women. Having won 167 seats in the National Assembly of Pakistan out of a total of 313, the Awami League had the clear mandate to form a government at the centre on its own. While there was widespread euphoria all over the eastern province at the massive victory for the AL, the ruling coterie in Islamabad and their cohorts were numbed at what had transpired on the election night. The Bengalis had spoken, but the Pakistani rulers were not ready to listen to what they had said at the polls.

Prior to the elections, the powers had believed that no party would be able to win an absolute majority in the National Assembly. The major winners, that is, the AL in East Pakistan and the Pakistan People's Party (PPP) in West Pakistan, therefore, would have to find a common ground, seek compromises and form a coalition government that would accommodate their divergent positions on governance. The decisive electoral victory of the AL had, in fact, struck at the very roots of the traditional power brokers in Pakistan. The result of the elections was a clear reflection of the people's aspiration for a representative government. It also signalled the end of exploitation of East Pakistan by the policymakers sitting in Islamabad. There was popular optimism that stability and democracy would no longer be disturbed by a vested few.

For Pakistan's ruling clique, the very thought of Bengalis exercising power, was unthinkable. A change of strategy was, therefore, called for. While the AL had won an absolute majority in the National Assembly of Pakistan, Bhutto's PPP failed to achieve anything resembling a clear mandate. It only managed to win a total of 88 seats in the National Assembly, all in West Pakistan, and controlled only two of the four provinces there.

Notwithstanding the limitations the electoral results imposed on the PPP, the wily and crafty Zulfiqar Ali Bhutto decided to play the role of a spoiler. In this, he found a willing partner in the military establishment. As Bhutto continued to raise impediments by staking a claim to be part of the central government, the Pakistan military was taking initial steps to significantly strengthen its numbers in East Pakistan.

In Chittagong, meanwhile, the Bengali officers in the army were watching the evolving scenario with trepidation and anger, particularly the fact that the Pakistani military, with help from Bhutto, was bent on denying power to Sheikh Mujib. This was all we talked about! On the 28 February 1971, I was called by the Commanding Officer (CO) to the office and asked to take over charge as Acting Adjutant of the battalion as Captain (Capt) Akhtar, the Adjutant, had to go on leave to his home in West Pakistan for a couple of weeks. Hence, the CO felt it necessary to have someone as Acting Adjutant and he chose me for the job.

With this turn of events, all key posts in 8th East Bengal Regiment, except that of the CO, were manned by Bengali officers: Major (Maj) Ziaur Rahman was the second in command; the senior-most company commander was Maj Mir Shawkat Ali; Capt Oli Ahmed was the Quartermaster; and I was the Acting Adjutant. Such an alignment of key jobs in the battalion for the Bengalis was to have a decisive impact on events that were to unfold in March.

On 7 March, Bangabandhu made his historical speech in Dhaka's Ramna Maidan to a massive gathering. In his around 18 minutes of address, Sheikh Mujib was unequivocal in his warning to those who mattered in Islamabad that time was fast running out and the patience of the people must not be tested any further. He catalogued the atrocities that were already being committed in various parts of East Pakistan by members of the army and called upon Pakistan's military leader, Gen Yahya Khan, to come and investigate them. He further demanded that the army return to the barracks, martial law be withdrawn forthwith and powers be transferred to the elected representatives without any delay. He called upon the people of East Pakistan to turn their homes into fortresses and be prepared to face the enemy with whatever they had. He reminded all that having shed blood already, we were prepared to shed more blood and that the people of this land shall be liberated, 'Insha Allah' (with Allah's blessings). He ended his fiery oration with a warning, 'This time the struggle was for our liberation; the struggle this time was for our independence.' Thunderous applause and sky-piercing shouts of 'Joy Bangla' greeted his every word.

He also announced a programme of non-cooperation with the Pakistani authorities, where public offices, transport services, banks and courts would run only as he decided. The message was not lost in Islamabad. As subsequent events show, the Pakistani military quickly set in motion plans to use its might to foil the political process, especially in East Pakistan, and Zulfiqar Ali Bhutto was fully complicit in this scheme. In the East though, the speech set in motion a series of events that helped transform the people. They knew that it was only a matter of time before the long struggle for emancipation would turn into a full-scale fight for independence.

Within about an hour of the historic speech, I got a telephone call from Lieutenant Colonel (Lt Col) M.R. Chowdhury, Chief Instructor at the East Bengal Regimental Centre (EBRC). He asked me to immediately pass a message to Maj Ziaur Rahman to meet him at Chittagong's Niaz Stadium after dark. He wanted the same message to be given to Capt Oli Ahmed. He said that a secret meeting had been convened of some senior Bengali officers to take stock of the situation and what might follow in the coming days in the light of Sheikh Mujib's public ultimatum to the authorities in Islamabad and Rawalpindi. Later that evening Maj Zia told me that at the meeting, Lt Col M.R. Chowdhury shared the information that Brig Majumdar had gathered from reliable sources that there was a plan by the Pakistani Army to disarm all Bengalis in the armed forces, including in the police and other paramilitary outfits. It was also agreed by those present there that this would not be tolerated and any such attempt by the Pakistan Army would be resisted strongly. In the meeting, it was agreed that efforts would be made to coordinate things with East Bengal battalions in Jessore, Joydebpur, Saidpur and Comilla, although this would be difficult and risky. They all agreed on the need to establish contacts with the political leadership. As Maj Ziaur Rahman walked away towards his house, I stared into the darkness, vaguely trying to recall in my mind the events of the day, one that would profoundly impact a nation's life.

On the night of 21 March 1971, five of us Bengali officers had a secret meeting with a group of local AL leaders in Chittagong University. Our group was led by Capt Rafiqul Islam, Adjutant, East Pakistan Rifles (EPR) in Chittagong. Other members were: Capt Harun Ahmed Chowdhury, second in command of the EPR wing in Kaptai; and Capt Khalequeuzaman Chowdhury, Capt Oli Ahmed and myself, all three from 8th East Bengal Regiment. Maj Ziaur Rahman had earlier given us the green signal for attending the meeting. From the AL side, there was Mr Hannan, Dr Zafar, Mr Ataur Rahman Kaiser and one or two others whom we didn't know. During the meeting, we made it clear to the AL representatives that Pakistan was moving a large number of troops into East Pakistan, mostly in civilian guise. Also, a ship carrying huge quantity of arms and ammunition had already reached Chittagong Port. It was clear to us that these actions were aimed at launching a military crackdown on the Bengalis. We assured them that we were prepared to face any such assault, at least initially. What was needed was a decision from the political leadership on the next course of action in the face of these alarming developments. The AL side assured us that the discussions in the meeting would be conveyed to the political leadership in Dhaka. Till then, we needed to wait, but had to remain alert. Under the situation prevailing at that time, such a meeting was fraught with risks, but such high risks had to be taken.

The battle lines were now clearly drawn. These lines were crossed on the fateful night of 25 March, culminating in the dismemberment of Pakistan and changing the landscape of South Asia forever.

The War of Liberation

It was midnight of 25–26 March 1971. I was doing road patrol duty near the Chittagong Cantonment. I had with me 12 sepoys and a total of four rifles only. As I approached the Baizid Bostami Mazar Sharif, I was stopped by Naib Subedar Habibur Rahman of my battalion, who was on patrol duty in that area. Habib told me that tremendous firing was going on inside the cantonment. I got out of my Dodge and heard for myself the relentless sound of guns firing. Sensing something wrong, I immediately rang my unit and told Capt Oli Ahmed, who was the duty officer, about what was happening. He told me to try and further ascertain the situation. Soon after that, one Havildar Moniruzzaman, who was in EBRC, along with five other soldiers, came rushing towards me. Trembling in shock, he said that 20 Baluch of the Pakistan Army had attacked the EBRC and had killed Lt Col M.R. Chowdhury, some Junior Commissioned Officers (JCOs) of the EBRC and innumerable recruits, who were all sleeping in their barracks. Some officers had also been arrested.

On hearing this, I immediately rushed to my battalion, which was located at Solashahar Market, and passed the information on to Capt Oli Ahmed. Soon after that, the West Pakistani officers were arrested and Maj Ziaur Rahman declared mutiny against the Pakistan Army and assumed command of the battalion. Fearing that we might be attacked by the Pakistan Army, Maj Ziaur Rahman and other senior officers decided to move the battalion to a safer location. So, during the night, 8th East Bengal, under the command of Maj Ziaur Rahman, left its lines and marched on foot and reached Kalurghat area a little after dawn, where we established our hideout. Here, we were joined by Capt Harun of the EPR, who had come from Kaptai. The troops led by Capt Harun and our own troops combined to become the first elements of the Bangladesh Liberation Army. The other officers were Maj Mir Shawkat Ali, Capt Khalequzzaman, Capt Sadek, Capt Oli Ahmed, Lt Mahfooz and myself. This was on 26 March 1971. The same evening, Maj Ziaur Rahman made us take an oath to fight for the independence of Bangladesh and be prepared to sacrifice our lives if necessary. On 27 March, we opened the first Bangladesh radio station from Chittagong from which Maj Ziaur Rahman spoke and asked for the recognition of Bangladesh. The same night, at about 12.30 a.m., I marched into the city with a section of the battalion. At Chatteshari Road, we were confronted by the Pakistani Army, who fired at us from a building. After throwing some grenades into the house, we withdrew to Kalurghat.

On 29 March, I led a platoon into the heart of Chittagong city, in spite of the fact that the Pakistan Army was already occupying most of the city. We took up position at Ispahani Hill near Askar Dighi. From Ispahani Hill, we had a very heavy exchange of fire with the Pakistan Army. With my mortars, I shelled the Circuit House, which was the Army Headquarters. During late afternoon, the Pakistan Army tried to surround us with a company strength. By then, we were running out of ammunition and so, I had to return to Kalurghat. The very fact that we fought right inside the city, shaking the Pakistan Army, with no casualty on our side, was a big victory for us. Our mortar shelling killed eight Pakistanis and wounded some more.

The same evening at about 7 o'clock, I was called by Maj Ziaur Rahman and asked to take up position at Chowk Bazaar, thus blocking the only route which the Pakistan Army could use for reaching Kalurghat. I was given a fresh platoon for this purpose. Early next morning, I heard some firing going on in Boalkhali, a village nearby. Someone came and informed me that two Pakistan Army commandos had entered that village and were firing at the villagers. So, I took 10 of my men and slowly approached the village. Soon, we saw the commandos. We took up lying position and once they were within range, we opened fire. One of the commandos was killed on the spot and the other one was seriously wounded. The villagers, who were waiting with sticks and rods, pounced upon him and beat him to death. Later, I collected a map, their weapons and a piece of paper which showed that they were from the 3rd Commando Battalion of the Pakistan Army.

At Chowk Bazaar on 31 March, the Pakistan Army tried to break through our position, but were beaten back. I wanted my position to be strengthened because I felt that the enemy would make all possible attempts to break through Chowk Bazaar. Capt Harun Ahmed Chowdhury of the EPR came and joined me with a platoon. He had a machine gun with him, and the two platoons were so deployed that the Chowk Bazaar defence became almost impregnable.

Repeated attempts were made by the Pakistan Army to get through our defences at Chowk Bazaar, but all in vain. On 4 April, they launched two companies, supported by tanks, against us. We were left with no other alternative but to get into a street fight. Fortunately, our mortars came to our help. In the street fight, there were some casualties on the enemy's side, but none on ours. Being outnumbered, and since defence against tanks was not possible, we had to withdraw from Chowk Bazaar to Kalurghat. Two buildings were blown up by the tank shells just after we vacated them.

The battle at Chowk Bazaar lasted for five days. During our stay there, the civilians were of great help to us. They gave us food, tea and anything else we needed. After moving to Kalurghat, we built a strong defence on both sides of the bridge.

Also, on 30 March, the Pakistan Air Force (PAF) had rocketed our radio station, but it was a sheer waste of ammunition because we had already removed the transmitter from there. After the PAF rocketed the empty radio station, the Pakistan Army reported that Maj Ziaur Rahman had been killed in the radio station. This was part of their false propaganda.

On 1 April, on the Comilla–Chittagong Highway, an EPR force ambushed a commando company. About 100 dead bodies, including that of a Lieutenant Colonel and a Captain, were later recovered by the Pakistanis from there. Till then, that was the heaviest number of casualties inflicted on the army by us in a single operation. It was indeed a great battle.

After retreating to Kalurghat, we decided to follow a 'hit-and-run' tactic. With our limited strength and being severely under-equipped, we could not afford to launch any large-scale offensive operations. At the same time, as we had built a strong defence at Kalurghat bridge, our hit-and-run policy worked very effectively.

On 5 April, Pakistan Army forces tried to attack our position at Kalurghat, but were beaten back by Capt Harun with his EPR troops. Capt Harun himself was firing a light machine gun in that operation. This defeat had a serious effect on the morale of the Pakistani Army. They withdrew by four miles and took up position in a tannery factory on the Kaptai Road.

On 7 April, we saw some men of the Pakistan Army occupy an under-construction cinema hall near Ispahani Jute Mill. Maj Mir Shawkat Ali and I launched a joint operation against them. He fired upon them with his automatics from close range, while I fired three 83 mm Blendicide rockets into the particular room that the army was occupying. The rockets blew up the room, with very few Pakistan Army's men managing to escape alive—most were killed and some were wounded. In this operation, I lost my sepoy, Naeb Ali. He died a hero, one of the first *shaheeds* of the Bangladesh Liberation Army. The local people gave him a befitting and emotional funeral.

Our job was not to give the enemy any rest. As part of that plan, Lt Mahfooz and his platoon attacked them at the tannery factory late at night on 9 April. The Pakistan Army was taken by complete surprise and this attack shook them up badly. They must have suffered heavy casualties in this action.

> The fateful day of 11 April dawned. It was a bright morning and with me, there were: Capt Harun; Shawkat Hussain, a student of Chittagong University; Shawkat Alley of Dhaka University; Fazlur Rahman, a local student; and Hashmi Mustafa Kamal, a cadet from the Marine Academy. These young men had been with us from the beginning. We had given them the basic training on weapons and they had taken part in all the action we had fought till then. Their courage and sense of patriotism was boundless.

It was about 8 o'clock in the morning when we heard heavy firing somewhere quite close. Suddenly, we saw a large number of Pakistan Army troops advancing towards us. I ordered my troops to open fire and took defensive position inside my bunker. Capt Harun moved to the railway guard room nearby and was firing on the advancing enemy. The Pakistan artillery was shelling our position heavily. I told Capt Harun to take cover, but when he started moving, he got hit by shrapnel. As he fell on the bridge, I asked my troops to move him to the rear. During Capt Harun's evacuation, I gave covering fire. Soon, I realised that we could not stay there for long, so I asked my troops to start retreating. I told them that I would join them shortly. By then, about five of my men had been wounded. The enemy had also lost some men. When all my men had withdrawn, I got out of my bunker and started firing at the enemy while standing in the open. This was when I was hit by a bullet. I collapsed on the bridge and when I tried to get up and run, I could not move as there was no strength in my legs. There was nobody to evacuate me as all my men had withdrawn by then.

The Pakistan Army men walked up to me and started abusing me. Some even kicked me as I lay flat on my back, bleeding profusely. Instead of killing me, the

Pakistanis decided to take me as a prisoner. They picked me up and took me to the Martial Law Headquarters at Chittagong Circuit House. All the while, I was being subjected to a variety of abuses, including being repeatedly called a traitor. At the headquarters, the authorities decided to give me some necessary medical treatment. So, I was sent to the Naval Base Hospital at Chittagong. There the doctor discovered that the bullet had entered my left thigh, pierced right through my stomach, shattered my right hip and was lodged in the femur. The same night I was operated upon and the bullet was taken out. Three days later, I was shifted to the Chittagong Combined Military Hospital (CMH). On the way, two sepoys of the Pakistan Army tried to choke me to death. God, once again, bestowed his mercy on me and their brutal attempt failed.

The same evening, while I was lying in my bed in the CMH, Maj Meher Kamal of the Pakistan Army attacked me. I had known Maj Kamal well as he, like me, was from the East Bengal Regiment and at that time, was posted to the EBRC. At first, he started hitting me with his fist on my face and nose and then, he started stabbing me with a bayonet. He stabbed me repeatedly on my chest and once on my cheek right below my left eye. All this stopped when a nursing orderly rushed in and physically pushed him out of the ward. I was shaking from the whole trauma. When the CO of the CMH came in a few minutes later, I told him that either he should kill me or give me some protection against such attacks.

The doctors at the CMH declared that there was not enough facility for my treatment in Chittagong and so, on 24 April, I was flown to Dhaka and was admitted in the military hospital there. Instead of keeping me in the ward, I was kept inside a makeshift tent under a mango tree out in the open, and no treatment was given to me. Although the doctors said I should be taken to the CMH Rawalpindi, the authorities decided not to because I was a traitor, and also because I was to be interrogated by the Army Intelligence. I was supposed to stay in the hospital for at least eight weeks, but was removed on a stretcher to the Field Interrogation Centre (FIC) after 12 days. There, I was subjected to 10 sleepless nights. If I dozed off, the sentry would hit me with the rifle butt. It was clear to me that the Pakistanis could not accept the genesis of the armed uprising. Their contention was that we had planned this whole thing. At last, I asked for paper and pen and wrote down my "confessional" statement, saying all what we had done in Chittagong prior to 25 March and the events thereafter. I left out no details. I wrote down my statement while lying flat on a stretcher and a powerful light bulb hanging over my head all night.

> I concluded my statement recalling the words of a college classmate from way back in 1965 when he said, "The existence of East and West Pakistan as one Pakistan is an absurdity". As it is, they felt like two separate countries. There is nothing common between these two people, except religion. Thus I was extremely happy with the result of the general elections of December 1970. I knew, it was only a question of time before we parted ways. I did not know, however, that it would happen so soon.

On 18 May, I was shifted to Prisoner's Camp No. 1, located inside Dhaka Cantonment. This place was a scene of brutality beyond imagination. All prisoners were generally subjected to ruthless beating by the Pakistan Army sepoys. Even in this seriously wounded condition and lying on a stretcher, I was not spared and was beaten mercilessly on 19 May, as a result of which I could not have my food for a couple of days. I was beaten time and again over the next few days. There were many prisoners in that camp and nobody was spared the brutality let loose by the guards in the camp. A.K. Shamsuddin, a top civil official, was beaten to death inside the camp.

This beating officially stopped in June, but unofficially, it continued in the cells where the civilians and other ranks of the army and the air force were staying. The food that we were given was of a quality which even a stray dog would not want to eat. However, by the end of June, the quality of food improved somewhat. The treatment meted out to us also changed slightly. The FIC people would come once in a while to take some officers for interrogation. Some of them never came back and this included at least one Bengali Captain. Much later, we came to know that he was tortured to death. The official version was that he was 'killed while trying to escape'!

Around early July, the officers were shifted to Shere Bangla Nagar and housed in buildings that were part of the Second Capital. Here, the living conditions were much improved. We were also allowed to see our families once a month or so. The days passed by and some officers were released turn by turn.

Towards the very end of August, a Major from the Pakistan Army intelligence asked me to be a state approver. He said that if I agreed, I would not be given the death penalty for mutiny. He gave me three days to consider his offer. He also admitted that he needed this to 'justify our actions'. After the third day, I told him bluntly that I refuse to be a state approver. The Major was furious and warned me about the consequences of my decision to not cooperate with their nefarious design. I looked him in the eye and said, 'Sir, I am not afraid to die'.

On 1 September, I was issued the chargesheet, containing six charges, the first of which was 'abetting mutiny'. This charge alone was enough to give me the capital punishment. I mentally prepared myself for the worst, but I was never afraid. I knew what I had done was right and I had no regrets.

On 19 November, my parents came to see me in the prisoner's camp. This was their second visit since my captivity. My father told me that he has been approached by the authorities saying that I should apologise to the Pakistanis in writing for my acts of treason and seek mercy from the President. They also told him that if I did that, I would be spared the death penalty but and given a lighter sentence and dismissed from the Army. I told my father that I have done nothing for which I should apologise and I shall never seek mercy from the Pakistanis. My father just said, 'I understand your decision. May Allah bless you'. My brother, who was also there, kissed me on the forehead and said, 'We are proud of you'.

On 28 November, I was moved to solitary confinement. This for me was hard because of my physically disabled condition. I was told that the move was in preparation for my trial by a military court on charges of 'Treason', along with abetting mutiny. Again, I mentally prepared myself for the worst, but I knew that the Almighty will bestow His mercy on me.

Then came the day we were all waiting for. It was the 4th of December 1971. From early morning, Indian Air Force aircrafts had been playing havoc in and over Dhaka. The Pakistan Air Force could barely fly any of their fighter aircrafts after the second or third day of the war. From my prison window I watched with uncontrolled excitement as the scene was being played out right in front of my eyes. I anticipated that it was only a question of time before the Pakistan Army laid down its arms and Mukti Bahini and the Indian military proudly marched into Dhaka. My dreams came true on 16 December. At that time, I was in the cantonment, where I had been shifted after the building in which I was being kept in the Shere Bangla Nagar caught fire after being hit by the Indian Air Force.

On 16 December, we received the news of the surrender of the Pakistanis with tremendous jubilation. The false pride of the Pakistan Army, their sadistic ego and the war mania they were nursing had ended forever in utter ignominy. Rarely in military history can one find such disgrace and shame which the Pakistan Army had to face.

On 17 December, six of us army officers who were prisoners, proudly walked out to free and liberated Bangladesh. The damage done to me by the Pakistani Army on 11 April never healed. My left hip was shattered and I still walk with support. Throughout my eight months and six days in captivity, I was given no medical treatment whatsoever except for the first operation. Instead, I was subjected to the most brutal form of physical and mental torture.

Conclusion

In an article in *The Express Tribune*, Khalid Ahmed has quoted Ikram Sehgal, a retired Pakistani Army officer from the East Bengal Regiment, on the conduct of the Pakistan Armed Forces during the Bangladesh Liberation War as saying:

> When soldiers make war on women and children, they cease to be soldiers. That is why in the final analysis, when it came to real combat, they could not face up to bullets which is their actual job as soldiers...the terror that was unleashed by them in East Pakistan between March and November 1971 is simply inexcusable.[1]

On 23 January 1972, 25 of us wounded freedom fighters, military and civilians, were flown to East Berlin, capital of the then German Democratic Republic (GDR) for medical treatment. The GDR was the third country in the world to recognise independent Bangladesh, after Bhutan and India. The GDR government had offered to provide this treatment as a gesture of friendship.

Noted author Salman Rushdie, in his 1983 book, *Shame*, has described Pakistan as it was created: '...that a country divided into two Wings a thousand miles apart, that fantastic bird of a place, two Wings without a body, sundered by the land-mass of its greatest foe, joined by nothing but God...'.[2] Salman Rushdie's cynical view of Pakistan was not misplaced. The year 1971 proved that religion alone was not enough to keep Pakistan united. What was crucially missing was an inclusive democratic mindset, not a unity based on religion alone.

In 1971, the people of Bangladesh had won. It was a proud and momentous time for us as a nation. For many though, the victory had come at a huge cost. For the widow of Lt Col M.M. Rahman, my school principal, killed by the Pakistanis in Jhenaidaha in April, the pain of the loss of her husband would live with her forever. For the families of my friends, Capt Salahuddin Mumtaz, and 2Lt Anwar, my roommate in Jessore, both of whom made the supreme sacrifice, the war brought more pain than joy. This was also the case for the families of my sepoy, Naeb Ali, who was killed in Chittagong in the early stages of the war, and Subedar Major T.M. Ali and Sepoy Motuk Miah, both killed in action in Sylhet towards its very end. They, and thousands more like them, did not live to see the fruition of their sacrifice: a free Bangladesh.

Freedom does not always come without pain and sacrifice. I bow my head in paying my deepest respect to those brave Bangladeshis who made the supreme sacrifice for their motherland. My gratitude is equally due to the brave members of the Indian military who shed their blood for our freedom. As a nation, we owe all of them an eternal debt. It is because of this shared sacrifice that, today, we stand tall having achieved an identity that we can rightfully call our own.

Being a prisoner of war in the hands of a brutal Pakistan military for a major part of the war, I had little or no knowledge of what was happening in the international arena with regard to the situation in Bangladesh. It was only after liberation that I became aware of the critical role that the Government of India under Prime Minister Indira Gandhi had played in shaping global public opinion in favour of Bangladesh and the involvement of India in it. She did this even in the face of open opposition from the Nixon administration, from China and from almost the entire Islamic world. The situation had reached such a critical point that by December, it had paved the way for the Indian Armed Forces to get directly involved in the final days of the war. This led to the emergence of a free and independent Bangladesh on 16 December when the Pakistan Army in Bangladesh surrendered to the joint forces of the Mukti Bahini and the Indian Army.

Current Indian External Affairs Minister, Dr S. Jaishankar, describes India's political, diplomatic and military involvement in the Bangladesh Liberation War in 1971 as a 'Triumphal one'.[3] It indeed was. It is this piece of irreversible history that had laid the foundation for the relations between our two countries and the two people. The task for us now is to build on it based on the universal principles of mutual benefit and mutual respect.

The Bangladesh Liberation War was not just for a geographical territory, nor was it only for the red and green flag. It was the culmination of the people's long quest for political, social and economic emancipation. Over the last half a century of the existence of Bangladesh as a state, the country has achieved much in the socio-economic area. Challenges, however still remain for us as a nation. We need to remain focussed on ensuring a democratic, inclusive, non-communal, just and exploitation-free Bangladesh. These are the values and goals for which so much was sacrificed by so many.

NOTES

1. Ikram Sehgal, *The Express Tribune*, Karachi, 14 October 2012.
2. Salman Rushdie, *Shame*, London: Jonathan Cape, 1983, p. 178.
3. S. Jaishankar, *The India Way*, Uttar Pradesh: HarperCollins, 2020, p. 74.

5

Land Warfare in the Eastern Theatre

1971 Indo-Pak War

P.K. Chakravorty

India has fought three wars with Pakistan, in 1947–48, 1965 and 1971, all initiated by Pakistan. Though India responded with alacrity and military precision to these wars, it is the 1971 Indo-Pak War that was a classical victory for it. This war witnessed the dismemberment of Pakistan and the creation of Bangladesh. The war also resulted in India becoming an important regional power in South Asia. The 1971 war was the result of the political turmoil which occurred post-general elections conducted in 1970 in Pakistan. This paper will focus on land warfare as it pertained to the eastern theatre of operations. I would like to add here that I was fortunate to serve with Field Marshal Sam Manekshaw, Lieutenant General (Lt Gen) J.S. Aurora, Lt Gen Sagat Singh, Lt Gen J.F.R. Jacob, Lt Gen I.S. Gill, Lt Gen Nirbhay Sharma, Major General (Maj Gen) Ian Cardozo, Brigadier (Brig) P.K. Ghosh and Colonel (Col) D.K. Chand. During the war, it was indeed inspiring to hear and discuss the nuances of the land campaign with these illustrious leaders.[1]

Evolution of Plans and Strategy

The central thesis of operations in the eastern theatre during the 1971 war was to liberate East Pakistan in a short intense war. India had to exploit air supremacy and launch offensive actions from numerous directions to reach the centre of gravity, which was Dacca, capital of East Pakistan. In order to attain the same,

India was fortunate to have Maj Gen J.F.R. Jacob (later Lt Gen) as the Chief of Staff, Eastern Command, in whom the Army Commander and the Chief of Army Staff had implicit faith. He was clear about the geographical challenges:

1. Broad deltaic plain subject to frequent flooding and a small hilly region near Chittagong. Offensive operations would be difficult during the monsoons.
2. Numerous rivers, most of them originating in India, with the Padma, the Jamuna and the Meghna being the major ones. Offensive operations would entail river crossing with land expedients or by helicopter.
3. Roads were few and had numerous culverts and bridges.
4. Built-up areas were densely populated and could easily be defended. It was best to bypass and move to the centre of gravity.
5. The Indian border was stretched across many states and most of the areas were connected by metre gauge railway lines. It was indeed difficult to logistically build up launch pads in Tripura due to communication problems.
6. Eastern Command had land borders in Sikkim and Arunachal Pradesh with China. To minimise Chinese interference, the mountain passes needed to be closed, which naturally moved the campaign to winter.

These challenges definitely impacted the contours of the offensive strategy. By May 1971, Maj Gen Jacob had formulated the strategic outline as under:

1. The final objective was to be Dacca, the geopolitical and geostrategic heart of East Pakistan.
2. Thrust lines were to be selected to isolate and bypass Pakistani forces to finally reach the objective.
3. Subsidiary objectives were to be selected with the aim of securing communication centres and the destruction of the enemy's command and control capabilities.
4. Areas which were well defended and fortified were to be bypassed and dealt with later.
5. Preliminary operations to be aimed at drawing out the Pakistani forces to the border, leaving key areas in the interior lightly defended.[2]

Eastern Command, which was tasked to launch the operations, had to provide security to the country against Chinese aggression, which could emanate from Sikkim and Kameng sector in Arunachal Pradesh. Further, it had to contain the insurgencies in Nagaland, Manipur and Mizo Hills. There was also a commitment to defend Bhutan in the event of a Chinese offensive. Since it was not practicable to deal with war on two fronts, it was decided that it is best to wait for winter when the passes would close and minimum strengths could be kept for holding action against the Chinese. Accordingly, troops to be left for the Chinese would be two divisions in Sikkim and two divisions in Arunachal Pradesh, catering for a division contingency in Bhutan. As regards counter-insurgency tasks, about two brigades would be available for Nagaland, Manipur and Mizoram.

From the Eastern Command resources, troops available for operations would be 8 Mountain Division less a brigade, 23 Mountain Division, 20 Mountain Division and 57 Mountain Division. Out of this, some divisions did not have their artillery component. Army Headquarters (HQ) decided to allot 9 Infantry Division, 4 Mountain Division, 340 Mountain Brigade Group and a battalion group of 50 Parachute Brigade.

Actions Before Issue of Operational Instructions from Army HQ

At the outset, administrative planning had to be done before the monsoons set in; thus, this had to be done before the Army HQ operational instructions were issued. Poor road and rail communications, particularly in Tripura, meant early preparations. The Sub Area HQ was moved from Assam to Tripura to organise infrastructure. Orders were issued for the placement of one month's requirement of ammunition, stores and supplies to commence immediately at Teliamura in Tripura, one division at Dharamnagar in Tripura, two divisions at Krishnanagar in West Bengal, one division at Raiganj in north Bengal and one division plus at Tura in Meghalaya.

Tentative allotment of troops to task at the preliminary stage was as follows:

1. *North-western sector*: 20 Mountain Division, with 340 Mountain Brigade Group under command, was to capture Bogra.
2. *Western sector*: 9 Infantry Division and 4 Mountain Division were to capture Jessore, Magura and if opportunity permitted, to move to Dacca using the inland water flotilla. A corps HQ was needed to command this force and HQ 2 Corps was soon to be raised.
3. *South-eastern sector*: It was proposed to allot 23 Mountain Division, 8 Mountain Division less a brigade and 57 Mountain Division. HQ 4 Corps was to command this force. The Chief of Staff was to be left behind to look after any issues on the Chinese front. The objectives were

to secure the area up to the Meghna, to include Chandpur and Daikundi. Ahead there was a requirement of helicopters to cross this major water obstacle and move on to Dacca.

4. *North-eastern sector*: Eastern Command proposed that they needed another division plus on the Jamalpur–Tangail–Dacca axis. The parachute battalion could be utilised to drop at Tangail.
5. *Mukti Bahini*: Support of them were visualised for all phases of the operation.

In August 1971, a meeting was held in the operations room of Eastern Command. The Chief (Gen Sam Manekshaw), Army Commander (Lt Gen J.S. Aurora), Director Military Operations (DMO) and Maj Gen Jacob were present. The DMO spelt out the objectives, maintaining that if the Indian Army captured Khulna and Chittagong, which were entry ports, the war would come to an end. The Hardinge Bridge on the Padma was also to be secured. The only one who disagreed was Jacob. He explained that in the event of hostilities, we should utilise our naval superiority and have an effective blockade in place. Further, Khulna was only a minor port. As far as Chittagong was concerned, it was almost peripheral, away from the centre of gravity, too far to the east. He maintained that the geopolitical heart of East Pakistan was Dacca. Capture of Dacca was imperative for India to control Pakistan. Manekshaw asked Jacob if by taking Khulna and Chittagong, Dacca would automatically fall. Jacob said that this was unlikely and therefore, Dacca should be the key objective. Manekshaw made changes to the plan and in the planning period, for most part, bypassed the Army Commander and dealt directly with the Chief of Staff, Jacob.[3] The operational instructions were issued and each formation war-gamed their plans. Original plans underwent suitable modifications after discussions. As far as possible, built-up areas were to be contained and the aim was to reach key areas in depth.

Mukti Bahini

Mukti Bahini is the appellation of the forces of the Bangladesh War of Liberation. The precursor of the organisation was the Mukti Fauj, which was preceded by the Sangram Parishads formed in the cities and villages by student and youth leaderships in early March 1971. The Mukti Bahini included fighting elements from two main streams: members of armed forces of erstwhile East Pakistan; and members of the urban and rural Sangram Parishads.[4] There were two distinct groups in it, namely, the Niyomito Bahini (regular army) and the Gano Bahini (the people's army). The Niyomito Bahini had under it the Swadhin Bangla

Regiment and the Mukti Fauj. The Gano Bahini was divided into three parts: Suicide Squads, Scorpion Squads and Toofan Bahini (storm troops). The Swadhin Bangla Regiment was the backbone of the organisation, comprising of members belonging to regular army regiments, the East Bengal Regiment and the East Pakistan Rifles.[5]

On the request of the provisional Government of Bangladesh, the Government of India directed the Indian Army to provide necessary assistance to the Mukti Bahini. This was known as 'Operation Jackpot'. Their operational HQ was located at Calcutta. Col M.G. Osmani was the head, with Wing Commander Khondkar as his deputy. The sector responsibility was given to the following officers:

1. Major (Maj) Zia, responsible for Chittagong;
2. Maj Khalid Musharraf, Comilla;
3. Maj Safiullah, Mymensingh;
4. Wing Commander Bashar, Rangpur;
5. Lieutenant Colonel (Lt Col) Zaman, Rajshahi;
6. Maj Usman, Kushtia;
7. Maj Jalil, Khulna; and
8. Tiger Siddiqui opted to operate from his own area in Tangail, as did Noorul Kadar and Toha.

The forces were to be trained for three months. Once trained, they would penetrate deep into East Pakistan to form cells and function as guerilla forces. Further, a large number of personnel were to make the existing East Bengal battalions up to strength, as also man the additional battalions and arty batteries that Col Osmani planned to raise. In addition, about 400 naval commandos and frogmen were trained, particularly for attacking port facilities and vessels. For example, a Mukti Bahini gunboat, mounting a 40 mm Bofors air defence gun, captured, sank or damaged some 15 Pakistani ships, seven gunboats, 11 barges, two tankers and 19 river craft. There were a number of small team actions which were also fruitful, such as the forces assisted the Indian Army in the advance to Sylhet.[6] These were indeed creditable achievements. It is to the credit of Indian Army officers, like Captain (later Col) D.K. Chand, who operated with the Mukti Bahini, which began at the Jalalpur camp in the foothills of Shillong. Overall, the achievements of Mukti Bahini were a key factor in the liberation struggle. Their contributions were a crucial element in the operations prior to and during full-scale hostilities.

Pakistani Order of Battle

At the helm of Pakistani forces was Lt Gen A.A.K. Niazi, along with HQ Eastern Command. The Pakistani order of battle at the commencement of hostilities was as follows:

1. *North-western sector*: 16 Infantry Division, under Maj Gen Nazar Hussain, with HQ at Nator. The division deployed 23 Infantry Brigade of four battalions in the area of Dinajpur–Rangpur; 205 Infantry Brigade in the area of Hilli–Ghoraghat; and 34 Infantry Brigade in the area of Rajshahi–Naogaon.[7]
2. *Western sector*: 9 Infantry Division was deployed in the area of Jessore. Maj Gen M.H. Ansari was the General Officer Commanding (GOC). Around Jessore was deployed a squadron of armour, two field regiments and one mortar battery. In addition, 107 Infantry Brigade was deployed in the same area, whereas 57 Infantry Brigade was deployed in Jhendia–Meherpur–Jibannagar. Some elements were dispersed to indicate a large quantum of troops in the area. They simulated large quantum of signal traffic in the area.
3. *South-eastern sector*: The area was under 14 Infantry Division. Maj Gen Abdul Majid Quazi was the GOC. They had deployed a squadron of armour, two field regiments and one heavy mortar battery in the northern part of this sector. The HQ was initially at Dacca, but later moved to Bhairab Bazaar. The 17 Infantry Brigade was in the area of Akhaura–Kasba–Brahman Baria; 313 Infantry Brigade was at Maulvi Bazaar; and 202 Infantry Brigade was at Sylhet. The 39 Infantry Division, commanded by Maj Gen Rahim Khan, occupied the southern part of this sector, with HQ at Chandpur. The 117 Infantry Brigade was in area of Maynamati; 53 Infantry Brigade of two battalions was in area of Feni; and 91 Infantry Brigade, comprising of one regular battalion, was at Faujdahat–Ramgarh. The remaining part of the brigade was deployed in the area of Chittagong, including its hill tracts.
4. *North-eastern sector*: HQ 36 Infantry Division was formed from the Director General of East Pakistan's Civil Armed Forces. It had under its command 93 Infantry Brigade, together with one battery deployed in the area of Jamalpur–Mymensingh. One brigade worth of troops was located in Dacca.
5. *Additional troops*: In addition to these regular troops, each division was given large numbers of East Pakistan civil armed police.

Relative Strength

It is evident that Indian forces were numerically a little more than the Pakistani regulars. Though there was need for an additional division and a brigade for the north-eastern sector, 6 Mountain Division and 123 Infantry Brigade could not be employed due to the possible threat from China. There were formations like 8 Mountain Division, which had no artillery; and 57 Mountain Division, which had limited artillery. Further, there was scarcity of light armour and bridging equipment.

Preliminary Operations

Pakistani troops started shelling around end of October 1971. As the border outposts were under artillery attack, it was decided to let troops go into East Pakistan up to a depth of 16 kilometre (km) to silence the Pakistani artillery. This resulted in 'improvement of defensive posture'. Formations were instructed to carry out the following tasks:

1. *2 Corps*: Invest enemy defences in the area of Afra and capture Mohammadpur.
2. *33 Corps*: Clear Pachgarh and advance as far south as possible towards Thakurgaon; capture Hilli.
3. *101 Communications Zone Area*: Capture Jaintiapur and Kamalpur; advance to Bakshiganj; intensify Mukti Bahini activity in Tangail; and threaten Mymensingh, Haluaghat, Phulpur, Shamganj and Durgapur.
4. *4 Corps*: Capture Gangasagar and clear up to Saidabad; establish a battalion block in the area of Debigram; isolate Akhaura and Brahman Baria; eliminate Pakistani border outposts in the area of Narayanpur; capture Rajpur and threaten Akhaura; secure Shamshernagar and Kalaura; and isolate Feni.

All this assisted in greatly ascertaining issues and improving our defence posture. In the western sector of 2 Corps, Chaugacha was firmly in the hands of Mukti Bahini by 29 November. The 9 Infantry Division reached halfway between the border and Jessore. Similarly, 4 Mountain Division captured Jibannagar, Uthali and Darsana. In 33 Corps sector, 71 Mountain Brigade captured Thakurgaon. Outskirts of Hilli were captured, but heavy resistance was encountered at Hilli. In 4 Corps sector, the salient east of the line Chargam–Karimganj had been captured and Kalaura invested. In the Akhaura area, Gangasagar had been captured. Further south, the whole of Belonia Bulge had been cleared. In 101

Communications Zone Area sector, 95 Mountain Brigade met heavy resistance in the capture of Kamalpur.

These preliminary operations reinforced Eastern Command's strategic concept that fortified positions had to be bypassed. The Pakistanis were thrown off balance and the strategy of drawing the Pakistanis to the border began to work. Gen Niazi concentrated on the defence of Jessore, Jhendia, Bogra, Rangpur, Mymensingh, Sylhet, Bhairab Bazaar, Comilla and Chittagong. He ordered these towns to be the nodal areas for defence. This strategy left open subsidiary axes, which Indian forces proposed to use.

Bridging Equipment, Movement of Stores, Signal Communications, Vehicles and Scarcity of Artillery

East Pakistan was a land of rivers and it was crucial to have bridging equipment for successful operations. By mid-August 1971, Eastern Command received Bailey pontoon bridge and folding boat equipment. Assault boats arrived late and were in position only a few days before the operations began. The chief engineer and his staff left no stone unturned to get the entire equipment ready for operations.

It was a herculean task to move stores to the corps' maintenance areas. A wise decision was to commence the movement in July and the dumping was complete before the operations commenced. The most difficult were the areas earmarked for 4 Corps in Tripura. These were established at Teliamura, Udaipur and Dharamnagar. Some 30,000 tonnes of stores were moved to these locations. Regarding others, 14,000 tonnes was moved to Krishnanagar for 2 Corps; 7,000 tonnes to Raigarh for 33 Corps; and 4,000 tonnes to Tura for 101 Communications Zone's thrust to Dacca.

Signal communications were highly underdeveloped, particularly in Tripura and Meghalaya. Further, the existing network was inadequate. Eastern Command had to create a new signal communications infrastructure for the entire launch pads, from 4 Corps in Tripura, 2 Corps in Krishnanagar to 101 Communications Zone in Tura, Meghalaya. The 33 Corps was the only formation where communications could be provided with lesser effort. Greater reliance was placed on electronic teleprinter circuits which were secure and successful.

Innovation was the order of the day. Mountain divisions were short of vehicles and there was a huge requirement of transport. Army HQ was unable to provide vehicles but offered 100 chassis. These were driven to the vehicle depot at Panagarh, which was holding a large quantity of vehicles to be discarded. During September–October 1971, the old vehicle bodies were removed and fitted on to these chassis;

and this served the purpose. Further, teams were sent as far away as central India to hire more than 2,000 civil load carriers. To overcome shortage of spares for small arms and tanks, Brig Sethna approached his friends in civil trade, who procured these items and handed them over to the units.

The divisional artillery of the formations being launched were mostly mountain guns. The 8 Mountain Division had no artillery and there were only two 5.5 inch Medium Regiments both deployed on the Chinese border. There was no other option but to take artillery resources from the Chinese border for operations against the East Pakistan. Later, one Medium Regiment possessing 130 mm guns was allotted by Army HQ. Further, HQ 2 Artillery Brigade was placed under HQ 2 Corps. Apart from these, huge dumping of ammunition was undertaken well before the operations. The best part was that once operations started, troops never had to look back.

Progress of Operations

Full-scale hostilities commenced on 4 December 1971 and most of the formations were engaged against Pakistani defences. The Indian Army offensive proceeded as follows:

1. *2 Corps sector*: 9 Infantry Division was knocking on the doors of Jessore by 6 December. Pakistanis withdrew from Jessore and moved to Daulatpur, Khulna and east of Madhumati River. While 9 Infantry Division moved towards Khulna, HQ Eastern Command wanted it to move towards Faridpur. The 4 Mountain Division captured Darsana and Kotchandpur by 5 December. Magura fell on 8 December and the Madhumati ferry was contacted. After the capture of Magura, 62 Mountain Brigade commenced the advance towards Faridpur. The brigade moved to the west bank of the Madhumati and was preparing for the crossing. In the meantime, 7 Mountain Brigade of 4 Mountain Division, which was sent to Kushtia, ran into stiff opposition from a depleted brigade and a squadron of light tanks. At this juncture, 62 Mountain Brigade, which was poised towards Faridpur onwards to Dacca, was diverted to Kushtia, thus delaying the advance to Faridpur onwards to Dacca. The focus on Kushtia led to crossing of the Madhumati on 14 December. This delayed utilisation of 2 Corps for possible use against Dacca.
2. *33 Corps sector*: Operations in this sector were primarily confined to securing of the Hilli–Gaibanda waistline, advance to Bogra and advance

to Rangpur. The 20 Mountain Division had positioned 165 Mountain Brigade to hold a firm base in the Balurghat Bulge and 340 Mountain Brigade for investing Dinajpur from the south. Two brigades, 66 and 202 Mountain Brigades, were to be utilised for the main thrust to Pirganj. While 66 Mountain Brigade captured Phulbari, 202 Mountain Brigade could not proceed beyond Hilli. The plans underwent a change and the two brigades maintained the momentum to Pirganj. The 66 Mountain Brigade met with stiff opposition at Bhaduria, and this could be cleared only by 11 December 1971. Meanwhile, 340 Mountain Brigade made a rapid advance and captured Pirganj on 7 December, Palashbari on 9 December, Gaibanda and Phulchari ferry on 10 December, securing the waistline and isolating Pakistani forces in the Dinajpur–Rangpur belt. The brigade pressed on further south and in an enveloping move, captured Gobindganj on 11 December. Hilli finally fell on 11 December and the next was advance to Bogra. By executing enveloping movements, 340 Mountain Brigade, 165 Mountain Brigade and 202 Mountain Brigade could capture the outskirts of Bogra. The next step was the advance to Rangpur, which was undertaken by 66 Mountain Brigade, followed by 202 Mountain Brigade. They were able to capture Miktapur against light opposition, and Rangpur had been invested from the south-west and south by two brigades.

3. *4 Corps sector*: The Corps Commander, Lt Gen Sagat Singh, was clear that time was limited and it was extremely necessary to cross the rivers and threaten Dacca. With this aim in mind, the first task was the isolation of Sylhet by 8 Mountain Division. On 6 December, 59 Mountain Brigade captured Kalaura. By 5 December, 81 Mountain Brigade had captured Munshi Bazaar and on 7 December, after heavy resistance, they isolated the Maulvi Bazaar defences. The Pakistanis were somehow convinced that Sylhet must hold out. They moved 311 Infantry Brigade to Sylhet from Maulvi Bazaar, reinforcing 202 Infantry Brigade. This was advantageous to 4 Corps as it found the passage over Meghna River practically uncontested. Meanwhile, 57 Mountain Division encircled and captured Ashuganj by 5 December. They now advanced towards Brahman Baria. By 9 December, the Pakistanis withdrew, blew up the Coronation Bridge and pulled back to Bhairab Bazaar. In the meantime, 23 Mountain Division was able to execute advances towards Laksham–Comilla and Chandpur. Comilla was vacated on 9 December and about 1,500

personnel surrendered between Comilla and Daudkandi. Laksham was also occupied on 9 December. The Meghna Bulge was secured and Maynamati was invested by the corps commander. This was followed by Heli-landings across the Meghna (covered later in the paper). Dacca was being threatened and tremendous psychological pressure mounted on the East Pakistan Army Commander, Gen Niazi.

4. *101Communications Zone*: The task of 95 Mountain Brigade was to capture Mymensingh. In October, the brigade moved to the concentration area at Tura in Meghalaya.[8] The enemy garrison at Kamalpur finally surrendered to 95 Mountain Brigade on 4 December 1971. Jamalpur was encircled and held out until 11 December and 95 Mountain Brigade resumed its advance south of Jamalpur on 12 December. In the meantime, 2 PARA was para-dropped at Tangail on the evening of 11 December and captured Poongli Bridge on the Jamuna.

Heliborne Operations Across the Meghna

In order to threaten Dacca, operations had to be undertaken to cross rivers. As bridges had been destroyed by the enemy force, heliborne operations and para landings had to conducted. The 4 Corps left no stone unturned to cross the Meghna using helicopters. Group Captain Chandan Singh, Commander of Air Force Station Jorhat, had Mi-4 helicopters. He started directly interacting with Gen Sagat Singh, GOC 4 Corps, with effect from 3 December 1971. On 6 December, 110 Helicopter Unit, under Squadron Leader Sandhu, arrived at Kailashahar. The first heliborne operations were launched with 4/5 Gorkha Rifles over Sylhet. The next was the crossings over the Meghna.

On 8 December 1971, Chandan Singh was asked to meet Maj Gen Gonsalves, the GOC of 57 Mountain Division at Brahman Baria. The GOC was stuck on the east bank of the Meghna River as the Pakistanis had demolished the bridge connecting Ashuganj and Bhairab Bazaar. As Bhairab Bazaar was held in strength, he wished to lift a battalion group to Raipura. It was decided to initially undertake an armed reconnaissance. On 9 December, an armed reconnaissance was undertaken, with Gen Sagat Singh participating in it. A helipad was selected and 11 Mi-4 helicopters were available for the mission. The operations commenced at 1400 hours on the same day. In this mission, 27 sorties were carried out by day and 30 sorties were done by night, and 4 Guards was heli-lifted successfully.

Gen Sagat Singh, on 11 December, directed that an entire brigade and an artillery regiment be airlifted across the Meghna. This entailed 150 sorties, with each helicopter undertaking about 14–15 sorties. The helicopters, being serviced at Agartala, had to airlift the troops to Narsingdi. By mid-day on 11 December, the sorties commenced and continued till early morning of 12 December. In all, 135 sorties were undertaken and a total of 1,628 troops were landed with arms, ammunition, artillery and rations.[9] Moving to Narsingdi involved crossing six water courses. Though there were a few engine breakdowns and forced landings, the helicopters did a great job.

The troops reaching close to Dacca built up the psychological pressure. The next was to lift troops of 23 Mountain Division from Daudkandi to Narayanganj, which was about 30 km to the south-east of Dacca. This started on 14 December and 80 sorties by day and 42 by night were undertaken. All of this contributed to threaten Dacca, leading to its surrender. Both Gen Aurora and Gen Sagat Singh stated these little helicopters, Mi-4, were worth their weight in gold.[10]

Airborne Assault

The 2 PARA, led by Lt Col K.S. Pannu, undertook the first airborne assault in enemy territory. The operation took place on 11 December at Tangail in Bangladesh. The battalion group included a para field battery from 17 Para Field Regiment, 411 Para Field Company and other components of the arms and services. On 9 December, the battalion was moved to the two mounting bases at Dumdum and Kalaikunda. Maj P.K. Ghosh was infiltrated through 95 Mountain Brigade by the Mukti Bahini to Tangail. He selected the dropping zones (DZs) for the mission. The task was to capture Poongli Bridge and the adjacent ferry on the Lohajung River near Tangail, approximately 70 miles north-west of Dacca. The aim was to defeat the enemy forces withdrawing from Jamalpur and Mymensingh towards Tangail. Link up was to be established by 95 Mountain Brigade. The pathfinders took off around 1400 hours on 11 December from Dumdum and 20 minutes later, the battalion group were airborne. The drop was widespread, about 2.5 miles. After a quick rendezvous, the pathfinders marked the DZ and were ready to receive the main drop. The battalion regroup after the drop was quick and they moved to Poongli Bridge. The bridge was captured and a Pakistani brigade withdrawing was disintegrated. Link up took place with 101 Communications Zone Area units on the evening of 12 December. After 13 December, the battle progressed but Pakistanis offered stiff resistance. On the morning of 16 December, a message was received that the Pakistan had agreed to surrender.[11] Rest was left to Maj Gen Jacob to negotiate with Gen Niazi.

Negotiating the Surrender

The Indian Air Force bombed the governor's house on 14 December and the governor, in panic, resigned. At the time, news channels had reported that 5,000 paratroopers had landed at Tangail instead of a battalion group. Further, 101 Communications Zone and troops of 4 Corps were threatening Dacca. Gen Manekshaw wisely asked the Pakistanis to surrender. India issued a unilateral ceasefire from 1500 hours on 15 December. On 16 December, Maj Gen Jacob was directed by the Indian Army Chief to go to Dacca and get a surrender from Gen Niazi. He landed at Dacca and read out the terms of surrender. Gen Niazi insisted that he agreed only to the ceasefire. However, Gen Jacob pulled Niazi aside and insisted that they surrender. He gave him 30 minutes to consider and after that, Gen Niazi reluctantly agreed and the ceremony took place the same evening.[12]

Issues Meriting Importance

It is more than half a century since the 1971 Indo-Pak War and the creation of Bangladesh. A few issues merit attention here that helped us win the war:

1. Clarity of objective is essential. Dacca was most important and this was possibly clear to HQ Eastern Command, who could swing the campaign in India's favour.
2. Importance of ensuring one front is dormant while undertaking operations. Care was taken to ensure that the Chinese front was guarded but remained inactive. Even today, as far as possible, a war on two fronts should be avoided.
3. The importance of air dominance for operations by land or sea.
4. Intelligence remains the key to success in operations. Signal intelligence provided key inputs to the entire campaign. Even today, there is a dire need of good intelligence.
5. Lack of light armour and artillery. These remain short even today. We need to address these issues with speed and military precision. This is particularly needed for operations in riverine and mountainous regions, including high altitude.
6. Civil–military cooperation is of utmost importance.
7. Integration between the three services is a requirement, which is correctly being addressed currently.
8. Logistics need detailed planning, and preparation must begin early to ensure successful operations.

9. Need for developing capabilities for launching amphibious operations is extremely important.
10. Heliborne operations and airborne operations are extremely important for speedy execution of tasks.
11. Media, in all its forms, has an important role. Foreign correspondents and media played an important role in the 1971 war. In the current environment too, social media plays an important role as part of information warfare, and thus must be managed correctly.
12. Military diplomacy is extremely important. As seen in 1971, Maj Gen Jacob was simply brilliant in convincing Lt Gen Niazi to surrender.

NOTES

1. I was fortunate to be posted in a mountain corps, forming part of Eastern Command where these luminaries met and spoke about the complexities of the eastern theatre. Further discussions with them took place at other locations where close interaction was possible.
2. J.F.R. Jacob, *Surrender at Dacca: Birth of a Nation*, New Delhi: Manohar, 1997, p. 60.
3. Ibid., pp. 66–67.
4. 'Mukti Bahini', *Banglapedia: National Encyclopedia of Bangladesh*, available at www.en.banglapedia.org, accessed on 26 June 2021.
5. Praveen Davar, 'Mukti Bahini: A Force of Freedom', *The Telegraph*, 29 April 2021, available at www.telegraphindia.com, accessed on 26 June 2021.
6. D.K. Chand, 'Memoirs of a Guerilla Force Commander', in D.C. Katoch and Q.S.A. Zahir (eds), *Liberation: Bangladesh–1971*, New Delhi: Bloomsbury India, 2015, pp. 41–48.
7. Jacob, *Surrender at Dacca*, n. 2, p. 102.
8. Hardev S. Kler, 'Making of a Plan, the Capture of Dhaka', in Katoch and Zahir (eds), *Liberation: Bangladesh–1971*, n. 6, p. 65.
9. Chandan Singh, 'The Meghna Crossing', in Katoch and Zahir (eds), *Liberation: Bangladesh–1971*, n. 6, pp. 218–22.
10. Ibid.
11. Nirbhay Sharma, 'The Story of Indian Army's First Airborne Assault', in Katoch and Zahir (eds), *Liberation Bangladesh–1971*, n. 6, pp. 133–40.
12. J.F.R. Jacob, 'Niazi Bested', in Katoch and Zahir (eds), *Liberation Bangladesh–1971*, n. 6, pp. 229–38.

6

The Battle of Garibpur

Vijay Yeshvant Gidh

The infantry battalion of 14 Punjab (Nabha Akal), raised as Nabha State Force on 24 October 1757, not only fought with distinction during both the World Wars, but also in most of the wars and operations fought by the Indian Army post independence. It also handed India its first victory in the Battle of Garibpur, a precursor to the 1971 Bangladesh Liberation War.

1971: Prevailing Scenario

Indian Army's 14 Punjab, as part of 42 Infantry Brigade, 9 Infantry Division, was deployed on the border in the Krishnanagar, Krishnaganj and Gede area in April 1971, to prevent the illegitimate ingress of refugees and to check the East Pakistan troops chasing the refugees.

The battalion later moved to Kalyani for infantry-tank cooperation training with 'B' Squadron of 45 Cavalry equipped with PT-76 amphibian tanks. Operationally oriented training was also carried out for launching an attack deep into the enemy territory on foot, self-contained for 24 hours; as well as negotiating riverine terrain.

The battalion was concentrated near village Bamandanga in the Bayra salient on 16 October 1971, and subsequently moved to Gobardanga, where intensive training was carried out with engineer expedients and improvised means to cross water obstacles. Bunker clearing/bursting drills were also perfected during day and night.[1]

Situation on the International Border

In the east, the situation on the Indo-Pakistan border was worsening due to genocide by the Pakistan Army. In view of the military actions by the Mukti Bahini, Pakistani forays and provocations inside Indian territory increased, leading to Indian casualties. The 14 Punjab was concentrated near the international border, where it was tasked to train the Mukti Fauj volunteers and successfully dominate the border.

By end of November 1971, the enemy actions had reached a level where it became necessary to protect Indian interests by occupying selected enclaves in East Pakistan. On 16 November 1971, the battalion was further moved for a new operational role in an entirely new sector of Bayra.

The Assigned Task

The battalion, under the command of Lieutenant Colonel (Lt Col) RK Singh, was initially tasked to occupy a battalion defended area in Fatehpur, which was located 6 kilometre (kms) inside East Pakistan. The task was later revised 'to secure the area of Garibpur by first light 21 November 1971'.[2]

The battalion was tasked to advance well inside to secure enemy territory in order to interdict the Chaugacha–Jessore road and trap the withdrawing enemy from Chaugacha, or prevent any reinforcements joining from Jessore (See Maps 1 and 2). The unit was allotted 'Charlie' Squadron of 45 Cavalry consisting of 14 PT-76 tanks, one platoon of 102 Engineer Regiment under command, with 87 Battery of 6 Field Regiment in direct support and remainder 6 Field Regiment and 78 Medium Regiment in support.

Importance of Garibpur

The hamlet of Garibpur, located in the Bayra salient 9 kms inside East Pakistan, astride the highway from India to Jessore via Chaugacha, was an important crossroad for both the nations. In the event of full military option being exercised, 9 Infantry Division had the initial task to capture the prestigious cantonment and vital communication centre of Jessore; and one of its axis of advance was the Chaugacha–Jessore highway. Its control created a road map for Indian forces to eventually defeat Pakistani troops in December 1971.

© GIS Section, Manohar Parrikar Institute for Defence Studies & Analyses (MP-IDSA). Map not to scale.

Map 1. Orientation Map

2 Corps Plan: An Outline

The newly created 2 Corps consisted of 9 Infantry Division and 4 Mountain Division (Map 3). The 9 Infantry Division's main thrust was planned along the Bayra–Garibpur–Jessore axis, while a secondary attack would be made along the Benapol–Jessore line. The role of 4 Mountain Division was to move along the Darshan–Jibannagar–Kotchandpur axis, with a secondary thrust along the Chuadanga–Jibannagar axis.

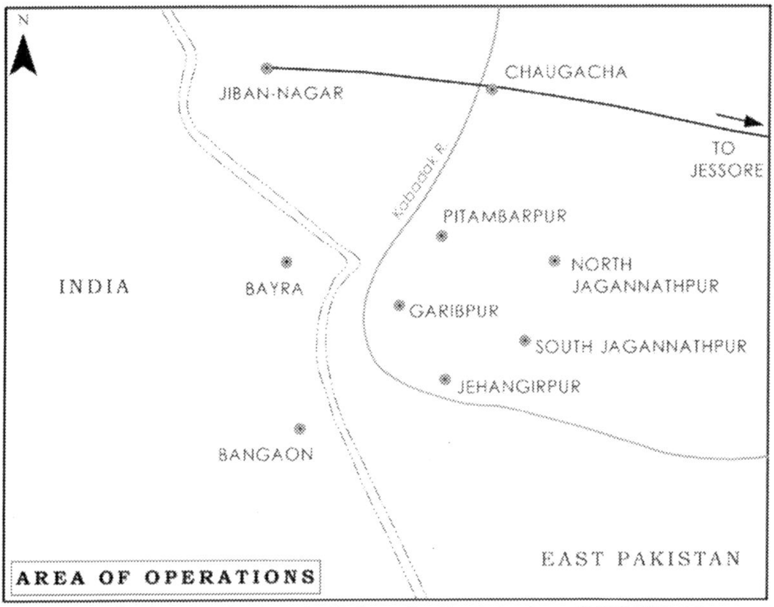

Map 2. Area of Operations

As mentioned earlier, India's 9 Infantry Division had the initial task to capture Jessore. Meanwhile, Pakistan's 9 Infantry Division was responsible for the defence of this sector, with 9 Division Headquarters located at Jessore. Pakistan 107 Infantry Brigade was responsible for the defence of Jessore.

Reconnaissance

A night before the attack, on night 19–20 November 1971, a strong patrol of 14 Punjab was sent across the border to reconnoitre a suitable area ahead of Fatehpur. Major (Maj) A.P. Viswanathan, Officer Commanding, Alpha Company led this patrol, which comprised elements of rifle companies to ensure that all the companies would have route guidance on arrival into positions. The move of the unit was supposed to be a surprise, but following a skirmish with an enemy patrol, the Pakistanis were alerted of the impending attack.

Advance to Fatehpur—A Tragic Start

The 14 Punjab commenced its advance at 7 a.m. on 20 November 1971. The Kabadak River on the border had to be crossed. For this, the engineer troops were building a bridge across the river, which was about 40 metres in width and 5

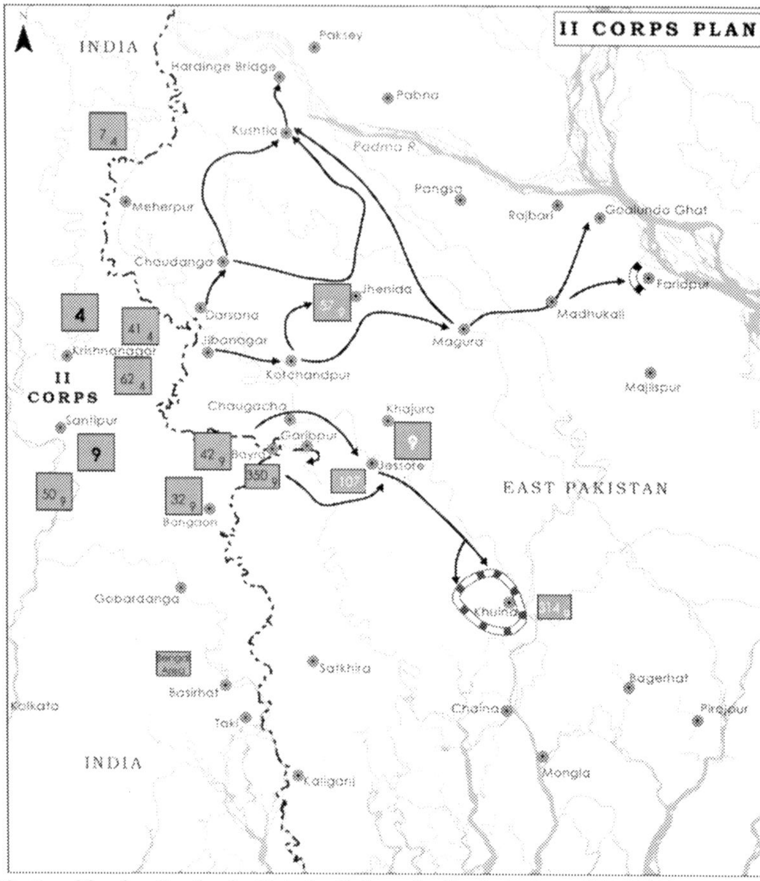

Map 3. The 2 Corps Plan

metres in depth. As this process would have taken many more hours, it was decided that since the battalion had arrived on the river banks, they would be ferried across on motorboats steered by engineer troops.

Bravo Company under Maj K.M. Machiah, was nominated as the vanguard company. The only crossing expedients available for the entire battalion were one assault boat with one out board motor (OBM), with a sitting capacity of 16 men, and a Class-5 raft with a maximum capacity of 20 men. In order to prepare the first wave to cross fast with the help of the available crossing aids, the men were fully equipped with arms and ammunition. No safety belts were available as the boat was meant for the exclusive use of the engineer crew for their work to lay the bridge.

In the first wave, one section with medium machine gun (MMG) detachment, totalling 16 men, got on board at about 9.30 a.m. to cross the Kabadak River. The boat, while approaching the other side, overshot the berthing area. The engineer operator of the OBM took a sharp U-turn and in this manoeuvre, the boat overturned and capsized. All the occupants fell into the river, entrapped in swamp and weeds under the upside-down boat, each swimming and struggling hard to save his life. Two engineer divers at once jumped in to save the drowning men. However, out of 16 soldiers, only seven were saved and nine got drowned.[3]

This unpredictably calamity, may be termed as an imponderable of war. The mishap affected the morale of the troops. They were dismayed and disheartened. However, it is to the credit of the unit officers, particularly the second-in-command, Maj Inderjit Singh who motivated the troops by citing the sacrifices made by Guru Govind Singh. The company groups slowly and carefully commenced crossing the river with proper safety measures. The entire battalion was able to cross by last light.

It is to the credit of the unit that this catastrophe did not deter them to get on with the impending operational task.

Advance to Garibpur

The infantry battalion of 14 Punjab along with 'C' Squadron, 45 Cavalry equipped with 14 PT-76 tanks, reached the Garibpur position by last light on 20 November 1971. There was just enough time for Lt Col R.K. Singh to issue orders to his company commanders before the early winter night set in.

The Battalion Headquarters, under Maj Inderjit Singh, Captain (Capt) M.P.S. Bajwa, Adjutant, Mortar Platoon under Capt V.S. Butalia and other heavy stores reached around 10.30 p.m.

Assessment of the Enemy

A battalion of Pakistani 107 Infantry Brigade was located at Chaugacha, while the remainder brigade and 9 Infantry Division was in Jessore. Since the Garibpur position would outflank the Pakistani battalion at Chaugacha, there was likely to be a strong enemy reaction.

Deployment and Preparation of Defences

Initial Deployment of Battalion

Capt Bajwa, the Adjutant, narrated the salient aspects of the deployment:

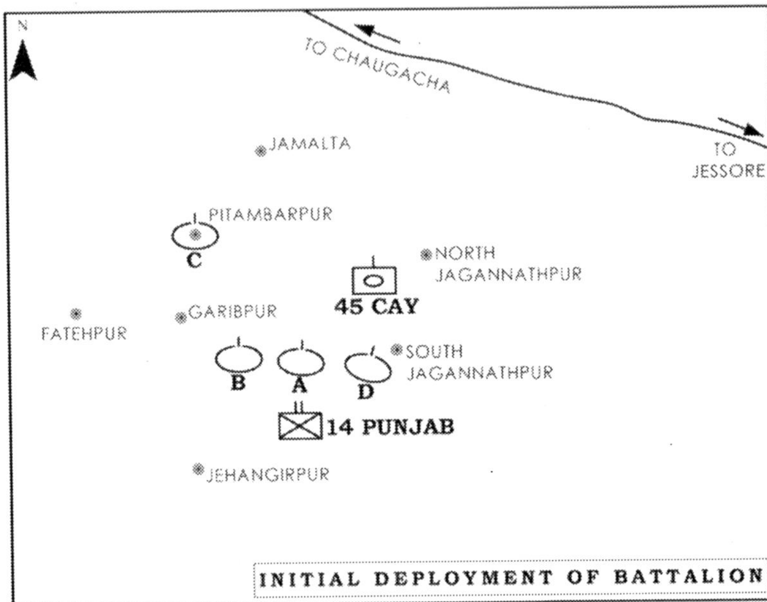

© GIS Section, Manohar Parrikar Institute for Defence Studies & Analyses (MP-IDSA). Map not to scale.

Map 4. Initial Deployment of Battalion

The companies were allocated their area of deployment. Maj N.S. Narang, 'C' Squadron Commander, 45 Cavalry, was ordered to deploy his tanks in conjunction with two recoilless guns to cover the enemy armour advance from the direction of road Jessore–Chaugacha and the east between Garibpur–South Jagannathpur.

Delta Company under Capt Balbir Singh, with one section MMGs and a recoilless gun, occupied a company-defended locality in South Jagannathpur to cover the tank approach with elements of armour. Charlie Company under Maj N.J.S. Bains, with a section of MMGs, occupied a company defended locality further north at Track Junction near Pitambarpur, where the two tracks converged from Chaugacha.

Alpha and Bravo Companies under Maj Vishwanathan and Maj Machiah occupied the gap between Çharlie and Delta Companies. By 3 a.m. on the 21st, the battalion was in position and the men were feverishly at work to get the defences ready by first light.

The Battalion Headquarters was located near Garibpur. Since strict radio silence was to be maintained, the Signal Platoon was instructed to lay lines to all companies and mortar position. Somehow, the linesman were unable to find Charlie Company location of Maj Bains, hence no line could be laid to Charlie Company.

It was past midnight when Maj D.S. Narang had deployed his tanks. The tank troops were commanded by Capt Tejinder Singh Sidhu, located near Alpha Company-defended locality: the other troop was commanded by Capt B.S. Mehta, which was deployed towards south eastern side, near Delta Company at the farthest end: and the third troop was commanded by a Junior Commissioned Officer (JCO).[4]

Bold Deployment of Protective Patrol

Maj Inderjit Singh explained why it was essential to send an officer patrol with an Artillery Observation Post (OP) officer ahead of the defences:

> It was tactically important to locate the enemy gun area, as we had encountered enemy fire during our move. So I advised the Commanding Officer to send an officer patrol along with Artillery OP to engage enemy gun area.
>
> A patrol with Capt G.S. Gill, the MMG officer and the artillery observer, Capt P.P. Chaturvedi from 6 Field Regiment, were moved north towards Singhajhuli–North Jagannnathpur to cover the enemy movement on road axis Jessore–Chaugacha.
>
> In the cold and foggy early hours of 21 November, Capt Gill heard the unmistakable sounds of enemy tanks moving south from the Chaugacha–Jessore road. The fog and poor visibility allowed the patrol to remain close to the enemy columns and report on them accurately.
>
> Capt Chaturvedi, provided with a fine opportunity, brought down some good concentrations on the closely massed Pakistani columns. In the poor visibility and the noise of tanks and own artillery fire, the patrol was nearly encircled, but resolutely broke away. Capt Chaturvedi was wounded and was bravely carried by Capt Gill and others till they finally made their way back to the Company. They were both awarded Vir Chakra (VrC).[5]

Capt Bajwa narrated an interesting incident:

> It was around 5.30 am on 21 November 1971 that all of a sudden, I heard Capt Gill mumbling on the radio set, "*Sir, etthe dushman de bahut tanks te infantry ekathe ho rahe ne*". [Sir, many enemy tanks and infantry are seen closing in this area]. He, thereafter, went off the air. I immediately informed the Commanding Officer about this important message.[6]

Although radio silence had been lifted, Charlie Company of Maj Bains was still out of communication. Later it was found that his radio operator had carried a faulty AN PRC-25 (radio set).

The Enemy Response and Our Counter Response

As visualised, the Garibpur position outflanked the Pakistani battalion at Chaugacha and there was violent response by Pakistani 107 Infantry Brigade at first light, 21 November to 14 Punjab's entry across the Bayra salient. It became known later through the prisoners taken, that Pakistan's 6 Punjab, elements of 21 Punjab, 22 Frontier Force and 3 Independent Armoured Squadron of Chaffee tanks made up the attacking force.

Pakistani Infantry and Armour Attacks

Phases of Operation

During early winter morning, heavy fog had enveloped the surrounding area. At about 3.30 a.m. on 21 November, our patrol deployed near Singajhuli passed on a message regarding roaring sound of tanks from the direction of Jessore. At 5.30 a.m., Capt Gill reported on radio link that he could see enemy armour and infantry lining up for assault in the forming up place (FUP). All companies were warned to be ready for the impending enemy attack. However, Charlie Company was still out of communication.

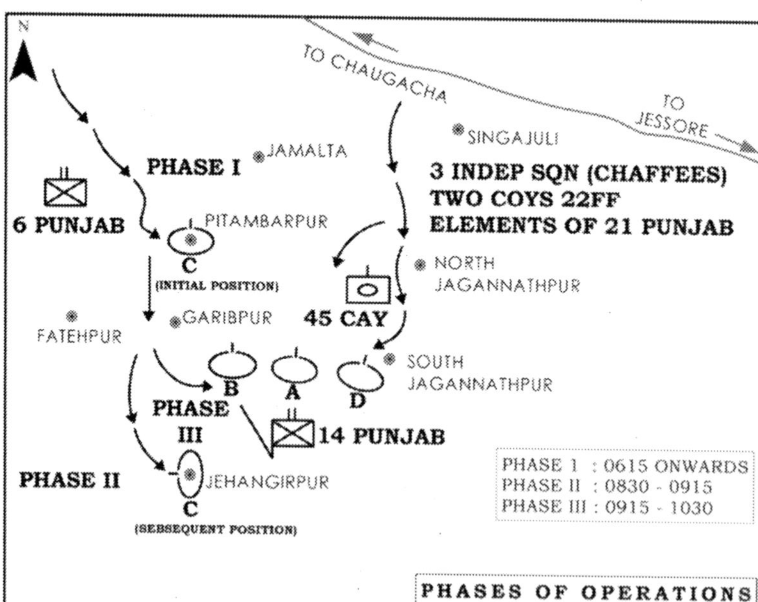

© GIS Section, Manohar Parrikar Institute for Defence Studies & Analyses (MP-IDSA). Map not to scale.

Map 5. Phases of Operation

The Pakistani thrust lines having become apparent, thanks to the good work of the patrols operating ahead of the defences, readjustments to muster the recoilless rifle (RCL) guns and the PT-76 tanks at the required places were carried out.

Enemy artillery guns opened up and started pounding our defences to support their assaulting armour and infantry. As dawn broke out on 21st November, the enemy launched an attack by two infantry battalions supported by a squadron of armour equipped with M24 Chaffee tanks.

The troops of 14 Punjab battalion group rose splendidly to the occasion and the well-organised drills and training stood to good effect in those crucial hours.

An Intense Infantry Encounter

Around 6 a.m. on 21 November 1971, enemy activity was observed opposite Charlie Company from Chaugacha built-up area side. The enemy attempted to encircle the company and a fierce encounter commenced.

Maj N.J.S. Bains was very nostalgic when he narrated his personal experiences of the Garibpur battle:

> The Commanding Officer, Lt Col R.K. Singh ordered me to occupy a company-defended location at Track Junction, ahead of village Pitambarpur, where the two tracks converged from Chaugacha. The location was about 1 km from the forward defences of 14 Punjab. It was already dark by the time Charlie Company moved to the given location. I deployed the Company and sent two patrols ahead of the defences for early warning of the enemy. Our radio set was also non-functional.
>
> During the night, the enemy sent two patrols, probably to find out our strength and location. At first light on 21 November, enemy activity was observed opposite our Company location from Chaugacha built-up area. It was sheer coincidence that when I banged the company radio set, it started functioning!
>
> As the enemy was forming up for the attack in front of our location, I requested the battery commander to give me fire immediately as the enemy was preparing to attack our location. The artillery fire was very effective as we could see the enemy suffering heavy casualties and retreating.
>
> Soon it was realised that the defences occupied by the company at night were too far from the main battalion defences and not fit for fighting a cohesive defensive battle. So we were informed to move the company further south, to the alternative location behind near Jahangirpur.
>
> I gave orders to my company to move to the alternate position. After marshalling the company, we executed a well-organised move almost in the

> face of the enemy. This location was in an open rice field and we were now ready to take on the enemy, if they followed us.
>
> Readjustment by Charlie Company was taken as a withdrawal of Indian troops and enemy commander ordered the remainder infantry and armour squadron to encircle my company from the south western direction.
>
> Soon it was seen that the enemy (which we learnt later was 6 Punjab of Pakistan) followed us; they were forming up in front about 500-600 metres away, and getting ready to attack us. The column of tanks, which were coming towards us were taken on by our armoured squadron. By now the enemy started shelling our location and preparing to attack us.
>
> I instructed the company to put on their bayonets and be prepared for hand-to-hand fight. Now heavy enemy small arms fire was coming on us, while we engaged the enemy with our small arms, MMGs and 2" mortar giving us supporting fire.
>
> Subedar Malkiat Singh, the Platoon Commander of my company, enthused the troops by moving under the enemy's small arms and artillery shelling at the cost of his life. He displayed conspicuous gallantry, for which he was awarded a Maha Vir Chakra (MVC). The enemy retreated, suffering heavy casualties, dead and seriously wounded.[7]

Capt Bajwa, in fact, remembered how Maj Bains suddenly came on air and requested for defensive fire DF [SOS], as the enemy had closed in and was forming up for the final assault. The artillery fire was promptly given by the Battery Commander, Maj Kailash Nath, who ensured an accurate barrage of fire to break the enemy attack.

The enemy tanks had come in the open and most of the tanks rushed towards southern direction towards Delta Company of Capt Balbir Singh with the aim to encircle Charlie Company from south-west. They were unaware about the deployment of the entire battalion, which was supported by tanks.

By this time, the 'C' Squadron, 45 Cavalry had swung into action and Maj D.S. Narang had readjusted the position of all the three troops. In the close fighting that ensued when the other Chaffees closed in, Maj Narang was hit and killed while directing his tanks standing up in the cupola, but not before taking out two Chaffee tanks. He was later awarded MVC for displaying indomitable courage in the face of the enemy. Capt B.S. Mehta, being the second-in-command, took over the charge.

The Main Frontal Attack

In the meantime, Delta Company, led by Capt Balbir Singh in the south, had fought fiercely and was successful in repulsing the repeated enemy attacks. Capt Balbir Singh shared some fond memories of the Garibpur battle:

> My Delta Company was last in the order of march and we advanced mounted on the tanks of 'C' Squadron, 45 Cavalry. We did not meet any enemy enroute and dismounted as we reached the outskirts of Garibpur village.
>
> After sometime, Commanding Officer came and indicated the general area where my company was to take up defensive position. I was lucky to have about 15 mins of daylight which helped to decide the deployment of my platoons and supporting elements. We immediately started preparing our defences as early morning the enemy attack was imminent.
>
> During the early hours of 21 November, we found enemy tanks coming at full speed towards our location. Our tanks started engaging them, but because of the fog it was difficult to engage them accurately.
>
> During the tank duel, a charging enemy tank sneaked through the fog close to Delta Company locality, within 25 metres of the positions. I instructed the RCL detachment commander, Havildar Lekh Raj, to engage the enemy tank charging into our company location. He himself loaded the shell and fired at the last tank which was visible to him. The enemy tank instantly went up in flames. This Non Commissioned Officer (NCO) was awarded VrC for his outstanding courage.
>
> The leading two enemy tanks had come very close to our defences, probably unaware of our presence. On seeing our tanks at 25 metres, they stopped and started aligning their guns. Before they could do so, our tanks blasted them. Enemy troops who jumped out of the tanks were engaged by our troops. The enemy troop commander, Lieutenant (Lt) Bhatt, was among those killed.
>
> Other enemy tanks which were following the leading tanks of Lt Bhatt were engaged by Capt B.S. Mehta and Capt Tejinder Sidhu. Witnessing the tank-to-tank battle in real life was an experience beyond imagination. After a few minutes, all the enemy Chaffee tanks were in flames. The enemy infantry, which was following the enemy tanks, were engaged by own troops. After seeing the three enemy tanks up in flames ahead of them, the infantry withdrew and started engaging us from village Jaganathpur. Luckily very accurate and intense artillery fire was brought on the enemy infantry which silenced the enemy small arms fire to a great extent.[8]

Later during the day, while searching the dead bodies of enemy troops, an enemy soldier was found who had hidden in the paddy field. When he tried to escape, Capt Balbir chased him for 40–50 metres and apprehended him.

The Attack on Battalion Headquarters

Capt Bajwa mentioned:

> By this time, Pakistan's 6 Punjab elements, which had earlier attacked Charlie Company, had now moved south towards Garibpur and attacked the Battalion Headquarters from the north-western direction. As Adjutant, I was busy controlling the battle when all of a sudden someone shouted, "*Sahib dushman sade pichhe walon attack kar riha hai.*" [Sir, the enemy is attacking from our rear]. I quickly reorganised the Battalion Headquarters defences and asked the Signal Platoon and Intelligence Section boys to readjust their defences to face the most unexpected threat from the rear.
>
> Meanwhile, I saw one of our tanks, which was passing by the Battalion Headquarters and requested him to chase the enemy, who was in the process of forming up in the wooded area of Garibpur. The Signal boys led by Capt P.S. Mankotia along with other Battalion Headquarters personnel, followed the tank which was by now chasing the enemy while firing his MMG. The enemy was totally confused and started retreating. This sudden action by us ensured breaking up the enemy attack towards Battalion Headquarters and mortar position.[9]

Maj Inderjit Singh too narrated an interesting incident:

> The protective patrol gave us adequate early warning of the impending enemy attack at first light, 21 November. The enemy assaulted our position; there was intense engagement of artillery, tank-to-tank battle along with our RCL guns engaging tanks and small arms fire.
>
> During the battle, one shell landed 6 metres away from my trench with the splinters flying all across. I was not hit but one of the shrapnel tore apart the skull of Lance Naik Piara Singh who was in the neighbouring trench with my *sahayak*.
>
> When the enemy started withdrawing, they came near our defences. We imagined that it was another assault through Garibpur village. Own tank nearby blasted the village. During that time, I could personally see a Pakistani Army JCO probably hiding behind a tree. Later on checking the area, the JCO was brought near our trench. Our doctor checked him and declared him dead. However, after sometime the JCO opened his eyes. He looked around and then died. On checking, we found a letter in Urdu written to his wife. In the letter he had written: '*Fatima, hamari Eid toh tab hogi jab*

> *ham apne watan wapas ayenge. Pehle to Bengali maarte the, ab Hindustan ki fauj hamare peeche hain*'. [Fatima, our Eid will be celebrated when we return home. Earlier the Bengalis were after us, now it is the Indian Army].[10]

The Role of Medical Personnel

Capt H.C. Vishwakarma, Regimential Medical Officer (RMO) posted with 14 Punjab, shared some nostalgic memories of the Garibpur battle:

> As a young RMO, I moved with the battalion to Garibpur on 20 November 1971. During the midnight darkness, we established a temporary Regimental Aid Post (RAP) with solitary Nursing Assistant (NA) Naik/NA B.R. Kharat (instead of two authorised) and Medical Platoon elements, 150 metres ahead of the Battalion Headquarters.
>
> During early morning of 21 November 1971, Pakistan Army elements of armour with Chaffee tanks and infantry attacked 14 Punjab. A fierce battle ensued effecting heavy casualties on enemy side with some casualties of ours. They were evacuated by our Medical Platoon elements to RAP, about 10-12 troops initially who were given prompt first aid by me and my NA. More casualties kept on coming for life-saving first aid at RAP. After requisite documentation, the serious ones were evacuated to Advanced Dressing Station (ADS) of 409 Medical Battalion during reasonable lull period.
>
> When we were attacked by Pakistani forces and bullets were flying all over, our Medical Platoon, and NA fired 70-80 rounds on the enemy located 100-150 metres away. We were lying on the ground, since there were no bunkers or proper trenches dug.
>
> A Pakistani soldier was brought after capture to RAP with extensive wound of left leg. I tended to him on priority following Geneva Convention and my professional ethics.
>
> Another enemy soldier was brought to RAP with large infected wound of right thigh in a moribund condition, as he was found lying in the field following injury. He was given intravenous plasma by me lying down beside him, holding the IV Plasma bottle to resuscitate him. The shelling and firing going around Battalion Headquarters made it impossible to stand.
>
> More casualties were attended by me and my NA along with Medical Platoon personnel, disregarding personal safety and upholding the battalion honour.
>
> On 22 November, we were subjected to air attack by enemy Sabre jets. The RAP was withdrawn behind the Battalion Headquarters.
>
> The Garibpur battle and other subsequent incidents during the war were a real-learning experience for me.[11]

By about 10.30 a.m. on 21 November 1971, the enemy's momentum of assault had petered out and it was very clear that Nabha Akal, with its affiliated units, had carried the day. Possessing numerical superiority, the Pakistani troops were in a position to decimate the Indian intrusion. However, the Punjab battalion, known for its long history and valour, rose to the occasion and thwarted the enemy attack. The winter sun rising up through the fog revealed a large number of enemy causalities, including 10 destroyed enemy tanks and three abandoned ones in good running condition.

Terrain and Climate Prevailing in the Area and Its Impact on Operations

The terrain in the area of operations was generally plains. As Garibpur is a tiny and predominantly agricultural hamlet, there were paddy fields around, water-logged at places. The battle was largely confined to the open fields.

The climate was bit cold and foggy, it being the onset of winter in late November. During the early hours, there was poor visibility on account of the fog, with restricted observation. The Pakistani tanks were unaware of the exact positions of the Indian tanks and field defences due to the early morning fog. This played a vital role, as it helped the Indian troops deployed in defences.

As mentioned earlier, the protective patrol sent ahead of the defences on the cold and foggy early morning of 21 November was able to observe the enemy tanks moving south from road Jessore–Chaugacha. The fog and poor visibility allowed the patrol to remain close to the enemy columns and Capt Gill was able to provide early warning as well as report on their movements accurately. It also helped the Artillery OP officer, Capt Chaturvedi to bring down accurate artillery fire on the enemy columns.

Reactions and Participation of Mukti Bahini and Locals

The attitude of the Mukti Bahini and locals of the area was friendly and helpful. The Mukti Bahini was happy to assist the Indian Army and provided volunteers, who helped as guides, and also provided information. After the fighting was over during the Battle of Garibpur, the locals helped the battalion in burying the dead soldiers.

During Brigadier (Brig) R.K. Singh's visit to Garibpur during Vijay Diwas, 16 December 2013, the people of Garibpur and surrounding areas were ever grateful for the contribution and sacrifices of the Indian soldiers in the liberation of Bangladesh in 1971.

List of Officers of 14 PUNJAB (NABHA AKAL) who participated in Indo-Pak War 1971

- Lt Col (later Brig) RK Singh, Commanding Officer (Was awarded Maha Vir Chakra).
- Maj (later Col) Inderjit Singh, Second-in-Command (Later commanded 19 PUNJAB).
- Maj (later Lt Col) AP Viswanathan, Officer Commanding, Alpha Company (Later commanded 14 PUNJAB).
- Maj (later Lt Col) KM Machiah, Officer Commanding, Bravo Company.
- Maj (later Lt Col) NJS Bains, Officer Commanding, Charlie Company.
- Capt (later Col) Balbir Singh, Officer Commanding, Delta Company (Was awarded Sena Medal).
- Capt (later Col) VS Butalia, Officer Commanding, Support Company and Mortar Platoon Commander (Later commanded 14 PUNJAB).
- Capt (later Brig) MPS Bajwa, Adjutant (Later commanded 27 PUNJAB and commanded a brigade in Kargil War, winner of YSM).
- Capt SS Samyal, Quartermaster and Administrative Company Commander.
- Capt (later Lt Col) PS Mankotia, Signal Officer.
- Capt (later Col) GS Gill, Medium Machine Gun Officer and Commando Platoon Commander (Was awarded Vir Chakra).
- 2/Lt (later Lt Col) HS Kaushal, Company Officer.
- 2/Lt (later Maj) ML Bajaj, Intelligence Officer.
- 2/Lt (later Brig) PK Chowdhury, Company Officer (Later commanded 14 PUNJAB).
- 2/Lt (later Capt) Amarjeet Kumar, Company Officer.
- Capt (later Col) HC Vishwakarma, Regimental Medical Officer (Was awarded Mention-in-Despatches).

The Battle of Garibpur from the Enemy's Point of View

Brig Hayat Khan, Commander Pakistan 107 Infantry Brigade, who was in custody as a prisoner of war (POW) at Ramgarh Cantonment, narrated his version of the battle during interrogation. He stated in his interrogation report that he had definite information that one Sikh company of Indian Army, that is, Charlie Company (under Maj Bains), had taken up position near Pitambarpur road junction. He was not aware of the remaining battalion (14 Punjab) having fetched up and deployed in area of Garibpur with a squadron of armour and other supporting elements. So, he ordered his brigade, comprising of 6 Punjab, 21

Punjab and 22 Frontier Force, along with 3 Independent Armoured Squadron consisting of Chaffee tanks, to encircle the Indian Army's lone company (Charlie Company) from the southern and south-western direction and prevent them from escaping towards the Indian territory. The aim was to capture them at first light, and show to the United Nations team that Indian troops were fighting inside Bangladesh, though war was still not declared.[12]

The Air Battle

Around 9.25 a.m. on 22 November 1971, three enemy F-86 Sabres strafed the battalion defences at Garibpur, knocking out one PT-76 tank and injuring some troops on the ground. Around 2 p.m., three Pakistani aircrafts roared in freely, when Maj Kailash Nath, the Battery Commander, got a smoke shot fired in the enemy position at Singhajhuli. This deception paid good dividends as all the enemy aircraft diverted their attack on their troops at Singhajhuli.

At about 2.45 p.m. the same day, three more Pakistani aircrafts roared in and were having a free run, when suddenly, four Indian Gnat aircrafts from No 22 Squadron, based in Kalaikunda, appeared in the sky. In the first aerial combat between the two sides since the 1965 war, all three enemy aircrafts were shot down in the ensuing dog-fight. Two of the Pakistani pilots, Flying Officers Khalil Ahmed and Parvez Mehdi Qureshi, ejected safely but were captured by the Indian troops and treated as POWs.[13]

Our troops on the ground had an uninterrupted view of the air battle, which gave the battalion a tremendous fillip. Once more, the diminutive Indian Gnats flown by the Indian Air Force (IAF) pilots had established their mastery over the Sabre jets.

The result was that since the interception of the three Sabres over Garibpur, the PAF stopped sending fighter-bombers to support of their own troops and the subsequent Indian formations were now free to continue their advance towards Jessore.

Chivalry and Honour of Both Sides

Of the two Pakistani pilots who ejected, one was Flying Officer (Fg Offr) Khalid Ahmed, brother of the Pakistan diplomat Aziz Ahmed Khan, who did two postings in India, the last as one of Pakistan's most popular High Commissioner to India.

The second captured pilot, Fg Offr Parvez Mehdi Qureshi, a Sword of Honour at the Pakistan Air Force Academy (PAF), later on become the Chief of Air Staff (CAS) of the PAF in 1996. Not many people recognised Qureshi as the same pilot who was a '*guest*' of India after the Bayra air battle on 22 November 1971.

When the news was reported in India, Group Captain Donald Lazarus (then a Flying Officer), who had shot him down in 1971, sent him a letter congratulating Qureshi for his achievement in becoming CAS. He mentioned that Qureshi may not recall his earlier meeting with Lazarus in the air. Lazarus did not expect a reply to the letter, but to his surprise, a Staff Officer for Qureshi wrote a reply acknowledging receipt of the letter and thanking Lazarus for the greetings. Lazarus received a further surprise, when a letter came signed by the Pakistan CAS himself. Air Chief Marshal Qureshi expressed his thanks to Lazarus for his wishes and complimented on the '*fight*' shown by the Indian pilots on the occasion.

Lazarus, who also happened to be an instructor at the prestigious Defence Services Staff College at Wellington, preserves this letter quite carefully. It speaks volumes about soldiering, chivalry and honour on both sides![14]

Importance of the Battle of Garibpur

The Battle of Garibpur, where one battalion group was able to defeat an enemy attack by two infantry battalions supported by armour and PAF, will go down in the annals of warfare as a classic example indeed. In the process, two Pakistani infantry battalions (6 Punjab and 22 Frontier Force) and 3 Independent Armoured Squadron were badly mauled.

On the tactical level, due to the overall pullback of Pakistani troops in each sector, the Pakistanis vacated Chaugacha without a fight. The success at Garibpur on 21–22 November was particularly significant, as it allowed India's 9 Infantry Division to gain considerable ground towards Jessore and resulted in the virtual destruction of the lone Pakistani armoured squadron in the area.

Later, after the declaration of war in early December, it allowed 9 Infantry Division to walk into Jessore unopposed, which was the initial objective.

Excerpts from National Newspapers

The successful battle of Garibpur was laudably commended in the newspapers and magazines. It is important to note that the 1971 Indo-Pak War had not been declared when this battle was fought on 21–22 November 1971.

The Times of India, on 27 November 1971, carried an article by their special correspondent from Bayra, which mentioned about the tank battle fought at Garibpur, located 5 miles inside East Bengal, which we won decisively. Eleven Chaffee tanks of 20 Lancers of the Pakistan Army had been knocked out in the 7-hour tank battle which started at 6 a.m. and ended at about 1 p.m.[15]

Col C.L. Proudfoot, military correspondent of the Indian Army, was specially deputed to brief the press and military attaches of other countries posted in India on this sensitive issue. The reports based on the briefing by late Col Proudfoot appeared in the newspapers. An Indian Army spokesman described the Bayra fighting was 'limited offensive action' on the part of Indian Army troops, who had returned to their bases on Indian side of the border after the operation.[16]

Lessons Learnt

1. *Intelligence*: No attack should be launched without proper information, as undertaken by the enemy in this battle. Its offensive capability was blunted for the subsequent battle as the whole squadron supporting 107 Infantry Brigade was destroyed in the first action. Similarly, without exact information of the enemy's locations or dispositions, 14 Punjab was also inducted in Garibpur area. Hence the need for carrying out reconnaissance and patrolling prior to any operation.
2. *Artillery Support*: The fire support provided by own artillery was very effective. The accurate and prompt artillery fire, particularly DF [SOS] was responsible for breaking the enemy's assault. Hence, intimate fire support by own artillery is a must for conducting any operations.
3. *Air Support*: There was no air support available to the battalion initially, when three enemy Sabres strafed our defences at Garibpur on two occasions on 22 November. It was only at 2.45 p.m. the same day that, four Indian Gnats aircrafts appeared in the sky and engaged with the Pakistani aircrafts, shooting them down in the ensuing dog-fight. Hence, this emphasises the importance of air support to ground troops.
4. *Motivation and High Morale*: The troops of 14 Punjab and affiliated units were imbued with high morale and were greatly motivated. Hence, the importance of junior leadership.
5. *Combined Arms Operation*: The Battle of Garibpur was fought very well by 14 Punjab, ably supported by 'Charlie' Squadron, 45 Cavalry and the artillery component. The Engineer troops allotted to the battalion also played an important role in assisting the unit in engineer tasks, while the RMO, with his NA, played a crucial role in treating battle casualties. This intra-service cooperation helped in defeating the fierce counter-attack launched by the enemy infantry and armour. It needs to be presented as a good case of combined arms operation.

Casualties, POWs and Honours and Awards

Our losses, including the affiliated units, were 28 killed and 42 wounded, while four PT-76 tanks were destroyed.[17] In contrast, 13 Chaffee tanks of Pakistan were neutralised, which included three captured in running condition. Three enemy aircrafts were lost in the air battle, while 300 soldiers, including three officers were killed and many wounded. Six enemy POWs were apprehended.[18]

The Battle of Garibpur brought a total of 40 well-deserved gallantry awards to the battalion, its affiliated troops and the IAF. While Lt Col R.K. Singh was awarded the MVC, the unit earned another MVC posthumously, two VrCs and two Sena Medals. The attached troops won one MVC (Maj D.S. Narang) posthumously, two VrCs and two Sena Medals. The three IAF Gnat pilots (Flight Lieutenants R.A. Massey and M.A. Ganapathy and Flying Officer D. Lazarus), who shot down the Sabre jets, were awarded a VrC each.[19]

Conclusion

The Battle of Garibpur was a significant military victory that blunted the enemy's counter-attack capability and adversely affected their morale. This eventually paved the way for the Indian victory over Pakistan 50 years ago.

As we commemorate the Golden Jubilee of the 1971 Indo-Pak War, this battle stands out as a worthy curtain-raiser to the famous victory of the Indian defence forces. However, the unit was denied a well-deserved award of Battle Honour 'Garibpur' Battle, since it was fought prior to commencement of hostilities on 3 December 1971. One of these Pakistani Chaffee tanks captured in running condition by 14 Punjab occupies a place of pride in the Punjab Regimental Centre at Ramgarh Cantonment, Jharkhand today.

NOTES

1. R.K. Singh, *The Battle of Garibpur: Indo-Pak War 1971*, 2nd edition, New Delhi, IMR Media Pvt Ltd, 2014, p. 29.
2. Ibid., p. 41.
3. Ibid., pp. 39–40.
4. Narrated to the author by Brig M.P.S. Bajwa on telephone from Jalandhar on 16 August 2021.
5. Narrated to the author by Col Inderjit Singh on telephone from New Delhi on 16 August 2021.
6. Narrated by Brig Bajwa on 16 August 2021.
7. Narrated to the author by Lt Col N.J.S. Bains on telephone from Panchkula on 17 August 2021.
8. Narrated to the author by Col Balbir Singh on telephone from Chandigarh on 17 August 2021.

9. Narrated by Brig Bajwa on 16 August 2021.
10. Narrated by Col Inderjit on 16 August 2021.
11. Narrated to the author by Col H.C. Vishwakarma on telephone from Ranchi on 17 August 2021.
12. Singh, *The Battle of Garibpur: Indo-Pak War 1971*, n. 1, pp. 133–35.
13. Ibid., pp. 153–56.
14. P.V.S. Jagan Mohan and Samir Chopra, *Eagles Over Bangladesh*, New Delhi: HarperCollins, 1972, Footnote, pp. 104–05.
15. Singh, *The Battle of Garibpur: Indo-Pak War 1971*, n. 1, pp. 143–45.
16. Ibid., p. 143.
17. Ibid., p. 66.
18. Ibid., pp. 66–67.
19. Ibid., p. 69.

* * *

APPENDIX

List of Officers Interviewed

Maj (later Col) Inderjit Singh
Capt (later Brig) M.P.S Bajwa, YSM
Maj (later Lt Col) N.J.S. Bains
Capt (later Col) Balbir Singh, SM
Capt (later Col) H.C. Vishwakarma

7

Eagle Unleashed

IAF Strategy and Operations

Diptendu Choudhury

In a surface-centric continental security-dominant military environment, the history of India's air power usage has been restrained and inadequate. In all the wars that India has fought after independence (1947–48, 1962, 1965 and 1999), there has been inadequate leveraging of air power. The strategic options provided by the unfettered use of air power have neither been fully understood nor exploited in the Indian context, except for a short duration of two weeks in the 1971 war. Consequently, the extent of the role of the Indian Air Force (IAF) and the outcomes it produced in India's most significant war remain largely unknown to the nation, other than a passing mention of its actions in Longewala, Tangail or Dacca. Any analysis of air power must take into account that it is the only war where the IAF did not operate under any political constraints, its full potential was utilised and that it was fought on two fronts, each with its own peculiarities and challenges.

The important outcomes created by the unfettered employment of offensive air power were lost in the euphoria of victory and Bangladesh's independence. The success of the air campaign on both fronts was due to the strategic vision of Air Chief Marshal Pratap Chandra Lal. Having been the Vice Chief of Air Staff during the 1965 conflict, on taking over reins of the IAF, he swiftly implemented all important lessons of the previous war. Thus, the IAF was not only at its peak of operational readiness and training status but, most importantly, it also had an air strategy in place, which coincided with national and military strategies.

The Prelude

A five-year plan was made by the Ministry of Defence for the expansion of 45 Squadron IAF in 1964, in which the older fleet of Vampire, Mystere and Toofani aircraft were to be replaced with modern fighters, bombers, reconnaissance and transport aircraft, helicopters and better weapons. However, the 1965 war, and subsequent fiscal constraints, slowed down the expansion, but '[f]ortunately, by 1971, their efficiency and strength had increased just enough to meet the challenge.'[1] As the possibility of war increased, the IAF reorganised itself, setting up Air Defence Control Centres for air defence (AD) in each of its commands, as well as Maritime Air Centres (MACs) at Bombay, Cochin and Vishakhapatnam for maritime air operations, providing cover to the navy on strike missions and protecting the coasts and merchant shipping.[2]

A resolute political leadership set unambiguous and decisive national aims and objectives, delegated responsibilities and thereafter, left the military to get on with their job. As recorded by Lal:

> The Chiefs were kept in constant touch with the developments in the subcontinent and what the Cabinet was thinking about them. There was full and free exchange of ideas amongst the Chiefs. The period of waiting and watching from 26 March to 3 December was well spent during which the Chiefs of Staff Committee, the inter-service Committees, the Service Headquarters and the Ministry of Defence worked in a smooth and coordinated manner.[3]

Thus, the synergy and cooperation amongst the national and military leadership enabled an achievable two-front strategy.

Pakistan's military strategy was based on the premise that defence of East Pakistan lay in West Pakistan. As a result, it kept the bulk of its air force assets and military, including its strike forces, in the west, underscoring the fact that Pakistan's real power centre lay in the west. Since it could not resolve the uprising in its east wing politically, it chose to force military action, thereby dragging India into the war. Pakistan believed that this would not only give it another opportunity to possibly wrest Kashmir, but in case East Pakistan seceded and managed to gain independence, it could be conveniently blamed on India. From the Indian perspective, a war in the east would inevitably force Pakistan to open the front in the west for several reasons: (i) to defend its rather flawed 'defence of East Pakistan lay in West Pakistan' strategy; (ii) to project India as the aggressor in the east, thus creating the perception internationally that it was compelled to open the western front; and (iii) to apply military pressure in the west to slow down India in the east till the United States (US) and China, post their historic rapprochement, came to its rescue.

Broadly, India's two-front strategy was aimed at defeating the enemy, gaining as much ground as possible and establishing a base for the creation of Bangladesh in the east, while keeping the Pakistanis at bay in the west. This was based on two key pragmatic assessments: a limited window of operations in the east, where even a war of two to three weeks could be foreclosed with international intervention; and any territorial gain in the west would have to be handed back once the United Nations Security Council (UNSC) and international pressure came to be applied post-conflict.[4] Therefore, with the deterioration of the situation, the military objectives were laid down clearly:

1. To assist the Mukti Bahini in liberating a part of East Pakistan, where the refugees could be repatriated to live under their own Bangla government.
2. To prevent Pakistan from capturing any Indian territory of consequence in Jammu and Kashmir, Punjab, Rajasthan or Gujarat. This was to be achieved by offensive defence and not merely passive line holding.
3. To defend the integrity of India in case of a Chinese attack in the north.

IAF's Air Strategy

Based on the above-mentioned military objectives, under Lal's leadership, the IAF worked out its broad 'air strategy' for both fronts of operations:

1. Defence of the home base(s).
2. Assist the army in the field and to do it, gain and maintain favourable air situation (FAS) over tactical areas. Mount reconnaissance, interdiction and other operations having a direct bearing on the outcome of the land battle.
3. Conduct counter air operations (CAO), that is, reduce the effectiveness of Pakistan Air Force (PAF) by destroying its aircraft and bases.
4. Provide air transport support to own surface forces, mainly the Indian Army (IA).
5. Provide maritime support to the Indian Navy (IN).[5]

This was further expanded into separate front-specific air strategies. For the eastern front, it was:[6]

1. Eliminate the PAF at the earliest. Given the preponderance of army's offensive in an obstacle-bound riverine terrain and the limited window of operations, time was of essence. Elimination of enemy air attack, which could severely impact IA's progress, was therefore an imperative.
2. Render maximum assistance to the army in the form of offensive air support, transport and helicopter support and airborne operations. Again, the terrain dictated that speed and rapid mobility was critical to the IA, which would need extensive transport and helicopter operations. Offensive air support would enable interdiction of vital enemy military assets and lines of communications. Finally, to provide dedicated close air support (CAS) to the IA.
3. Assist the navy to isolate East Pakistan from West Pakistan, and prevent PAF's interference with operations of naval ships and air assets. This, once again, underscored the need for air superiority as, without it, the IN's aircraft carrier and aircraft would not be able to operate in the region.
4. Ensure AD of the area of responsibility (AOR) and the steel towns of Bihar and Orissa, which were lucrative strategic targets for the PAF.

While the eastern front was the key time-bound priority, it was clear that given Pakistan's strategy, it would definitely attack on India's western front. The three-pronged air strategy for the west was:[7]

1. Defence of the IAF home base(s). This obviously flowed from the lessons of the previous war where a large number of aircraft were lost on ground due to PAF air strikes.
2. Assist the army and navy, including gaining and maintaining FAS over tactical areas. This flowed from the challenges of disjointed and independent operations by the army and the IAF in 1965, and hence an FAS to enable greater freedom of own surface operations was clearly laid down as an operational priority. Given the strength of the PAF in the west, air superiority was not an option due to two facts. First, the combat aircraft force ratio of 1.4:1, though in IAF's favour, was inadequate due to: the wide frontage of operations; wide range of air operations to be undertaken; commitment of forces to the east due to the two-front nature of the war; and the ever-present Chinese threat. Second, due to limited IA objectives on the western front, coupled within the limited window of two weeks, FAS was the only viable option.
3. The next priority was CAO against enemy air bases and radar stations,

> including attacks on strategic targets which had a vital role in supporting the economy and war potential of the enemy. The inclusion of strategic air strikes against Pakistan's economic and war-waging centres of gravity (CoGs) was a first for the IAF.

The prioritised strategy was to be achieved by adopting an approach which, in the modern-day context of air warfare, is called a concept of operations (CONOPS). The offensive CONOPS that evolved in Lal's words—'through a process of discussions amongst joint planners and Chiefs of Staff and senior AF Commanders', was the 'target system' strategy. All the important enemy targets were clubbed under three target systems. The first system to be targeted was the enemy air, through aggressive offensive operations against its air defences while guarding own airspaces. This was to wrest the control of air in India's favour so as to prevent the PAF from interfering with India's surface operations. The second was targeting the most important strategic CoGs of the enemy so as to not only cripple its war-fighting capability but also its capacity over a longer time frame. This involved targeting all forms of energy, which included fuel storage tanks, oil refineries, gas plants, hydroelectric power plants, power stations, etc. Enemy transportation was the third system identified, which meant targeting key road and rail communication networks and choke points which linked Pakistan's hinterland to the Karachi Port, enabling the movement of goods, supplies, logistics and manpower.[8] It is through the perspective of IAF's strategy and CONOPS that its performance in the war must be analysed.

Rollout of the Air Strategy (East)

The two-front strategy forced the IAF to rebalance its combat resources on both fronts in order to overwhelm the PAF for achieving swift air superiority in the east, while maintaining a credible and favourable ratio of combat squadrons for a holding/limited offensive war in the west. On the east, the IAF initially deployed four squadrons for AD and six squadrons for strike roles, comprising of a total of 161 fighter aircraft, five helicopter squadrons and seven transport squadrons. The PAF had one squadron of Sabres, with 16 aircraft, and an assortment of trainer, helicopter and transport aircraft. While the 10:1 ratio may seem like an overkill, there were several factors that had to be taken into consideration, such as: India's aim of supporting the Mukti Bahini in the formation of Bangladesh; the PAF's grounding of all Bengali pilots in March 1971, coinciding with the military crackdown in the east;[9] and the removal of Air Commodore (Cmde) Z.

Masud, the PAF Air Officer Commanding (AOC) in the east, due to his refusal to use the PAF against its own people; he was replaced by Air Cmde Inam-ul-Haq in March 1971.[10]

According to the history of the PAF, air operations in the east had begun in March with 14 Squadron, with the transport element playing a lead role in round-the-clock sorties to flush out the rebels.[11] This meant AD against the PAF which had started to regularly enter Indian airspace on such missions, and subsequently led to the shooting down of PAF Sabres over Boyra. In the event of a war in the east, the IAF's key objectives of air superiority against the PAF and support to the army would need adequate strike squadrons. The final factor was countering the ever-present threat from China, which had made clear to the US that in case of an Indo-Pak conflict, it would militarily intervene on behalf of Pakistan.[12] This meant that India, at all times, would have to cater for the China contingency.

Air Superiority and Outcomes

The pre-emptive strike by the PAF in the west, on 3 December 1971, triggered the war. The IAF carried out strikes against airfields at Kurmitola, Tejgaon and Chittagong on the night of 3–4 and 4–5 December with the Canberras; and during the day, strikes were carried out with Hunters and Su-7s. Though the airfields were hit, they were not put out of action because of incorrect choice of weapons and initial enemy air opposition. The goal was to deny the use of these airfields, thereby taking the PAF out of the fight. This was vital as air superiority would enable full freedom of air operations, keep the surface operations free from enemy air interference and allow wholehearted assistance to the advancing IA. The initial limited success in neutralising the PAF airfields was because air-to-ground rockets proved ineffective in causing the desired level of damage on the runway surface. This led to eight MiG-21s being employed innovatively in airfield strikes, armed with 500 kilogram (kg) bombs delivered in steep dive attacks. The persistent attacks and exceptional results achieved in cratering the runways ensured they were no longer usable by the PAF, and their pilots were flown out to West Pakistan through Burma on 8–9 December. Post-war inspection revealed bomb craters of 46 direct hits on Tejgaon and 20 on Kurmitola runways.

Effectively from 6 December, the IAF had gained total air domination over the skies of East Pakistan,[13] enabling it to fly 2,002 sorties and restricting the PAF to only 30 sorties.[14] This automatically increased the availability of aircraft and air effort for close support and interdiction missions. It also enabled airborne operations and special heliborne operations in direct support of the army, which were to play a decisive role in the victory. The air superiority allowed the relatively slower Sea Hawk fighters to operate from the aircraft carrier, *INS Vikrant*, and carry out attacks in the coastal areas and facilities without enemy air interference. Another contribution from the morale point of view was the formation of the fledgling Mukti Bahini Air Force called 'Kilo Flight' in October 1971, where an assortment of nine defected Bengali PAF and civilian pilots were given training by Indian pilots. The IAF donated a Dakota, a DHC-3 Otter and an Alouette III aircraft, all of which were modified with weapons to form the Flight, which operated from Dimapur. The IAF leadership, aware of the immense significance, allowed Kilo Flight the symbolic privilege of opening the air war over East Pakistan by ensuring the Bengali pilots took the first shot.[15]

Joint Operations

The lessons learnt from challenges faced in providing CAS to the army in the previous war led to several initiatives: coincidence of the AORs of the IA and IAF commands; establishment of the Advance Headquarters (HQs) alongside the respective IA commands; and the creation of Tactical Air Centres at the corps level to enable decentralised vetting and prioritisation of close support requirements. These initiatives, coupled with improved communication and tactical procedures, enabled the forward air controllers (FACs), who operated jointly at the brigade levels, to access the air effort more efficiently, and also reduced the mission response timelines.[16] Extensive training and exercises of the FACs, ground liaison officers of the army at the IAF bases and the joint operations staff in the west and east, in the preceding months, paid immense dividends in the conduct of CAS missions. Most importantly, these initiatives led to much greater mutual trust and confidence at all levels between the two services, ensuring more efficient use of air effort and reduction in wastages, unlike the previous war. Some wastages did occur in 1971 as well, but such confusion is inevitable in the fog of war as the field commander 'tends to call on every available resource to fight his battle'.[17]

The complete command of air in the east, which was achieved in 36 hours, allowed re-tasking of the MiG-21s and Gnats from AD and CAO roles to CAS role in support of the army. The IAF actively supported the IA in all corps sectors, preceding all thrusts. The thorough disruption in enemy rail and road communications had made the enemy totally dependent on the waterways for movement of troops, ammunition and supplies.[18] By 8 December, AD missions had stopped, with a corresponding increase in the effort towards surface operations.

Over two-thirds of IAF offensive missions were in direct assistance of the army's land battle. Concentrated air attacks within one day destroyed almost all gunboats and steamers[19] on the rivers used by the enemy, denying it the flexibility and mobility it had enjoyed in the riverine obstacle-intensive terrain. Interdiction missions by Gnats, Hunters and Canberras carried out aggressive attacks on all water vessels, sparing only local boats, unless found to be carrying troops. S.N. Prasad notes: 'the attacks were carried out so thoroughly that thereafter few gunboats or steamers were seen plying in the Bangladesh rivers.'[20] Over and above the interdiction targets, the ammunition factory at Joydebpur, which supplied the Pakistani Army, was struck several times till it was destroyed.[21]

Air Power Effects

The signal message of 9 December from Lieutenant General (Lt Gen) A.A.K. Niazi to President Yahya, admitting for the first time the criticality of the situation, is illustrative of the effects of IAF missions. Lieutenant Colonel (Lt Col) Siddiq Salik, who was the Public Relations Officer of the Pakistan Army, records:

> *One:* Regrouping readjustment is not possible due to enemy mastery of skies. Population getting extremely hostile and providing all out help to the enemy. No move possible during night due intensive rebel ambushes. Rebels guiding enemy through gaps and to the rear. Airfield damaged extensively, no mission last three days, and not possible in future. *Two:* Extensive damage to heavy weapons and equipment due enemy air action. Troops fighting extremely well but stress and strain now telling hard. Not slept for last 20 days. Are under constant fire air, artillery and tanks. *Three:* Situation extremely critical. We will go on fighting and do our best. Four: Request following immediate strike all enemy air bases this theatre. If possible, send (*sic*) reinforcements airborne troops for protection dacca.[22]

By the end of the war, the IAF had flown 1,353 sorties towards CAS missions, of which a lion's share of 507 sorties were towards supporting 4 Corps under Lt Gen Sagat Singh, whose aggressive and innovative offensive strike thrusts received a special mention by both K.V. Krishna Rao and Lal.[23] The commitment of the IAF towards supporting the army is underscored by the fact that of the 13 combat-related aircraft losses, nine fighters and five pilots were lost to anti-aircraft guns and ground fire. The air superiority in the east also enabled the rapid redeployment of a Hunter and Su-7 squadron to bolster the western front.

Combat Support Air Operations

With large number of bridges and ferries destroyed, the rivers and innumerable rivulets presented a serious obstacle that slowed down the movement of advancing forces. Mi-4 helicopters were extensively used for Heli-lift operations between 7–15 December, flying a total of 409 sorties, forward deploying 4,803 troops and 100,070 kg of weapons and equipment, by day and night. This rapid movement of troops and equipment across obstacles and rivers enabled leapfrogging and bypassing of the enemy to capture key objectives.[24] The first Heli-lift of a battalion from Kailashahar, across the Surma River, in full view of the Pakistani brigade at Sylhet, was a deception master plan by Lt Gen Sagat Singh. The noise and the continuous movement of helicopters ferrying the battalion created an impression of a large force being inducted, locking in the Pakistani forces who were expecting an attack.[25] In reality, the Indian forces were able to bypass the enemy who were 'completely passive and paralysed. The capture of Sylhet was facilitated, because of this operation and the better part of the enemy division was bottled up there.'[26]

The second was an even more daring and innovative night Heli-lift of a battalion across the Meghna River in the darkness of 10–11 December to Baidya Bazaar: 'Again, this operation had resulted in panic in the enemy ranks and early capture of Dacca.'[27] The IAF Mi-4s, operating ex-Agartala where they had to return periodically for refuelling, moved 650 troops using '80 hand-held battery powered torches of the kind normally used in any household' to mark the helipads.[28] The IAF also carried out the casualty evacuation of 899 soldiers from forward areas by helicopters, and thereafter airlifted them to Guwahati/Calcutta by Dakotas, which contributed greatly to the morale of the troops.[29]

The total air superiority also allowed the iconic airborne paradrop operation over Tangail to be conducted on 11 December. The massive air operation, involving 23 Packet, 22 Dakota, six AN-12 and two Caribou aircraft, para-dropped 784 troops, weapons and equipment within a span of 50 minutes, without any losses. A resupply drop of 40 troops and 45 tonnes of equipment, by five AN-12 and one Packet aircraft, followed on 12 December.

Fall of Dacca

The capture of Dacca, interestingly, was not a part of the army's initial strategy. According to Lt Gen J.F.R. Jacob, on 13 December, Manekshaw ordered Eastern Command to capture all towns which had been bypassed while advancing into Bangladesh, and Dacca was not named in this list of towns.[30] Krishna Rao posits that while Dacca had to be kept constantly in view as the final objective, its final capture would depend on the progress of operations.[31] The dramatic advances made by the Indian forces, the increasing international pressure, entry of the American aircraft carrier, *USS Enterprise*, into the Bay of Bengal as a coercive signal,[32] all seemed to indicate an imminent United Nations (UN)-called ceasefire.[33] An untimely ceasefire of all hostilities would have allowed a desperate and vital reprieve to Yahya and prevented the fall of East Pakistan. This was a critical factor which the military leadership had anticipated prior to the war, which necessitated rapid consolidation of the gains rather than the capture of Dacca.

Being the capital of East Pakistan, capture of Dacca was central to the creation of Bangladesh, but time seemed to be running out. A strategic window of opportunity opened up when the IAF wireless experimental unit at Eastern Command picked up an encrypted message, at 1045 hours (hrs), that a cabinet meeting was to be held at 1200 hrs on 14 December. The meeting was to be chaired by Dr A.M. Malik, Governor of East Pakistan, and attended by General (Gen) Tikka Khan, the Martial Law Administrator, and the PAF AOC, Major General (Maj Gen) Rao Farman Ali, among others. According to P.V.S. Jagan Mohan and Sameer Chopra:

> Army Command and Eastern Air Command immediately grasped the importance of the communique. Malik and his cabinet had the capacity to take momentous decisions on the course of action: prolonging the war and shoring up the defence of Dacca. Or even arranging for a ceasefire rather than surrender. The meeting had to be disrupted, perhaps to remove the 'decision making capability'; a strike on the meeting would paralyse East Pakistani decision.[34]

The pilots were briefed about the target at 1055 hrs, with instructions to strike it by 1120 hrs, which included a flying time of 20 minutes. What followed is a classic example of strategic effects caused by the swift response, accuracy and lethality of air power. The target was reached using a locally obtained Burma Shell tourist map and six MiG-21s struck the governor's house in Dacca with 192 rockets, followed up by a 30 millimetre (mm) cannon attack by two Hunters. The effects of the air strike were observed first hand by John Kelly, United Nations High Commissioner for Refugees (UNHCR) representative, and a journalist, Gavin Young, who broadcast around the world on wire:

> The jets made a shattering row. The ground crashed and heaved...Malik produced a shaking pen and a sheet of paper. The Ministers mumbled and held on together. Between one crash and the next Kelly and I looked at the

> paper and saw that it was addressed to the President Yahya Khan and that Malik had at last resigned. That was the end to the Governor's House. That was the end of the last Government of East Pakistan.[35]

Amidst intense enemy air activity, Governor Malik informed the president about the futility of further operations and after mid-day rocket attack by six enemy fighters, he and his cabinet resigned. The grim reality of the situation in East Pakistan dawned on Yahya Khan and at 1332 hrs, he replied in a signal message: 'You should now take all necessary measures to stop the fighting and preserve the lives of all the armed forces personnel, all those from West Pakistan and all loyal elements.'[36] Lt Gen A.A.K. Niazi immediately met the US consul with a proposal for a ceasefire, and sent a copy to Yahya. The message was intercepted by Indians, who stepped up their air attacks to maintain the pressure, and eight 500 pound bombs were dropped on Niazi's command post in Dacca cantonment. The new site selected for the Pakistani Eastern Command in Dacca town was thus bombed even before the HQ started to shift.[37]

By 14 December, under relentless air attacks, Pakistani troops occupied Dacca University campus. After the IAF faced heavy small arms fire in the first air attack, on 15 December, the university was repeatedly struck by 40 sorties, which, according to Air Vice Marshal A.K. Tiwary, totally neutralised the Pakistanis. The intensity of IAF attacks is borne out by Air Cmde Inam-ul-Haq, the PAF AOC, according to whom the IAF activity over the Dacca complex was so intense that the stock of anti-aircraft artillery (AAA) ammunition, which was to have lasted for months, was exhausted in a fortnight and only one day's ammunition was left on the day of the surrender.[38] As a day, 14 December was also unique as IAF Hunters made history by landing in the captured Jessore airfield.[39] As the end game neared, the air offensive was stepped up to support the army in the mopping up and against the final Pakistan resistance, rising from 91 sorties on 14 December to 152 on 15 December.

Finally, at 4.30 p.m. on 16 December, the Pakistan Army surrendered at Dacca race course, in the presence of an estimated one million people of the new country of Bangladesh.[40] Ironically, the greatest acknowledgement of the IAF's role came from the enemy. On being asked why he had surrendered, Niazi pointed to the wings on Group Captain Chandan Singh's chest and said:

> This has hastened the surrender. I and my people have had no rest during day or night, thanks to your Air Force. We changed our quarters ever so often, trying to find a safe place for a little rest and sleep so that we could carry on the fight, but we have been unable to do that.[41]

Rollout of the Air Strategy (West)

The need for Pakistan to launch an offensive in the west to support its strategy is endorsed by Niazi, who wrote that the fate of not only the eastern garrison and East Pakistan but whole of Pakistan hung on the outcome of the offensive in the west.[42] Pakistan's aim was to secure significant territory in Jammu and Kashmir, which could be retained after the war, and launch a major armoured offensive across the front ranging from Jammu to Ganganagar. India's military strategy was therefore centred on safeguarding its own territory, where it would remain defensive initially, and if Pakistan were to initiate a war, then it would retaliate by going on the offensive to secure limited objectives. In fact, 'There was no question of any effort at dismembering West Pakistan, as mischievously propagated in certain quarters.'[43] In the northern sector on the western front, limited attacks had been planned to strengthen Indian defensive positions. A Pakistani thrust was expected in Poonch and to counter it, two thrusts were planned: one in the north between the Beas and Basantar rivers; and the second along the Ravi axis. In the southern sector, two Indian thrusts were planned in the Rajasthan sector: one in Barmer sector towards Chor; and other in south towards Rahimyar Khan.[44] The IN was actively involved in the strategy for conducting offensive operations against the Pakistan Navy centred around Karachi, after ensuring safety from the PAF in a joint IAF–IN operation in the area coinciding in time and space.[45]

In the west, the IAF had 24 fighter/fighter-bomber squadrons and four bomber squadrons deployed, which included two squadrons of legacy Mysteres, as well as Vampires, totalling 419 combat aircraft, while PAF had 13 fighter/bomber squadrons, totalling 288 aircraft. This translated into a force ratio of 1.45:1 in IAF's favour in the beginning of the war on 3 December, which increased to 1.6:1 after 8–9 December, when one squadron each of Hunter and MiG-21 was redeployed to the west.[46] However, including the F-86 Sabres, F-104 Starfighters and MiG-19, from Jordan, Iran, China[47] and Saudi Arabia,[48] which supplemented the PAF inventory by two additional squadron worth of fighters, as reported, the actual combat ratio came down to 1.4:1. Although the IAF's priority of operations was AD, support to the army and navy and then CAO, for a better grasp of the impact of air power on joint operations, in the subsequent narrative sequence, AD and CAO have been combined, followed by support to the IA and maritime air operations.

AD and CAO

Post-1965, the IAF bases were significantly bolstered by construction of additional forward airfields; and their AD improved with blast-protected concrete aircraft pens and infrastructure. There was an extensive medium and high-level radar coverage, which was integrated with radar-controlled guns and surface-to-air missile (SAM) systems and woven into the base Air Defence Centres of all fighter airfields.[49] The radar coverage was also strengthened by moving units from the east to fill critical gaps in the west. In some vitals sectors, radars were inducted as a redundancy in key areas of operation. Important cities, economic installations and airfields were defended with a variety of AAA weapons and SAM systems. A Low-Level Reporting System (LLRS), consisting of a chain of mobile observation posts equipped with radio/telephone communication system, was set up and integrated into the AD network to fill low-level radar cover gap.[50] Maj Gen Fazal Muqueem Khan acknowledges that India had a balanced and integrated AD which was well-knit into formidable and deep defence zone. In addition, he gives credit to IAF's expansion and modernisation, as well as crystallised strategic options, contingencies, updated plans and all aspects of operational command and control.[51] The war in the west started with the 'pre-emptive' strike on 3 December, when the PAF struck Pathankot, Amritsar, Awantipur and Srinagar between 1740–1745 hrs, with only 18–26 aircraft, with the aim of diminishing the capability of IAF to operate from its forward airfields.[52] As per Prasad, six Starfighters and 10 Sabres were used in an attack which proved ineffectual,[53] underscoring the efficacy of IAF's passive AD measures and aircraft dispersion in blast pens, due to which no IAF aircraft was lost on ground, and neither claimed by the PAF.[54]

The CAO kicked in on the first day of war itself, when the IAF retaliated swiftly within two-and-half hours,[55] with 23 missions by night against seven major PAF airfields. To sustain the pressure, the attacks were continued through two nights by Canberras and fighters from the IAF's newly formed unit, Tactics and Combat Development and Training Squadron (TCDTS) (renamed Tactics and Air Combat Development Establishment [TACDE] after its upgradation in 1972). Specially created in February 1971, this small unit evolved strike and combat tactics and carried out extensive weapon trials before the war, from May to July. Also, tactical seminars and exercises were held and tactical standard operating procedures (SOPs) were prepared for the IAF. The unit struck back repeatedly on the first night of the war, with its MiG-21s and Su-7s hitting seven airfields and counter air targets 180–200 kilometre (km) deep in enemy territory, at low levels, with no moonlight or navigational aids and marginal fuel reserves, delivering 500 kg bombs with great accuracy.[56] The use of MiG-21s and Su-7s in such circumstances was a first for the IAF, and possibly the world. Despite shortage of equipment, operating two types of aircraft and from temporary locations, the contribution of TCDTS was considerable,[57] flying 174 sorties by day and 119 by night.[58]

All told, the IAF's total counter air effort in the west added up to 423 sorties against PAF airfields and radars, where it lost 17 aircraft.[59] Of the total air effort, 141 sorties were flown on third night and fourth day. Of these, it is the daytime 118 CAO sorties which cost the loss of seven aircraft—four in air combat and three to AAA. However, according to Khan, 10 aircraft were lost in air combat and seven to AAA in the daylight raid, a claim which neither bears scrutiny nor finds a mention in the *History of the PAF* by Hussain and Qureshi. Still, there is no denying the high attrition rate of 6 per cent suffered in the daytime attacks over PAF airfields. Tiwary attributes this to several factors, ranging from single attack direction, multiple attack passes, set attack patterns, dive attacks in dense AAA zones over the target areas, to inadequate tactical routing through safe areas, vulnerability of low-level missions to ground fire and inadequate AD escorts in general, in the initial days. While the tactical aspects are definitely pertinent in hindsight, one cannot take away the courage and commitment of the pilots flying deep into enemy territory, often at the extremities of aircraft range, into heavily defended PAF bases. High combat losses in the opening rounds of war are a reality due to high-risk offensive counter air, vital for the control of the air. William Momyer explains: 'The most precious thing an air force can provide to an army or navy is air superiority, since this gives to surface the ability to carry out their own plan of action without interference from an enemy air force.'[60] Therefore, the losses must be seen in the perspective of strategic outcomes created by the IAF's CAO in the west.

Maj Gen D.L. Palit writes that, within 24 hours, the IAF had broken the back of the PAF,[61] which is said to have lost 50 aircraft on the western front as per official records.[62] Pushpindar Singh puts this loss at 51,[63] of which 23 PAF aircraft were lost on the ground. Palit claims 25 aircraft were lost on ground, which later assessments place at 30.[64] Whether it was 23 or 30 PAF aircraft that were lost on ground, the fact is that it wrote off between 8–10 per cent of its fighter fleet—a loss which impacted its strategy and combat performance. The IAF's planned strategy of FAS could not have been achieved without the CAO, where 15 enemy airfields were targeted. Of these, six were forward airfields without any PAF deployments, but were targeted nevertheless, to render them unavailable and deter their use to forward deploy fighters. This was critical as forward deployment would not only have allowed the PAF to challenge the FAS but also enabled greater support to Pakistan Army, which in turn would have directly impacted our land operations, both in the tactical battle area (TBA) and the maritime domain. The aggressive and persistent counter air targeting was due to a lesson well learnt from the past, where the restrictions imposed—preventing striking the PAF airfields—cost the IAF dearly.

Effects of CAO

The outcomes of the CAO were:

1. The PAF relocated by falling back from three forward bases to depth bases in the north, and it was also denied the use of four forward bases in the Rajasthan sector. In addition, it relocated two squadrons for the south (Karachi).
2. It forced the PAF to adopt a defensive strategy concentrated on AD of depth air bases.
3. Operating from depth bases compelled PAF operations to shift to medium altitudes and fly high-low-high mission profiles, which could be picked up on radar and intercepted by the IAF.
4. The increased distance adversely impacted its offensive capacity due to reduced weapon carriage capability vis-à-vis fuel. It also reduced the support the PAF could provide to its army.
5. It significantly reduced the PAF interference in IA's surface operations.
6. It allowed IAF to focus on targeting the energy and transportation 'systems'.

The efficacy of the strategy is borne out by Khan:

> The defensive strategy of the PAF in fact, gave the IAF a free hand to interdict Pakistan communications and other strategic targets and keep pressure on Pakistan troops in the forward areas. The situation as it emerged seemed that, while the PAF had complete air superiority over their bases, the IAF could operate without hindrance in the forward areas and over Pakistani vital communications along her borders.[65]

The PAF perspective that it achieved air superiority over its air bases is incorrect since IAF continued to carry out 282 sorties of CAO from 5 December to 17 December, including eight sorties on the last day of war. While FAS was the goal, effectively the IAF had gained air superiority over Pakistan's area of tactical operations, where its energy and transportation 'systems' were to be engaged. Niazi writes: 'Indian aircraft had command of the skies over West Pakistan as PAF was nowhere putting up effective resistance.'[66] This was also endorsed by Palit, according to whom the IAF had established air superiority in the western front by 4 December evening.[67]

In Assistance of the Army

As per the official history records, out of 4,509 sorties flown in the west, 41.3 per cent were flown in direct assistance of the surface campaign, 45.9 per cent were towards AD, 8.9 per cent were towards CAO, 0.8 per cent were towards strategic strikes and 3.1 per cent were towards reconnaissance. Krishna Rao writes that given IAF's CAO and FAS strategy, CAS availability was limited and desired results were not obtained wherever Pakistan positions in defence were well concealed and camouflaged. However, when Pakistan armour and guns were in the open, like in the Sialkot and Longewala sectors, 'the Air Force dealt with the target very effectively.'[68] There are two aspects here. On the issue of limited air effort, the facts do not support his perception and this is explained in the subsequent paragraph. On the issue of efficacy of the IAF's ability to destroy camouflaged and dug-in targets being lesser than destroying targets in the open needs no clarification. This is a well-established problem which is common to all the services the world over, given the high speeds, firing ranges and limited cockpit visibilities of fighter aircraft.

The Pakistani ground operations began on 3–4 December night, preceded by the ineffective PAF counter air strike. The attack in Poonch sector was beaten back by the Sikhs who fought valiantly. The IAF also carried out strafing of the enemy using the slow Harvard aircraft, which was effectively used in the narrow-wooded valleys and proved to be a morale booster for the IA.[69] The innovative exploitation of the AN-12 transport aircraft in the bombing role proved effective in Poonch sector. The AN-12s also bombed the enemy's Changa Manga ammunition depot in the forests for two days and attacked Pakistani artillery concentration around the Haji Pir pass successfully.[70] The bombing attacks over troop concentrations in Kahuta, called for by the Chiefs of Staff Committee in the forest north-west of Poonch, forced the enemy to call off the attack; and the targeting of forward assembly areas on 9–10 December caused the second enemy offensive to fizzle out.[71] The 40 tonnes of bombs dropped over the enemy by night, where the flashes of the enemy guns revealed their positions, leading to their neutralisation, was confirmed by Lt Gen Candeth to Lal.[72] In the battle for

Chamb, the attempted Pakistan armoured thrust led to the enemy losing 23 tanks, with the majority of the kills by IAF aircraft.[73] Khan records that Indian artillery fire and heavy air activity led to heavy casualties and the bridgehead being withdrawn.[74] Hunters and Su-7s carried out extensive close support sorties, and the Canberra's bombing at night helped stabilise the position.[75]

The IAF chief, closely monitoring the slow offensive operations in the Shakargarh bulge, was concerned if the IAF effort was adequate. He was assured by Candeth that the slow progress was not due to lack of IAF effort, but the extremely cautious approach of the corps commander. Air effort towards assisting surface operations was in plenty but could not be utilised due to non-availability of worthwhile targets.[76] It was also used in a wasteful manner against targets that could have been better engaged by the surface forces themselves.[77] In the Punjab sector, at Hussainiwala, the enemy attacked the IA position across the river and cut off the defending Punjab Regiment. Over two dozen sorties of 'timely and extremely effective air strikes' by Su-7s, which kept the Pakistan armour at bay,[78] helped to cover the withdrawal of the beleaguered unit,[79] a fact which even Khan records: 'as many as six IAF air strikes to keep up the pressure'.[80]

The fairly serious reversal in Fazilka sector saw extensive engagement by IAF Mysteres,[81] which, despite taking heavy losses, prevented a breakthrough by Pakistan armour.[82] Further south in the Rajasthan sector, the Pakistan Army launched a massive offensive planned by their chief, hoping to capture Jaisalmer airfield. On 5 December, at Longewala, IAF Hunters responded to calls for CAS by the divisional commander and carried out 17 sorties against the enemy armour which had beleaguered a company of 23 Punjab Regiment. On the first day itself, 15 tanks and one armoured recce vehicle were destroyed, and 23 were damaged, thus immobilising them. The 12 Infantry Division recorded the famous SOS message (translated) sent by the Pakistan forces under attack:

> The enemy air force has made our life miserable. Each aircraft goes and another comes and dances above us for up to twenty minutes each. Forty of our equipment have been destroyed. Let alone advance further, even retreat has become difficult. Provide air support immediately, otherwise retreat will be impossible.[83]

In the words of the legendary Ian Cardozo: 'By the evening of 6 December, nearly thirty-seven tanks lay burning/damaged in this belt of the Thar Desert. The battle of Longewala was, in fact over.'[84]

According to Khan, 'The enemy was the master of the skies.'[85] The IAF efforts towards CAS and assistance to the army was continuous and carried on till the last day of the war. Indeed, it provided extensive assistance to army's offensive; was instrumental in precluding major Pakistan offensives in Suleimanke, Fazilka and Longewala; and provided critical support in defensive battles, especially wherever the IA was beleaguered. An important aspect which needs to be remembered whenever there is a debate on the large ratio of AD sorties is that a huge portion of the AD combat air patrol was over the TBA, providing cover over both offensive and defensive battles of the army. This was pivotal in preventing PAF interference, ensuring FAS, and thus enabling extensive CAS by the IAF. The PAF claimed 922 missions in direct support of the Pakistan Army.[86] However, according to Indian official records, 'this must be considered a gross exaggeration' and best estimates put it around 500.[87] Compared to this, the 1,862 sorties of CAS to the IA clearly indicates the quantum of air effort which was possible due to the FAS. Of the total 50 fighter losses, 20 were lost during counter air for establishing FAS and the balance were lost to small arms/enemy AAA; and there was no loss to enemy air while providing close support. Also, the PAF could launch only 10–15 sorties per day in support of its army from 6 December onwards.[88] Given the scale of the operations and the frontage, this amounted to negligible enemy air interference to the IA operations.

An Innovative CONOPS at Work

The 'target system' CONOPS of the IAF also paid significant dividends. The first 'energy system' target attack was on 4 December on oil tanks at Keamari, Karachi, by Hunters from Jamnagar. In this attack, two tanks were set on fire, which burned for four days, as recorded in the history of Pakistan Navy. The mission was launched due to the initiative of the squadron commander of the operational training unit (OTU), who was keen to use the latest Mk 56 Hunters with 235 gallon drop tanks against Karachi. The chief operations officer of Jamnagar, busy with strike planning of other targets, cleared him. After landing back from the successful attack, the OTU was redeployed immediately to Jaisalmer and the Karachi oil tank strike outcome was not officially recorded.[89] According to *The New York Times* of 5 December 1971:

> Raids on Karachi Reported Meanwhile, Indian bombers were said to have attacked targets in Karachi, and air raid sirens wailed in Rawalpindi and other West Pakistani cities. There were five raids on Karachi on Saturday, The Associated Press reported, and civil defense source there said one Indian plane had been shot down by antiaircraft fire.

The reported loss of a plane was incorrect but nevertheless, it endorses that the air strike did take place. This strike was incorrectly attributed to the Indian Navy, which successfully engaged the Karachi oil complex only on its second strike, which took place on 8 December.[90] The IAF attacked oil storage tanks in Drigh Road, Attock refinery and the Sui gas plant, along with its storage facilities. Mangla Dam, Suleimanke Headworks and power stations were also targeted.

The 'transportation systems' too were targeted extensively and were included in the interdiction campaign against the Pakistan Army. These included strikes on Karachi harbour, road–railway links of Sindh–Punjab, Hyderabad–Gadra Road, Jhelum–Wazirabad, Montgomery–Pattoki, Rati–Khanpur reti, Bahawalpur, Vihari, etc. Rail junctions and yards of Lahore, Okara, Raiwind, Lodhran, Larkana, Zafarwal, Narowal, Jassar, Ghotki, Larkana, Khairpur, Khudian, Wazirabad, etc., were all targeted by fighter and bomber strikes. On 15 December, Western Air Command continued interdiction of the whole transportation system between Sialkot and Sukkur, reducing Pakistan road and rail traffic to a trickle.[91] In the west, 50 trains, 20 locomotives and about 400 wagons were destroyed.[92] Several permanent and temporary boat bridges were regularly targeted. The extent and persistence of IAF's air superiority over the operational areas allowed it to operate without hindrance in forward areas, including over Pakistani vital communications along the entire border. Pakistan was ill prepared to meet the Indian interdiction onslaught due to the sudden change in IAF strategy from destroying the 'enemy air' system to destroying lines of communication and industrial targets.[93] Another understated success was its pre-planned AD radar deployment, which was effective in keeping IAF fighters over the TBA clear of enemy combat air patrol aircraft.[94]

While Pakistan may have perceived the shift from a PAF-centric CAO-intensive operations to a deliberate surface support and offensive targeting as a change of strategy, the fact is that it was a pre-planned, integrated and a concurrently run CONOPS. The target system strategy was undeniably successful and as Prasad posits: 'the strategic bombing drove home the fury of the war of the war to the people of Pakistan'. The Karachi attack destroyed millions of gallons of fuel; the Attock refinery was set on fire producing no dividends from 1971–72; and the cooling tower of the Sui gas plant was damaged, reducing the production to 50 per cent till April 1972.[95] Strategic effects were evident as 'Pakistani fuel reserves were considerably reduced',[96] which impacted their war effort both in terms of supply and distribution, and had to be imported from Iran.[97] Prasad summarises:

> Though only a small percentage of IAF's offensive effort was directed towards strategic/economic targets the results outweighed the efforts. Pakistan lost a

> large chunk of her fuel resources during the conflict and there was a considerable reduction in her power generation also. A longer war, in all probability, would have meant a disaster for Pakistan.[98]

The significant aspect is that the IAF flew a total of 11,549 sorties in 14 days,[99] of which 6,604 were combat sorties, with an average aircraft utilisation rate of 40 per cent (as against an initial planned rate of 75 per cent, reducing to 70 per cent after five days and then to 60 per cent of the available strength),[100] assessed on the basis of both fronts put together. This means that the IAF had spare capacity to fight if the PAF had been more aggressive, or if the war were to last longer. It also underscores the efficacy of IAF's operational planning, force utilisation and combat persistence while fighting against trained and capable opposition.

Combat Support Operations

Strategic photo reconnaissance was carried out by Canberras and tactical photo recce capacity was built up by modifying Hunters, Sukhois and MiGs, which was also called fighter reconnaissance (FR). These were used for both tactical recce for the army and bomb damage assessment (BDA) after air strikes. Post-mission photo development, analysis and dissemination from joint perspective emerged as an area needing attention,[101] as also brought out by Candeth[102] and Krishna Rao.[103] Electronic warfare employment was very nascent and used in a limited manner for communication jamming. Transport aircraft and helicopters performed a huge and unsung role, airlifting thousands of personnel and tonnes of wartime loads, ammunition and equipment on both fronts. In the east, the IAF created history with Heli-bridging and airborne drop. In the west too, a drop was catered for but not executed. These enabled IAF units to move swiftly between bases, and also shift fronts. The AN-12s were innovatively used for bombing missions with significant results. Caribou and Otter aircraft played a vital role in supporting operations in the short airstrips in the North-East. Transport aircraft were also used as radio relays for deep strikes into enemy territory by night. Helicopters were extensively exploited in the east in support of land operations. Army's requirement of transport support to airlift two brigades from the east to the west was met. While helicopters took on field-level casualty evacuation, over 800 casualties were flown by transport aircraft to hospitals in the rear areas.[104]

Maritime Air Operations

A smaller and yet notable part of the IAF support to the surface forces was towards maritime operations. The IAF had a maritime organisation in place on both seaboards in the form of MACs, under AOC Maritime Air Operations in Bombay. Lal writes that 13–14 aircraft were allotted to each MAC and 545 hrs of air effort were flown in nearly a hundred missions since mid-October, prior to the war. The maritime reconnaissance (MR) role was undertaken by a squadron of Super Constellation aircraft and strike role by a squadron of Canberras. Since the naval plans were not defined, air power requirements were not clear. The operations in the east was centred around *INS Vikrant*, which was free to come into operations with the sinking of the Pakistani submarine, *PNS Ghazi*, off Vishakhapatnam. The air superiority enabled full freedom of naval operations and enabled *INS Vikrant* to play an active offensive role, with its Belize and Sea Hawk aircraft striking port facilities, naval infrastructure and Pakistani merchant shipping in and around Chittagong and Cox's Bazar. It also assisted in contraband control and apprehension of merchant shipping and enabled amphibious landing.[105]

On the west front, the withdrawal of Pakistan Navy into Karachi harbour and limited submarine operations allowed the IN to dominate the Arabian Sea. The IAF's offensive strikes to support the navy were conducted over Masroor airfield and Karachi between 3–5 December and paralysed the PAF AD system.[106] This enabled the navy's abortive missile boat strike on 5 December to go through without any PAF response, with combat air patrol by Hunter aircraft providing cover to the post-strike exit of the missile boats. The continued attacks by Canberra's over Masroor and Drigh Road caused considerable damage and contributed in keeping the PAF at bay, thus enabling the second missile boat strike by the navy on 8 December night to go through successfully without air interference. The IAF MR aircraft carried out regular missions for shipping, including searches for *INS Khukri* which was sunk by a Pakistani submarine. A total of 96 sorties were flown by the IAF in support of the navy in the west.[107]

The Final Analysis

By all standards, it was a unique war, fought simultaneously on two widely separated fronts. Two nations went to war and three emerged. India defeated Pakistan decisively in the east and captured approximately 93,000 prisoners of war. Also, it was in a dominant position in the west militarily, with Pakistan's offensive having failed. According to official history, Pakistan was in no position to continue the fight on account of: a politically unstable internal situation; oil and ammunition stocks being reduced to two weeks by the IAF; no replenishments possible due to the IN's blockade; and the IA being in a better position territorially.[108] Further, despite all promises, neither China nor the US did anything tangible to rush to the aid of their protégé. However, Muslim nations extended their support to Pakistan, and also provided military assistance. For that matter, India too did not receive any direct support, except aid and international sympathy for the refugee crisis. The Soviet Union emerged as a significant friend and this was to shape the future Indo-Soviet relations and regional geopolitics. Given the circumstances, there was definitely a section of Indians who believed that the war in the west should have been continued till Pakistan was decisively defeated. Whether this would have ended the challenges of the Indo-Pak issues is debatable, but India chose to end the war on its terms.

The IAF air strategy and CONOPS proved successful. It achieved total air supremacy in the east. On the west, while the goal was FAS, it actually managed to gain air superiority in the forward TBAs and in-depth up to the north–south vital communication network. This played an overarching role in enabling total freedom for both the army and the navy from enemy air opposition and interference in the conduct of their operations in the east. On the western front too, the PAF was neither able to support the Pakistani Army adequately nor was it able to cause any significant attrition or interference in IA's ground campaign. In the east, the IAF was able to cause a serious mobility paralysis for the Pakistan Army by taking out the rail and waterway transportation system.

The IAF interdiction and CAS not only caused significant attrition to the enemy military but also severely affected their morale. The fall of Dacca was certainly swifter due to the relentless air strikes on enemy positions, which actually impacted their will to fight. Without air power, Dacca could easily have become a long-drawn battle of house-to-house fighting, like the Battle for Stalingrad in World War II. As per Niazi's four-layered defence of Dacca fortress plan, the final battle was to be fought in the built-up areas,[109] which would have not only been militarily debilitating but also a time-consuming battle. This delay would have enabled strategic space to Pakistan to force a ceasefire through international intervention and would have denied India the ascendancy of a decisive surrender. The attack on the governor's house amidst relentless air strikes on Dacca was therefore justifiably the strategic tipping point for the final surrender. The IAF's extensive role supported the other services and, on occasions, even played a pivotal part in both offensive and defensive battles. The Meghna River crossings, the Tangail paradrop and the thwarting of three major enemy armoured thrusts at Chamb, Fazilka and Longewala remain examples of classic air power effects.

The first unfettered offensive employment of air power in war by India actually enabled a swift decisive outcome in a limited and high-intensity campaign. If the IAF had been constrained like it was in the previous war, it is debatable if the war could have been won so swiftly, with such extensive enemy attrition and significantly lower own losses. Niazi's words are illustrative: 'To capture Dacca, the Indians would have had to fight hard and suffer heavy losses in destroying my force, but to their good luck, the blunders of our High Command enabled them to turn what would have been a military stalemate into a victory.'[110] The war definitely would have lasted much longer without the use of offensive air, and would have possibly precluded any decisive outcome due to international intervention. Air power, in this case, not only prevailed upon the enemy air but also force-multiplied the surface campaign towards defeating the enemy army.

Tailpiece

An interesting anecdote is highly illuminative of the spirit of the IAF pilots. Squadron Leader D.S. Jaffa—who was Lal's staff officer in the war and chose to go back to his squadron to fight—was shot down and taken a prisoner of war. He was interrogated by Brigadier General Chuck Yeager, famous for being the first pilot to break the speed of sound, and sent by the US to assess aircraft wreckage of Soviet origin. When told by Jaffa that there was no special guidance equipment provided by the Russians which explained the accuracy of IAF strikes, he asked:

> 'Then how come your pilots were finding the targets so accurately by night? Not a single failure.' 'Come on', Jaffa taunted, 'Why can't you accept the simple fact that a little bit of accurate flying with a compass, a speedometer, and a wrist watch will take you unerringly to wherever you want to go, every time! So, tell me what are you really after?' As the visitors were saying their goodbye Jaffa looked at the American and said, 'Are you going to place the Seventh Fleet in the Arabian Sea next? For this part of Pakistan' There was no reply. The Yankee shrugged his shoulders and walked out.[111]

NOTES

1. S.N. Prasad et al. (eds), *History of the 1971 India-Pakistan War*, New Delhi: History Division, Ministry of Defence, Government of India, 1992, pp. 270–74.
2. Ibid., pp. 280–81.
3. P.C. Lal, *My Years with the IAF*, New Delhi: Lancer, 1986, p. 167.
4. Ibid., pp. 171–72.
5. Ibid., p. 420.
6. Ibid., pp. 594–95.
7. Prasad et al., *History of the 1971 India-Pakistan War*, n. 1, p. 420.
8. Lal, *My Years with the IAF*, n. 3, pp. 181–83.

9. P.V.S. Jagan Mohan and Sameer Chopra, *Eagles over Bangladesh: The Indian Air Force in the 1971 Liberation War*, Harper Collins, 2013, pp. 33–40.
10. Ibid., p. 33.
11. Syed Shabbir Hussain and M. Tariq Qureshi, *History of the Pakistan Air Force 1947–1982*, Karachi: PAF Press, May 1982, p. 189.
12. Prasad et al., *History of the 1971 India-Pakistan War*, n. 1, p. 143.
13. Siddiq Salik, *Witness to Surrender*, New Delhi: Oxford University Press, 1979, pp. 131–32.
14. Mohan and Chopra, *Eagles over Bangladesh*, n. 9, p. 370.
15. Ibid., p. 95.
16. Lal, *My Years with the IAF*, n. 3, pp. 175–76.
17. Ibid., p. 177.
18. A.K. Tiwary, *Indian Air Force in Wars*, New Delhi: Lancers, 2012, p. 174.
19. Prasad et al., *History of the 1971 India-Pakistan War*, n. 1, p. 615.
20. Ibid., p. 604.
21. Tiwary, *Indian Air Force in Wars*, n. 18, pp. 189–90.
22. Salik, *Witness to Surrender*, n. 13, p. 196.
23. K.V. Krishna Rao, *Prepare or Perish: A Study of National Security*, New Delhi: Lancer, 1991, p. 201; and Lal, *My Years with the IAF*, n. 3, p. 177.
24. Jasjit, p. 146.
25. Lal, *My Years with the IAF*, n. 3, pp. 210–11.
26. Krishna Rao, *Prepare or Perish*, n. 23, p. 201.
27. Ibid., p. 201.
28. Lal, *My Years with the IAF*, n. 3, p. 213.
29. Prasad et al., *History of the 1971 India-Pakistan War*, n. 1, p. 616.
30. J.F.R. Jacob, *Surender at Dacca: Birth of a Nation*, New Delhi: Manohar, 2001, p. 129.
31. Krishna Rao, *Prepare or Perish*, n. 23, p. 199.
32. Prasad et al., *History of the 1971 India-Pakistan War*, n. 1, citing Jack Anderson of Washington Post, p. 672.
33. Jasjit, p. 167.
34. Mohan and Chopra, *Eagles over Bangladesh*, n. 9, pp. 327–29.
35. Gavin Young, *Worlds Apart: Travels in War and Peace*, London: Hutchinson, 1987, p. 51.
36. Salik, *Witness to Surrender*, n. 13, p. 207.
37. Fazal Muqueem Khan, *Pakistan's Crisis in Leadership*, Islamabad: National Book Foundation, 1973, pp. 187–88.
38. Prasad et al., *History of the 1971 India-Pakistan War*, n. 1, p. 617.
39. Mohan and Chopra, *Eagles over Bangladesh*, n. 9, p. 337.
40. Krishna Rao, *Prepare or Perish*, n. 23, p. 196.
41. Lal, *My Years with the IAF*, n. 3, p. 221.
42. A.A.K. Niazi, *The Betrayal of East Pakistan*, New Delhi: Manohar, 1998, p. 85.
43. Krishna Rao, *Prepare or Perish*, n. 23, pp. 206–10.
44. Tiwary, *Indian Air Force in Wars*, n. 18, p. 195.
45. S.N. Kohli, *We Dared*, New Delhi: Lancer International, 1989, pp. 36–44.
46. Tiwary, *Indian Air Force in Wars*, n. 18, p. 197.
47. Sajit Gandhi (ed.), *The Tilt: The U.S. and the South Asian Crisis of 1971*, National Security Archive Electronic Briefing Book No. 79, 16 December 2002, available at https://nsarchive2.gwu.edu/NSAEBB/NSAEBB79/, accessed on 11 July 2021.

48. Pushpindar Singh, Ravi Rikhye and Peter Steinman, *Fiza'Ya: Psyche of Pakistan Air Force*, New Delhi: The Society of Aerospace Studies, 1991, p. 64.
49. Ibid., p. 248.
50. Prasad et al., *History of the 1971 India-Pakistan War*, n. 1, pp. 422–23.
51. Khan, *Pakistan's Crisis in Leadership*, n. 37, p. 235.
52. Ibid, p. 240.
53. Prasad et al., *History of the 1971 India-Pakistan War*, n. 1, p. 414.
54. Khan, *Pakistan's Crisis in Leadership*, n. 37, p. 240.
55. Ibid.
56. Teshter Master, *Moonlight Marauders*, Partridge India, 2018, pp. 50–68.
57. Lal, *My Years with the IAF*, n. 3, p. 258.
58. Pushpindar Singh, *Himalayan Eagles, Vol. II*, New Delhi: The Society for Aerospace Studies, 2007, p. 179.
59. Tiwary, *Indian Air Force in Wars*, n. 18, p. 201.
60. William A. Momyer, *Airpower in Three Wars*, Maxwell AFB, AL: Air University Press, 2003 (reprint), p. 178.
61. D.K. Palit, *The Lightning Campaign*, New Delhi: Thompson Press Ltd, 1972, p. 78.
62. Prasad et al., *History of the 1971 India-Pakistan War*, n. 1, p. 455.
63 Singh, *Himalayan Eagles, Vol. II*, n. 58, p. 65.
64. Palit, *The Lightning Campaign*, n. 61, pp. 78, 142.
65. Khan, *Pakistan's Crisis in Leadership*, n. 37, p. 241.
66. Niazi, *The Betrayal of East Pakistan*, n. 42, p. 127.
67. Palit, *The Lightning Campaign*, n. 61, p. 78.
68. Krishna Rao, *Prepare or Perish*, n. 23, p. 249.
69. Ibid., p. 213.
70. Gulshan Luthra, 'IAF's Innovative Use of Transporters as Heavy Bombers', *India Strategic*, April 2013, available at https://www.indiastrategic.in/topstories1980_IAF_use_transporters_heavy_bombers.html, accessed on 19 July 2021.
71. Palit, *The Lightning Campaign*, n. 61, p. 83.
72. Lal, *My Years with the IAF*, n. 3, p. 235.
73. Palit, *The Lightning Campaign*, n. 61, p. 85.
74. Khan, *Pakistan's Crisis in Leadership*, n. 37, p. 198.
75. Prasad et al., *History of the 1971 India-Pakistan War*, n. 1, p. 436.
76. Ibid., p. 437.
77. Lal, *My Years with the IAF*, n. 3, p. 240.
78. Prasad et al., *History of the 1971 India-Pakistan War*, n. 1, p. 380.
79. Lal, *My Years with the IAF*, n. 3, p. 261.
80. Khan, *Pakistan's Crisis in Leadership*, n. 37, p. 207.
81. Krishna Rao, *Prepare or Perish*, n. 23, p. 236.
82. Lal, *My Years with the IAF*, n. 3, p. 265.
83. Ibid., p. 282.
84. Ian Cardozo, *1971: Stories of Grit and Glory from the Indo-Pak War*, Penguin Random House India, 2021, p. 127.
85. Khan, *Pakistan's Crisis in Leadership*, n. 37, p. 212.
86. Ibid., p. 242.
87. Prasad et al., *History of the 1971 India-Pakistan War*, n. 1, p. 448.
88. Data extrapolated from Prasad, Lal, Jasjit, Tiwary and Chopra and Mohan.

89. Sushant Singh, 'December 4, 1971: When Navy got Credit for IAF's Strikes on Karachi Oil Tanks', *The Indian Express*, 4 December 2015, available at https://indianexpress.com/article/explained/december-4-1971-when-navy-got-credit-for-iafs-strikes-on-karachi-oil-tanks/, accessed on 22 July 2021. Interestingly, the OTU was the unit involved in the Longewala battle.
90. Available at https://www.indiannavy.nic.in/sites/default/files/Transition-to-Triumph-07Apr16.pdf, p. 276, accessed on 22 July 2021.
91. Prasad et al., *History of the 1971 India-Pakistan War*, n. 1, p. 442.
92. Lal, *My Years with the IAF*, n. 3, p. 322.
93. Khan, *Pakistan's Crisis in Leadership*, n. 37, p. 241.
94. Lal, *My Years with the IAF*, n. 3, p. 246.
95. Ibid., p. 182.
96. Palit, *The Lightning Campaign*, n. 61, p. 143.
97. Lal, *My Years with the IAF*, n. 3, pp. 182, 298.
98. Prasad et al., *History of the 1971 India-Pakistan War*, n. 1, p. 451.
99. Ibid., p. 452.
100. Tiwary, *Indian Air Force in Wars*, n. 18, p. 243.
101. Lal, *My Years with the IAF*, n. 3, p. 323.
102. Tiwary, *Indian Air Force in Wars*, n. 18, p. 245.
103. Krishna Rao, *Prepare or Perish*, n. 23, p. 249.
104. Prasad et al., *History of the 1971 India-Pakistan War*, n. 1, p. 447.
105. Available at: https://www.indiannavy.nic.in/sites/default/files/Transition-to-Triumph-07Apr16.pdf, p. 324, accessed on 22 July 2021.
106. T.M. Asthana, 'Jointness in War', in Jasjit Singh (ed.), *Role of Indian Air Force in 1971 War*, New Delhi: KW Publishers Pvt. Ltd, 2013, p. 120.
107. Prasad et al., *History of the 1971 India-Pakistan War*, n. 1, pp. 444–47.
108. Ibid., p. 686.
109. Niazi, *The Betrayal of East Pakistan*, n. 42, pp. 203–08.
110. Ibid., p. 219.
111. Dhirendra S. Jaffa, *Death wasn't Painful*, New Delhi: Sage, 2014, pp. 45–46.

8

Sagat and Helicopters

True Pillars of Victory

Rajesh Isser

India's support to the hapless people of then East Pakistan is worthy of remembrance. In supporting the Mukti Bahini and subsequent War of Liberation, India not only saved millions of future Bangladeshis but also helped create a new nation. The Pakistan Army-led genocide was worse than words can describe. I can vouch for this because of witnessing it as a child. The following short account clearly shows the genocide that took place during the 1971 Liberation War and why India's intervention must be regarded as a great and historical humanitarian effort.

A Personal Trauma of the Author

My father was in the Foreign Service, and we had come back to India in end-October 1971 just a few months before the war. Our otherwise blissful time of three years in Dacca included the almost eight months under house arrest by the Pakistani Army. This included the full high commission with families. All of us were confined to a multi-storey complex at Kakrail, with only one officer allowed to go along with a coolie to Shanti Bazaar, once a week, to do the whole community's shopping. No school, no outings, and yet we kids made the most of it. The current COVID lockdowns and restrictions do not compare! The entire lot was evacuated by two planes of Swissair and Aeroflot one fine day sans any luggage. Everyone lost everything.

Even as small kids we saw it all from our windows and roofs of the six-storey building. I witnessed the genocide first-hand along with others in the mission. The horror of killings at point blank, screaming of women being gang-raped, naked men being paraded and made to crawl on the hot asphalt roads. The worst was the massacre at Shanti Bazaar. One fine Sunday, there was a big commotion in the building, and everyone went to the roof. One could see the huge marketplace at a distance which used to get packed on Sundays. A few fire engines had gathered and armed forces in huge numbers with vehicles mounted with machine guns. In an orchestrated move, they blocked Shanti Bazaar's all exits just when it was most crowded. And then they set fire to the ring of shops that surrounded it and fired at people running away. The fire engines stopped the fire from expanding to unintended places. Later in life, during school lessons of history, I would compare it with Jallianwala Bagh massacre in India during British rule.

Sometime in March of 1971, the Awami League organised a night procession with burning torches or *mashaals*. We watched the unending procession for hours from our roof. That is how popular the movement for justice had become. But the repercussions were quick and heavy. A vivid example was the Dhobi Ghat cluster right behind our building. You could see all the activities from the roof or windows facing it from our building. Two days after the march, it became a flurry of activity. Pakistan security and army surrounded the village and made sure no one escaped. All the women and old were herded out somewhere in vehicles. The women were taken into the huts, and the screams and cries all day long told their own story. All the men and grown-up boys were beaten and tortured in the open for the whole day in a telling public display. At night, there were distinct gunshots that continued for some time. That ghat never got inhabited till we were evacuated eight months later in October.

The only thing that we were allowed to carry back to India was my little sister's (3 years then) doll which was taller than her. On landing at Palam at a ground reception, my sister and her doll became a star attraction of news reporters—she was there on all front covers the next day along with the horror stories that families related. Many years later, my parents told us that it was a touch-and-go situation with everyday full of uncertainty of whether we would survive or not.

Assisting the Birth of Bangladesh

If there is any home-grown campaign in India that truly boosts the concept of jointness, it is the war for liberating Bangladesh. The multiplying effect of synergy between the three services created magic on the eastern front, while containing damage in the west. The whole gamut of joint support structures, such as Advance Headquarters (HQs), Tactical Air Centres (TACs), forward air controllers (FACs), ground liaison officers (GLOs) and others, worked in a coherent manner to achieve air superiority in the east and effective offensive air support in the west. The blitzkrieg on the ground in East Pakistan, ably supported by a well-coordinated air campaign, demonstrated the air–land battle concept well before it came into common parlance in the 1980s and the 1990s.[1]

Wars, it is said, are fought in the minds of the Generals, Air Marshals and Admirals. Nothing could be truer than what was demonstrated in the lightening moves of the Indian Army/Indian Air Force(IAF) combine in the east. Learning from the Vietnam campaign, the IAF top brass, in collaboration with Lieutenant General (Lt Gen) Sagat Singh, General Officer Commanding (GOC) 4 Corps, conceived a series of special heliborne operations (SHBO) that leapfrogged Indian infantry into the centre of gravity of General (Gen) Niazi's forces. Indeed, the early surrender was due to the speed of advance that even took the Indian Army HQ by surprise! This was surely the best example of what mutual respect and faith in each other's capabilities could bring about among the Indian Armed Forces.

While the historical focus remains on the pioneering SHBO that redefined tactics, commanders at all levels displayed remarkable ingenuity and creativity to grab every opportunity for denting the enemy's might—special armed operations by helicopters along with the Mukti Bahini is one such story. Though a drop in the ocean in the overall scheme of things, the effect it had on the morale of local fighters and populace was immeasurable. Recent campaigns of North Atlantic Treaty Organization (NATO) underline support as lynchpin for success; the Indian Armed Forces demonstrated it well in 1971.

Innovative Employment of Helicopters

While helicopters as war machines, vital suppliers and gunships were first employed in France's Algerian campaign in 1950, it was the Vietnam War that brought them to the fore as a game-changer in such dirty wars. Helicopter employment was only limited by a commander's creativity and risk-taking limits. The whole world sat up and took notice—and so did a few Indian commanders during the war for liberation of East Pakistan in 1971. Lt Gen Sagat Singh was the maverick corps commander of 4 Corps, one of the formations which was tasked with offensive operations towards Dacca from east. He was not very well liked by peers and superiors for his maverick attitude, but he had seen what the Mi-4s could do during the 1966 Mizoram campaign by Indian joint forces, that is, SHBO and vertical envelopment of adversarial forces. Supporting him in leveraging the potential of the Mi-4s were pilots and crews of helicopter units (HUs) of the IAF. Together they orchestrated the most audacious series of operations over one week with just over a squadron worth (11–15) of Mi-4 helicopters from 110 and 105 HUs. They, in fact, did the unthinkable and produced a miracle that only a fog of war throws up.

Using Mi-4s to launch whole battalions and brigades across innumerable waterways that included the mighty river Meghna and its tributary, Surma, Sagat and Group Captain Chandan Singh first bypassed and bottled-up the Sylhet garrison with merely a battalion, and then Heli-lifted two brigades to the doorsteps of Dacca. This left Dacca vulnerable and forced its garrison to surrender.[2] Though Sagat was made to wait for other formations to catch up, the series of heliborne operations that he executed could well be considered to be gamechangers that accelerated the collapse of the Pakistan Army in East Pakistan and the creation of Bangladesh.[3]

The Air–Land Battle Concept in the East

Concept of Operations: Indian Army[4]

The Army Commander, Lt Gen Jagjit Singh Aurora, had reminded his formation commanders that the battle in East Pakistan would be a fluid one and his operational instructions should be used as a basis for general guidance. Thus, though the final objectives would remain unaltered, formation commanders should be prepared to constantly review thrust lines and intermediate objectives as per changed situations. These modifications involved bypassing sizeable enemy strongholds, which not only indicated a significant change in concept but also expressed a growing confidence and realisation by the Eastern Command that a swift advance into the vitals of East Pakistan would threaten Dacca and bring about a total collapse and defeat of the Pakistani forces. Initial plans catered for securing the line of the Brahmaputra and Meghna rivers. Further detailed planning could only be done taking into consideration the progress of various thrusts. It was envisaged that 4 Corps would cross Meghna between Daudkandi and Bhairab Bazaar and advance towards Dacca. The 101 Communication Zone Area with 95 Mountain Brigade (Mtn Bde) group of four battalions, 2 Para group, followed by 167 Mtn Bde, would advance towards Dacca from the north. It was felt that these forces would be supported in their advance to Dacca by Siddiqi Force, a large group of freedom fighters which had been operating with good effect in Tangail district.

Contingency plans were also made for elements of 2 Corps to cross the Padma River at Goalundo, for which suitable inland water transport craft were placed at Dhubri to assist 95 Mtn Bde or move elements of 20 Mountain Division, if required. Army HQ reserve of 50 Independent Para Brigade was to provide one complete battalion drop and two company drops. It was appreciated that the most important area for the main drop was Tangail in order to ensure early pressure on Dacca. Second priority was given for two-company drops to assist in securing Magura if necessary. Due to the limited availability of Mi-4 helicopters, all these helicopters were allocated to 4 Corps to enable them to ferry troops as required. The air effort allotted to the army was sufficient to cater for an average of 120 sorties per day. Naval forces were to blockade Chalna and Chittagong and the naval air arm was to be used in the area of Chittagong–Cox's Bazaar.[5]

The Mi-4 units had seen continuous operational service in India's north-east, supporting the army's counter-insurgency operations in Nagaland and Mizoram, lifting commando teams into action and helping to pre-empt hostile infiltration to and from China. They had often suffered hits from small arms fire; on one occasion, a Mi-4 even returned to base with a poison-tipped arrow sticking in its undercarriage! The operational climax for the Mi-4s in IAF service came during the 1971 war, when it played a key role in the Indian Army's blitzkrieg-style advance to Dacca.

Whilst the 2 Corps battled its way from the western side, the 4 Corps thrust came from three directions in the east, across 155 miles (250 kilometre [km]) of border between East Pakistan and Meghalaya to the north, through to the Feni salient in the extreme south of Tripura. One column moved in from Silchar–Karimganj area towards Sylhet, another along the Akhura–Asjuganj axis and the third in the south with the objective of containing Comilla and cutting off Chittagong. Whilst battling against the two Pakistani divisions ranged against them, 4 Corps had to contend with the most formidable riverine terrain, criss-crossed by rivers and streams that make the area a logistic nightmare for any offensive action.

Supporting the advance was 110 HU, with 10 Mi-4s on strength and another two Mi-4s attached from 105 HU.[6] Mi-4s were intimately involved in the spectacular progress made by the army, particularly by 8 Mountain Division. 110 HU transported troops, guns, ammunition and equipment, evacuated casualties and conducted reconnaissance for the field formations in the sector. On 7 December 1971, 254 troops were airlifted from Kailashahar to the Sylhet sector in the face of heavy ground fire. Next day, another 279 troops and 97 tonnes of equipment were airlifted from Kalaura, mostly at night. An additional 584 troops and 125 tonnes of supplies and nine field guns were lifted between 9 and 10 December to reinforce the build-up against Sylhet, which was held by the Pakistani 313 Brigade. The 110 HU then moved to Agartala for the heliborne operations from Brahmanbaria to Raipura.

The Mi-4s could be said to have forced the pace of the army's relentless drive, which now saw heliborne infantry leapfrogging past natural obstacles and enemy defences, with Gnats strafing and rocketing strongholds, in a textbook display of coordinated air power. The biggest operational task yet undertaken by the IAF's helicopter force was between 11 and 15 December. On 11 December, 1,350 troops and 19.2 tonnes of equipment was airlifted from Brahmanbaria to Narsingdi, including in particular the lead battalion, 4/5 Gorkha Rifles of 59 Mtn Bgde, spearheading 8 Mountain Division's intrusion in Sylhet. The Gorkhas and their equipment were lifted across the Meghna River to south-east of Sylhet, forcing the much larger enemy force to abandon defences and, for fear of being cut off by the heliborne forces, pull back into the town.

Heliborne Operations

These operations are essentially troops being dropped behind enemy lines from a helicopter by landing, being light on wheels or from a hover. From 7 December onwards, helicopters began transporting troops, light guns, ammunition and fuel. In three days of operations, these helicopters had flown over 120 sorties to lift nearly 1,200 troops and 10 tonnes of load. Over 50 of these sorties were carried out by night. These operations facilitated the capture of Sylhet and certain other features in the same sector. Night movement of troops in large numbers caught the Pakistan Army by surprise. Besides fully armed troops in thousands, the load in hundreds of tonnes included RCL guns, gun shells and mortars, small arms ammunition and rations.

The IAF's small helicopter force could fairly claim credit for the speed of advance of the Indian Army in East Pakistan. It is well recognised and documented by the Indian Army that 110 HU was a key factor in the lightning campaign, where speed of advance was of the utmost importance. Two additional units worthy of special mention were 15 and 24 Squadrons, whose Gnats provided escorts to the heliborne operations and close support over the entire Brahmanbaria–Sylhet axis. Other Mi-4 and Alouette III units, including 112 HU in the Jessore sector, conducted casualty evacuation, communication and reconnaissance flights. Some Mi-4s and Alouette IIIs were equipped as gunships and operated in this role both in the east and the north-west of India, recalling their earlier role in 1965, when they hunted infiltrators with machine guns and anti-personnel bombs in Kashmir.

The Mukti Bahini Air Force

The birth of a 'Bangladesh Air Force' took place as 'Kilo Flight'. It was the Mukti Bahini's combat aviation formation, set up in October 1971, well in advance of the formal declaration of war in December. It consisted of one DHC-3 Otter plane and one Alouette III helicopter, both carrying rocket pods and machine guns for launching hit-and-run attacks on Pakistani targets, and one DC-3 Dakota for logistical missions. Nine Bengali pilots and 58 ex-Pakistan Air Force personnel were trained and supported by Indian forces clandestinely. It trained at Dimapur in Nagaland, and this unit was the first to launch airstrikes on Pakistani targets in East Pakistan on 4 December 1971, by attacking oil depots at Narayanganj and Chittagong. After the war, it formed the core of the nascent Bangladesh Air Force.

It was on the night of 3 and 4 December that Otter aircraft of this air force attacked fuel dumps at Chittagong and an Alouette helicopter raided the fuel dumps at Narayanganj. Both the missions were successful. On 4 December, this Flight at Kailashahar airfield was placed at the disposal of GOC 8 Mountain Division, operating in the Maulvi Bazaar/Sylhet sector. The GOC demanded attacks by night on convoys, river barges and streamers on the Meghna, north of Bhairab Bazaar. The Flight flew five sorties between 4 and 7 December, hitting bunkers and troops concentrations at Maulvi Bazaar, and also destroyed two steamers and several 3-tonne trucks carrying troops.

Between 7 and 12 December, the Alouette helicopter was constantly and effectively used as an armed escort during the special helicopter operations at Sylhet, Raipura, Narsingdi and Baidya Bazaar. It engaged targets, as directed by the FAC, at night also. After the first night raid on Chittagong fuel dumps, Otter aircraft were utilised for armed escort/recce on a few missions only, in the same areas as the Alouette. The overall returns from this Flight were not very encouraging, perhaps because it had no definite tasks. Thus, the contribution of this Flight to the war effort was rather small. However, as far as raising the morale of the Mukti Bahini was concerned, it did serve the desired purpose. During the period of operations, the total flying effort of Kilo Flight was: Alouette, 77 sorties/68 hours; and Otter, 12 sorties/23 hours.

A Herculean and Colourful Effort

The type-wise breakdown of helicopter effort under the command of HQ, Eastern

Air Command (EAC), for conduct of air operations in the eastern theatre from 3 December to 17 December1971is given in Table 1.

Table 1: Summary of Flying Effort: 3–17 December 1971

Type of Aircraft	*Sorties*	*Hours*	*Load (tonne)*	*Troops Carried*	*Casualties Carried*
Mi-4	1,397	992:05	185.7	5,136	866
Alouette	894	726:35		809	282
Bell	113	84:00			31
Total	2,404	1,802:40	185.7	5,945	1,179

Source: Author's compilation from war diaries.

The first-hand personal accounts of pilots who took part, as well as unit diaries of the time, truly bring out the dynamic and fast-changing issues that exemplify true jointness. These are gleaned from unit war diaries and personal accounts (written debriefs available in units and Air HQ).[7] Some extracts from unit records of 110 HU are given next.

First-hand account (extracts) of Flight Lieutenant (Flt Lt) Pushp K.Vaid:

> ...But by the time I was going for my third trip it was already dark. Also the Pakistan army had seen the helicopters and started surrounding the field we were landing in and were firing at us as we came into land. On my third flight, I must have seen as many as five hundred bullets or more coming towards me. I couldn't count of course but they looked like a lot of bullets along with tracer bullets. Amazingly not one bullet hit us. I warned all others pilots to keep a look out and to reduce the time on the ground to minimum. We all finished our three trips and shut down for fuel at our bases. All of us checked our helicopters and not even one bullet had hit any helicopter.
>
> While we were getting ready to start flying again, Group Captain Chandan Singh, who was in charge of the Air Force side, said that we won't fly at night and that we will start flying next morning. That really upset the army. They had not planned their soldiers or the ammunition or the food or the radio. They were not even sure of what or who had gone so far. All the helicopters had been filled up as the soldiers arrived with the idea that we will keep flying till everything had been moved. There was a big discussion between the army and the 110 HU supervisors. Eventually, after nearly three hours, it was decided that one helicopter will go, and if it came back the others will be sent...After the sortie, at base we discovered that the cable to the fuel gauge had been hit. This was mended and then we continued flying with the rest of the helicopters right through the night till we had dropped the entire brigade at Sylhet.[8]

Account of wartime activity by Air Commodore (Air Cmde) C.M.Singla (Retd):

> ...At Dimapur, I was asked to pick up an armed Chetak from Tezpur which had just been modified by and airlifted from BRD. It had one rocket pod on either side and each pod carried seven rockets. These could be fired in pairs or in salvo. In addition, on the helicopter floor, a twin barrel machine gun was mounted.
>
> ...Then onwards, we operated as self contained and mobile hitting outfit. We moved frequently to support troops as they advanced. I was ordered to fly in command on all armed missions. On one night, troops were to be inducted by Mi-4 helicopters. I was to give air cover. The Forward Air Controller told me on R/T that he was my pupil at Bidar. Our effective rocket firing over several missions that night was witnessed by a senior officer who flew as a passenger with us initially. Being an unstable platform, in our dive to aim and engage targets with rockets pairs, we had to come pretty low and close to the targets. We took some bullet hits that night. Subsequently, we hit & burnt ammunition trucks, boats ferrying troops by night and enemy concentrations. The helicopter had now got pierced by bullets all over. The engineers did a good job of repairs and despite vibrations etc. we remained operational throughout the war.[9]

Extract from 110 HU War Diary:

> On 16th December 1971, Flight Lieutenant Ravindra Vikram Singh (9524) Flying (Pilot) was flying the C-in-C and Chief of Staff of Bangladesh with other passengers to Sylhet. At a height of 1 km, his aircraft was hit by enemy ground fire at 1720hrs, where one bullet, after piercing the cabin injured the Chief of Staff of Bangladesh, hit an oil pipe, and resulted in leak of hot oil into the cabin. Pulling up immediately to 1.5 km of height, he checked that the reductor oil pressure had started dropping to zero giving limited time for action. It was by then dark and returning back to base or to any other airfield was impossible. He manoeuvred out of enemy area, selected a suitable field at Fenchuganj after approximately 15 minutes flying under trying circumstances in complete darkness and made a successful landing saving the aircraft and lives of C-in-C and chief of Staff of Bangladesh along with other passengers and crew.[10]

110 HU's Legacy

The 110 HU was raised on 19 February 1962 with Mi-4 helicopters at Tezpur. During the 1971 Bangladesh Liberation War, within a brief period of 12 days, it was instrumental in demonstrating the flexibility of air power by successfully undertaking the first-ever SHBO in war. It was utilised for 'vertical envelopment' extensively and carried out the famous Heli-bridging operations in which the Indian Army was moved with creditable swiftness that finally brought a formidable enemy to his knees. The relentless operations changed the face of the tactical battle area in the theatre of operations (east of Dacca) in East Pakistan. The SHBO missions contributed majorly to the most decisive liberation campaign ever in military history. A depiction of the progress of SHBO (north to south) is given in Map 1.

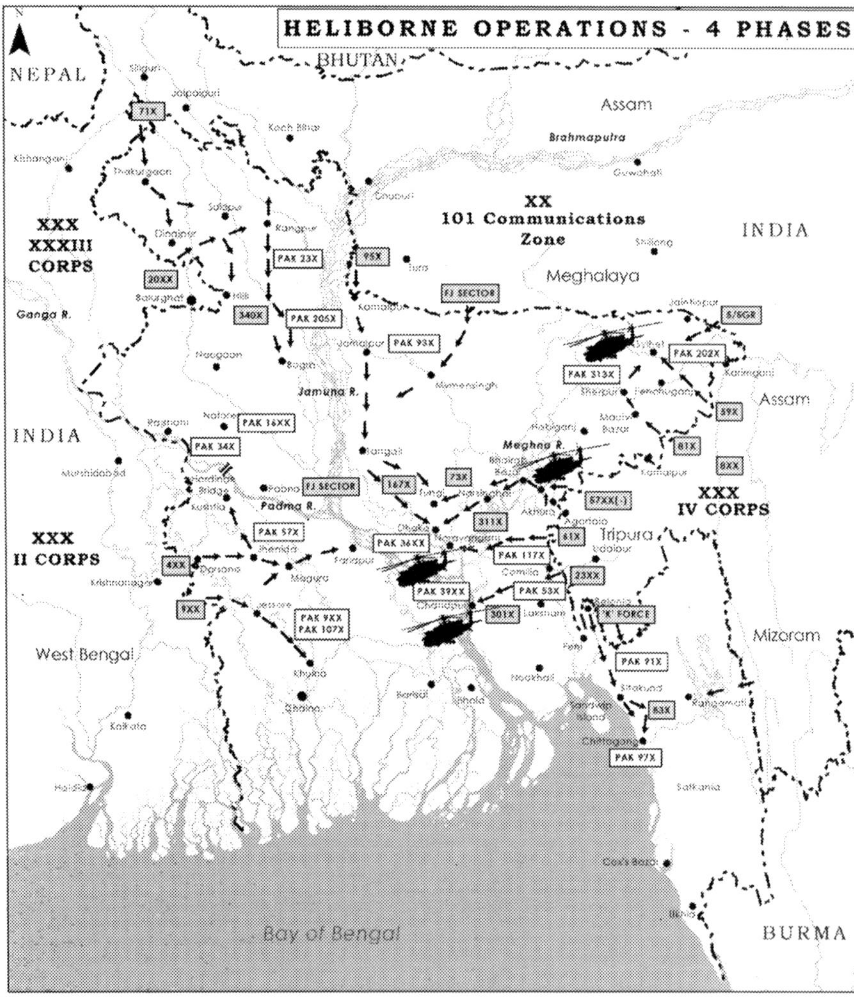

Map 1. Heliborne Operations-4 Phases

An extract from 110 HU War Diary gives further clarity:

> It had been assessed at higher formations that Sylhet town, a district and communication centre, was an important place from the military point of view and its fall would inflict a severe setback to Pakistan Army. Thus, HQ 4 Corps tasked 4/5 Gorkha Rifles of 59 Mountain Brigade to capture Sylhet and inducted Mi-4 helicopters of 110 HU to undertake SHBO missions to accomplish the ground plan. The main task was to heli-lift a battalion (4/5 GR) to Mirpara (outskirts of Sylhet) to secure the railway bridge over river Surma and occupy Sylhet airport/radio station to further operations. The challenges for the Unit helicopters did not end with Sylhet and the Unit was subsequently tasked to undertake extensive SHBO missions for furtherance of corps objectives as the battle progressed from different axes at Raipura, Narsingdi and Baidya Bazar.
>
> 10 Dec 1971—Raipura (SHBO). The 4 Corps Commander decided not to stop on the east bank of the Meghna River but to get across if possible to Dacca. The bridge across River Meghna was blown up and it was left to the helicopters to heli-bridge a sizeable force across the river. The operation to cross River Meghna began shortly before last light on 10 Dec 71 when about 100 troops were ferried to landing pads. By the time the second wave of helicopters arrived it was quite dark but the helicopters landed safely. The movement of troops continued throughout the night and the next day. Though the normal capacity of Mi-4s was to carry 14 troops, the number of troops was increased to 23 men per trip.
>
> 11 Dec 1971—Narsingdi (SHBO). The Unit was given the biggest task of SHBO when eight helicopters of 110 HU were moved to Narsingdi from Brahmanbaria. By 0730 hrs every helicopter had done three sorties each. After refuelling at Agartala the second wave took off at 0900 Hr and carried out three sorties each. Two more details were flown. In all, a total of 834 troops and 58,600 kg of load were airlifted on 11 Dec 71 involving 99 sorties. More sorties could have been carried out but the Army could not cope up with the swiftness with which the SHBO was carried out.
>
> 12 Dec 1971. 35 sorties were carried out at Narsingdi, airlifting 234 troops and 18,520 kg of load. Due to heavy ground fire, there were 30 casualties and one helicopter was sent to Sylhet for evacuation of these casualties. One helicopter met with an accident due to fire in air.
>
> 13 Dec 1971. 282 troops and 14,850 kg of load were airlifted in 30 sorties on 13 Dec 1971. On 14th, 12 helicopters were positioned at Daudkandi early morning where they were employed to move a battalion of troops across the River Meghna to Baidya Bazar, barely seven miles from Narayanganj on the outskirts of Dacca. By evening 810 troops and 22,650

kg of load were airlifted in 79 sorties. From the time that the SHBO operations into Narsinghdi began on 10 Dec evening, till the landing of a battalion at Baidya Bazar, the pilots had already flown for 36 hours continuously, doing 409 sorties.

15 Dec 1971. SHBO missions continued and 1209 troops and 38,100 kg of load were airlifted to Baidya Bazar. One aircraft met with an accident but the morale of the Unit continued to be high. The next day, most helicopters were taken up for maintenance and inspection. One helicopter which was sent to Sylhet for casualty evacuation airlifted 16 casualties while two other helicopters were utilised for Army communication sorties during the day. In the evening five helicopters took part in the Dacca Surrender Ceremony.

SHBO and Casualty Evacuation (Casevac) Missions Flown by 110 HU in December 1971

Table 2: Summary of SHBO by 110 HU

Sl. No.	*Mission*	*Sorties*	*No. of Troops*	*Total Load (kg)*
1.	SHBO Sylhet	66	1,117	22,600
2.	SHBO Raipura	57	650	10,400
3.	SHBO Narsingdi	164	1,350	91,950
4.	SHBO Baidya Bazaar	200	2,019	60,750
5.	Casevac	-	269	-
	Total	**487**	**5,136**	**1,85,700 (185.7 tonnes)**

Source: Extracted from 110 HU War Records.

As is evident from Table 2, 110 HU was an integral part of the 1971 operations east of Dacca. The Mi-4 helicopters undertook extensive Heli-bridging operations in the riverine-dominated terrain of East Pakistan where all the major bridges had been blown up by the enemy. These operations were led ably by the Commanding Officer (CO) of 110 HU, Squadron Leader (Sqn Ldr) C.S. Sandhu. He was later awarded the Vir Chakra for leading these pioneer SHBO missions in war. The enormity of the task undertaken can be judged from the fact that almost 500 sorties were flown in the direct face of enemy fire during these operations.

A Deeper Analysis of Achievements

Gen Sagat, the Unpredictable

In late November 1961, in operations for liberation of Goa, 50 Parachute Brigade, which Sagat was commanding, was tasked to execute a subsidiary thrust from the north. However, his brilliance and out-of-the-box ideas took over soon. Hostilities at Goa began on 17 December 1961, when a unit of Indian troops attacked and occupied the town of Maulinguém in the north-east, killing two Portuguese soldiers. On the morning of 18 December, Sagat moved the brigade into Goa in three columns: 2 Para advanced towards the town of Ponda in central Goa; 1 Para advanced towards Panaji; and the main thrust of the attack—comprising 2 Sikh LI as well as an armoured division—advanced on Tivim.

Although the 50 Para Brigade was charged with merely assisting the main thrust conducted by 17 Infantry Division, its units moved rapidly across minefields, roadblocks and four riverine obstacles to be the first to reach the capital of Panjim on 19 December 1961. The brigade achieved objectives much beyond its initial purview. On entering the capital, Sagat famously ordered his troops to remove their steel helmets and wear the Parachute Regiment's maroon berets.

Again, as a Major General commanding 17 Mountain Division in Sikkim on the Sino-Indian border, he and his division performed in unexpected and brilliant ways during the Nathu La and Cho La clashes, achieving a decisive tactical advantage after defeating the People's Liberation Army (PLA). This included bypassing of higher instructions and use of barbed wire and artillery without permission. However, these were precisely the issues that gave the PLA a bloody nose and something to think about. In his stint as GOC 101 Communication Zone in Shillong, he oversaw the operations in Mizoram, which included SHBO of special troops in IAF Mi-4 helicopters.

It is unfortunate that Gen Sagat did not have the best of relations with either the Army Commander, Lt Gen Aurora, his immediate superior, or with the Army Chief, Gen Sam Manekshaw. In fact, Gen S.K. Sinha, in a foreword to Maj Gen Randhir Sinh's book, compares Sagat's fate to that of Patton for the unfair treatment by his army and government.[11] Dacca was not spelt out as an objective of the Indian operations by Army HQ. Gen S.K. Sinha writes, 'From the very beginning he [Sagat] had set his eyes on Dacca and made preparations for it.'[12]

Every Constraint to Tie Down Sagat

In the pre-1962 Indian Army, where conventional thinking straitjacketed the military thought process, Sagat's approach was so exceptional and 'out-of-the-box' that his boldness and savoir faire were considered more of an aberration.[13] Gen Aurora was an adherent of the direct approach and disliked Sagat's propensity for risk-taking. It is only in the pre-war battles under Sagat, especially after the Battle of Dholai, that the level of casualties convinced Aurora of the value of bypassing fortified positions. These pre-war incursions helped Sagat in not only assessing enemy capabilities but also indoctrinating his primarily counter-insurgency troops. By end November, Sagat had a clear blueprint in his mind, but did not share it with the higher commanders. Closer to the 'Meghna Heli-bridge' dates, he was extremely reticent and non-communicative with Gen Aurora. In fact, in a documented conversation between the two on 7 December, Aurora asserted his 'No Dacca', but to no avail as Sagat launched the biggest operation of the war, the Meghna Air Bridge, on 9 December.[14]

Besides the mental constraints, there were numerous restrictions placed on 4 Corps. First, the troops were mostly 'light' from insurgency action areas. They were highly inadequate in transport, artillery and engineering resources. In a terrain of highly riverine morass, it made campaigning almost impossible. Second, the mandate restricted Sagat to only containing or isolating Comilla, Chittagong, Sylhet, and to secure Agartala. Nothing beyond east bank of Meghna was allowed by Eastern Command's operational instructions. Third, on ceding to his relentless demand for helicopters, 4 Corps was allotted 110 HU with its ageing Mi-4 helicopters. Even then, only a company drop was authorised. Another issue was that barely a few pilots were trained to fly by night. To top that, most troops taking part in SHBO were seeing a helicopter for the first time. Finally, because of the distances, 4 Corps hardly got any air support, and this stepped up only after 11 December when everyone realised that Dacca was within reach.[15] Gnats were moved to Agartala to provide direct support, which they did effectively. In a nutshell, Army HQ and Eastern Command of Indian Army had done all they could to 'fix' Sagat's corps east of Meghna River.

Even before the Sylhet operations from 4 December onwards, close air support was denied to 4 Corps due to other priorities. Air Chief Marshal (ACM) P.C. Lal notes in his book, 'Air attacks against defended positions produced little damage, but they had considerable psychological effect.'[16] The biggest contributor to morale and effective higher guidance were the hundreds of recce sorties by helicopters, tens of landings in forward locations by Sagat himself and his almost daily face-to-face with commanders in thick of action. Many helicopters took enemy hits, including Sagat's own IAF pilot and helicopter. Very importantly, this allowed him to have an accurate situational awareness and grasp windows of opportunities.

The start was the seizure of Sylhet by the gallant 4/5 Gurkhas.

> The first Special Heli-Borne Operation of the Indian Army was not a pre-planned operation. It just popped up, out of nowhere and was executed exceptionally well by a small team of 10 Mi-4 helicopters. The operation

> was a brain child of the legendary Corps Commander Lt. Gen. Sagat Singh who saw a small window of opportunity to tie down enemy forces in Sylhet town of East Pakistan and subsequent capture of the town.[17]

By 14 December, Sagat was successful in moving 73 Brigade, 301 Brigade, 311 Brigade and Shafiullah's 'S' Force across the Meghna, giving 4 Corps two clear short approaches to Dacca. This was the coup de grace, just as the Sylhet feint and debacle had unsettled Niazi's centre of gravity.

If a truly objective review is done chronologically to decipher what really made Dacca fall in December 1971 and create a new nation of Bangladesh, the honours would undoubtedly go to the manoeuvring chaos engineered by Lt Gen Sagat Singh commanding 4 Corps. Unfortunately, just as the Army Chief and Eastern Command GOC of that time brushed this under the carpet because of their dislike for this larger-than-life persona, military historians, barring a very few, have also chosen to do the same.

In the process, the courage, innovation and sheer boldness of helicopter pilots and aircrew of the IAF remains an untold story. As this narrative progresses, there will be little doubt left that it was this teaming of a brilliant but maverick general and IAF's helicopter pilots that unnerved Gen Niazi and upset the Pakistani centre of gravity in the east.

Helicopter Contribution Played Down

ACM Lal's book, *My Years with the IAF*, is the most popular and authentic narration of IAF's contribution in various operations.[18] Yet, the account seems to downplay the achievements of helicopters in them. For example, when writing about the 1962 war, the book just briefly mentions how the fleet was raised, and also gives a cursory account of downing of Sahgal's helicopter by the Chinese. A vast contribution in then North-East Frontier Agency (NEFA) and Ladakh (for example, Galwan resupply) is completely missed out.

Similarly, in the 1965 war write-up, ACM Lal painstakingly documents all fighter and transport aircraft operations, but completely omits the Herculean effort of helicopters in general, and Mi-4s based in Srinagar in particular. The Mi-4s were modified in a record time of a week to the armed role with frontguns and bomb racks in the cargo cabin. Almost 80 sorties of interdicting Razakars were done in operations starting three months before war broke out. This invaluable support finds a worthy mention in a book by Lt Gen Harbaksh Singh (Retd).[19]

While Lal does mention SHBO in 1971 under Gen Sagat, it seems more of an effort to bring out the fact that jointmanship worked because, as a paratrooper, he understood air power capabilities and limitations. It must be remembered that Sagat's track record of dynamism was documented starting from liberation of Goa, Sikkim (1965–67) against the Chinese to the Mizo operations (SHBO). He was not an original paratrooper but was given the command of the para brigade directly. Perhaps ACM Lal's omissions are understandable in light of the fact that he expired before the book could be put together. It was compiled by Mrs Ila Lal, with advice and vetting by senior IAF officers.

Gen Sagat's creativity, high situational awareness and grounded understanding came from his innate qualities of vision and forward thinking, along with ample risk propensity. Even during the SHBO episode, there are ample instances of Sagat bulldozing his way through the maze of IAF rules and regulations and having his way. This was his very nature, focused on goals and thinking many steps ahead of everyone else.

While the Tangail paradrop is claimed as India's biggest and most successful such operation, it must be correctly placed in its contribution to the creation of Bangladesh. It was carried out on 11 December to interdict the access to Dacca from Mymensingh, essentially to isolate the brigade there and stopping reinforcements to Dacca. By this time, Gen Niazi had already been unnerved by Sagat's confounding manoeuvring with heliborne forces at multiple points. Between 9 and 10 December, the Meghna air bridge and river crossings were well accomplished. The damage to the core of Niazi's fortress strategy was done.

More importantly, Tangail had a completely friendly population and was dominated by resistance fighters, which ensured full cooperation and no risks. There was no air or ground opposition. The date of 11th is contextual as the morale of Pakistan forces was at rock bottom. Therefore, when taken in the overall context, the airborne operations were a sideshow in comparison to the SHBO across Meghna River.

Another issue in playing down the contribution of COs and pilots of helicopter units is the IAF's singular focus on the role of Group Captain Chandan Singh, a transport aircraft pilot and station commander in Jorhat. He was deputed to raise the nascent Bangladesh Air Force with Otters, Dakotas and an armed Alouette. He first met Sagat on 3 December, well after CO 110 HU (at Kumbhigram) had planned the Sylhet SHBO with Gen Sagat. In fact, before the formal war, on 29 November, 110 HU had carried out SHBO north of Rangamati to interdict fleeing Mizo National Front cadres. Around the same time, Pakistan Army too had carried out SHBO with its special forces to counter Indian action in Belonia Bulge. Chandan joined the SHBO fray only on 7 December at the execution phase.

Despite being central to the victory, the 'bosses' decided that minimum visibility should be given to helicopter pilots during the surrender ceremony. In the words of Pushp Vaid, flight commander of 110 HU: 'I was told that pilots not needed for flying duties should be left behind. However I ignored the instructions—I reasoned that after risking their lives and flying to their limit, my pilots and flight engineers deserved to see this once-in-a-lifetime surrender ceremony.' Maj Gen Randhir Sinh, talking of the final surrender ceremony at Dacca, claims: 'The young pilots, so much instrumental in creating this history had left only one of their colleagues to guard the helicopters.'[20] Flt Lt Krishnamurthy clutched an outraged Gen Jacob while peering over his left shoulder to witness the signing of the surrender in the iconic photograph. It actually aptly summed up who the real architects of the victory were, and efforts to deny their legacy. The Ministry of Defence's official history of the war covers 'Heli-bridging' in two pages in chapter 14 (pp. 607, 608), but devotes the rest 27 pages to operations by fighter aircraft.[21]

Was Dacca ever an objective? The official history debates this extensively and clearly states a play-safe approach with no formal orders.[22] It is clear that the actions by Gen Sagat Singh caused a major crisis in the mind of Gen Niazi, and the attendant fallout thereafter. In fact, in the closing chapter of the official history of the 1971 war, it is unambiguously stated:

> Sagat Singh in particular stood out as a General any army could be proud of, not only because he had the largest Corps to handle over the longest front but also because he surmounted the stiffest obstacles of the Meghna and Lakhya rivers. A close look at the capture of Dacca, thus makes the exploit shine brighter than ever.[23]

Conclusion

Adapting in the 'Fog of War'

Adaptability in battle has two faces: the ability to sense a change in situation demanding a change in response; and the ability to commit to that requirement. What does complexity leadership entail in terms of fast-changing or asymmetric warfare? The Australian Army replaced the famous orient, observe, decide and act (OODA) loop with an act, sense, decide and adapt (ASDA) loop that deals better with non-linear, complex and unpredictable states. In the ASDA cycle, action is first because in uncertainty, one needs to prod to elicit a requisite response for assessments to be made. Decisions are made based on these assessments, followed by deeper reflection and adaptation. However, the situation prevailing for decisions to be taken will dictate what to apply, that is, OODA, ASDA or something else.[24]

The 1971 war is illustrative. 'Dacca was never an objective even in the final operational instruction by Army HQ to Eastern Command.'[25] However, the famous probes by Mi-4s, ordered by Gen Sagat Singh of 4 Corps, caused chaos and a fateful decision by Gen Niazi to defend Sylhet by two brigades rather than defending Meghna River crossings towards Dacca. It allowed 4 Corps to reach the doorsteps of Dacca days earlier than thought to be possible. Deeper reflection allowed the Indian Army to quickly go for the jugular and reach the doorsteps of Dacca. This example of mental flexibility and agility is not unique; it is ever-present in battlefields with the victors.

Helicopters in general, and Mi-4s in particular, stood out as game changers in the 1971 war. More importantly, it was open minds and the pervasive spirit of jointmanship that really achieved much more than just the additive totals of capabilities of the services. Achieving air superiority over the entire East Pakistan enabled the Indian Army and the IAF to do the unthinkable, namely, help liberate Bangladesh.

NOTES

1. Rajesh Isser, 'Game Changing Helicopter Employment', in Anil Chopra (ed.), *The 1971 Indo-Pak Air War*, New Delhi: KW Publishers Pvt. Ltd, 2021, pp. 165–82.
2. I. Cardozo, 'The Battle for Sylhet', *Scholar Warrior*, Spring 2020, pp. 98–105.
3. R. Isser, 'Asymmetric Competition ahead for Indian Air Power', *Journal of Defence Studies*, Vol. 15, No. 1, January–March 2021, pp. 1–24.
4. R. Isser, *The Purple Legacy: IAF Helicopters in Service of the Nation*, New Delhi: Pentagon Press, 2012, pp. 63–64.
5. J.F.R. Jacob, *Surrender at Dacca: Birth of a Nation*, New Delhi: Manohar, 1997, pp. 129–32.
6. P.C. Lal, *My Years with the IAF*, New Delhi: Lancer, 1986, pp. 207–16.
7. Isser, *The Purple Legacy*, n. 4, pp. 81–83.
8. Debrief of Flt Lt P. Vaid in War Diary, 110 HU, extracted by the author, December 2012.
9. Personal account of Air Cmde C.M. Singhla, Files Air HQ, October 2012.
10. 110 HU War Diary, extracted in December 2012 by author.
11. Randhir Sinh, *A Talent for War: The Military Biography of Lt Gen Sagat Singh*, New Delhi: Vij Books India/United Service Institution of India, 2013. Foreword by Lt Gen S.K. Sinha (Retd).
12. Ibid.
13. Ibid., p. 69.
14. Ibid., p. 161.
15. H. Massand, 'Offensive Air Operations in the Eastern Theatre', in Chopra (ed.), *The 1971 Indo-Pak Air War*, n. 1, p. 101.
16. Lal, *My Years with the IAF*, n. 6, p. 211.

17. Sumit Walia, '1971 War: Battle of Sylhet—The First Special Heli Borne Operation', *Indian Defence Review*, 18 December 2019, available at http://www.indiandefencereview.com/news/1971-war-battle-of-sylhet-the-first-special-heli-borne-operation/, accessed on 5 September 2021.
18. Lal, *My Years with the IAF*, n. 6.
19. Harbaksh Singh, *War Dispatches: The Story of the Indian Army's Western Command*, New Delhi: Lancer International, 1991.
20. Sinh, *A Talent for War: The Military Biography of Lt Gen Sagat Singh*, n. 11, p. 9.
21. Ministry of Defence, *The Official History of the 1971 Indo-Pak War*, pp. 592–618.
22. Ibid., pp. 789–92.
23. Ibid., p. 792.
24. R. Isser, 'Is Indian Airpower Preparing for Tomorrow's War?', *VIF Brief*, August 2019, p. 14, available at www.vifindia.org, accessed on 1 November 2020.
25. Lal, *My Years with the IAF*, n. 6, pp. 207–16.

9

Operational Aspects of the 1971 War in the Maritime Domain

Srikant B. Kesnur, M. Doraibabu and Ashish Kale

The outcome of the elections in Pakistan in December 1970 was a shock to the dominant West Pakistani ruling elite since the Awami League won a clear majority in the federal as well as provincial assemblies, thereby laying legitimate claim to form the government.[1] Since the verdict was not palatable to practically anyone in West Pakistan, a political stalemate led to violent protests in the East, which slid into a civil war. General Tikka Khan, the military governor, himself conceded that 'the West Pakistani troops killed as many as 30,000 people'.[2] Presumably, the real figure was much higher. India was flooded with nearly 10 million refugees.[3] Feeding, accommodating, and caring for this massive influx of refugees was a near impossible task for India.[4] The ensuing months witnessed substantial diplomatic activity wherein India tried canvassing the United Nations and many other nations for political and diplomatic assistance to create conditions for the refugees to go back.[5] However, this was to be of no avail. By end of April 1971, the political decision had been taken, to prepare for military intervention in East Pakistan, by the end of the year, in case a satisfactory political situation had not been found by then. Accordingly, Naval Head Quarters (NHQ) prepared itself for the ensuing war. Operational plans were made and discussed. War-gaming of various scenarios was done iteratively to refine efficacy of plans and liquidate shortcomings. Accordingly, tasks were assigned to the Western and Eastern Naval Commands and forces allocated. The Operational Commanders carried out intensive training and rigorous work-up of units. The maintenance agencies such as Dockyards went into overdrive to bring ships, including the aircraft carrier, INS Vikrant into the best material state possible. Op-logistics also received considerable attention and bases such as Okha were augmented to function as Forward Operating Bases (FOB) for ships. The Navy's success in December 1971 was the outcome of the way in which these preparatory activities eventually synthesized into a gamut of operations which had far-reaching strategic outcomes.[6]

The Western Theatre

A Brief Synopsis of Maritime Operations in the Western Theatre

The Naval leadership's concept of operations was straightforward: take the offensive, attack Karachi, lure the Pakistan fleet to battle and sever the Sea Lines Of Communication (SLOC) between West and East Pakistan. By end November–early December 1971, assessments by the operations staff at NHQ made it evident that hostilities were imminent and the possibility of a pre-emptive attack by Pakistan was very high. On 2 December, the then Chief of Naval Staff (CNS) Admiral SM Nanda issued orders to the ships of the Western Fleet to sail from Bombay Harbour as soon as possible, which proved to be just in the nick of time.

The Western Fleet was deployed with the objective of posing a threat to Karachi. This would consequently result not only in bottling the Pakistan Fleet at Karachi but also causing the Pakistan Navy (PN) to centre their attention on the *IN*'s Western Fleet, thereby allowing the missile boats to execute their pre-planned attacks from the Saurashtra Coast. Three missile boat attacks were initially planned and were codenamed as Operation Trident (night of 4/5 December), Operation Python (initially planned for the night of 6/7 December but later executed on the night of 8/9 December) and Operation Triumph (initially postponed and later cancelled). To mitigate the risk of air attack, the Western Fleet was to remain outside the 250-mile arc from Karachi during the day and make forays inwards at night. This arc represented the seaward radius of operation of the Pakistan Air Force aircraft.[7]

As per the operational plans, the missile boats were to be escorted by frigates, which were equipped with enhanced radars and command and control facilities, to the vicinity of Karachi under the cover of darkness so that the lethal missiles could be launched at the ships in the harbour and on port installations.[8] The withdrawal of the missile boats had to be expeditious as they would be within the coverage of the shore-based radars in Karachi and would therefore be under the risk of retaliatory action after the initial surprise of the attacks was overcome.

The first missile attack, Operation Trident was successfully executed on the night of 4/5 December by the missile boats INS Nipat, INS Nirghat and INS Veer, escorted by the frigates INS Kiltan and INS Katchall. The oil tanks at Keamari were set ablaze and the PN destroyer Khaiber, minesweeper Muhafiz and the Liberian registered commercial ship MV Venus Challenger were sunk. The latter was carrying a critical load of arms and ammunition for the Pakistan Armed Forces.

The second missile boat attack was carried out on the night of 8/9 December by the missile boat INS Vinash, escorted by the frigate Trishul. For the second time, the oil tanks at Keamari were set on fire. The attack caused the Panama registered vessel Gulf Star to sink and damaged the PN's fleet tanker Dacca and the British vessel Harmattan. The damage inflicted was so high that PN promptly recalled all ships into the safety of the inner harbour and even ordered the reduction of their war outfits of ammunition thereby signalling its inability to engage any further with the *IN*.[9]

On 9 December 1971, two anti-submarine frigates INS Khukri and INS Kirpan were deployed on a mission to locate and hunt down the Pakistan Daphne class submarine Hangor, whose presence in the Indian waters was 'threatening Indian shipping'. In this engagement, the PN submarine PNS Hangor torpedoed the Indian frigate INS Khukri which happens to be the only ship we lost in that war.

The *IN* launched its entire available force for Operation Falcon post the sinking of INS Khukri to rescue the survivors and conduct massive anti-submarine operations including the deployment of anti-submarine ships, shore-based surveillance aircraft, Alize and Seaking anti-submarine helicopters to hunt the Pakistan submarine Hangor. For four days, ships reported carrying out attacks on probable submarine detections. A total of 67 survivors were rescued and yet the search for the submarine proved elusive as PNS Hangor evaded detection. Finally, on 13 December, the search operation was called off as the Indian forces were beginning to approach within the range of shore based Pakistan Air Force (PAF).

The third missile boat attack, Operation Triumph, was planned to be undertaken on 10 December. However, since Operations Trident and Python had already neutralised the targets, there remained no great strategic gains to be made by a third attack. Moreover, the hunt for the Pakistan submarine and Search

& Rescue (SAR) operations for the survivors of INS Khukri, as also the loss of the element of surprise after the first two attacks, caused the Flag Officer Commanding-in-Chief (FOC-in-C) West to further postpone the attack and then ultimately cancel it altogether.

The Western Fleet carried out a wide range of operations—multi-dimensional surveillance, SLOC protection, and capture of enemy merchant ships, contraband control, anti-aircraft (AA)/Anti-Submarine (A/S) operations, and providing mutual support to the missile boats, all in order to establish Sea Control in the North Arabian Sea. The Western Fleet achieved the objective of rendering the PN ineffective as they bottled the latter up in Karachi Port.

Lessons from the Missile Boat Attacks

Ingenious Deployment of Missile Boats

The ingenious 'out of the box thinking' and a spirit of taking the offensive to the enemy by attacking Karachi, the primary and most heavily defended port of Pakistan, led to unprecedented success. The missile boats were towed/escorted by bigger ships and released closer to the enemy shore, to overcome their limited endurance.[10] The deployment of these small Soviet-built crafts on the high seas and use of radar-homing missiles which devastated ships and shore targets in Karachi were, undoubtedly, a display of the Navy's ingenuity and innovative spirit at work.[11] Ironically, the Pakistani Navy too had been offered six of the same Osa class missile boats by the Soviets in July 1968 but they declined the offer due to their limited range, endurance, lack of anti-aircraft defence and poor sea keeping due to their size.[12] Given these limitations, the PN perceived them to be suitable only for harbour defence. Resultantly, PN did not anticipate the *IN's* innovative tactics of using the missile boats in an offensive role. Loss of ships and damage to harbour infrastructure resulted in considerable panic in Karachi. Further, neutral merchant ships in Karachi harbour began to seek permission from Government of India for safe passage out of the harbour. In effect, these ships acknowledged the supremacy of the *IN* in the waters around Karachi and the north Arabian Sea.[13]

PN Dependence on PAF

Pakistan's Naval leadership was confident that any surface threat posed by the Indian ships to the West Pakistan coast could be dealt with by their nation's Air Force. This confidence was bolstered by their information that Vikrant had been deployed to the Bay of Bengal. In hindsight, this proved to be a costly assumption as the *IN* missile boats pressed home their attacks with devastating results.[14]

Training and Modifications to Support the Operation

Several modifications and training sessions were resorted to in order to use the missile boats the way they were. The crews of both the towing vessels and the missile boats worked up relentlessly to reduce the time required to connect/disconnect to the briefest possible.[15] A new necklace was designed, and strengthened elbows were fixed on the rear struts with the help of the Naval Dockyard to divide the strain over a larger area.[16] The cumbersome steel-wire-rope (SWR) bridle was replaced with nylon hawsers. This innovation made towing easier to handle, and in the long run, the use of the SWR cables was ceased, and the *IN* adopted nylon hawsers for towing as a standard practice. The missile boats did not have cooking or bathing facilities, which limited sea sorties for the crew to less than ten-hour periods. To overcome this limitation, a small galley was added and the water tank was enlarged to hold 5 tons.[17]

Effect on Enemy Morale

The Indian Naval forces in the West, through the missile boat attacks, had exemplified sound preparation, superior tactics and offensive action.[18] Effective use of the element of surprise led to the enemy being caught completely off guard. The Pakistani Navy which had been convinced that the *IN* would never dare to attack its impenetrable stronghold was left surprised and demoralised.[19]

The Advent of Missile Warfare at Sea

The missile boat attacks on 4 and 8 December 1971 ushered the *IN* into the realm of missile age. Any such paradigm change would not have been possible without meticulous training, confidence, professionalism and their integration into the fleet's tactics.[20] The top leadership was visionary in this regard and communicated effectively between all echelons.

Need for Maritime Domain Awareness (MDA) and Identification-Friend-or-Foe (IFF) Systems

After the attack, the Trident Task Force was to rendezvous Kiltan off the Dwarka Coast, but mistook her to be a Pakistani Naval warship and nearly fired at her. However, this 'blue-on-blue' situation was averted at the last moment. This illustrated the need for having good MDA, seamless information sharing and IFF systems. However, this has to be seen contextually against the technology available at that point of time. The *IN* today has hoisted those lessons and has made MDA one of the key aspects of its operational philosophy. Indeed today, the advancements made in MDA, satellite based communications and C^4I^2SR[21] systems make the *IN* of today more formidable force than what it was in 1971.

Need to have well-defined Task Organisation and Command & Control

The initial plans envisaged INS Trishul to be the accompanying escort to the missile boats in the Trident Task Force. However, this was changed to INS Kadmat leading to the reworking of the procedures and plans. At the last minute Kadmat was replaced by INS Kiltan. INS Kiltan had never worked up or trained with the missile boats. This resulted in some co-ordination problems as the missile boats had planned, exercised and developed confidence with one set of ships but ended up being escorted by another one. It was probably this reason that at the last minute, Cdr BB Yadav, the Squadron Commander of Missile Boats Squadron (K 25), decided to embark INS Nipat to provide direct leadership and cohesion to his force. These events highlight the need to have task organisation structures laid out well in advance by the leadership so that training and plans can be aligned tightly.

Before INS Nipat and INS Veer sailed from Bombay, a briefing was held in the Maritime Operations Room (MOR), where the Missile Boat Commanding Officers (COs) and K-25 were briefed that INS Kiltan and INS Katchal would accompany the missile boats and since Commander (later Commodore) Gopal Rao, CO INS Kiltan, was senior to K-25, he would be the Officer in Tactical Command (OTC) of the Force till the group arrived 75 miles from Karachi. Thereafter, the escort force (Kiltan and Katchal) would fall back, and the missile boats would proceed under the Tactical Command of K-25. However, on the evening of 4 December 1971, when the Trident Force was on its way to Karachi, Headquarters Western Naval Command (HQWNC) sent a signal informing that Escorts were to remain in company of the missile boats throughout. Though the signal was silent on who would assume the Tactical Control, INS Kiltan assumed that since she was the senior-most ship in company, she would retain Tactical Command. However, K-25 and the missile boats were clear that having arrived 75 miles of Karachi, K-25 was in Tactical Command, irrespective of the fact that INS Kiltan was in company. This dichotomy manifested itself when immediately after the missile attack on ships, the missile boats reversed course and withdrew at high speed while Kiltan continued on a northerly heading. K-25 claimed he decided to withdraw taking into account the likely confusion between friendlies due to the dispersal of own forces and the possible development of air and surface threat.[22] However, CO Kiltan's stand was that K 25 was not authorised to order withdrawal. This was his prerogative as the OTC.[23] Vice Admiral Kohli, the then C-in-C WNC, was of the opinion that a serious command and control problem had engulfed the Trident force which could have led to serious difficulties and that, it was just as well that the attack was broken off by K-25.[24] This brings out the need to have a clear understanding of command and control by all concerned at any point in time. Any changes made to the orders also need to be explicit in their communication.

Communication Gaps and Differences of Opinion

There were differences of opinion between the Chief of Naval Staff (CNS) and Flag Officer Commanding-in-Chief (FOCINC) West regarding the missile boat attacks. There were also differences of opinion between the FOCINC West and the Fleet Commander regarding the employment of fleet ships. There were certain differences between CO Kiltan and K-25 regarding command and control as brought out above. Whether these differences may have jeopardised any mission is hard to evaluate. However, it is necessary not to 'over read' them. Firstly, in any campaign of such nature spread over a large canvas such differences are natural and, arguably, healthy since they contribute to overall development of plans. Secondly, whatever the differences (and they are matter of public record) all personnel concerned closed ranks once plans were finalised and war was fought. The takeaway from these episodes is to recognise the fact that such things may happen in future and we must guard against the possibility of differences of opinion, necessary as they may be, diluting the combat effort.

Action Information Organisation (AIO) and Exchange of Information

During Op Trident, after firing the initial missiles on the contacts detected on radar, it was expected that when there were no contacts on radar, all the ships of the Task Group should have continued to close Karachi and, from the predetermined point promulgated by INS Kiltan, each missile boat should have fired one more missile at Karachi thereby inflicting maximum damage on the adversary installations. However, the missile boats turned back mistaking the anti-aircraft tracer rounds fired from Karachi, to be enemy aircraft thereby possibly missing out on an opportunity to inflict more extensive damage.[25] This, however, has to be balanced by the fact that the missile boats had limited AIO facilities and could not have an adequate picture to be built up for the Command.[26] The facilities for such command and control on the Petyas (the escorting ships) were also limited. But apparently, the existing facilities were not used to best advantage.[27] It may be possible to argue, in hindsight, that they could have maintained a better surface plot.[28] Coordination of AIO between the escort ships and the missile boats could have possibly been handled better. It seems from the differing accounts given by Commodore Vijay Jerath in his book, *25 Missile Boat Squadron* and by Commodore KP Gopal Rao in his article, 'Distortion of Indian Naval History—1971 Period (*Indian Defence Review*, July 1990)' that either an accurate surface plot was not maintained or that information was not passed or not received adequately. Either way, this implied that knowledge of the friendlies and the enemies in the area was not completely available to the units, and therefore, possibly the missile boats after achieving the damage turned back, leaving us open to the question, "Could they have inflicted greater damage if they had better situational awareness?".

Communication

Anomalous Propagation (ANAPROP) conditions which are prevalent in the Arabian Sea during certain months often result in communication interception over very long ranges. To overcome this, ships communicated on Very High Frequency (VHF), made use of communication code in Russian and, otherwise, tried to communicate within loud hailer range, thereby denying Pakistanis the valuable chance to decipher the messages in time. Concurrently, the Pakistani Naval Code was broken by our signal intelligence teams which gave us a big advantage. However, there were one or two occasions when the ships out of Very/Ultra High Frequency (V/UHF) range did not switch over to secondary communication circuits on H/F and this resulted in loss of communication. In some cases, the 'fog of war' increased by the fact that there were different IFF codes between ships which was not checked prior to the operation.[29] Over the years, these lessons have been analysed by the *IN* and substantial emphasis were laid on development of seamless communication policies and facilities.

Flexibility of Plans

Operation Python was launched further seaward than Trident and took place in more unfavourable sea conditions causing the operation to be delayed to the night of 8/9 December. After the first missile attacks on Karachi, the PN was keeping the approaches to Karachi from Saurashtra under close surveillance, and it would not have been possible for the missile boats to approach Karachi from that direction undetected. Moreover, NHQ had intercepted Pakistani Navy's signals of the Pakistani Air Force strafing its own Frigate PNS Zulfiqar, in a clear case of mistaken identity. Consequently, concern was raised in the mind of the CNS, Admiral SM Nanda that it would not be prudent to expose the Python task force to such a high probability of attack by an alerted enemy.[30] Therefore, Flag Officer Commanding Western Fleet (FOCWF) not only decided to launch the second missile attack from west-southwest but also altered the Fleet's course westward.[31] Thus, the second missile attack also went in undetected.

Fleet Action off Makran Coast

At the same time that the Trishul group had been detached to attack Karachi, FOCWF had detached the Mysore group to bombard Jiwani Port with the aim of distracting PN Ships away from Python Task Force. On the evening of 8 December, 75 miles south of Jiwani, the Mysore group, encountered, boarded and apprehended Pakistani merchant ship Madhumati registered in Karachi but masquerading as a neutral. FOCWF assessed that the aim of creating a distraction was achieved and decided not to waste ammunition bombarding worthless targets on the Makran coast. To some, this produced the impression that the Fleet had not done much in terms of offensive action or having a 'glory moment' of its own. However, as brought out earlier, the Fleet had carried out many operations and gained sea control in the north Arabian Sea apart from enabling Missile Boat attacks. There were no worthwhile targets at sea. On the other hand, many Senior Officer including Admiral Nanda felt that the Fleet could have bombarded Jiwani, Gwadar, or Pasni on Makran Coast with the objective of raising own morale and demoralising the enemy.[32] This is an issue that has adherents to both points of view and can be discussed by students of the subject in future.

A Brief Synopsis of The Sinking of INS Khukri

The presence of a Daphne Class Submarine off the Gujarat Coast, south of Diu, was intercepted by the Navy's communication intelligence stations and having assessed that it posed a potential threat, the Western Naval Command took the decision of conducting anti-submarine operations. Despite being aware that the latest Daphne class submarine was far more advanced than the *IN's* submarines and surface ships, urgent operational orders were drafted in consultation with Captain M.N. Mulla, the Senior Officer (F 14) of the 14th Frigate Squadron (14 FS). Since the 14 FS comprising INS Khukri (F-14), and INS Kirpan (INS Kuthar was not available as explained later), as well as few Seakings, were the only force available for the mission, it was decided to use them as 'Hunter Killers' and the ships set sail on 8 December for the submarine's last known position. As per the plan, the Seaking helicopters were asked to operate closer to Bombay while the Frigates were to operate closer to Diu in the northern sector.

There were two ships against a submarine. Conditions at sea favour a submarine in warm waters. Moreover, the ships had sensor equipment with far lesser capabilities as compared to the submarine. On 9 December, PNS Hangor fired a torpedo at Khukri and was able to sink it along with 18 Officers including the Commanding Officer Captain M.N. Mulla and 176 sailors. It even fired two torpedoes at Kirpan that missed either due to the torpedo misfiring or due to Kirpan's evasive action. Realising that the ship was torpedoed, Captain Mulla stayed on the bridge assisting others in the limited time span he had as most of the ship's crew was trapped in the lower decks. Captain Mulla preferred to go down with the men and the ship following the old maritime tradition. The heroic act of Captain Mulla and his valiant crew still serves as an exemplary act of unyielding spirit and indomitable courage. At that moment when INS Khukri was torpedoed, INS Kirpan realised she too was a target and took evasive measures. She fired Anti-Submarine (A/S) mortars at the torpedo bearing, but when her mortars became inoperative, she cleared the area at full speed as per the Standard Operating Procedure (SOP). She returned to the location the next morning after rendezvousing with INS Katchall to continue the hunt as well as assist Search and Rescue (SAR) operations.

The loss of Khukri posed several other questions of which the following stand out:

(a) How much did the absence of Kuthar affect the overall combat capacity and whether this brings to light sub optimal maintenance by ship's crew/ dockyard staff.

(b) Should the Seakings have operated directly under the OTC/ SAC at sea than the shore authorities?

(c) Should *IN* have been experimenting with a new sonar during war especially considering that the sonar under trial required slower speeds for optimal performance whereas normal anti-submarine tactics required much higher speeds?

(d) Operationally, the question most discussed is whether it would have been more prudent to sidestep the submarine totally and let it be. Its position did not pose a threat to Western Fleet which was much to the West and the deduction of the submarine being a 'threat to Indian shipping' seems far-fetched. Even the missile boats operating there and, unlikely targets by themselves, could have been directed to use high speeds and operate close to Coast or further west to sidestep the Hangor.

(e) If it was indeed a threat should the weight of attack have been more and should more ships and air-borne anti-submarine warfare (ASW) efforts been directed to this effort as was done after the attack.

Lessons from the Sinking of INS Khukri

Improved Focus on All Things ASW

The sinking of INS Khukri was a signal for the *IN* to improve its ASW capabilities. Long-range sonars and longer range weapons had to be inducted if ships were to have a fighting chance against modern submarines and their homing torpedoes. The incident resulted in the navy's emphasis, in post war years, on development of indigenous sonars, improvement of ASW drills, induction of potent Maritime Reconnaissance (MR) ASW aircraft, development of better torpedo evasion techniques, compliance to life jacket and life raft release inspections and drills and better damage control arrangements especially in combat. ASW tactics were revised to cater for situational decision making, and of putting air ASW assets under the control of the Scene-of-Action Commander (SAC). Systematic efforts began to keep up with the rapid advances taking place in submarine and ASW, sonars, anti-submarine weapons, torpedo homing mechanisms and torpedo decoys and integrate all this into an effective anti-submarine doctrine. Post 1971, major tactical exercises and debriefs were organised under NHQ's direct supervision to emphasise these concerns. These helped to gradually standardise ASW doctrines and enhance operator efficiency.[33]

Development of Indigenous Tactical Publications

One consequence of the legacy of British training in initial years was the commonality of tactical publication being used by both navies. Hence, the Pakistani submarine commander knew exactly which search plan was being carried out. Even if it is argued that the course of events would not have been any different, if we had put together and used our own search plans, it would have made the submarine commander's task less easy.[34] Consequently, the post war years saw greater focus on *IN* devising indigenously developed tactical publications and doctrines.

The Eastern Theatre

A Brief Synopsis of Operations in the Eastern Theatre

The Eastern Fleet carried out contraband control, severed the SLOCs between East and West Pakistan, thereby preventing reinforcements/supplies to Pakistan forces in the East or their potential escape. INS Vikrant and her squadrons of aircraft—Seahawks and Alizes—carrying out sustained operations, inflicted heavy damage, on the enemy installations and airfields at Cox's Bazaar and Chittagong and at many other places and also on enemy shipping. The *IN* achieved the important feat, right at the outset of war, of luring and sinking the Pakistan submarine PNS Ghazi off Visakhapatnam.

A riverine operation was mounted by 'Force Alpha', a maritime task force comprising two gunboats Padma and Palash, loaned from the West Bengal government, Chitrangada, a watercraft of the Border Security Force (BSF) and INS Panvel, a seaward defence boat, as the command ship. The Force undertook a maritime attack from the riverine route on the port complex of Chalna and Mongla, thereby achieving an offensive on the adversary from the sea, and further affected the enemy's war waging potential which was being sustained through shipping at these crucial river harbours.

By 9 December, a need was felt for amphibious landing operations to be conducted at Cox's Bazaar. For this purpose, two Landing Ship Tank (LSTs), INS Gharial and INS Guldar along with a merchant vessel Vishwa Vijay were used. The operation was to be carried out using an infantry battalion 1/3 Gurkha, two companies of 11 Bihar and 881 Light Battery with Army Service Corps (ASC) and medical platoons. An amphibious landing was attempted on 15 December at the Reju Creek, South of Cox's Bazaar.[35] However, due to the difficulties faced in landing the troops only one platoon could be landed and later the amphibious landing of troops was moved to Cox's Bazaar. This issue has been discussed in more detail later in this paper.

By 10 December, the Navy controlled all the approaches to Bangladesh ports. East Pakistan harbours and installations at Chittagong, Chalna, Khulna, Mongla, and Cox's Bazaar had been subjected to round-the-clock attention from the air. The PN merchant craft that had assembled at Narayanganj and Barisal which could have been used for troop transportation had been sunk or disabled. Mongla and Chalna had already been evacuated.[36] Ultimately, Pakistan forces in East Pakistan surrendered on 16 December 1971.

Lessons from Operations in the Eastern Theatre

Deception and Destruction of Ghazi

Being well aware that Pakistan would deploy its submarine PNS Ghazi to sink the aircraft carrier, the Eastern Naval Command, before the war broke out, was successful in convincing the Pakistanis that INS Vikrant was in Visakhapatnam whereas, in fact, she was in the Andamans. Large quantities of rations were ordered from the local contractors to indicate the presence of the carrier in and around Visakhapatnam.[37] INS Rajput was used as a decoy to try and deceive the enemy into believing that she was the Vikrant and was sailed about 160 miles off Visakhapatnam. She was directed to generate high volume of dummy signal traffic to masquerade as a big unit. As another deception measure, an intentional breach of security was done by making an unclassified signal—a private telegram from one of Vikrant's sailors, asking about the welfare of his mother who was seriously ill.[38] Consequently, the PN, based on the intelligence received, directed PNS Ghazi to occupy Zone Victor (codename for Visakhapatnam) to lie in wait for Vikrant. This was the position where it was finally sunk on the night of 3rd/4th of December 1971. In a communication recovered from the wreck, Commodore Submarines in Karachi sent a signal to PNS Ghazi on 25 November informing that "Intelligence indicates Carrier in Port" and that she should proceed to Visakhapatnam with all dispatch. Hence, *IN*'s efforts of deception succeeded, and the Fleet was able to operate with greater freedom with the Ghazi now eliminated.

Importance of War Watching Organisation

In the weeks before the war, special efforts were taken to contact various fishing communities in and around Visakhapatnam and motivate them to act as visual lookouts over the vast expanse of waters for anything out of the ordinary, e.g., a periscope or a snort, that they may see when out fishing. They were briefed exactly on what to do with any information gathered. Integrating the vast network of fishermen to act as the eyes and ears of the Navy was a precursor of the War Watching Organisation that has today become well entrenched in Naval plans. Today, it has come a long way and the Navy constantly maintains a close liaison with coastal and fishing communities under the National Committee for Strengthening Maritime and Coastal Security (NCSMCS) construct.[39]

Offensive Use of Naval Air Power

During the 1965 war, INS Vikrant was kept inside Bombay harbour and did not go out to sea. In 1971, if a situation like that of 1965 war repeated itself, INS Vikrant would have been considered to be a 'White Elephant' and hence it was imperative for INS Vikrant to be deployed. Despite the cracks and leaks in INS Vikrant's boilers and the risks that were encountered in deploying it, the CNS was resolute in his decision to use the carrier in an offensive role under all circumstances.[40] The Dockyard and the ship's crew used imaginative and innovative means to make repairs and modifications and the *IN* was able to harness its combat potential despite some limitations.[41] When the balloon went up on 4 December, a high volume of air strikes were carried out by Vikrant's Alizes and Seahawks on Chittagong, Cox's Bazaar, Mongla, Chalna and Khulna. This was achieved despite Vikrant's speed limitations and marginal wind conditions which placed aircraft at risk during launch and recovery.

The cumulative effect was that in addition to substantial destruction or damage of several port cities of East Pakistan, about 11 merchant ships (totalling 57 thousand tons) and three PN Ships Jessore, Comilla and Sylhet were destroyed.[42] Without INS Vikrant, the limited number of ships that constituted the Eastern Fleet could not have coped with the many merchant ships in the area.[43] Thus, Vikrant's assistance in contraband control was invaluable and its effective implementation helped the *IN* to establish a strangle-hold on East Pakistan's SLOCs.

Success of Force Alpha

With the aim of mounting a sneak attack on Chalna and Mongla using the riverine route, a small task group called Force Alpha (Force A) was created with elements of the *IN* personnel, Mukti Bahini and erstwhile Bengali East Pakistan Navy personnel who had defected. In an example of good jointmanship, the task force operated directly under the orders of the Eastern Command (Army) at Fort William and not the Eastern Naval Command.[44] This was possibly the *IN's* first and only riverine operation. Force Alpha's story is of a disparate group assembled from limited resources scoring big in the war. They braved navigational and other challenges to penetrate deep into enemy heartland. They risked capture with attendant consequences. Be it the interception of Pakistani merchant ships or the destruction at Khulna, the naval task force proved its mettle due to good leadership.[45]

Mechanisms for Prevention of 'Blue on Blue' Incidents

On the morning of 10 December, while undertaking a raid through the Pussur river, the ships of Force Alpha were engaged by Gnat fighter jets of the Indian Air Force (IAF). Analysis of this 'Blue-on-Blue' incident reveals that it was precipitated by the IAF fighters' lack of identification of the yellow flags as was pre-arranged, as well as the fact that Force Alpha was not supposed to go to Khulna—it was an impromptu and brave decision taken when it was found that the Pakistani troops had withdrawn from Mongla. Even if Commander MNR Samant, the Senior Officer of the Force, had informed his headquarters of his decision, it is doubtful whether the information would have reached the Gnats in the few hours that it took Force Alpha to go up the river from Mongla to Khulna.[46] Such incidents can be prevented only by having more jointness whereby real-time information sharing of ongoing operation in a theatre is known to all elements of the three services. Further, at the tactical level, having IFF systems on maximum or all units is necessary. However, these are easier said than done as they need to balance requirements of security and compromise of plans.

Lessons from the Amphibious Landing

The Eastern Army's rapid advance between 4 and 8 December led to an assessment that Pakistani troops might attempt to escape southward into Burma past Cox's Bazaar. To prevent this from happening, it was decided, albeit at a very short notice, to mount an amphibious landing of a battalion of troops at Cox's Bazaar at dawn of 12 December. However, assessing that the landing might face opposition at Cox's Bazaar, the landing was ultimately carried out on 15 December on a beach further south near the town of Ukhia. This landing operation is now regarded as not having achieved its objectives. Army troops earmarked had not trained in amphibious operations and the surge in numbers did not, possibly, cater for sufficient life belts, scramble nets or suitable landing craft and most importantly, the troops from the 1/3 Gurkhas had never been to sea. The *IN* had limited amphibious assets—two LSTs along with a requisitioned coal carrier, Vishwa Vijay—and, therefore, if a landing were to be planned, it required more careful planning and extensive rehearsals. However, this could not happen as there was no clear joint operational scheme existing at that time and, admittedly, because the time was short. It, therefore, comes across as an *ad hoc* decision. V. Adm Hiranandani attributes this to the 'lack of detailed planning'.[47] These constraints were exacerbated by the fact that the planners neither had adequate intelligence of the area, nor proper charts, nor survey information of feasible beaches, all of which are understandable retrospectively. In view of these circumstances, the initial plan was to beach the landing craft and refloat them at high tide whereby the troops would land 'dry shod'. However, as this entailed risks to the ships, the plans had to be changed at short notice thereby resulting in the unfortunate outcome.[48] However, what must not be forgotten in this is that 600 troops were landed, that it sent the tottering East Pakistan further signal of our resolve and it sealed off escape routes for the fleeing West Pakistan personnel.

There were many lessons to be learnt. Amphibious operations are, arguably, the most complex joint operations in the collective repertoire of armed forces. They mandate formalising clear Command and Control structures, extensive joint training and elaborate procedures. There is little room for error as command errors or incompatibilities are often at the origin of failures. This was seen in the landings on 15 December 1971 when the landing ships did not reach the designated beach on time as tidal conditions had changed. Three Gorkha soldiers drowned and Gharial almost broached. For the *IN* which, since 1971, has built up formidable amphibious capabilities, the 'unsuccessful or partially successful' landings of the war offer several lessons about jointness in planning, execution, training, doctrine development and logistics. This extends to the other two services as well and several efforts have been made in this regard over the past decade to bridge the gaps.

A Brief Synopsis of the Enterprise Incident

By 10 December 1971, the Pakistani offensive in the West had ground to a halt. The Pakistan Army in the East had made its first tentative move to obtain a ceasefire. On the same day, President Nixon of USA ordered the creation of Task Group (TG) 74, consisting of the nuclear propelled aircraft carrier *Enterprise*, an amphibious assault ship *Tripoli*, three guided missile escorts, four destroyers, supply ship and a nuclear attack submarine, and sent it steaming from the Gulf of Tonkin, towards Bay of Bengal. Whether this was a desire to help an ally in Pakistan or prevent its further 'dismemberment' or perceived Indian threat to West Pakistan is not for this paper to analyse. Nor does this paper seek to discuss the many back channel negotiations that may have taken place in Embassies and Capitals of the countries concerned. Meanwhile, the USSR responded by sending a group of warships northwards from the Soviet Indian Ocean fleet.

In India, the reactions to the TG 74 deployment ranged from some public consternation or perplexity regarding American motives; however, it was met with poise at the highest political level aided by clear understanding by the Navy at operational level. In Delhi, PM Indira Gandhi was briefed by Naval Intelligence on the gamut of operations TG 74 was capable at sea. The collective judgement of the situation was that USA was unlikely to get involved in the war. Consequently, the Indian government displayed an unfazed attitude to the TG steaming towards the Bay of Bengal.[49]

In the meanwhile, the US Navy's Chief of Naval Operations, Adm Zumwalt halted the TG at Singapore for two days since his advice had not been taken while the orders had been given by the civilian administration. Then, on 12 December, they were ordered to proceed to the Bay of Bengal through the Malacca Strait in broad daylight so as to be as conspicuous as possible. The original orders for the TG were to deploy to a position off East Pakistan. But Adm Zumwalt felt that this would put them in harm's way and he convinced the powers to change their deployment area to a position that was South-East of Sri Lanka. By 15 December, the day Pakistan forces in East Pakistan surrendered, TG 74 was in this station, thousands of kilometres away from the combat zone.

Lessons from the Enterprise Incident

The reconstruction of events yield interesting insights of how, in sensitive situations, naval deployments can convey signals of intent and how these signals are interpreted at different levels, nationally and internationally.[50] Although the naval leadership's immediate reaction was of incredulity and concern, they quickly went about assessing the development and determined its responses to various possible events that may or may not unfold. Indian Naval leadership assessed that the Task Force 74's primary intention was to frighten the Indian Forces into withdrawing their forces from the operational area and let the PN ships break out.[51] Admiral Krishnan, FOCINC East, decided that it must be ensured that Chittagong airport, which had already been bombed and rendered useless to the Pakistanis, must remain in that condition. Also, the five merchant ships that had been camouflaged and concealed by the enemy to be used for evacuation of troops were located after a thorough aerial search and destroyed. That way, with the merchant ships gone, even if the TG 74 was to provide an impregnable air umbrella, the evacuation of Pakistan's trapped army would not be possible.[52] Hence, effective operational assessment by the naval leadership helped convert an unacceptable situation to a manageable one.

Commendably, the *IN* leadership considered all the important variables when deciding on moves to counter the presence of USS Enterprise and come up with viable counter strategies. Having studied the possibilities by which the entry of the Seventh Fleet in the scene of action could pose a threat to *IN*'s smaller Carrier Battle Group (CBG) around INS Vikrant, they also drew a plan which would render swift and maximum damage on the enemy installations before the arrival of the Seventh Fleet, thereby making it difficult for the latter to make any significant contributions to the success of their aims.[53] At the strategic level, it had been correctly assessed that the US ultimately would not risk getting drawn into a war in which it had no real purchase.

Subsequent recollections of some of the naval personnel involved in the war did indicate their thought process. They concluded that the US Navy presence showing was more in nature of strategic signalling to coerce India and be involved when their political leadership thought opportune. While USSR with their own naval forces provided deterrence to such scenarios, the *IN* exhibited imperturbability at the apex level (the oft quoted statement of Adm SM Nanda that he had directed his forces to invite the US Navy Captains for a drink on board) while at the operational level plans were mooted to interdict the Seventh Fleet by deploying ships (INS Beas) and a submarine, and if it came to crunch the Vikrant with her aircraft. While it would have been a hugely asymmetrical force, it would have sent a signal of Indian resolve.[54]

In retrospect, the whole incident turned out to be a futile gesture but provided a lesson to India in coercive realpolitik. To the political elite, it reinforced the case for having a navy with strong sea-denial capability to insulate the nation against foreign interference.[55] After the war, the USS Enterprise incident awakened awareness at the higher decision-making levels in India of the finesse with which the naval forces could facilitate diplomacy. This awareness combined with the public appreciation of the Navy's other achievements in the 1971 war, helped to reinforce naval proposals for a stronger Navy.[56]

Miscellaneous Lessons and Takeaways

Submarine Operations

Strategic Considerations Behind Submarine Operations

The political restrictions imposed in Rules of Engagement (ROEs) for submarines requiring 'positive identification' (i.e., visual identification by periscope) prior to targeting, affected their attack capability especially in SLOC interdiction. The PN also had similar restrictions. Consequently, *IN* submarines drew no blood, but a PN submarine sank INS Khukri off the Indian coast in a well-executed tactical action. The *IN*'s ASW weakness was apparent. The ROEs have to be seen in the context of the Law of Armed Conflict and neither side perhaps wanted to precipitate post-hostilities legal issues especially if neutral ships of other countries were involved. Given a choice, perhaps a better line of action would have been to have declared 'War Zones' and sink any ship transiting through those, after a suitable warning period. Only the submarines could have achieved this with impunity in enemy waters.[57] However, it is interesting that no such restrictions were imposed on surface units and during the two missile boat attacks off Karachi, three merchant ships were sunk or disabled. The Venus Challenger and the British-owned merchant vessel Harmattan were sunk and the SS Gulf Star suffered heavy damage. If the *IN*'s missile boats could attack merchant shipping, then the Indian submarines too could have been given some relaxations to carry out the missions. But by absolutely restricting them, they were rendered completely ineffective.[58] The explanation perhaps lies in the fact that the Laws of Armed Conflict at Sea prohibited targeting of neutrals by submarines, and it was a strategic consideration of not dragging other nations into the war or widening the scope of conflict that made Admiral Nanda prescribe restrictive submarine ROEs.

Effect of Submarine Deployment

Even though the Submarine arm of the Navy was in its infancy and its deployment was done with some hesitation, the work done by them was commendable as it acted as deterrence by limiting the area of adversaries' shipping. During the war, the presence of the Indian submarine INS Karanj along the enemy coast forced the enemy to confine their shipping to a narrow area and operate only during the dark hours thereby effectively imposing heavy navigational restrictions on them. Consequently, the adversary not only had to step up their aerial reconnaissance but was also constrained to bottle up its warships in havens along the coast.[59]

Viewed from submariner's perspective though, the ROEs were considered restrictive. While INS Kursura and INS Karanj were deployed off West Pakistan, INS Khanderi was deployed in the East. The recollections of Cmde KS Subramanian, CO INS Virbahu and RAdm Arun Auditto, CO INS Kursura[60] bring out their 'frustration' at not being able to attack shipping while operating freely in proximity of enemy territory.

New Hardware Inductions

The procurement and induction of some contemporary naval hardware in the years preceding the war also played a pivotal role. The *IN* had only some months earlier acquired eight missile boats of the Osa class and their crews, freshly trained in the USSR, were highly skilled and motivated. Further, the Navy also commissioned five Petya Class anti-submarine vessels, four submarines of Kalvari Class, INS Amba the submarine depot ship and smaller Seaward Defence Boat Class of vessels in the period. Indian Naval pilots were also highly trained and those who were away from flying duties were reinstated onboard the Vikrant. They flew together as a team irrespective of rank or seniority, and the Seahawks and Alizes were airworthy and operational, which together made Vikrant a formidable platform even though she was aging and had only three boilers out of four operational. The *IN* had also recently inducted the formidable Seaking helicopters from the UK, colloquially called 'Flying Frigates' because of their advanced capabilities. However, they were flown to Bombay post-haste just when the war broke out and their crews lacked tactical weapon training since their weapon fits were still being inducted.[61]

This factor contributed to success in the war and owes much to the efforts of Adm AK Chatterji, the CNS preceding Adm Nanda. As seen from the loss of Khukri and success of other platforms, induction of contemporary systems and capabilities to counter those of the potential adversaries is an ongoing and critical necessity for the Navy and the same has been enshrined in the Indian Maritime Doctrine (INBR-8).

Effect of Guerre de Course

The economic dependence of Pakistan on imports of raw material, fuel, food and military supplies by sea made its ports irresistible targets. The *IN* therefore decided to choke the jugular by effectively policing the Pakistani trade routes even as they had blockaded the port of Karachi and enforced contraband control. During the operations, several merchant ships and dhows were intercepted, boarded and seized.[62] Consequent sinking of merchant shipping off Karachi, and the resultant stoppage of all shipping traffic to and from West Pakistan, highlighted the magnitude of effect that *guerre de course* (trade warfare) can have on a strategic level.

Investment in Signals Intelligence (SIGINT)

Radio interceptions by SIGINT units paid huge dividends. During the period preparatory to the war, first fledgling steps towards joint planning were taken, not only amongst the three services but also with the paramilitary forces and the essential services. Lieutenant General JFR Jacob, Chief of Staff of Headquarters Eastern Command, insisted on Eastern Command having its own signal intercept unit, as he felt it would be futile waiting for information from Delhi.[63] This unit was not only able to intercept Pakistani communications between its western and eastern wings but also break the Pakistani Naval Code.[64] Therefore, our Headquarters were able to know in advance much of what the Pakistani Navy was planning. SIGINT conveyed to the *IN,* both in Delhi as well as in Visakhapatnam, that the submarine PNS Ghazi had entered the Bay of Bengal. Many other such important signals regarding Naval and merchant vessel traffic were shared with all Service Headquarters. This helped the *IN* to analyse the information and decide on the next course of action with a smaller Observe–Orient–Decide–Act (OODA)[65] loop than the adversary.[66] This was augmented by the tactics adopted by the *IN*'s Signal Branch, of creating huge dummy traffic to mislead the listening Pakistani intelligence posts and to cover the actual deployment of our forces. This helped confuse the Pakistani Naval Forces and thereby the *IN* succeeded in carrying out the systematically planned attacks.[67] The importance of Signal Intelligence is as relevant today as it was in 1971.

A Case for Indigenous Ship Building and Maintenance-Repair-and-Overhaul (MRO) Facilities

The war also brought into focus, the sub-optimal material state of some of our ships. For instance, within 72 hours of sailing on 2 December, INS Kuthar had a major blow-up in the engine room and some personnel were injured. She had to be taken in tow by INS Kirpan to return to Bombay and escorted by INS Khukri. In effect it meant that the problem of one ship resulted in three ships being removed from the chessboard. INS Vijeta, one of the two missile boats attached with the Fleet for Op Python, also suffered a breakdown on the day after sailing from Bombay and had to be towed back by INS Sagardeep. Similarly, due to a last-minute defect INS Talwar had to drop out of the Karachi strike group during Op Python. In essence, 50 per cent of the combat capability of the force was denuded. Any material defect in war does not just affect the ship but has other repercussions as well, as it affects the entire force. Throughout the period the ships were at sea, there were machinery breakdowns which intermittently reduced the speed of the Force and enhanced vulnerability for that duration. The technical crews of the ship responded to the challenges, repairs were carried out and ships were able to get back. One reason for the material state of the ships was that many of these ships were 'hand-me-downs' or bought second-hand from the British and were old. Most of their maintenance was done through British agencies. The Naval Dockyard and the Base Repair Organizations in the ports of Mumbai, Goa, Kochi and Chennai had to work hard to keep the ships in fighting trim.

This conflict was also a lesson for our dockyards and maintenance facilities, to remain abreast of best maintenance practices and technologies to ensure peak availability of units during war. This restates the need for self-reliance in ship-building and dockyards to ensure timely maintenance and quality refits of the ships and submarines.[68] To be fair to the Naval Dockyards incorporation of lot of new equipment meant that their canvas had widened; they had to simultaneously learn about the new Russian ships which had different maintenance philosophies while nursing many old British ships which needed extensive housekeeping. The need for continuous, uninterrupted, long haul and top-class maintenance is one of the key takeaways of the war especially since future wars might not give notice like this one. Navy's emphasis on self-reliance and indigenisation, on being a builder's rather than buyer's navy, to a large extent, is shaped by the experiences of this war.

Need for Jointmanship

There were also some shortcomings in planning, jointmanship and execution. Jointness whenever or wherever it occurred was either on a tactical level or through *ad hoc* mechanisms set up by the operational commanders. A comprehensive joint operational scheme was conspicuous by its absence.[69] Whatever coordination occurred was factually tactical. Greater economy of effort and effectiveness of limited military assets would undoubtedly have accrued through the greater coordination and planning associated with jointness. For instance, the IAF and *IN* had no discussions on airspace management. In fact, a fighter from the Vikrant fired its guns at a UN aircraft bound for Dacca. Fortunately, it missed.[70] The *IN* had initially planned to use its carrier wing to support IV Corps' advance from Tripura. That could not materialise for two reasons. First, the carrier borne aircraft had their hands full in attacking ports and shipping. Second, they had hardly trained jointly with the IAF for joint offensive air support.[71]

Leadership

The war brought out the quality of naval leadership at several levels. Adm Nanda, the CNS, had seen how the Navy was restricted from playing a major role in the 1965 war. He had determined that 'should another opportunity arise' the Navy would not be left behind and would make significant contributions to the war. He was able to convince the political apex with his bold and offensive plans for 1971. He was also responsible for the modicum of jointness achieved with the Army and Air Force at the level of the Service Chiefs, a fact to which Field Marshal

SHFJ Manekshaw attests.[72] Adm Nanda worked painstakingly to bring about a change in the outlook of the Western Command which designed more of a defensive strategy. He faced opposition from some of the staff at the NHQ and other places as they were not in favour of strikes against Karachi. His working style made sure everyone was involved in the planning process. His decision to allocate the *IN*'s sole aircraft carrier INS Vikrant to the Eastern Fleet was a very well thought out decision that ultimately paid dividends.[73] Nanda was a visionary with the big picture in mind while allowing his staff to work out the details.

Another key figure in the naval leadership calculus was Vice Admiral N Krishnan, the Flag Officer Commanding-in-Chief East during the 1971 war. The Eastern Naval Command was continuously worked up under this very demanding and a hard taskmaster C-in-C. His intellect and operational savvy greatly contributed to the plans for the war. As he had commanded INS Vikrant earlier, he knew about its operational capabilities. His willingness to take risks with the aircraft carrier's deployment and the consequent success achieved were attributable in a large measure to his ability to be daring while judiciously viewing the larger picture.[74]

Vice Admiral SN Kohli was the Flag Officer Commanding-in-Chief West during the 1971 war. Despite the initial differences with the CNS and coming across as somewhat cautious (or prudent as others may aver), Kohli set about preparing the war plans with meticulousness and as the war progressed he assumed a bolder stance and shouldered the responsibility for all the actions which were unfolding in the Western Theatre. He was disheartened by the loss of INS Khukri, after which he devoted much of his time until the war came to an end in the Maritime Operations Room (MOR), thinking of possible solutions by which such an incident could have been avoided.[75]

At other echelons, the short but high tempo naval war brought out the varied leadership and other skills of people like VAdm J Cursetji, the VCNS, RAdm EC Kuruvilla and RAdm SH Sarma, the Commanders of the Western and Eastern Fleet respectively; Capt MN Mulla, the gallant Captain of Khukri; Cdr BB Yadav, the K-25; Cdr MNR Samant, the Senior Officer of Force Alpha; Capt OS Dawson at Directorate of Naval Operations and Capt MK Roy at Directorate of Naval Intelligence; Capt Swaraj Prakash; CO INS Vikrant, to name just a few. At the ground level, instances of bravery and overcoming of heavy odds by the men, were the norm rather than the exception, such as during the missile boat attacks, the sinking of the Khukri, the attacks by Vikrant's aircraft, operations by Force Alpha, the Fleets that remained at sea for long durations. All of this was aided by good planning at NHQ and other Headquarters.

Conclusion

In the previous wars, the Navy could not play a major role either due to the government's decisions or due to the inability in the apex to understand the role of the Navy. However, in 1971, where the two wings of Pakistan were separated by sea, gave an opportunity for the Navy to be more involved. The Navy responded effectively through the actions in the Eastern and Western theatres and contributed to the final outcome by inflicting large scale destruction. Through decisive actions and strangulation by ensuring that the enemy forces could not flee or get resupplied, the Navy played a key role.

The *IN* could achieve success in the war because of the stronger willpower and resolve demonstrated by the Indian Naval officers and sailors which in turn stemmed from the top leadership. They were ready to take risks to attack the adversary with whatever they had and at the same time accepted or worked around the shortcomings. The most crucial and vital factor which helped gain victory was their offensive spirit aimed at carrying the battle to the enemy and destroying Pakistani Naval vessels and shore installations.[76] The *IN*'s offensive stance in the war helped to create a completely new paradigm that the *IN* should not be confined to playing a marginal role in India's wars or 'play second fiddle' in future.[77]

Cumulatively, all of this made the political apex and the common people more aware of what the Navy can do and this accorded greater recognition for the Service. It showcased to the political leadership, the powerful tool of statecraft that a Navy can be and the need for the country to be a sea power to achieve economic, political and military goals at sea. All of this subsequently helped in the growth and development of the *IN* as there was greater commitment, budget allocation and understanding of the Navy's role. While 1971 war has been the Navy's finest hour, it has also been the springboard for subsequent development of the *IN*. Fifty years later, we are a bigger, better and one of the most potent navies in the world.

Finally, we also need to hoist the signal that the outcomes that we analyse about war are always in hindsight. There must be appreciation that any war, anywhere in the world, will have its fog and friction and will never play out perfectly as per plans. The 1971 Indian Navy campaign must be seen in that light and the fact that in overall terms it was extremely successful. Considering the resources and other constraints, the conduct of the war at both planning and execution levels were excellent. As with all such conflicts there were many takeaways for the future and the lessons learnt from the 1971 war continue to guide us as we navigate the course ahead.

***Authors' Note*:** *While an attempt has been made in this chapter to give a synopsis of various naval operations of the 1971 Indo-Pak War before delving into the lessons, constraints of space preclude greater elaboration of the background and presume readers' knowledge in this regard.*

Acknowledgements: The authors are thankful for the research assistance provided by Ms Uma Kabe. The opinions expressed in the paper are the authors' personal views and do not reflect the official position of the Indian Navy or the Government of India.

NOTES

1. Richard Sisson and Leo Rose, *War and Secession: India and the Creation of Bangladesh*, Berkeley: University of California Press, 1990, p. 32. As per Table 2 on p. 32, the Awami League and supporters won 162 out of 313 seats, a clear majority. Its major opponent, the Pakistan People's Party, won 81 seats. Its leader, Bhutto, spearheaded the obduracy which eventually led to a Civil War in the East.
2. Owen Bennet Jones, *Pakistan: Eye of the Storm*, Karachi: Oxford University Press, 2002.
3. J.N. Dixit, *India-Pakistan in War and Peace*, New Delhi: Books Today, 2002, pp. 201–02.
4. Rear Admiral SY Shrikhande (Retd), *East Leaves West: An Operational Art Redux of the Little Known Indo-Pak War of 1971 that Liberated Bangladesh*, Joint Military Operations paper submitted to the US Naval War College in May 2003, p. 3.
5. Vice Admiral G.M. Hiranandani, *Transition to Triumph*, Lancer Publishers, 2000, p. 18.
6. Ibid., p. 118.
7. Admiral S.M. Nanda, *The Man who Bombed Karachi*, Harper Collins Publishers India, 2015, p. 219.
8. Ibid., p. 220.
9. Hiranandani, *Transition to Triumph*, n. 5, p. 203 and Nanda, *The Man who Bombed Karachi*, n. 7, p. 221.
10. Hiranandani, *Transition to Triumph*, n. 5, pp. 106, 198.
11. Admiral Arun Prakash (Retd), 'Lessons of Maritime Success Story', *The Tribune*, 31 January 2021, available at https://www.tribuneindia.com/news/features/lessons-of-maritime-success-story-205892, accessed on 14 September 2021.
12. Hiranandani, *Transition to Triumph*, n. 5, p. 106.
13. Ibid., p. 213; Admiral S.N. Kohli, *We Dared: Maritime Operations in the 1971 Indo-Pak War*, Sangam Books Ltd, 1989, p. viii.
14. Lieutenant Commander (Retd) Madanjit Singh Ahluwalia, *Torpedoed at Sea: The Saga of INS Khukri*, Notion Press, 2016, p. 7.
15. Ibid., p. 81.
16. Hiranandani, *Transition to Triumph*, n. 5, p. 125.
17. Ahluwalia, *Torpedoed at Sea: The Saga of INS Khukri*, n. 14, p. 83.
18. Ibid., p. 105.
19. Kohli, *We Dared: Maritime Operations in the 1971 Indo-Pak War*, n. 13, p. 38.
20. Ibid.
21. Command, Control, Communications, Computers, Intelligence, Information, Surveillance and Reconnaissance.

22. Hiranandani, *Transition to Triumph*, n. 5, p. 187.
23. Commodore (Retd) KP Gopal Rao, 'Distortion of Indian Naval History-1971 Period', *Indian Defence Review*, July 1990, p. 46.
24. Hiranandani, *Transition to Triumph*, n. 5, p. 191; Kohli, *We Dared: Maritime Operations in the 1971 Indo-Pak War*, n. 13, p. 54.
25. Hiranandani, *Transition to Triumph*, n. 5, pp. 188–89.
26. Ibid., p. 191.
27. Ibid.
28. Commodore (Retd) Vijay Jerath, *25 Missile Boat Squadron*, Prakash Books, 2013, p. 177.
29. Ahluwalia, *Torpedoed at Sea: The Saga of INS* Khukri, n. 14, p. 94.
30. Hiranandani, *Transition to Triumph*, n. 5, p. 198.
31. Ibid.
32. Interview with Adm SM Nanda, *Quarterdeck*, Published by Naval Headquarters, 1996, p. 8.
33. Hiranandani, *Transition to Triumph*, n. 5, pp. 210–11.
34. Ahluwalia, *Torpedoed at Sea: The Saga of INS* Khukri, n. 14, p. 13.
35. Hiranandani, *Transition to Triumph*, n. 5, p. 139.
36. Ibid., p. 134.
37. Ibid., p. 142.
38. Ibid.
39. The National Committee for Strengthening Maritime and Coastal Security (NCSMCS) is a national-level forum and an apex review mechanism for maritime and coastal security, in which all concerned ministries and government agencies are represented.
40. Hiranandani, *Transition to Triumph*, n. 5, pp. 119–20.
41. Ibid.
42. Hiranandani, *Transition to Triumph*, n. 5, p. 140; Vice Admiral N. Krishnan, *A Sailor's Story*, Punya Publishers, 2011, p. 64.
43. Hiranandani, *Transition to Triumph*, n. 5, p. 184.
44. Ibid., p. 154.
45. Cmde Srikant B. Kesnur and Lt Abhijeet Patil, 'INS Panvel: The Small Ship That Scored Big In The 1971 War', *The Daily Guardian*, 16 December 2020, available at https://thedailyguardian.com/ins-panvel-the-small-ship-that-scored-big-in-the-1971-war/, accessed on 29 September 2021.
46. Hiranandani, *Transition to Triumph*, n. 5, p. 184.
47. Ibid., p. 181.
48. Ibid., p. 173.
49. Ahluwalia, *Torpedoed at Sea: The Saga of INS Khukri*, n. 14, p. 65.
50. Hiranandani, *Transition to Triumph*, n. 5, p. 157.
51. Ibid., pp. 161–67.
52. Ibid., p. 168.
53. Ibid.
54. Nanda, *Quarterdeck*, n. 32, pp. 9, 28.
55. Admiral Arun Prakash (Retd), 'Lessons of Maritime Success Story', n. 11.
56. Hiranandani, *Transition to Triumph*, n. 5, p. 170.
57. Ibid., p. 212.
58. Hiranandani, *Transition to Triumph*, n. 5, p. 202; Nanda, *Quarterdeck*, n. 32, p. 7.
59. Kohli, *We Dared: Maritime Operations in the 1971 Indo-Pak War*, n. 13.
60. Nanda, *Quarterdeck*, n. 32, pp. 35–36. This point has been further reiterated in a recent

article by Adm VS Shekhawat for *The Tribune* newspaper. Shekhawat was CO INS Karanj during the war.

61. Cmde Ranjit Rai (Retd), *A Nation and Its Navy At War*, Lancer International, 1987, p. 46.
62. Nanda, *Quarterdeck*, n. 32.
63. Admiral Arun Prakash (Retd), 'Lessons of Maritime Success Story', n. 11.
64. Hiranandani, *Transition to Triumph*, n. 5, p. 130; Major General (Retd) Ian Cardozo, AVSM, SM, *The Sinking of INS Khukri*, Roli Books, 2006, p. 34.
65. 'Observe-Orient-Decide-Act'. Having a smaller OODA loop prevents the adversary from seizing the initiative.
66. Hiranandani, *Transition to Triumph*, n. 5, pp. 174, 181.
67. Nanda, *Quarterdeck*, n. 32, p. 217.
68. Hiranandani, *Transition to Triumph*, n. 5, p. 246; and Ahluwalia, *Torpedoed at Sea: The Saga of INS Khukri*, n. 14, p. 4.
69. Shrikhande, *East Leaves West: An Operational Art Redux of the Little Known Indo-Pak War of 1971 that Liberated* Bangladesh, n. 4, p. 12.
70. P.C. Lal (Air Chief Marshal), *My Years with the IAF*, New Delhi: Lancer, 1986, p. 187.
71. Ibid., p. 210.
72. Nanda, *Quarterdeck*, n. 32, p. 11.
73. Rai, *A Nation and Its Navy At* War, n. 61, p. 166.
74. Ibid., p. 32.
75. Ibid.
76. Kohli, *We Dared: Maritime Operations in the 1971 Indo-Pak War*, n. 13, p. 98.
77. Nanda, *Quarterdeck*, n. 32, pp. 178, 185.

10

The Protection of Sea Lines of Communication during the 1971 War

Somita Chakraborty

Continuous flow of essential commodities in domestic market is one of the most crucial requirements for the survival of a country. In the modern world, as no country is self-sufficient, effective disruption of the supply chain can bring about terrible economic and political upheaval and change in peacetime, while shrinking economic strength as well as war effort of a belligerent at the time of war. As a result, protection of sea lines of communication (SLOCs) has always been an important part of military strategy. Before the World War II era, protection of sea lanes was mainly a naval affair. In a multipolar world, where the economic and military capacity of major powers was near about equal, military solution was a natural and preferred option. However, after World War II, diplomacy gained prominence and led to change in the protection system of sea lanes. The wide gap between the superpowers and other powers, regarding economic and military strength, opened up the new arena of diplomatic initiative. The process of protection of sea lanes in the post-war world, therefore, includes policymaking and foreign policy along with defence strategy.

The geographic location and maritime history of India shows the inviolable relation between sea trade and economic strength. Independent India, for a long time, failed to combine its geostrategic advantage with regional and international politics to guard the prime source of its economic security, that is, sea routes. In the 1960s, India faced two wars with two of its neighbours, China and Pakistan. Both the 1962 and 1965 wars had crucial impact on India's economic condition, military build-up and foreign policy. In this context, the paper attempts to trace India's strategy and effort to protect its sea lanes and continuous flow of shipment during the 1971 war.

India in the Indian Ocean

Geographically, India has open access to one of the biggest oceans of the world, the Indian Ocean. The long coastline of the Indian Peninsula is surrounded by the Indian Ocean and two of its large marginal seas, the Bay of Bengal and the Arabian Sea. Enriched by this geographical advantage, prosperous maritime trade has become an intrinsic part of maritime history of India. By the thirteenth century, India's sea trade was well established over a vast area, extending from the Mediterranean Sea to the South China Sea.[1] Within that time, the Chola Empire of India, with its vigorous naval strength, set up a precedence of protection chain for India's sea trade through the Strait of Malacca.

Decline of the Chola naval power reduced security of the shipping lanes and ended an era of Indian naval superiority over the Indian Ocean. Two hundred years later, when the European traders reached the Indian Ocean and deployed patrolling to harass both Indian and Arab shipment under a strategy to monopolise the sea routes to India,[2] the established Indian kingdoms of that time, such as the Mughals, Calicut and Maratha power, hardly could do anything to protect Indian trade. With their coastal naval power, they had capacity to hamper European trade near Indian coast, but could not secure Indian trade in the high seas.[3]

By the mid-nineteenth century, Britain had established its monopoly over sea routes to India, as well as a protection chain from the Strait of Malacca to the Suez Canal (1869). In this protection chain, India played the key role. Taking the peninsula of India and Colombo and Trincomalee of Sri Lanka as the main points, Britain established a protection chain including Aden, Egypt, Maldives, Seychelles, Mauritius, Cape of Good Hope and St. Helena to protect trade routes through the Persian Gulf, the Red Sea and round the Cape route.[4] To protect eastbound trade, it established hold over Myanmar and had a small security facility in the Andaman and Nicobar Islands (A&N Islands). This British strategy of inadequate protection for eastbound trade was mainly influenced by the geopolitical condition of the Western Pacific. By the late nineteenth century, Britain had control over Malaysia, a strong naval base in Singapore as well as firm grip over Australia and

New Zealand. On the other hand, France had control over Indochina; the United States (US) had control over the Philippines; and Japan had control over Korea. In case of China, all these powers had heavy influence in its economic, military and political affairs. In 1904, Britain entered into an alliance with France and Japan; and it had already established a close relation with the US by then. As Russia and Germany had little presence in this region, this made the framework more favourable for Britain and protected its eastward trade till World War II.

In the beginning of 1940s, this geopolitical arrangement received a shattering blow. Japan's victory march in the Western Pacific, failure of British allies, fall of Singapore and presence of Japan in Myanmar shook the British strategy. Realising the consequence, in 1942, Britain evacuated A&N Islands, leaving India's eastern shore and trade routes near about unprotected. Japan captured the islands and turned it into a base. The short-lived Japanese war effort in the Indian Ocean followed the strategy of control over trade routes. For that, it continued attacks on British merchant ships in the Bay of Bengal and the Arabian Sea, raided Colombo and Trincomalee and established submarine patrolling up to Madagascar.[5] Success of the US in the Midway (1942) restricted Japan, but its war effort established the strategic importance of India to protect the vital sea lanes through the Indian Ocean.

The end of World War II led to major changes in the international political structure. Long military engagements had exhausted the economic might of Britain and other European powers. In comparison, geographical isolation and gigantic industrial strength saved the US from any major economic scar. Besides that, with the know-how of nuclear device, the US maintained the position of the sole superpower of the world till 1949, when the Soviet Union exploded a nuclear device.

Against this background, Britain decided to transfer power to India. During this process, the main focus of apex British administration was the security of British sea trade through the Indian Ocean. Knowing the strategic importance of India, a lot of hesitation and discussion prevailed among the British administrators regarding transfer of A&N to India. Hold over the islands, with a strong base in Singapore, would make the Strait of Malacca a private canal for Britain. Interestingly, during that period, Lord Wavell, the then Secretary of State of India, while writing a letter on the security of independent India, prophetically predicted the future deciding factors of independent India's foreign policy. He was sure that, growing industrialisation and increasing seaborne trade, with inadequate naval power, would push India either towards Russia or the Western powers.[6]

This historical discussion establishes that, for centuries, India's position has remained a pivotal point for trade and protection chain in the Indian Ocean. Geographically, India is situated close to the Malacca Strait and is adjacent to several important trade routes through the Indian Ocean. In this regard, the geographic location of the two island chains, that is, the A&N in the Bay of Bengal and Lakshadweep in the Arabian Sea, is highly significant. In the Bay of Bengal, several busy sea lanes are located adjacent to the A&N Islands. Among them, the Preparis Channel and the Coco Channel are situated to the north of A&N and the Great Channel or the Six Degree Channel is in the south. Three more channels, that is, the Duncan Passage, the Ten Degree Channel and the Sombrero Channel, pass through A&N. Among the three, the Ten Degree Channel is the most important because of its busy traffic.In the same way, the Nine Degree Channel, one of the most important shipping lanes of the Indian Ocean, passes through the Lakshadweep chain of islands in the Arabian Sea. Another important sea route, the Eight Degree Channel, is located to the south of the Lakshadweep Islands. Ships in the Indian Ocean, between the Suez and the Malacca, are bound to use these channels according to their destination. Alongside these trade routes, besides some small groups of islands—for example, the Seychelles, Maldives, Lakshadweep and A&N—and single island country, Sri Lanka, the large Indian Peninsula is the only available landmass which stretches into the Indian Ocean and is positioned parallel to the Strait of Malacca and the Red Sea. While the geographic position places it in the vicinity of several busy trade routes, the large landmass increases the capacity of India to sustain any war effort. This exclusive geostrategic dimension of India, historically, has made it a centre point for trade, transhipping and protection chain.

Economic Condition of India and Security Structure of the Indian Ocean Till 1965

The colonial exploitation and drainage of resources, mainly at the time of two world wars, exhausted India's economic condition. The British policy during World War II caused large-scale shortage of food grains and led to famine in Bengal (1943). Four years later, India became independent as one of the poorest countries of the world, with majority population struggling with poverty and hunger. Thus, improving the economic condition became priority for the policymakers. They also had the responsibility to protect a large landmass and long coastline. In this defence–development dichotomy, considering the incontestable military supremacy of the superpowers and weak military strength of the close neighbours,

Indian policymakers chose development over defence and tried to secure territorial sovereignty through diplomacy.[7] However, in the immediate years after independence, when India was building its defence through diplomacy policy, it did not pay much attention to its own dependence on the seaborne trade and the security structure of the Indian Ocean.

After Partition, India lost its traditional trade route connections, through land and internal waterways, with other parts of Asia, for example, Western Asia and Southeast Asia. Hostile relations with Pakistan reduced the possibility even further. This left sea routes as the only option for India's foreign trade. Besides this geographic factor, scarcity of mineral oil and other oil products, such as diesel and kerosene, was another factor for the increasing importance of sea lanes. Sea route was the cheapest and safest mode of transportation for these commodities, which were crucial for the rapidly growing industrial and transport sector of the newly independent India. Despite growing strategic importance, India's shipbuilding sector was in a disastrous condition. The colonial rulers, for their own economic benefit, did not allow India's shipbuilding sector to grow. Later, during World War II, Japan's trade warfare considerably shrunk India's merchant fleet structure. Consequently, independent India had less than 60 ships to carry its huge seaborne trade. This resulted in more than 95 per cent of India's overseas trade dependent on foreign, mainly Western, ships.[8]

In the post-war era, the decline of Europe and the rise of the US and the Soviet Union as superpowers signalled the possible change of international system. Though the possibility did not disturb the already established British security structure, the growth of a new structure was clearly visible in the Indian Ocean. After 1947, the British protection chain in the Indian Ocean continued with several places and bases, including Madagascar, Kenya, Seychelles, Aden, several air bases in the Persian Gulf, Mauritius and Sri Lanka (Trincomalee till 1957),[9] along with small US presence in Bahrain (1949), to protect sea routes from round the Cape and Bab-el-Mandab to the Strait of Malacca. The trade routes through the Western Pacific, due to British hold over Singapore, Malaysia, Hong Kong, along with presence of the US in Japan, the Philippines (Subic Bay and Clark Bay), Vietnam (Da Nang) and its influence on Taiwan (after 1949), Australia and New Zealand, carried on with Western domination. Thus, in the immediate years after World War II, the vast region of the Indo-Pacific remained under the influence of Western powers. Geographically, to reach the Indian Ocean, the South China Sea is the shortest corridor for the US, just as the Suez is the shortest route for Europe. Therefore, continuation of the aforementioned security structure was a critical requirement for both the US and Britain. However, growing Soviet influence in the Western Pacific (China, North Korea, Vietnam, Indonesia), and in the vicinity of the Suez (Egypt), was a clear threat for Western commercial interests.

In the changed geostrategic framework, it was believed that India could serve as a key point for the Western camp to counter the Soviet influence. Failing to convince a non-aligned India, the US and Britain began to assist Pakistan in defence build-up. Thus, in the 1950s, Pakistan strengthened its defence and diplomatic capability through economic and military aid from the US. Also, its membership in the Southeast Asian Treaty Organization (SEATO) and Central Treaty Organization (CENTO) brought Pakistan close to the US, Britain, Iran and Turkey. India, which chose defence through diplomacy policy, overlooked the overwhelming US economic and military aid to Pakistan and latter's growing relation with Britain. Besides that, during the 1950s, India took a pro-Soviet stand on several occasions: for example, in 1956, India, along with other non-aligned countries, out-and-out disapproved the Franco-British–Israeli aggression on Egypt on the Suez crisis, but simultaneously only expressed distress on the tragedy of the Soviet intervention in Hungary. Therefore, when the security structure of the Indian Ocean, India's seaborne trade and naval build-up was dominated by the West, diplomatically India was tilting towards the Soviet Union. In a nutshell, India neglected its vital source of economic strength through the Bay of Bengal and the Arabian Sea, both diplomatically and militarily.

In the late 1950s, India's economic condition was also deteriorating rapidly. At independence, India had received a large sterling deposit in exchange of war requirements it supplied to Britain and allied forces at the time of World War II. Besides that, Britain also committed to bear India's war expenditure partially. However, the 1949 devaluation of rupee, increasing import bill, rapid outflow of foreign exchange due to moderate naval build-up and dependence on Western shipping, accompanied by insufficient growth of export, evaporated the large sterling deposit within ten years. This resulted in extensive balance of payment crisis, which limited India's economic strength.[10]

In this context, in the 1960s, India fought two wars against two of its close neighbours. The 1962 India–China War was mainly land-based and did not affect India's seaborne trade, though it restrained India's economic growth considerably. The sudden attack challenged India's defence with diplomacy strategy and questioned its neglect towards defence build-up. The war also revealed the unpreparedness of India's economic and military set-up to handle any unexpected defence crisis. Considering the land-based threat of 1962 Chinese aggression, India strengthened its army and air force. For this, in the next financial year, budgetary allocation for defence build-up became near about double. This immediate requirement was fulfilled by imposing heavy taxation and import duties. Imposition of import duties, on the one hand, increased prices of essential raw materials for the industrial sector. On the other hand, tax burden on petrol, diesel and income tax increased transport charges, prices of kerosene and other essential commodities of daily life.[11] Altogether, it affected every Indian household.

After the 1962 war, threat towards India's sea trade increased rapidly. Growing relations of Pakistan and Sri Lanka with China and the capacity of Chinese submarine to reach the Bay of Bengal became a concern for India. Meanwhile, India–Indonesia relation was also deteriorating. At that point, the US leased one submarine to Pakistan. It suddenly posed a two-way security threat to India's seaborne trade, from both the Bay of Bengal and the Arabian Sea, as China, Pakistan and Indonesia were all armed with submarine—a well-proven threat to the merchant fleet. Till 1962, India's own security was unacceptably insufficient for its valuable sea trade. India had an inadequate naval strength, mainly concentrated in the western waters, and the Indian Army was responsible for the security of the A&N. After the 1962 war, the responsibility of the A&N was handed over to the Indian Navy and naval facilities on the islands were increased to improve patrolling capacity of the navy. In 1964, a Five Year Defence Plan was formulated. Though the navy did not get adequate share in this plan, the policymakers began their quest for submarine around this time. A sincere long-term strategy for protection of sea lanes, however, materialised only after the 1965 war.

The Period Between the Two Wars, 1965–71

The 1965 war fully exposed India's security neglect of its eastern shore, ports and sea trade. In September 1965, when a number of Indian naval ships were present in the Bay of Bengal to protect A&N from Indonesian naval intrusions, Pakistan launched an attack on India's western front. With the beginning of war, all ships present in the eastern waters were recalled, leaving the eastern shore and ports completely unprotected. It was sheer luck that Pakistan had neglected its eastern wing; China, which had issued a warning, did not get involved in the war; and the Indonesian submarine reached Pakistan after the ceasefire. Indian sea trade, however, was not so fortunate. At that time, India owned 250 ships and had a large volume of trade with the US and Europe. In addition, due to the geographic location, all the merchant ships carrying both Indian and Pakistani cargo first visited Pakistan either in the Bay of Bengal or in the Arabian Sea.[12] India also had trade links with eastern wing of Pakistan through internal waterways. Therefore, at the time of the sudden outbreak of war, a number of ships and small vessels that were carrying Indian cargo were either already present in Pakistani ports and internal waters or on the way towards it.

In spite of that, initially, the policymakers did not extend protection at sea and tried utmost to confine the hostility within the nature of an armed conflict.[13] This lack of perception regarding the economic consequences of unprotected sea trade during conflict period, when the belligerent was a close maritime neighbour with considerable naval strength, left a large number of defenceless Indian vessels at the mercy of the adversary. It enabled Pakistan to detain three Indian merchant ships in Karachi Port, and also offload a large amount of Indian import cargo from the Indian, Pakistani and neutral ships presents in both East and West Pakistan at the time of war.[14] Later, when India began to retaliate militarily, it was too late. Diplomatically, India protested before the United Nations, where Pakistan justified its actions as its 'right of self-defence'.[15] Realising the growing maritime threats towards India's territorial and economic security, a number of leaders from the opposition and ruling party expressed their concern and proposed to build an independent fleet on the eastern shore.[16]

The war put additional strain on India's economic condition. Immediately after the war started, the US stopped aid to both India and Pakistan. India also experienced large-scale drought in 1965 and 1966, which worsened the situation. Inadequate agricultural output and consequent unavailability of food grains in the market led to mass dissatisfaction in several parts of the country.[17] In financial year (FY) 1965–66, India's export also experienced a downward slide.[18] To stabilise the economy, 'plan holiday' was declared for FY 1966–67, 1967–68 and 1968–69. The deteriorating trade growth, poor agrarian output, severe foreign exchange crisis, along with international pressure, led India to devalue rupee. Despite severe criticism even within the ruling party, it was assumed that devaluation would reduce the price of Indian products and make it more competitive in the international market.[19] However, after the 1967 Six Day War, Egypt closed the Suez for an indefinite period. This compelled all the ships bound for European and transatlantic market to take a detour around the Cape. The extra miles increased the cost of shipping as well as products. India had to pay US$ 200 million extra per annum for this detour.[20] The only relief, in the late 1960s, came from the agrarian sector, which witnessed remarkable growth in agrarian output due to the introduction of high-yielding varieties (HYV) of seeds.

Here, taking a pause from the topic under discussion, let us take a look at the security structure of the Indian Ocean and the political situation of the subcontinent between 1965 and 1971. In the post-war period, deteriorating economic condition of Britain restricted its military deployments and colonial engagements in different parts of the world. Further, the 1956 Suez debacle revealed the political position of Britain in the post-war international system. After Egypt nationalised the Suez, Britain, along with France and Israel invaded Egypt, but forced to withdraw under heavy pressure from both the superpowers. The incident sharply divided the world between the superpowers and the other powers and placed Britain, politically, with the latter. The British departure from Trincomalee (Sri Lanka), Kenya and South Arabia (including Aden) also was a clear sign of rolling back of the empire. In this background, in order to reduce the economic burden, Britain hastened withdrawal from its former bases in the Indian Ocean and the Pacific. By the mid-1960s, the US had a strong presence in the Western Pacific and a small naval force stationed in Bahrain. In 1966, Britain leased Diego Garcia to the US and paved the way for the latter to dominate the Indian Ocean. After the 1967 Arab–Israel crisis, the Soviet Union also increased its naval presence in the Indian Ocean. Further, the political condition of the subcontinent was changing rapidly. After the US stopped aid to both the belligerents of 1965 war, Pakistan quickly turned to its close friend, China, and received a large amount as aid. To restrict China, the Soviet Union reached out to Pakistan and brought the subcontinent under its aid diplomacy. In 1969, the Nixon administration came to power in the US. Realising the growing Soviet influence in the subcontinent, it immediately turned towards Pakistan and gradually increased its interest towards China. This created a peculiar situation for India, which had already established an in-depth dependence on the Soviet Union to fulfil its naval requirements.

During the same period, India's sea trade witnessed a steady growth. While in 1960–61 India's total trade was near about Rs 1,800 crore, within ten years, it rose to more than Rs 3,000 crore. In that period, India's dependence on petroleum and oil products also increased sharply. In 1971, India spent Rs 193.9 crore to import petroleum and oil products.[21] Moderate investment in shipbuilding, on the other hand, increased the number of Indian ships. In spite of rapid growth of volume of trade, in 1969, 15 per cent of India's overseas trade was being carried by Indian ships, compared to 8.2 per cent in 1961.[22] Considering all these aspects, India decided to increase its naval capability to protect its sea lanes through the Bay of Bengal and the Arabian Sea. Backed by strong public opinion, and upheld by the navy, print media and political leaders, a favourable environment had developed for strong naval build-up,[23] including a separate major base in the eastern shore. This, in turn, increased India's defence expenditure, which crossed Rs 1,000 crore per annum from 1969 onwards. In 1971, with an increase of Rs 169 crore, the revised estimate stood at more than Rs 1,400 crore.[24] Guarding the strongest source of India's economic security, therefore, became a necessity.

Protection of Sea Lanes During the 1971 War

The western and eastern wings of Pakistan were located in the two marginal seas of the Indian Ocean, namely, the Arabian Sea and the Bay of Bengal, respectively. India was the only land connection between the two wings. After independence, because of hostile relationship with India, Pakistan lost this only land connection. The other options were not viable as the distance between the two wings of Pakistan by air (via Sri Lanka) was 2,400 miles and through sea route, it was a journey of two weeks.[25] In 1971, amid growing tension between the two countries and the East Pakistan crisis, India carefully exploited this geostrategic advantage.

In January 1971, following the hijack and destruction of an Indian Airbus F-27, India cancelled overflight facilities of Pakistani aviation. To continue connectivity, Pakistan requested Sri Lanka, and was granted permission, for overflight, landing and refuelling facility for both civil and military aviation. Strategically and politically, it was not a welcome situation for India. Since 1963, Sri Lanka's pro-China approach and its growing maritime relation with China, was a concern for India.[26] Considering the situation, a growing Sri Lanka–Pakistan relation was a clear strategic gain for Pakistan. Moreover, during that time, Pakistan was transferring a large number of troops, arms and ammunitions from West Pakistan to its eastern wing, mainly by ship; but it was allegedly using aviation for the same purpose.[27]

Against this background, in the beginning of April 1971, an armed uprising was organised in Sri Lanka by a leftist terrorist group. Considering the request of Sri Lankan government, India immediately sent military assistance, which included naval patrolling and surveillance, along with assistance from Indian Air Force and Indian Army.[28] The US, Soviet Union, Britain and Pakistan also sent assistance. In short, Sri Lanka received prompt support from all those countries which were standing against each other on the East Pakistan crisis. Later, Sri Lanka remained silent on the Indo-Soviet friendship treaty and maintained strict neutrality at the time of war.

Also, by April 1971, millions of East Pakistani crossed international border and entered India as refugees. In spite of continuous diplomatic protests by India, the inactivity of the Western powers proved their silent support for Pakistan. At that juncture, in July 1971, using Pakistan's mediation and territory, the US reached out to China. Realising the emerging US–China–Pakistan triangle and its impact on India amid the East Pakistan crisis, within a month India signed the Treaty of Peace, Friendship and Cooperation with the Soviet Union. Though the possibility of cooperation between the two was already there, the timing and Article IX of the treaty, which declared mutual military assistance in face of any threat on peace and security, indicated clear Soviet support to India. From early October onwards, Pakistan began to concentrate troops near the western border of India, making the war inevitable.

Further, in 1971, India's economic condition was facing the burden of increasing imports, defence expenditure and spending on refugees. Any hampering of the flow of shipment or act of offloading import cargo, in that situation, could bring about severe economic problems for India. Politically, Pakistan already had close relations with China, and the Western powers had also shown their 'tilt'. In this context, how far did the Indo-Soviet treaty work for India, regarding protection of sea trade, at the time of war? In 1971, Britain had a strong naval and air power presence in the Arabian Sea, capable enough to endanger India's trade and security. The US, in turn, had a strong presence in the Western Pacific and its nuclear-powered attack carrier, *USS Enterprise*, was stationed off the coast of Vietnam;[29] and it maintained a small naval force in the Bahrain and its complete entry in the Diego Garcia was still awaited. Since the mid-1960s, the Soviet Union too had increased its naval presence in the Indian Ocean, and it also had a strong Pacific Fleet stationed at Vladivostok. Any misadventure, by any superpower, had the possibility to proliferate the crisis. After the Cuban Missile Crisis (1962), both the superpowers and the North Atlantic Treaty Organization (NATO) powers were highly sensitive regarding this issue. By signing the friendship treaty with the Soviet Union, India therefore managed to restrict the intervention of all external powers, leaving Pakistan alone to confront the Indian naval power.

Different decisions of the policymakers, since 1965, including: introduction of the submarine arm; building a separate naval base at eastern shore and its inauguration just before the war; cancellation of overflight facilities for Pakistani aviation; signing friendship treaty with the Soviet Union; and empowering Indian Navy to control Indian merchant shipping through Naval Control of Shipping Act of 1971, set the stage, gave ample scope and better chance to Indian Navy to implement its design to secure the flow of shipment during wartime. Submarine and air bombing are the two major wartime threats for merchant fleet. Capacity of submarines against merchant fleet was well proven in both the world wars and during World War II, Japan and the US established the importance of air cover for merchant ships.

In 1971, Pakistan had a strong submarine arm with four submarines, along with strong air power armed with US, French and Chinese aircraft. Pakistan, however, did not have any naval facilities in its eastern wing, and also had very few aircraft there. Considering all the merits and demerits of the adversary, the Indian Navy prepared a plan to protect important Indian ports, control the routes of merchant ships and establish patrols in the Bay of Bengal and the Arabian Sea to secure nearby vital sea lanes. To protect important ports of the western and eastern coasts, naval and air reconnaissance was established up to a particular extent and special care was taken to prevent any sabotage in the Indian harbours. Protection of shipping was established by coordinating routing and programming of ships, directing to keep them away from Pakistani coasts and by recalling Indian ships from the Gulf. To protect the sea lanes in the eastern water, patrolling was deployed from east of Sri Lanka to the Chittagong Port (Bangladesh). In the western part, patrolling was deployed from Colombo to the Eight Degree Channel and the Nine Degree Channel. Later, another patrolling was deployed in the west of the Nine Degree Channel to cover both the channels.

During that fateful fortnight, mysterious sinking of Pakistani submarine, *Ghazi*, in the vicinity of Visakhapatnam, headquarter of Eastern Naval Command, together with successful blockade in the Bay of Bengal, air strike in East Pakistan, missile attack on Karachi Port and 'Operation Falcon' (launched by Indian Navy in the Arabian Sea, in search of Pakistani submarine which torpedoed and sunk *INS Khukri*), completely disabled Pakistan's capacity to attack India's vital sea lanes.[30] Consequently, not a single Indian merchant ship was either captured or damaged. The foreign merchant ships, which initially expressed some hesitation regarding safety and security, continued to supply goods and commodities to the Indian ports.[31] During the war period, a total of 130 ships sailed through both the Bay of Bengal and the Arabian Sea to reach the Indian ports.[32] Even the supply of the war materials, such as crude oil tankers, reached the Indian ports completely unscathed and undisturbed.[33]

The war and its massive geostrategic effect resulted in several economic burdens. With the declaration of war, the US suspended development aid to India. Performance of Indian Navy and near about zero effect of the Task Force 74 on it hastened the US' naval entry in the Indian Ocean after the war. Besides that, the US–China–Pakistan triangle increased India's defence budget in the successive years. In a background of excessive refugee burden, a war and continuous growing defence expenditure, increasing price of goods and commodities, therefore, was an expected market scenario. However, a continuous flow of essential commodities controlled the expected scarcity of materials and consequent incapacity in agricultural, industrial and transport sectors. Availability of products in the domestic market, on the other hand, minimised the price hike. This economic scenario, in turn, strengthened the position of the policymakers at the time of further political bargain with its close neighbour after the war.

Conclusion

During the 1971 war, India, through a blitzkrieg campaign, achieved a decisive victory and permanently halved Pakistan's political and economic capability. Continuous flow of resources during the war period, through protected sea lanes, was one of the major strategic successes of this war. The most important factor of this well-designed strategy was its long-planned surprises, built during peacetime. From 1965 to 1971, India seriously observed the changing political and security structure in the region, particularly in the Indian Ocean, and acted accordingly. Gradual building of a base on the eastern shore and its inauguration just few weeks before the war suddenly increased the capability of the Indian Navy in the Bay of Bengal. It helped India to project equal strength to protect its sea trade in both the eastern and western waters. Signing a treaty with the Soviet Union was another factor. Gaining Soviet naval support in a bipolar world was a huge strategic win for India. Altogether, in the 1971 war, India achieved unprecedented success with regard to protection of SLOCs, when the foreign policy and defence strategy worked together.

The maritime history of India established the geostrategic importance of the country. Independent India, to reduce expenditure decided to defend its territorial sovereignty through diplomacy and ironically, left the strongest source of its economic security near about unprotected. The 1965 war revealed the consequence of this deliberate neglect. In spite of that, till 1971, India did not make any attempt to build maritime relations with countries strategically located adjacent to its vital sea lanes. It was sheer luck that, Sri Lanka turned neutral. Except this small blot, in 1971, both the military and political units of the country complemented each other's objectives and strategies and brought a watershed moment for the protection of SLOCs in independent India.

NOTES

1. R.C. Majumdar, *Outlines of Ancient Indian History and Civilizations*, Calcutta, 1927, pp. 285–95, 547, available at http://ignca.gov.in/Asi_data/19499.pdf, accessed on 22 July 2021; Santosh Kumar Das, *The Economic History of Ancient India*, Calcutta: Mitra Press, 1925, pp. 119–22; K.M. Panikkar, *India and the Indian Ocean: An Essay on the Influence of the Sea Power on Indian History*, London: George Allen and Unwin Ltd, 1945, pp. 24–33; I.A. Khan, 'Arabian Sea Trade in the 15th and 16th Centuries', *Proceedings of the Indian History Congress*, Vol. 39, 1978, pp. 908–09; and Satyindra Singh, *Under Two Ensigns: The Indian Navy 1945–50*, New Delhi: Oxford and IBH Publishing Co., 1985, available at https://www.indiannavy.nic.in/sites/default/files/Under-Two-Ensigns-06Apr16.pdf, accessed on 19 June 2021. For Europe, there were several routes, but all of them included both sea and land routes. For example, one of the major trade routes was through the Mediterranean Sea via the Red Sea and Alexandria (Egypt).
2. Panikkar, *India and the Indian Ocean*, n. 1, pp. 39–43; and Khan, 'Arabian Sea Trade in the 15th and 16th Centuries', n. 1, pp. 911–12.
3. Panikkar, *India and the Indian Ocean*, n. 1, pp. 40–64.
4. John McAleer, '"The Key to India": Troop Movements, Southern Africa, and Britain's Indian Ocean World, 1795–1820', *The International History Review*, Vol. 35, No. 2, 2013, pp. 294–316; and Panikkar, *India and the Indian Ocean*, n. 1.
5. Jeremy Black, 'Midway and the Indian Ocean', *Naval War College Review*, Vol. 62, No. 5, 2009, pp. 131–40; also see Panikkar, *India and the Indian Ocean*, n. 1, pp. 72–81 and Singh, *Under Two Ensigns*, n. 1.
6. Singh, *Under Two Ensigns*, n. 1, p. 65.
7. Raju G.C. Thomas, *The Defence of India: A Budgetary Perspective of Strategy and Policies*, Delhi: The Macmillan Company of India Ltd, 1978.
8. Rahul Roy-Chaudhury, *Sea Power and Indian Security*, London: Brassey's, 1995, pp. 147–55.
9. Joseph S. Roucek, 'Britain's Retreat from Aden and East of Suez', *Il Politico*, Vol. 33, No. 2, 1968, pp. 413–26; Hugh Hanning, 'Britain East of Suez: Fact and Figures', *International Affairs (Royal Institute of International Affairs)*, Vol. 42, No. 2, 1966, pp. 253–60; and S.U. Kodikara, 'Major Trends in Sri Lanka's Non-Alignment Policy after 1956', *Asian Survey*, Vol. 13, No. 12, 1973, p. 1123.
10. Thomas, *The Defence of India*, n. 7, pp. 104–05; and Roy-Chaudhury, *Sea Power and Indian Security*, n. 8.
11. Thomas, *The Defence of India*, n. 7, pp. 105–07.
12. Satyindra Singh, *Blueprint to Bluewater: The Indian Navy 1951–65*, New Delhi: Lancer International, 1992, pp. 462–65.
13. Christopher Greenwood, 'The Concept of War in Modern International Law', *The International and Comparative Law Quarterly*, Vol. 36, No. 2, 1987, pp. 292–93; and Roy-Chaudhury, *Sea Power and Indian Security*, n. 8.
14. Singh, *Blueprint to Bluewater*, n. 12, pp. 462–65; also see Roy-Chaudhury, *Sea Power and Indian Security*, n. 8, pp. 53–54.
15. D.R. Humphrey, 'Belligerent Interdiction of Neutral Shipping in International Armed Conflict', *Journal of Armed Conflict Law*, Vol. 2, No. 1, 1997, pp. 29–30.
16. Thomas, *The Defence of India*, n. 7, p. 206.
17. Francine R. Frankel, *India's Political Economy, 1947–2004: The Gradual Revolution*, New Delhi: Oxford University Press, 2005, pp. 249.

18. V.R. Panchmukhi, 'Foreign Trade and Trade Policies', in R.K. Sinha (ed.), *Economic Development since Independence: Forty Years of India's Development Experience*, New Delhi: Deep & Deep Publications, 1988, p. 352.
19. K. Sundaram, 'Political Response to the 1966 Devaluation: III: The Press, Business Groups and Economists', *Economic and Political Weekly*, Vol. 7, No. 38, 1972, p. 1931.
20. Thomas, *The Defence of India*, n. 7, p. 238.
21. Panchmukhi, 'Foreign Trade and Trade Policies', n. 18, p. 352.
22. Roy-Chaudhury, *Sea Power and Indian Security*, n. 8, pp. 147–54.
23. Thomas, *The Defence of India*, n. 7, pp. 202–09.
24. Ibid., p. 113.
25. Jagmohan Meher, 'Dynamics of Pakistan's Disintegration: The Case of East Pakistan 1947–1971', *India Quarterly*, Vol. 71, No. 4, 2015, pp. 302–09.
26. Kodikara, 'Major Trends in Sri Lanka's Non-Alignment Policy after 1956', n. 9, pp. 1127–28.
27. Ibid., p. 1134.
28. See Ibid., p. 1134; and Roy-Chaudhury, *Sea Power and Indian Security*, n. 8, pp. 62–63.
29. Michael Walter, 'The U.S. Naval Demonstration in the Bay of Bengal during the 1971 India-Pakistan War', *World Affairs*, Vol. 141, No. 4, 1979, pp. 299–302.
30. For Indian Navy's plan and operations, see G.M. Hiranandani, *Transition to Triumph: History of the Indian Navy 1965–75*, New Delhi, 1999, available at https://www.indiannavy.nic.in/sites/default/files/Transition-to-Triumph-07Apr16.pdf, accessed on 6 July 2021; D.K. Palit, *The Lightning Campaign: The Indo-Pakistan War, 1971*, Delhi: Lancer Publishers & Distributors, 1998; and Roy-Chaudhury, *Sea Power and Indian Security*, n. 8.
31. Roy-Chaudhury, *Sea Power and Indian Security*, n. 8, p. 72.
32. Palit, *The Lightning Campaign*, n. 30, p. 146.
33. Roy-Chaudhury, *Sea Power and Indian Security*, n. 8, p. 148.

11

Planning and Impact of Special Operations during the 1971 Indo-Pak War

Vinod Bhatia

The fortnight-long 1971 war between India and Pakistan in 1971 is a classic study in detailed planning, preparation, and a speedy, swift execution of military operations to achieve the desired political end-state. The war ended in less than two weeks with a decisive victory for India and resulted in the creation of Bangladesh, which was then known as East Pakistan.[1] Pakistan and the Pakistan Army were decimated into submission in the East, leading to the largest surrender of forces after the World War II. The Indian Armed Forces achieved the 'military objectives' and the 'desired political end-state' against all odds, capturing East Pakistan and liberating Bangladesh before the international community and the United Nations imposed a forced ceasefire. Speed was imperative. The Bangladesh resistance movement, Mukti Bahini, contributed in a major way in the unprecedented victory by disrupting and demoralising the Pakistan Army.

Political directions given by the Indira Gandhi-led government to the Indian Armed Forces were categorical:

- Liberate as much territory as possible in the east to set up a provincial Bangladesh government.
- Swift campaign of short duration in order to achieve objectives as there was a high likelihood of UN intervention.

- Defend Bhutan at all costs in case of Chinese intrusion.
- Ensure that conditions in liberated Bangladesh are conducive for the return of 10 million refugees residing in India.

Derived from the clear political objectives, the military aims were:

- Fight a holding, offensive–defensive battle in the west. In the east, ensure maximum speed of operations to force Pakistan to hand over the country to the provincial Bengal Government (established on 10 April 1971).
- Capture Khulna and Chittagong at the earliest and threaten Dhaka.
- To capture Dhaka.
- Launch operations in winter to negate any effective military intervention by China to support Pakistan.

Terrain—East Pakistan

To fully comprehend the enormity of the military objectives, especially in view of the restrictions of time imposed, speed of operations would dictate the success in the East Pakistan. Given the riverine terrain and the fortress-like defences constructed by the Pakistan Army, the task seemed near-impossible. Hence, planning and successful execution of special operations were critical to achieving the desired politico-military end-state. Prior to detailing the special operations, it is imperative to briefly analyse the terrain in East Pakistan and the relative force levels, to put it in context.

The terrain in erstwhile East Pakistan is mostly riverine interspersed with large tracts of marshy jungle astride the 700-plus kms of coastline along the Bay of Bengal. Lying at the confluence of the Ganga (Padma), Brahmaputra (Jamuna), and Meghna rivers, the terrain is prone to floods in the monsoons and drought in summers. The physiography is characterised by two distinctive features: a broad deltaic plain subject to frequent flooding, and a small hilly region crossed by swiftly flowing rivers.[2] Bangladesh has a total landmass of 1,44,000 sq km extending 820 km by 600 km. East Pakistan was located nearly 2,000 km from West Pakistan and shared a 4,096-km-long land border with India. On the south is a highly irregular deltaic coastline of 600 km, fissured with rivers and streams flowing into the Bay of Bengal.[3]

In the context of military operations, the major impediment to the maintenance of momentum and speed were the mighty rivers; the many crossings had to be captured and secured for the progress of operations (Map 1). The waterways comprise three mighty river systems:

- The massive Jamuna (Brahmaputra) river flows from the north till the confluence with river Padma, subsuming the waters of river Teesta.
- The mighty Padma (Ganga) flows from West Bengal in India till the confluence with river Jamuna 75 km west of Dhaka, a formidable obstacle for any offensive. The Padma is a 2,150-km-long river system, generally aligned from west to east, joining river Meghna at Chandpur nearly 100 km south of Dhaka.

Map 1. Terrain—Eastern Sector

- Meghna–Surma river at 670 km long is a major waterway formed by six rivers. These river systems all flow into the Bay of Bengal. Operations in the riverine terrain are the most challenging and time-consuming. Dhaka was and is a formidable objective, with three mighty river systems providing it with the requisite all-round defence.

Historically, airborne and special heliborne operations (special operations) have been successfully executed to maintain the momentum of attack and speed up operations. As speed and time were of essence in the Bangladesh war, the Indian Armed Forces planned and executed special operations with unprecedented success, surprising not only the Pakistan Army but also the world. It is a common narrative that India had limited time to achieve the objectives before the world powers (USA/UN) enforced a ceasefire. Special operations conducted by the Indian Armed Forces during the 13-day war from 3 December 1971, leading to the surrender by the Pakistan Army and the liberation of Bangladesh, make an interesting study. The many actions by Mukti Bahini that disrupted, degraded, and demoralised the Pakistan Army, as also the covert and clandestine operations executed prior to the declaration of war, are a study in themselves, and hence have not been analysed in this paper.

Special Operations

Special operations are defined as: 'Unconventional military operations, undertaken in a hostile or politically sensitive environment, to achieve political and military objectives at the national, strategic and operational level and to safeguard economic interests. Their arena extends the complete spectrum of conflict and ranges from direct action to covert and clandestine operations. These are undertaken mostly in concert with other elements of national power.'[4] Special operations were an integral and essential component of the planning process to ensure an early culmination of war by maintaining the tempo of operations in the Eastern Sector. On the Western Sector, special operations were planned and executed to disrupt and demoralise the enemy by typical commando raids. Prior to studying the special operations executed by the Indian Armed Forces, it will be prudent to briefly analyse the role and contribution of the Mukti Bahini, who were equally instrumental in the destruction of the Pakistan Army and the quick culmination of the war. The real-time intelligence, knowledge of the terrain, and the support of the people contributed to the war effort in a big way as also the success of the special operations. Pakistan Army somehow did not deploy forces to defend the road axis and avenues leading to Dhaka; however, most of the bridges, ferries, and crossings on the rivers were defended strongly to cause both attrition and delay and give time to the international community to step in and seek a ceasefire. However, two back-to-back operations by the Indian Army foiled the plan: one was the Meghna heli-bridge airlift on 9 December, and another, the Tangail airdrop on 11 December.[5] The special operations planned and executed during the war were:

- The airborne operations at Tangail to capture the Poongli bridge in the Eastern Sector, leading to the early capture of Dhaka.
- The special heliborne operations in support of 4 Corps offensive—Meghna crossing.
- The Chachro raid in the west.
- The raid on Mandhol—Western Sector (Poonch).

Airborne Operations—Tangail

This is the account of the first airborne operation launched by India against Pakistan post-Independence. The Bangladesh war of 1971, often called a 'lightning campaign', is well-recorded in the annals of military history. The para drop on 11 December at Tangail behind the enemy lines was India's trump card, which unhinged Pakistani forces in East Pakistan and ultimately led to the fall of Dacca (now Dhaka).[6]

Tangail is a major city in the Dhaka division. The main objective given to the airborne force was to secure the Poongli bridge on the mighty Jamuna. A secure crossing on the Jamuna river was essential to facilitate the uncontested advance of the ground forces astride the lightly held Manikganj–Dhaka axis, thus bypassing the strongly held Tongi–Dhaka axis. The success of all special operations is contingent on detailed planning, intelligence, preparation, training and leadership. The planning for the airborne assault had been initiated at the Army and Air Headquarters in New Delhi in early October.

With Major General Inder Gill, a die-hard paratrooper himself, as the Director of Military Operations in New Delhi, the Pakistan Army should have appreciated and factored the integration of special operations into the war plans of the Indian Armed Forces. General Inder Gill, a legendary paratrooper, was among a small team who executed Operation Harling to destroy the Gorgopotamos rail bridge in Greece behind enemy lines in the autumn of 1942 and was awarded the Military Cross for gallantry.[7] As a young Second Lieutenant of the Royal Sappers, his first parachute descent was a combat descent. Hence, the airborne assault at Tangail was integral to the early capture of Dhaka in the planning stages itself. Airborne operations need detailed planning and coordination at all levels, from the service headquarters to intermediary headquarters, and equally importantly, between the air task and airborne commanders.

Lieutenant General Mathew Thomas, the then commander of 50 (Independent) Parachute Brigade, writes in his blog:

> In the third week of Oct 1971, I was called up to Army HQ to discuss the proposed airborne operations with Army and Air HQ. I had a preliminary discussion with the Director of Military Operations (DMO) Maj Gen Inder Singh Gill PVSM, MC who was also the Colonel of the Parachute Regiment. He was fully aware of the pros and cons involved in executing the intended airborne tasks, nevertheless heard me out, my assessment and proposals patiently. He cleared a lot of my doubts with suggestions as to what was practically feasible. Finally, we had a plan for the use of paratroops should a war situation be thrust on us.[8]

Lt Gen Mathew Thomas goes on to detail the options during the planning stages of the airborne operation. He writes that Lieutenant General J.S. Aurora, another accomplished paratrooper, wanted the airborne operation to be carried out along the Jamalpur–Tangail–Dacca axis as the major part of his forces was advancing along this axis, which incidentally was also the shortest route to Dhaka. Accordingly, likely Drop Zones (DZs) were selected in the vicinity of crossings on Jamuna river near Tangail, as also along with a ferry on Lohajang river. On the capture of the crossings along Jamuna, the advancing columns under Major General GS Nagra would not only get an uncontested run to the outskirts of Dhaka but also interdict enemy columns withdrawing from Jamalpur and Mymensingh from reinforcing the Dhaka defences. A well-respected Mukti Jodha, Tiger Siddiqui, with large numbers of the Mukti Bahini, had effective control in and around Tangail, and hence, he could be contacted to assist the airborne force, enhancing the probability of success. The advancing columns of 101 Area would then link up with the airborne force, duly supported by Tiger Siddiqui's Mukti Bahini, thus setting the stage for the 'Battle for Dhaka'. The timing of the airborne operation, however, was contingent on the Indian Air Force achieving a 'favourable air situation', or at best, 'air superiority', in the intended area of operations. The progress of the ground operations would have to be fine-tuned to fit in with the airborne assault(s) as it was imperative that the link-up between the airborne assault forces be at the earliest.[9] The Service Headquarters issued a joint directive for the airborne assault on 29 October 1971, setting in motion the preparation and detailed planning of India's first-ever airborne operation. In early November 1971, a Joint Planning Cell was established at Advance Headquarters Eastern Air Command, conjointly staffed by Air Force and Parachute Brigade officers, for detailed planning and coordination. In mid-November, Captain P.K. Ghosh of the Parachute Brigade Signal Company, a bold and adventurous officer, fluent in Bangla, was infiltrated into the Tangail area and tasked to establish contact with Tiger Siddiqui to persuade him to provide detailed intelligence and to support the airborne drop. On 16 November 1971, the final Joint Army/Air Plan for airborne operations was issued, signed by Major General J.F.R. Jacob, Chief of Staff HQ, Eastern Command, and Air Vice-Marshal C.G. Devashar, Senior Air Staff Officer, Eastern Air Command.[10] This set the stage for the execution of the largest airborne assault ever by India, thus ensuring the early fall of Dhaka.

It is well documented that the US Task Force 74, led by the 75,000-ton USS Enterprise, then the world's largest nuclear-powered aircraft carrier, with 70 bombers and fighter aircraft, sailed into the Bay of Bengal on 11 December 1971, officially to evacuate the American citizens. But it was well known that the manoeuvre was aimed to deter India and prevent the liberation of Bangladesh.[11] The move of USS Enterprise coincided with the airborne operations. The US would have realised that the success of the airborne operation would lead to the inevitable fall of Dhaka and an end to the liberation war.

The 2 Para (Maratha) were selected for the airborne assault along with support elements of 17 Parachute Field Artillery Regiment, sappers, signallers, and medical staff of the units of the Parachute Brigade. The airborne operation was mounted on 11 December 1971 at 1423 hrs from Dum Dum (Calcutta) and Kalaikunda airfields with 46 aircraft. The Pathfinders took off from Dum Dum 30 minutes earlier to secure and mark the 'drop zone' and receive the main drop, duly aided by Tiger Siddiqui and his Mukti Bahini. The Pathfinder group secured and marked the drop zone by 1555 hrs on 11 December. As is the normal practice, the heavy and supply drop preceded the main drop. The entire battalion group, including the supply and heavy drop, was completed by 1650 hrs.[12] Forty-six aircraft, including the C-119 (Fairchild Packet), AN12, C-47 Dakota, and Caribou aircraft were employed for the airborne assault. The assault echelons, taking advantage of the surprise and shock effect, moved with speed to capture the objectives, Poongli bridge and ferry across the mighty Jamuna river, which the enemy was defending with a platoon each, supported by a few Razakars. Despite the Indian Air Force having achieved complete air superiority in the early days of the war over East Pakistan, Pakistan Army failed to appreciate the employment of airborne forces.

The 2 Para (Maratha) battalion group captured the assigned objectives of Poongli bridge and the ferry by 2000 hrs the same day, that is, within four hours of the heavy and supply drop on 11 December, thus furthering the swift advance by 101 Communication Zone under Major General Nagra. The capture of the Poongli bridge by the paratroopers also cut off Pakistan's 93rd Brigade, which was retreating from Mymensingh to defend Dhaka, which again contributed to the early fall of Dhaka. Advancing from the south, First Maratha Light Infantry, a sister battalion, broke through the Tangail defence to link up with the 2 Para (Maratha), thus securing both ends of the bridge. Around 1,000 paratroopers were airdropped at Tangail along with a battery of 75mm pack Howitzers, 106mm recoilless guns, jeeps, and other essential combat loads—the Tangail drop is one of the largest ever post-World War II.[13] Right up to the end of hostilities, Lieutenant General Niazi and his associates believed that India was employing a brigade strength of its paratroopers, and this further unnerved him. There was no Pakistani troop interference at the time of the drop; however, the inhabitants of the neighbouring villages panicked and began to run away from the area. Major General Sukhwant Singh writes that when the villagers heard the cry of 'Jai Bangla', they felt reassured and later flocked to the drop zone, all eager to carry loads and act as guides.[14] The Pakistan Army was on the run and its eventual defeat was now simply a matter of time.[15] However, the capture of the bridgehead was not without a fight by the enemy, which recognised the strategic implications of the special operations. A battalion of the Pakistan Army launched an immediate counter-attack to recapture the bridge but was defeated. Thereafter, Pakistan Army units launched two more counter-attacks on the night of 11/12 December from the northern and eastern directions with a battalion strength each, supported by Razakars. Both counter-attacks were beaten back by the paratroopers, with the enemy suffering heavy casualties. In all, the enemy suffered 143 killed and 10 wounded, 2 officers, 17 Other Ranks, and 10 Razakars were captured, together with considerable arms and ammunition and some vehicles.[16] The next morning, a desperate Pakistan Army, realising the criticality of recapturing the Poongli bridge on Jamuna, launched two more daylight attacks with nearly 500 men reinforced by Razakars.[17] These counter-attacks too were beaten back and the Poongli bridge and ferry were firmly in control of the Indian Army, thus facilitating the race to Dhaka by the 101 Communication Zone.

Deception and surprise were inbuilt in the plans and succeeded in deceiving the Pakistan Army into believing that the advance of 101 Communication Zone was diversionary. This was an intentional move by General J.S. Aurora to mislead the enemy into thinking that the Indian Army's advance into Dhaka would take place through the Comilla border.[18] To further reinforce the deception plan, General Jacob addressed a press conference in Calcutta on the night of 11 December after the drop saying that the Indian paratroopers had surrounded Dhaka city and that Dhaka was waiting to fall any day as it was surrounded by a division. However, in reality, the division was a battalion of paratroopers who had dropped not in Dhaka but over 100 km north in Tangail. Pakistani command was distressed by this bluff; it created a tremendous amount of psychological pressure on General Niazi to surrender.[19] The airborne assault at Tangail surprised the Pakistani leadership, thus speeding up the fall of Dhaka and an early end to the war. The support and the many actions by Tiger Siddiqui and his Mukti Bahini were critical to the success of the operation and fall of Dhaka. One of the most significant components of this plan was the landing of a battalion of paratroopers in Tangail.[20]

Writing for *ThePrint*, Lieutenant General Nirbhay Sharma, who was the Adjutant of 2 Para (Maratha) says:

> I was a young Captain and Adjutant of the battalion. Colonel K.S. Pannu, my Commanding Officer, asked me to carry a message. I, along with ADC to the GOC, Captain Hitesh Mehta, carried a handwritten message from General Nagra for General Niazi. It read: 'My dear Abdullah, I am here. The game is up, I suggest you give yourself up to me and I will take care of you.'[21]

General Niazi accepted the offer to surrender around 1045 hours on 16 December 1971. The 2 Para (Maratha) was the first to enter Dhaka.

Meghna Crossing: Heliborne Operations—Lieutenant General Sagat Singh's Masterstroke

If any one victory in battle were to be rated as the greatest victory in the history of warfare ever since man started recording history, then the criteria for judging it must be based on the following parameters:

- The final outcome of victory in battle.
- The comparative strength of the opposing forces.
- The losses in men and material.
- The time interval between conception, planning, execution and victory.[22]

If the above factors are to be considered, then the crossing on 9 December 1971 of the mighty Meghna by the Indian Army and Indian Air Force has to rank as one of the greatest and most brilliant feats of arms by any army and air force in the world since the dawn of history. No other single victory in battle has had a more profound an effect on the history of nations and humankind than this battle. In one swift masterstroke of brilliant conception, planning and execution, which from the beginning to the end was over in one day, a small force of a few hundred brave soldiers and 12 helicopters and their valiant crew created conditions for the liberation of an entire country and its hundred million citizens from the yoke of tyranny and forced an enemy army of over hundred thousand soldiers, sailors, and airmen to seek an abject ceasefire and surrender. This victory in a single operation helped create a new nation, Bangladesh, which had never before existed in history.[23]

Special Heliborne Operations (SHBO) was an emerging concept in the Indian Armed Forces in 1971. Lieutenant General Sagat Singh, one of the primary architects of the victory in the war, in an audacious manoeuvre employed infantry units and support arms to capture and establish a series of bridgeheads on the rivers in the assault and capture of Dacca. The most daring of these moves was the SHBO across the mighty Meghna river, which changed the course of the war. General Singh was a paratrooper, having had the distinction of commanding the coveted 50 (Independent) Parachute Brigade of Indian Army. Though belonging to the Gorkha Regiment, he completed his parachute jumps as Brigade Commander. He also led the Parachute Brigade in Operation Vijay, the liberation of Goa in 1961. Adept at seeking opportunities and thinking out of the box, he planned and executed the heli-lift across the Meghna river. Detailed planning, inter- and intra-service coordination, staff work, and training are essential to successfully execute an SHBO, and especially so with untrained infantry units and formations. But in 1971, General Singh practically pulled it off all by himself, along with a handful of his staff officers, Group Captain Chandan Singh, and his small Air Force of 12 Mi-4 helicopters. Sumit Walia writes in the *Indian Defence Review*:

> One wonders how did they manage to advance 110 miles in 13 days over 5 water obstacles – the toughest being the river Meghna which was 2.5 times wider than the Brahmaputra river. It was perhaps the widest river crossing conducted ever, that too while the enemy was present on both sides of river![24]

It came naturally to General Singh to keep scanning the ongoing battles in his area of operations for any opportunity to exploit. When he saw a small window of opportunity, he took a calculated risk and ordered the first heliborne operation in the history of the Indian Army. Using just 10 Mi-4 helicopters (under the command of Group Captain Chandan Singh), he got a battalion (4/5 Gorkha Rifles) heli-lifted in Sylhet. Emboldened by its success, he got a whole division landed across Meghna while the Pakistani forces sitting in Bhairab Bazar watched the spectacle—a remarkable feat that no one ever imagined. Readers must note that such humongous operations need meticulous planning at the Corps or Command level, followed by sand-model discussions and exercises.[25] He used

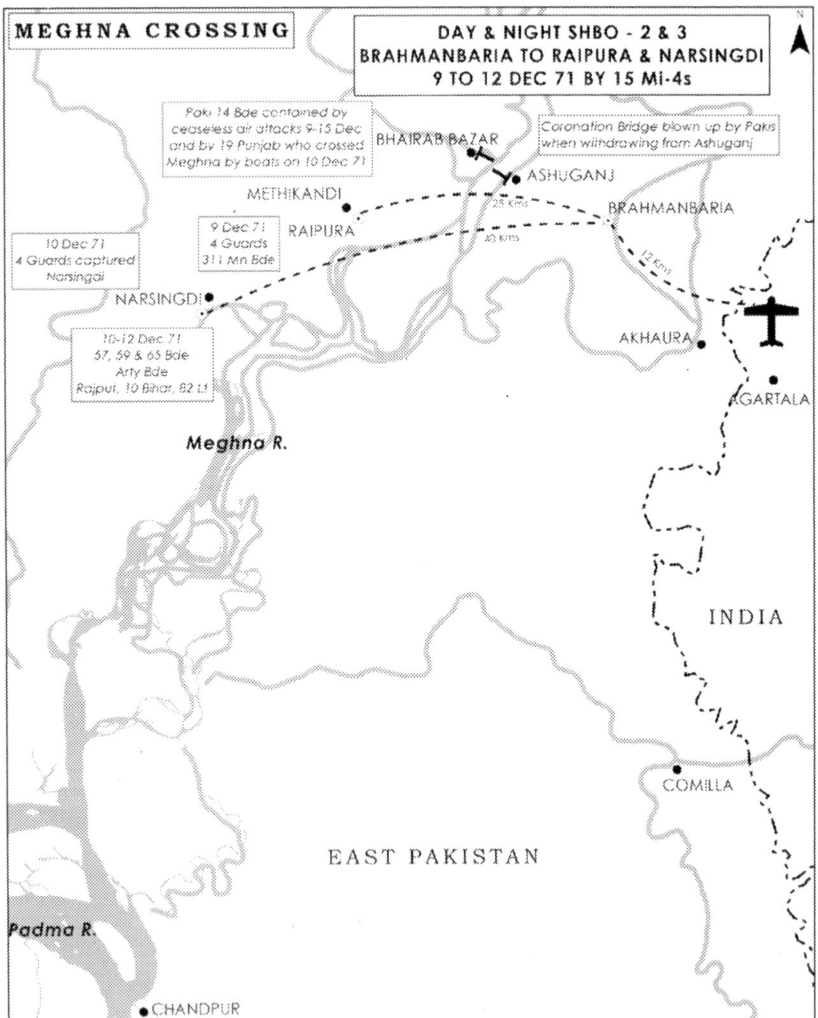

© GIS Section, Manohar Parrikar Institute for Defence Studies & Analyses (MP-IDSA). Map not to scale.

Map 2. Meghna Crossing

innovative campaign strategies to dislocate and surprise an already weakened adversary into complete capitulation. He was helped in great measure by the successful para-drop at Tangail, north of Dhaka, and the series of heliborne operations across the Meghna river at Narsingdi and further north at Sylhet, all of which caused a psychological collapse in Dhaka, brought on by what is called in military parlance 'vertical envelopment' (Map 2). Adding to General Niazi's woes was the constant bombing by the Indian Air Force and the pressure kept up on the coastal bastion of Chittagong by the Indian Navy.[26]

For the fall of Dhaka, it was essential to capture the heavily fortified city of Comilla, in the Chittagong division. The 57 Mountain Division had advanced and captured territories up to the Meghna river by 8 December; however, the Ashuganj bridge on the Meghna river was a major obstacle to be captured, secured, and crossed to maintain the momentum of advance. The enemy too had appreciated the value of holding the bridge in strength, and thus, the bridge was heavily fortified and defended. Assault across a river obstacle, especially a river like Meghna, which is 4,000 yards wide at the narrowest point, posed a major challenge. Any attack would be very costly and time-consuming. The advance of II Corps had also been stalled by a resolute defence by the enemy at Kushtia. Even when captured, the construction of a new bridge by army engineers would take unduly long, thus jeopardising the success of the war, which was time-sensitive, as international pressure led by the US for a ceasefire was gaining traction. General Sagat Singh then came up with the plan to heli-lift troops across the Meghna—success would ensure a quick culmination of the war, failure, however, would lead to a very high cost not only in terms of casualties but also as a failure to achieve the core objective of the capture of Dhaka. There were only 12 Mi-4 Soviet-built helicopters capable of carrying a maximum of 14 troops in one sortie. The infantry element being heli-lifted would be without any artillery support. Against all odds, the largest heli-lift by India thus was put into motion in a bold plan on 9 December, taking the enemy by surprise. 'Who Dares Wins' is the motto of the paratroopers.

The plan envisaged to lift troops in the available 12 Mi-4 helicopters from Raipura, on the southern side of Ashuganj bridge, and drop them north of Meghna at Narsingdi, thus facilitating the advance to Dhaka. This axis was lightly held by the Pakistan Army secure in the belief that the Indian Army will not be able to cross the mighty Meghna. The amphibious PT-76 tanks were tasked to ford across the Meghna and give direct fire support to the troops being heli-lifted. Group Captain Chandan Singh led the heliborne force employing the available Mi-4s.

The 4/5 Gorkha Rifles, also known as the Sylhet Gorkhas, were lifted on the night of 9 December to Raipura. They faced resistance from the Pakistan Army units deployed to defend the crossing. However, with the fire support and unmatched grit, they held on to their objective. In a non-stop ferry by the helicopters, 311 Infantry Brigade was heli-lifted in 110 sorties over a period of 36 hours. The Mi-4 helicopters, which are designed to carry a maximum of 14 troops, carried 23 in some sorties. This is one of the largest airlifts of troops in military history. On securing Raipura, the troops were again airlifted to secure Narsingdi. One of the most successful airlifts ever in military history was carried out, giving the Indian Army full access to Dhaka.[27]

The Meghna SHBO resulted in the complete collapse of the Pakistan Army in the East, leading to their ultimate surrender and liberation of Bangladesh. The Meghna crossing is unique in many ways, planned at the operational level with minimum resources and no support from outside the corps, executed with unprecedented speed, surprising the enemy, resulting in a complete collapse of the enemy's defensive battle. Speed was the essence that ensured success in face of odds—speed in decision making, speed in planning and in execution. The operation was planned and executed without any clearances from either the Service Headquarters or the Headquarters Command at Kolkata controlling the theatre. The most important aspect of the operation is the fact that despite the high risk, the casualties to own troops were negligible. The Mukti Bahini, in no small measure, contributed to the success with full support, creating chaos and delay among the enemy, and providing accurate intelligence. The SHBO by IV Corps under the leadership of the charismatic General Sagat Singh led to the eventual and early fall of Dacca.

The Raid on Chachro

The raid on Chachro military installations nearly 75 km deep inside Pakistan was a classic special operation. It was in the manner as conceptualised and conducted by Major David Sterling, popularly known as the 'Phantom Major'—he was adept at conducting vehicle-bound raids deep inside German positions, thus raising the Germans' costs for defending their installations and badly impacting troop morale and the decision-making abilities of the generals. The raid on Chachro by 10 Para Commando commanded by Lieutenant Colonel Bhawani Singh, belonging to the erstwhile royal family of Jaipur, had a strategic impact on the war in the Western Sector. The classic 'raid', immaculately planned and executed, shattered the morale of the enemy, and created a decision dilemma for the Pakistan

Army generals at the highest level. They grappled to discern the strategic intent of the Indian military in intervening deep inside West Pakistan, exposing the many weaknesses in their defences, as also the need to guard various military installations and echelons, thus diverting combat power from the primary role. Detailed planning, coordination and training are the prerequisites for the success of any special operation, especially one deep inside enemy territory. Among special forces operatives, such missions are euphemistically called 'a one-way ticket'.

Brigadier Abraham Chacko, who was then a newly minted subaltern in 10 Para Commando, writes:

> It was in December 1970, that we had the Army Chief, Sam Manekshaw, who came to spend half a day with us at Nasirabad. There was a close door meeting in the Commanding Officer's office, followed by a visit to the training area where we showed him demolition techniques and Heliborne deployment from a mock up helicopter. Immediately, after this visit, Bhawani went to Delhi. The tasks for the Paltan was evolving because two chiefs' visit to a unit at Nasirabad, which only had a Brigade HQ, could not have been a coincidence.[28]

The 10 Para Commando was mobilised to train and prepare for a deep vehicle-borne insertion into Pakistan in September 1971. The mission given to the commandos was:[29]

- Charlie Team to infiltrate along the Sarup Ka Tala and ginger up Ranger Wing Headquarters at Chachro by first light 7 December 1971.
- Alpha Team to disrupt lines of communication along Chachro–Umarkot axis and, if possible, destroy bridges along the canal in the green belt.
- Bravo Team to raid and destroy two rail bridges in general area Rahim Yar Khan to aid the advance of 12 Infantry Division along Tanot–Kishangarh–Islamgarh–Rahim Yar Khan.

Lieutenant Colonel Bhawani Singh's leadership was mainly instrumental in the success of the mission. He conceptualised the exact role and missions of the unit, properly equipped the troops with the requisite wherewithal to carry out the assigned mission and ensured meticulous planning and preparation. He was a soldier extraordinaire. Though Colonel Megh Singh is considered the father of special operations in India, it was Bhawani Singh who convinced Chief Sam Manekshaw on the strategic value of special operations. Brigadier Abraham Chacko writes about the great General Sam Manekshaw: 'If at any time you are tempted to feel scared, put your hands in your pocket and remember Sam. We firmly believed that no harm could come to us with him as our Chief.'[30]

The Chachro raid was actually a 'diversionary' to cause confusion and decision dilemma in the Pakistan General Headquarters (GHQ) and keep the Pakistan forces tied down in time and space, thus ensuring that the Indian Army achieves its strategic objective of holding action along the Western Front. The Alpha and Charlie Teams spearheaded the operation to insert 80 km inside Pakistan territory by vehicles and carry out a raid on the Chachro garrison. As planned, the raids were timed with the commencement of the war, with orders to insert given on 4 December. The insertion was by jeeps specially modified to navigate the desert terrain. Surprising the enemy in a bold action, the commandos launched daylight raids to capture Virawah and Nagarparkar, followed by the raids on Islamkot and Lunio. During these operations, the speed and ferocity of the attacks forced the enemy to panic and flee despite having superiority in numbers and position. The militia groups tasked with defending this region also did not fare any better. Logistical difficulties and the brief duration of the war saw the Sindh campaign halt just short of Umarkot. However, by the end of the war, about 13,000 sq km of Sindh was in Indian hands.[31] This was a dream special operation, creating havoc among the enemy ranks and a decision dilemma at the Pakistan GHQ. The excellent planning, preparation, equipping, training and the sheer audacity and ferocity ensured complete success. The best part was that the para commandos suffered no casualties. The unit was bestowed with the Battle Honour 'Chachro 1971' as well as with 10 gallantry awards. Lieutenant Colonel Bhawani Singh, the Commanding Officer, was awarded the Mahavir Chakra.

Operation Mandhol: Raid by 9 Para Commandos (9 Para SF)

The military objective in the Western Front was clear: fight a holding, offensive-defensive operations in the west to tie down maximum combat potential. This would contribute to the early collapse of East Pakistan, leading to the liberation of Bangladesh. However, Pakistan too intended to defeat India's war aims, and hence, their strategy and objectives were:

- Carry the battle into Indian territory in the west to make it the main theatre of war, thus delaying the Indian offensive in the east, forcing an early ceasefire through US and China.
- Capture maximum territory in Jammu and Kashmir (J&K) in a swift operation.
- Launch offensive in Chamb to cut off J&K and in Poonch.

Surprising the enemy, India launched its first-ever Special Operations

'Commando Raid' by foot insertion along a heavily manned and mined Line of Control on Mandhol gun position in the Poonch Sector. Though a tactical-level operation, it had strategic ramifications, instilling fear in the enemy by sheer daring and ferocity of the raid, forcing a defensive mindset, thus stymying the Pakistan Army offensive. The preparation and planning of the raid by 9 Para Commando [9 Para (SF)] had commenced early with the deployment of the commandos in the Nangi Tekri battalion of Poonch, a position which afforded direct visibility into enemy territory and its actions.

The 9 Para Commando was assigned a commando mission to raid and destroy an enemy artillery gun position in Mandhol, approximately 19 km southwest of Poonch. The insertion was planned by foot across the Poonch river. Six 122mm Chinese guns of a Pakistani battery were effectively interfering with the operations of Indian 93 and 120 Infantry Brigades. Colonel K.D. Pathak, who was part of the raiding party, says, 'We started around 5.30 pm on December 13 with one company comprising six officers and around 120 men of 9 Para Commando.'[32] According to Colonel Pathak, it was a very cold night, and they had to cross the Poonch river on foot to reach Mandhol. On reaching, they found the village had been vacated. The commandos located the enemy guns with the help of an old man. The raiding party then split into six, with the task of destroying one gun each. After a fierce fight, the commandos succeeded in destroying all the guns. During the fight, many soldiers of the Pakistan Army were killed and several fled. 'It was also an uphill task to return to our territory with wounded soldiers and the body of a soldier. Cots, taken from villages, were improvised and turned into stretchers to carry the wounded soldiers. We reached back at our post at 6.30 am.'[33]

Apart from the destruction of guns, ammunition and other vital equipment, the Pakistanis suffered 37 killed and 41 wounded. This raid, launched at a crucial time to enable India's 25 Infantry Division to progress the operations for the capture of Daruchian (a Pakistan-occupied post). The 9 Para Commandos suffered 16 casualties: two fatal, 14 wounded. For overall operations in this sector, the Para Commandos were awarded the Battle Honour 'Defence of Poonch' in the 1971 war. This is the only classical raid ever executed by the Indian special forces.[34]

The Indian Army, impressed by the unprecedented success of the raid, planned to disrupt the enemy at other locations. The C Team of 9 Para Commando was attached to 80 Infantry Brigade, Naushera Sector, on 17 December for a repeat performance at Chauki. But after the troops had moved to the forward assembly areas, the operation was called off due to the ceasefire.[35]

Though a tactical operation, the Mandhol raid had strategic implications. The raid instilled fear, demoralising Pakistan troops, and forcing them to deploy additional forces on protection and security duties to defend their installations and gun areas. This also led to the delay of a planned Pakistan offensive in the sector. It had so deep an impact on the Pakistan Army that it had to raise a second line of troops to secure their artillery guns, thereby making a change in its war doctrine.[36]

Mukti Bahini

The contribution of the Mukti Bahini in the liberation war has unfortunately been overshadowed by India's unprecedented victory, especially so in the final stages of the war. The key role of the Mukti Bahini was definitely a battle-winning factor. Beginning as the Mukti Fauj, the Mukti Bahini was born soon after the Pakistan Army unleashed mass rape and genocide on 25 March 1971 (Operation Searchlight). By the end of April, the number of volunteers who joined the Mukti Bahini was close to 2,50,000.

The Mukti Fauj was divided into 11 operational sectors, most of them along the periphery of the Indo-Bangladesh border. Each sector was allotted, on average, 2,000–3,000 sector troops and 6,000–7,000 guerrillas of the Gano Bahini. The operational policies were formulated by India's Eastern Command and the headquarters of Bangladesh Forces, and their implementation was entrusted to sector commanders. Although the Mukti Fauj and the East Bengal Rifles battalions fought pitched battles with the Pakistan Army, it was the Gano Bahini branch of the Mukti Bahini consisting of guerrillas that inflicted the greatest damage deep inside East Bengal. It was this guerrilla force that kept the Pakistan Army on tenterhooks.[37]

Mukti Jodhas of the Mukti Bahini struck deep inside East Pakistan, destroying command and communication networks and systems, bridges, railway network, administrative installations and infrastructure. They were a force multiplier supporting the Indian Armed Forces in all domains. The intelligence and local support they provided were critical not only to the overall war effort but also, in particular, in the planning and execution of special operations. It is not possible to detail the many operations and contributions of the Mukti Bahini. Suffice it to say that they were a battle-winning factor.

Conclusion

The 1971 India–Pakistan war is a must-study for military practitioners and strategists the world over. The Indian Armed Forces, with effective support from the Mukti Bahini, captured a well-defended and fortified East Pakistan riddled with massive river systems within a span of 13 days, which was akin to the 1939 German Blitzkrieg in World War II. The meticulous planning and the sheer audacity in the execution of special operations impacted the course of the war. The Indian Armed Forces achieved the derived military objectives in totality, thus ensuring the desired political end-state. Bangladesh was liberated at the end of the 13-day war after Indian troops entered Dhaka on 16 December 1971 to accept the surrender of nearly 93,000 troops of the Pakistan Army as prisoners of war.

NOTES

1. Karan Manral, '50th Anniversary of 1971 India-Pakistan War: All You Need to Know', *Hindustan Times*, New Delhi, 16 December 2020, available at https://www.hindustantimes.com/india-news/50th-anniversary-of-1971-india-pakistan-war-all-you-need-to-know/story-U1JwHfjrFvQaWr7Rp3dNHI.html, accessed on 3 August 2021.
2. James Heitzman and Robert Worden (eds), 'Bangladesh: A Country Study', Washington: GPO for the Library of Congress, 1989, available at http://countrystudies.us/bangladesh/25.htm, accessed on 10 August 2021.
3. Ibid.
4. Vinod Bhatia, 'Powerful Punch: A Restructured Special Operations Force Can be a Game Changer in India's Security Landscape', *Force*, available at https://forceindia.net/guest-column/guest-column-vinod-bhatia/powerful-punch/, accessed on 10 August 2021.
5. Ratnakar Sadasyula, 'Meghna Heli Bridge, Tangail Air Drop', *History Under Your Feet*, 12 December 2019, available at https://historyunderyourfeet.wordpress.com/2019/12/12/meghna-heli-bridge-tangail-air-drop/.
6. Nirbhay Sharma, 'As a Young Captain in 1971 Bangladesh War, I Gave Pakistan's Lt-Gen the Letter to Surrender', *The Print*, 11 December 2019, available at https://theprint.in/opinion/in-1971-bangladesh-war-i-gave-pakistan-lt-gen-letter-to-surrender/333068/, accessed on 12 August 2021.
7. Peter D. Pawelek, 'Europe Ablaze - Operation Harling: Destruction of the Gorgopotamos Rail Bridge, 1942', available at http://www.sa-snd.gr/docs-pdfs/operation%20harling.pdf.
8. Mathew Thomas, 'The Planning and Conduct of Airborne Operations in the Indo-Pak War of 1971 Part 2 : The Air Assault Op at Tangail (East Pakistan)—11 December 1971', *Musings of a Mutt from Meerut*, available at https://htppijump4joy.wordpress.com/2019/11/03/the-planning-and-conduct-of-airborne-operations-in-the-indo-pak-war-of-1971-part-2-the-air-assault-op-at-tangail-east-pakistan-11-december-1971/.
9. Ibid.
10. Ibid.
11. Asif Mahfuz, 'US Fleet in Bay of Bengal: A Game of Deception', *The Daily Star*, 16 December 2013, available at https://www.thedailystar.net/news/us-fleet-in-bay-of-bengal-a-game-of-deception.
12. Thomas, 'The Planning and Conduct of Airborne Operations in the Indo-Pak War of 1971 Part 2: The Air Assault Op at Tangail (East Pakistan)—11 December 1971', n. 8.

13. Sadasyula, 'Meghna Heli Bridge, Tangail Air Drop', n. 5.
14. Sukhwant Singh, '1971 War: Airborne Operations', available at http://www.indiandefence review.com/interviews/1971-war-airborne-operations/.
15. Nuran Nabi, 'The Tangail Landings: A Signal for Victory', *The Daily Star*, 26 March 2015, available at https://www.thedailystar.net/supplements/independence-day-special-2015/the-tangail-landings-signal-victory-73754.
16. Thomas, 'The Planning and Conduct of Airborne Operations in the Indo-Pak War of 1971 Part 2 : The Air Assault Op at Tangail (East Pakistan)—11 December 1971', n. 8.
17. Ibid., p. 18.
18. Ibid., p. 10.
19. Ibid., p. 16.
20. Ibid., p. 22.
21. Sharma, 'As a Young Captain in 1971 Bangladesh War, I Gave Pakistan's Lt-Gen the Letter to Surrender', n. 6.
22. Available at https://www.bharat-rakshak.com/ARMY/history/1971war/444-the-meghna-crossing.html, accessed on 8 August 2021.
23. Ibid.
24. Sumit Walia, 'Remembering the Undefeated Sarvatra (Lt Gen) Sagat Singh – Part-2', *Indian Defence Review*, Net Edition, 15 November 2019, available at http://www.indiandefencereview.com/news/remembering-the-undefeated-sarvatra-lt-gen-sagat-singh-part-2/.
25. Ibid.
26. Arjun Subramaniam, '1971 Bangladesh Liberation War: Meticulous Planning Was the Key', available at https://www.indianarrative.com/opinion-news/1971-bangladesh-liberation-war-meticulous-planning-was-the-key-42032.html, *India Narrative*, 17 January 2021.
27. Walia, 'Remembering the Undefeated Sarvatra (Lt Gen) Sagat Singh – Part-2', n. 24.
28. Abraham Chacko, *Memories of My Initial Years in 10 PARA SF and 1971 Indo Pak War (Operation Cactus Lilly)*, New Delhi: Centre for Joint Warfare Studies, available at https://cenjows.in/article-detail?id=364.
29. Ibid., p. 15.
30. Ibid., p. 3.
31. Ananth Karthikeyan, 'The Desert Raids of the 1971 War', *DNA India*, 16 December 2018, available at https://www.dnaindia.com/analysis/column-the-desert-raids-of-the-1971-war-2696445, accessed on 13 August 2021.
32. Ajay Sura, 'Operation Mandhol Forced Pakistan to Change War Plan', *The Times of India*, 16 December 2013, available at https://timesofindia.indiatimes.com/india/operation-mandhol-forced-pakistan-to-change-war-plan/articleshow/27444282.cms, accessed on 19 August 2021.
33. Ibid.
34. 9th Battalion The Parachute Regiment (Special Forces),Source 9 PARA SF: 'The Raid at Mandhol by 9 Para (SF)', *Scholar Warrior*, Spring, 2011, pp. 135–37, available at https://archive.claws.in/images/journals_doc/Spring%202011-%20Final%20Issue. 148-150.pdf, accessed on 19 August 2021.
35. Ibid., p. 137.
36. Sura, 'Operation Mandhol Forced Pakistan to Change War Plan', n. 32.
37. Praveen Davar, 'Mukti Bahini: A Force for Freedom', *The Telegraph Online*, 29 April 2021, available at https://www.telegraphindia.com/opinion/mukti-bahini-a-force-for-freedom/cid/1813965, accessed on 23 August 2021.

12

The Mukti Bahini
Three Dimensional Guerillas

Sandeep Unnithan

An archer letting off an arrow may or may not kill a single man, but a wise man using his intellect can kill even reaching unto the very womb.

—**Kautilya,** ***The Arthashastra***

The 1971 Indo-Pakistan War fought half a century ago remains one of the few twentieth century conflicts where armed forces of both sides deployed in all three dimensions—land, sea and air—as seen during the Second World War. The war marked the demise of Great Britain as a colonial power in Asia, Africa and the Middle East and was thus one of the direct causes of India's independence. The military leadership of India and Pakistan in 1971 had fought the world war together in the army of undivided India. A handful had been commissioned into service together, some of them in the same theatres of the war. The armed forces on both sides continued the training and traditions handed down by the British in the armed forces on both sides. The war continued to inspire the planners of 1971. Lt Gen JFR Jacob, Chief of Staff in the Eastern Command, cited the mass surrender ceremonies of the Imperial Japanese Army in South-East Asia as his inspiration for staging a public signing of the instrument of surrender by Lt Gen AAK Niazi in Dhaka on 16 December 1971.

Guerilla warfare was another aspect of the war clearly inspired by the World War II. The war saw irregular forces being raised and trained on an unprecedented scale across the globe. As German and Japanese forces rolled across Europe and Asia engulfing countries and former western colonies, the Allies supported bands of guerillas in Europe—the dogged French resistance in occupied France, Greek partisans or the Andartes in Greece, Italian partisans and Tito's communist partisans in Yugoslavia. 'An inner circle which British PM Winston Churchill called his "Ministry of Ungentlemanly Warfare" aided the partisans in assassinations and acts of sabotage across Europe'.[1] Closer home, two communist guerilla movements—Viet Minh insurgents in French Indo-China (later Vietnam) and the Chinese Communist Party in China, active during World War II—captured power in their respective countries soon after the war.

The three wings of the Indian armed forces raised a Mukti Bahini (Liberation Force), an army of over 1,00,000 guerillas raised from among the Bengali population of East Pakistan. Their creation was inspired by an Indian army leadership with combat experience of similar actions during the World War II. But their eventual composition and combat operations, especially in the maritime theatre, outstripped seen since the World War II. The Bengali guerillas had a land forces component and even small naval and air force wing. They were thus among the most unique guerilla forces of the twentieth century.

A History of Guerilla Warfare in South Asia

Guerilla warfare, literally 'small war', is the oldest form of warfare. 'It's not hard to see why this mode of warfare has become so prevalent. For one thing, it is cheap and easy: waging guerilla warfare does not require procuring expensive weapon systems or building an elaborate bureaucracy', the scholar Max Boot noted in his authoritative book *Invisible Armies*.[2]

It was Pakistan and not India that was the first to introduce guerilla warfare into the subcontinent as a means to achieve geopolitical outcomes. It failed on both occasions. On 22 October 1947, Pakistan Army officers launched Operation Gulmarg—the infiltration of approximately 20,000 Pathan tribesmen into the princely state of Jammu and Kashmir. Twenty tribal Lashkars of a thousand men each were created, ten each for the Srinagar and Poonch-Rajouri sectors. The princely state was yet to accede to either India or Pakistan. The tribal raiders were meant to capture the Kashmir Valley and the vital towns of Poonch and Rajouri. Their objectives were foiled as the Indian Army entered the state on 25 October 1947 and repulsed the raiders.

'Operation Gulmarg at no stage anticipated a spirited riposte as it was felt that the state forces of Jammu and Kashmir would capitulate within hours, and the Indian Army would be too preoccupied with managing the refugee and communal crisis to intervene in time', military historian Air Vice Marshal Arjun Subramaniam notes in his book *India's Wars: A Military History, 1947–1971*.[3]

In 1965, the Pakistan Army struck again. On 5 August, they launched 'Operation Gibraltar', infiltrating mujahid battalions and regulars into the Kashmir Valley. The 'Gibraltar Forces', as they were called, was said to have numbered approximately 4,000 to 5,000 and divided into approximately eight forces of five companies each. These companies of 110–120 were divided into infiltrating groups of 50 to 60 with regular Junior Commissioned Officers and a few soldiers embedded in the group to provide leadership.[4] By 21 August that year, the operation was crushed and many of the infiltrators captured by the Indian Army. Operation Gibraltar, quite unlike the rock base it was named after, had collapsed. Pakistan's Inter Services Intelligence (ISI) however, continued to use its Eastern wing to support insurgents in India's North East. As B. Raman, former Special Secretary, R&AW notes in his book *The Kaoboys of R&AW: Down Memory Lane*:

> Ever since 1956, the Naga hostiles under the leadership of the late Phizo were in touch with Pakistan's ISI. The ISI supported their struggle for independence and provided them with funds, training, arms and ammunition. It allowed them to set up sanctuaries and training camps in the Chittagong Hill Tracts (CHT) of East Pakistan. Between 1956 and 1967, many gangs of Naga hostiles went to the CHT for being trained by the ISI and then returned with arms and ammunition.[5]

The Ferment in East Pakistan

The Partition of the subcontinent in 1947 had created a bizarre geography of Pakistan—a country with two wings separated by 2,200 km of India's mainland. The ethnic Bengali-speaking eastern wing chafed at being reduced to second-class citizens in a country dominated by the western wing. Pakistan's Punjab province dominated the western wing, its armed forces and politics.

The run-up to Bangladesh's freedom struggle began in 1970, with Pakistan's first general elections of December 1970. Sheikh Mujibur Rahman's Awami League won elections to the National Assembly by a landslide. The Awami League won 167 of the 169 seats in East Pakistan while Zulfiqar Ali Bhutto's PPP won 83 out of 144 seats in West Pakistan. The results were a setback to the ruling military junta led by General Yahya Khan. They were loathe to hand over power to a party from its eastern wing. The election results were held in abeyance prompting increasing unrest in east Pakistan. On 23 March 1971 (now observed as Bangladesh's independence day), the Awami League replaced Pakistani flags with Bangladeshi flags. Two days later, the Pakistan army began its crackdown in the eastern wing, arresting Sheikh Mujibur Rahman and killing thousands of people including officers and men of the East Bengal Rifles which had mutinied.

The Pakistan Army began a genocide in its eastern wing targeting elements of the East Bengal Rifles (EBR), East Pakistan Rifles (EPR), paramilitary ansars, mujahids, Awami League office-bearers and students. They also targeted students, intellectuals, doctors, journalists and Hindus.

The start of the creation of the Mukti Bahini was the announcement on 11 April by Tajuddin Ahmed, the Prime Minister of the provisional government of Bangladesh that a liberation army was being created. The liberation army, Ahmed said, was being created from the elements of the EBR, EPR, police, ansars, mujahids and thousands of volunteers. He also ordered the creation of eight regional commands to fight the Pakistani forces, each headed by a Major or a Captain of the EBR or EPR. Colonel MAG Osmani, a retired Pakistan Army officer and member of the National Assembly was appointed Commander-in-Chief of the Bangladesh Liberation Army. The Mukti Bahini was initially around 2.5 lakh strong and drawn from the ranks of young men who had fled their homes in East Pakistan.

A provisional government of Bangladesh was created on 17 April 1971 on the border with India. The town was later renamed Mujib Nagar. From May onwards, the Bangladesh army based in India carried out raids to harass and disrupt communications in East Pakistan. Pakistani army reprisals triggered off a flood of refugees into India. By the end of May, 4.3 million refugees had flooded into India and by the end of July, the figure was 7.2 million creating an enormous socio-economic burden on Indian states bordering East Pakistan. This was one of the direct causes of the third war fought by the two countries which began on 3 December 1971.

The Man with a Plan

The creation of the Mukti Bahini had the explicit if not overt political backing of the government of Mrs Indira Gandhi.[6] The Mukti Bahini were raised through an operational directive issued by army chief, General SFHJ Maneckshaw to Eastern Army Commander Lt General Aurora on 1 May. General Maneckshaw directed Lt General Aurora to raise, equip and train the East Bengal cadres for guerilla operations in their own native land so as to immobilise and tie down the East Pakistan forces to protective tasks in East Bengal and subsequently, by gradual escalation of the guerilla operations, sap and corrode the morale of the Pakistan forces to impair their offensive capability against India.

The directive had its origins in a paper presented by (then) General Maneckshaw's Director Military Training, Major General (later Lt General) Inder Singh Gill. In the summer of 1971, no officer in the Indian Army knew more about guerilla warfare than Major General Inder Gill. Gill, the son of a UK-trained Sikh doctor and a Scottish mother, had been born and raised in Great Britain before the war. He was commissioned into the British Army as a 2nd lieutenant in the Corps of Engineers and had parachuted behind enemy lines in 1943 and had operated with the Greek partisans, the Andartes.

> In April 1971 while he (Major General Gill) was DMT, he presented a paper to the Chiefs of Staff Committee on what India could do in East Pakistan. Inder had developed strong convictions on the usefulness of Special Services Operations in the successful conduct of war, based on his experience in Greece. In his paper, he suggested organising the East Pakistani refugee youths, those in service with Pakistan's East Pakistan Rifles, East Militia Rifles, the Militia and Paramilitary Forces and the armed police, and the young political cadres of the Awami League that had established a government in exile, as commandos and guerillas for clandestine operations inside East Pakistan. He argued that, with some training, direction and motivation, they could be employed suitably for tasks that might be militarily productive in the event of war or even for creating war-like situations.[7]

The codename given to the Eastern Command's overall training effort for the Mukti Bahini was 'Operation Jackpot'. After a significant conference of the provisional government of Bangladesh, the eastern wing was divided into 11 sectors for operational purposes. These sectors reported to the Calcutta-based provisional government. Only one—Sector 10—was along the maritime boundaries and placed directly under the C-in-C Colonel Osmani. The numerical sectors inside East Pakistan liased with Indian sectors alphabetically named Sectors Alpha through Foxtrot-Juliet on the Indian side. The Indian sectors were headed by Brigadiers and had been set up for training and logistics and for coordinating Mukti Bahini operations.

Land Forces

The core of the land forces were made up of the East Pakistan Rifles and East Bengal Rifles. The original plan was to raise a force of 20,000 men by 30 September

1971. But subsequently the raising was stepped up, first by 12,000 men a month then by 20,000 men a month. By 30 November 1971, the strength of the force was increased to over 1,00,000 men.[8] Numerically that would make them second only to an estimated 3,00,000 Communist Vietnamese guerillas the 'Viet Cong' who fought in Southern Vietnam between 1953 and 1975.

At their peak in November 1971, their numbers were as follows:

East Bengal Rifles (EBR)	8,156
Mukti Fauj (MF)	9,660
Mujib Bahini and Uban Force	6,000
Freedom Fighters	83,028
Total	**1,06,844**

Of the above, 50,810 had started operating inside East Pakistan by the end of November 1971. All freedom fighters were given four weeks' training, including weapons training, field craft, raids and ambushes. Commando training included simple demolitions, operation of pocket-sized radio sets and transmission of Morse code messages at the rate of six words per minute. In August the period of training was reduced to three weeks.[9]

Air Force Component

The Mukti Bahini Air Force codenamed 'Kilo Flight' was raised on 4 October 1971. It included one Dakota, one Otter and one Alouette helicopter armed with rocket pods and medium machine guns.[10] On the night of 3–4 December, the Otter aircraft based at Kalashshahar, attacked the fuel dumps at Chittagong and the Alouette helicopters raided the fuel dumps at Narayangunj. At the outbreak of the war, this force was placed under the GOC 8 Mountain Division operating in Sylhet sector. It carried out five sorties between 4 and 7 December hitting bunkers and troop concentrations at Maulvi Bazar and also destroying two steamers and two 3-ton trucks carrying troops.

Naval Component

The Naval component of the Mukti Bahini was unlike any in the twentieth century. The core comprised eight Bengali sailors who had deserted the Pakistani submarine PNS Mangro in France in March 1971. They were attached to the Directorate of Naval Intelligence (DNI) who began to raise a force of limpeteers (naval saboteurs) trained on the battlefield of Palashi/ Plassey in Nadia District. The eight Pakistani sailors formed the core of what would be called Naval Commando Operations

(X). A total of 457 combat swimmers/limpeteers were trained under the operation also known as run by the DNI but supervised by the Eastern Army Command.[11]

The choice of this unique form of naval guerilla operation was no accident. Bangladesh is a riverine country. Around 11 per cent of her total area was covered by rivers and waters. The largest river, the Jamuna, was formed by a confluence of the Ganga and Brahmaputra. The Jamuna was 200 kilometres long and had an average width of 10 kilometres. An elaborate network of boats, barges and ferries was the only way to transport people and commodities around. In 1971, the limpeteers targeted the boats and vessels that transported supplies and personnel for the Pakistan Army. As a result, thousands of Pakistani soldiers were drawn away from offensive operations against the Mukti Bahini towards protecting waterways from naval saboteurs.

On the night of 15 August, over 170 combat swimmers of the naval wing carried out near simultaneous attacks on the ports of Mongla, Narayangunj, Chittagong and Chandpur destroying or disabling 25 vessels—the largest such attacks since the World War II.

By August this force was given two harbor utility craft converted into mine-laying gunboats—the MV Palash and the MV Padma. The combat swimmers also known as 'naval commandos' by DNI sank or disabled 1,00,000 tonnes of enemy shipping in East Pakistan waging what is called a war of 'guerre de course' or commerce destruction. This guerilla war targeted not just the merchant ships that carried out jute and tea which earned the Pakistan foreign exchange but also those bringing in arms, ammunition and food for its military garrison. The gunboats laid mines at the mouth of the Pussur river leading to East Pakistan's second largest port, Mongla, in September 1971.

Major General JFR Jacob, then Chief of Staff, Eastern Army Command, called the (naval commando missions) 'the most significant operations of the Mukti Bahini'.[12]

Assessment of Mukti Bahini Operations

While the Mukti Bahini's guerilla war sapped the morale of the Pakistan army, it is doubtful this campaign by itself would have achieved the liberation of Bangladesh. Just as Europe was liberated from the yoke of Nazi Germany by Allied armies converging in from eastern and western Europe, an independent Bangladesh was created by the hammer blows of Indian armed forces in December 1971. A multi-pronged Indian army ground-offensive bypassed the fortified towns and cities and captured the centre of gravity of the eastern wing—Dhaka. The Air

Force swept away the single PAF squadron based in the eastern province and flew close air support missions and logistic duties to aid the ground offensive. The Indian Navy fleet enforced a naval blockade and interdicted merchant ships fleeing with members of the Pakistani garrison. On 16 December 1971, the entire East Pakistan garrison numbering 92,208 persons had surrendered to the Indian armed forces.

The Mukti Bahini were hobbled by the lack of effective training—just three weeks as opposed to at least three months of training that would be needed to turn raw cadres into guerillas. They also had a shortage of experienced officers because of which they undertook only easy tasks. Their raids on Pakistani Border Outposts were ineffective. Where they succeeded however was in the gathering of intelligence which helped the Indian forces that were to move in.

Mukti Bahini operations also tied down large number of Pakistani forces into static guard duties. This was especially the case with the martime wing's sabotage operations which began on the night of 15 August 1971.

Every barge with ammunition sunk, meant the Pakistani army had fewer bullets to shoot at civilians and the Indian Army. Every attack by the naval commandos—whether successful or not—meant the Pakistan army had to pull its forces away from the borders into guarding the ports and waterways. The biggest contribution of the naval guerillas was to take pressure away from the land forces element of the Mukti Bahini. The guerilla camps were disbanded on the Indian side but the cadres went on to form the nucleus of the Bangladeshi armed forces after their War of Liberation. 'Left unstated was the fact that the Indian state had proved it was not entirely a stranger to irregular warfare, which it had been at the receiving end of since 1947'.[13]

Hybrid Warfare

The Pakistani deep state continued its pursuit of covert operations. It greatly expanded its understanding of such warfare during the Soviet occupation of Afghanistan between 1979 and 1988 where it trained and equipped the Afghan resistance, the Mujahideen, with the assistance of the CIA and other western intelligence agencies. The expertise and ordnance left over from the Afghan war was used to run covert wars against the Indian states of Punjab and Jammu and Kashmir, both of which continue till date. It was used to wage war against India's economic capital between 1993 and 2008 using an array of 'non-state actors'[14] while using its nuclear weapons to deter a conventional Indian military response.

The analyst Commodore C. Uday Bhaskar has termed this 'Nuclear Weapons

Enabled Terrorism' or NWET.[15] The Afghan expertise came in handy when the Pakistani deep state armed and trained the Taliban raised from among Afghan students and veterans of the war against the Soviets. The Taliban's Islamic Emirate of Afghanistan ruled that country between 1996 and 2001. After 20 years in the wilderness, most of them spent in havens in Pakistan, the Afghan Taliban fought a bruising insurgency against the western supported regimes of President Hamid Karzai and Ashraf Ghani.

In a written testimony to the United States Senate Committee on Armed Services in 2011, Admiral Mike Mullen, Chairman of the Joint Chiefs of Staff, said that 'the Quetta Shura [Taliban] and the Haqqani Network operate from Pakistan with impunity' and that these Pakistan government proxies 'were attacking Afghan troops and civilians as well as US soldiers'. Admiral Mullen termed the Haqqani Network, 'a strategic arm of Pakistan's Inter-Services Intelligence Agency'.[16]

By August 2021 the Taliban had captured power almost without firing a shot as members of the Ghani regime fled following the US withdrawal.

With the receding prospect of full-scale wars between nation states, insurgency and terrorism have become the dominant forms of conflict between nation states.[17] Iran and Russia have been proponents of the same. Iran's Islamic Revolutionary Guards Corps (IRGC) has supported guerilla forces in Yemen, Syria and Iraq.[18] A Russian Private Military Contractor (PMC) Wagner, believed to have ties with the Kremlin, has shown up in countries across Africa and Asia where Russia has interests but is unwilling to commit boots on the ground.[19] PMCs with their in-built deniability are effective means of ensuring deniability. The shift was first noticed by the Pentagon's Quadrennial Defence Report of 2006 which noted how 'in the post September 11 world, irregular warfare has become the dominant form of warfare confronting the United States'.

Covert warfare is one of the elements of what the US scholar Hoffman termed as 'hybrid warfare'. In his paper 'Conflict in the 21st century: The Rise of Hybrid Warfare', Hoffman said that:

> At the strategic level, many wars have had regular and irregular components. However, in most conflicts, these components occurred in different theatres or in distinctly different formations. In Hybrid Wars, these forces become blurred into the same force in the same battlespace. While they are operationally integrated and tactically fused, the irregular component of the force attempts to become operationally decisive rather than just protract the conflict, provoke overreactions or extend the costs of security for the defender.

The 1971 War was a rare and well-documented foray into the realm of hybrid warfare by the Indian state. Indian military leaders have since examined these options. Delivering the 9th YB Chavan Memorial Lecture hosted by the Manohar Parrikar Institute for Defence Studies and Analyses on 28 November 2018, then Army Chief General Bipin Rawat reflected on the dilemma before the Indian state as it considered two options:

> One is to engage in offensive Hybrid Warfare as a nation and the second is to defend against this threat proactively. In weighing these options, our standing in the global strategic framework, our reputation, our nation's sensibilities and training and organisation of our agencies need to be looked at comprehensively.[20]

General Rawat suggested the 'offensive option' was the least preferred option but it could consider 'limited hybrid' in support of 'proactive defence'.

> Creating unrest in our neighbour's territory should not be the first choice. Moreover, as evidenced in Pakistan, there are no good or bad terrorists. Sooner or later, such use of irregulars as a strategy destabilises the country internally. Also, it takes the focus away from development. Thus, in my opinion, in our case, we should prefer the proactive defence option against Hybrid war, through limited Hybrid in support of proactive defence is advisable. This will involve the whole of government approach.[21]

The 'limited hybrid' that General Rawat suggested involves the raising of irregular forces for limited objectives rather than prolonged support which could result in a blowback. These irregular forces could then be disbanded after the achievement of the objectives. Exactly as was the case with the Mukti Bahini in 1971. Fifty years after the 1971 War, its lessons remain as relevant as ever.

NOTES

1. Giles Milton, *The Ministry of Ungentlemanly Warfare: How Churchill's Secret Warriors Set Europe Ablaze and Gave Birth to Modern Black Ops*, Picador, 2017.
2. Max Boot, *Invisible Armies: An Epic History of Guerrilla Warfare from Ancient Times to the Present*, New York and London: Liveright Publishing Corporation, 2013.
3. Arjun Subramaniam, *India's Wars: A Military History, 1947–1971*, HarperCollins, 2016.
4. Ibid.
5. B. Raman, *The Kaoboys of R&AW: Down Memory Lane*, Lancer Publishers, 2007.
6. Gary J. Bass, *The Blood Telegram*, Penguin Random House India, 2013.
7. S. Muthiah, *Born to Dare: The Life of Lt Gen Inderjit Singh Gill*, Penguin Books India, 2008.
8. *The India–Pakistan War of 1971: A History*, Ministry of Defence, Government of India, Natraj Publishers, 2014.
9. Ibid.

10. Ibid.
11. Captain MNR Samant and Sandeep Unnithan, *Operation X: The Untold Story of India's Covert Naval War in East Pakistan 1971*, HarperCollins, 2019.
12. Lt Gen JFR Jacob, *Surrender at Dacca, Birth of a Nation,* Manohar, 1997.
13. Samant and Unnithan, *Operation X: The Untold Story of India's Covert Naval War in East Pakistan 1971*, n. 11.
14. Sandeep Unnithan, '1993: The Pakistan Army's First Attack on Bombay', *India Today*, 12 March 2021, available at https://www.indiatoday.in/india-today-insight/story/1993-the-pakistan-army-s-first-attack-on-bombay-1778600-2021-03-12.
15. Chitrapu Uday Bhaskar, 'Non-Use of Nuclear Weapons', *The Hindu*, 21 June 2011, available at https://www.thehindu.com/books/nonuse-of-nuclear-weapons/article2122710.ece.
16. Thomas Joscelyn, 'Admiral Mullen: Pakistani ISI Sponsoring Haqqani Attacks', *FDD's Long War Journal*, 22 September 2011, available at https://www.longwarjournal.org/archives/2011/09/admiral_mullen_pakis.php.
17. Jeremy M. Weinstein, *Inside Rebellion: The Politics of Insurgent Violence,* Cambridge: Cambridge University Press, 2007.
18. Frank Gardner, 'Iran's Network of Influence in Mid-East "Growing"', *BBC News*, 7 November 2019, available at https://www.bbc.com/news/world-middle-east-50324912
19. Nathaniel Reynolds, 'Putin's Not-So-Secret Mercenaries: Patronage, Geopolitics, and the Wagner Group', *Carnegie Endowment For International Peace*, available at https://carnegieendowment.org/2019/07/08/putin-s-not-so-secret-mercenaries-patronage-geopolitics-and-wagner-group-pub-79442
20. General Bipin Rawat's speech at 9th YB Chavan Memorial Lecture, MP-IDSA, available at https://idsa.in/keyspeeches/y-b-chavan-memorial-lecture-by-coas-gen-bipin-rawat
21. Ibid.

APPENDIX

Table A1: Total Casualties Suffered by Pakistan Forces in the Mukti Bahini Operations up to 30 November 1971

	Killed	*Wounded*
a) Regular	4,500	4,000
b) Paramilitary	909	674
Total	5,409	4,674
Grand total	10,083	

Source: The India–Pakistan War of 1971: A History, Ministry of Defence, Government of India, Natraj Publishers, 2014.

Table A2: Casualties Suffered by Mukti Bahini

a)	Killed	10,957
b)	Wounded	1,704
c)	Missing	839
	Total	13,500

Source: The India–Pakistan War of 1971: A History, Ministry of Defence, Government of India, Natraj Publishers, 2014.

13

Role of the United States in the 1971 War
Implications for India–US Relations

Saroj Bishoyi

India–US relations have transformed over the last two decades with the two countries having upgraded their relations to a 'comprehensive global strategic partnership' and their perceptions and interests are converging on a wide range of areas, including at bilateral, regional and global levels. However, this was not the case always, as they remained at loggerheads over a number of areas and their relationship was often characterised as 'estranged democracies'. The 1971 India–Pakistan War is one such example.

The crisis in East Pakistan (now Bangladesh) led to the India–Pakistan War of 1971, also known as the Bangladesh Liberation War. The war started on 3 December 1971 with 'Operation Chengiz Khan', when the Pakistan Air Force (PAF) launched pre-emptive air strikes on 11 north-western Indian airfields, including in Kashmir, Punjab and Agra. The very next day, on 4 December, the then US Ambassador to the UN, George H.W. Bush, who later served as the forty-first US president, brought up the issue at the UN Security Council (UNSC), where he accused India of being responsible for the war, and proposed a ceasefire and withdrawal of troops. After President Richard Nixon failed in his efforts to end the conflict, he ordered the US Navy's 7th Fleet on 10 December to enter into the Bay of Bengal to threaten the Indian activities.

This move by the Nixon Administration marked the lowest point in India–US relations, and the scars it created never left the Indian psyche. In response to this move, India activated Article IX of the Indo-Soviet Treaty of Peace, Friendship and Cooperation, which called for immediate consultations and appropriate measures in the event of a threat of attack from outside on any of the two countries. Following which, the Soviet Union sent a list of ships from Vladivostok towards the Bay of Bengal. The sending of the 7th Fleet by the US became a mere political but not an effective military measure. Defying US pressure, India signed the Treaty with the Soviet Union, the chief foe of the US, for 20 years on 9 August 1971 that assured India of military and diplomatic support in the event of a war with Pakistan, which seemed inevitable at that time.

Meanwhile, the US established its relations with China with the help of Pakistan, India's foe, which resulted in a convergence of US–China–Pakistan's interests, a move that India perceived as a serious security threat. Moreover, on 14 December 1971, columnist Jack Anderson published the minutes of Washington Special Action Group (WSAG) meetings of 2, 4 and 6 December 1971, revealing National Security Advisor (NSA) Henry Kissinger's statement to the WSAG relaying President Nixon's strong pressure to 'tilt' towards Pakistan.

Prime Minister Indira Gandhi ordered a unilateral ceasefire on 16 December after around 93,000 Pakistani soldiers surrendered to the Mukti Bahini and the Indian Army in Dhaka, and the war ended on 17 December. The 13-day war was one of the shortest wars in history, which ended with a decisive and glorious victory for India, and Bangladesh was liberated from Pakistan's military rulers. The US recognised Bangladesh in April 1972 and established its diplomatic relations with Bangladesh in May 1972. However, the role that the US played during the 1971 war deeply affected India–US relations and it continues to shape their ties to this day. With this background, the paper aims to analyse and examine the major reasons behind the divergent perceptions and approaches of the US and India towards the India–Pakistan War of 1971. It examines the different foreign policy goals, ambitions and perspectives of the two countries during this period and their overall implications for the war and India–US relations.

Divergent Foreign Policy Goals, Ambitions and Perspectives

India and the United States shared a mutually suspicious relationship following India's independence in 1947 till the beginning of the 1971 war, which was mostly due to the different foreign policy goals, ambitions and perspectives of the two countries. It was because of their divergent perceptions and approaches that they could not develop strong bilateral relations, despite having several overlapping political and strategic interests. The US foreign policy prioritised to contain communism and desired to create blocs of military allies to prevent the advancement of communism, in which India was not interested.

India has rejected this policy of alignment from the very beginning and has remained officially non-aligned. India's professions of non-alignment had no appeal for the US Administrations which only strengthened US' suspicions about India. Importantly, the US energies 'were largely focused on the economic and security problems of Western Europe'.[1] South Asia, particularly India, was not considered important to the US in its major foreign policy decisions of that time, including containment of communism, maintenance of international peace, security and stability.[2]

India's decision to not join the US-led military blocks attracted considerable criticism from the Washington. The US Secretary of State John Foster Dulles termed India's non-alignment policy as an 'immoral' policy. However, the major factors that encouraged India to adopt a foreign policy strategy of non-alignment were the desire for economic development, the nature of Indian political leadership, the character of Indian public opinion, the exigencies of security and political stability.[3] This policy was also derived from its desire to pursue an independent foreign policy free of external influence and the realisation that the developmental needs of a newly independent state would not permit heavy defence expenditure.

Moreover, India and the US differed on each other's role in world politics. Indian leaders, particularly Jawaharlal Nehru believed that India would be able to acquire an international political and moral role by abstaining from bloc politics.[4] Hence, rather than looking for an ally, India preferred a minimal superpower presence in the South Asian region. While the US branded India as a Soviet supporter, India considered the US as a hegemonic power.

India–US relations briefly improved during the 1962 Sino-Indian War. The US provided military and diplomatic support to India to counter Chinese aggression. The spontaneous US arms' assistance to India during the Sino-Indian War created goodwill for America amongst Indians. Then US Ambassador to India, John Kenneth Galbraith noted in his journal that the US support to India significantly enhanced 'American prestige' overnight and it was regarded as 'a first friend'.[5] However, this strong pro-American feeling began to evaporate, as India gradually recovered from the shock of the unexpected Chinese attack and as a sharp reaction set in because of the joint pressure of the US and the UK on India and Pakistan to hold a series of meetings for resolution of the Kashmir issue.

Then US Undersecretary of State, Chester Bowles observed that this was like taking advantage of Indians extremity to influence them to take actions they did not want to take.[6] Chester Bowles wrote that 'We had also—rather ineptly—seized upon India's acute need for US assistance as a lever to force India to make concessions to the Pakistanis in regard to Kashmir, which no democratic Indian Government could make and survive.'[7]

However, the US perceptions and attitudes towards the Sino-Indian War were largely determined by its negative image of China and strategic calculations.[8] The US Administration knew that if immediate military aid was not provided to India, then the Soviet Union could make political capital out of India's difficulties, which would facilitate the extension and intensification of communist influence in the Indian subcontinent. It demonstrated that the US was prepared to help India only to such an extent that did not undermine its own security and strategic interests both within the framework of its global as well as regional diplomacy.

The US policy towards India was also influenced by political considerations. As the world's biggest democracy, India was perceived as being important to America's long-term interests. The US policy makers insisted that every effort be made then onwards to assist the countries of South Asia within their capabilities to maintain non-communist governments. They did not wish that India should fall into the Soviet or Chinese spheres of influence. Senator John F. Kennedy called for urgent US participation in this contest to help India in its role as a 'counter' to communist China.[9] He declared that 'no thoughtful citizen' could ignore the US' 'stake in the survival of free government in India,' because 'India stood as the only effective competitor to China'.[10]

Above all, the US–Pakistan relationship became one of the main sources of conflict between India and the US. Since the beginning of Cold War, the US had been looking for new allies in Asia to contain the Soviet Union and China. India's continued adherence to the non-alignment policy and its decision to not join any military alliance, left no option for the US but to turn towards Pakistan. Pakistan's geographical location, its proximity to China and its position below Russia's belly was considered ideal for bases from where the US could operate. Pakistan provided the US a reliable friend in the region, and the US in turn provided Pakistan a security umbrella, including military and financial aid.

Pakistan and the US signed the Mutual Defence Assistance Pact in May 1954, despite strong opposition from India. In addition to this, Pakistan also joined the US-sponsored military alliances—the Southeast Asian Treaty Organisation (SEATO) in 1954 and the Central Treaty Organisation (CENTO) in 1955. It was however the remittance of US military aid to Pakistan as an important frontline US ally in South Asia that further alienated India from the US. India protested on the ground that Pakistan had no intention of using the arms aid against China or Russia and that the arms would only be used against India, which proved to be true in the 1965 India–Pakistan War. These arguments by India cut no ice because America's strategic interests demanded alignment with a willing Pakistan.

By the time the 1971 war started, India–US relations reached its lowest point. Henry Kissinger in his memoirs, *The White House Years* noted that the US relations with India reached a state of 'strained cordiality' by 1971.[11] This was despite the fact that there had been a strong American viewpoint that emphasised on the commonality between US and Indian foreign policy interests because of their commitments to democratic values, basic human rights, and willingness to cooperate on important bilateral or international issues. The economic and cultural ties were considered to be brighter spots in an otherwise indifferent relationship, and yet these were dependent on political and strategic relations. The US foreign policy towards India was largely characterised by the application of a global strategy focusing on the 'structure of superpower relationships'.[12] Therefore, the basic problem of India–US relations remained in the divergent foreign policy goals, perspectives and interests of the two countries. In essence, India and the US disagreed on key national security issues, which were considered vital to each other.[13] While the US took a global perspective on its relationships with South Asian countries, India perceived problems from a regional and national security standpoint.

India and the US' Perceptions and Approaches to the East Pakistan Crisis

India and the US viewed the East Pakistan crisis from different perspectives. Their divergent foreign policy goals and approaches to the crisis did not allow the kind of cooperation that was required to resolve the crisis amicably and, the bilateral relations strained on this critical issue. While India supported the Awami League (AL) leaders and the Mukti Bahini, the US sided with the government of Pakistan, which was committing brutal genocide in the East Pakistan. India requested the US to pressurise Pakistan to agree for a political settlement so that the refugees could return to their homes, as their continued presence was a threat to the Indian economy, as also to the peace, stability and security of India. However, the US treated the problem as an internal affair of Pakistan. It took global balance of power approach to the crisis and used Pakistan as a channel for its new China initiative.

India's Perceptions and Approaches to the East Pakistan Crisis

The 1971 India–Pakistan War took place against the backdrop of tensions between the West Pakistan (now Pakistan) and the Bengali-majority East Pakistan. The crisis started soon after the announcement of the Pakistan National Assembly election results in December 1970, which came as a big shock for President Yahya Khan and his supporters. Nobody had anticipated Awami League's total and decisive victory. Under the leadership of Sheikh Mujibur Rehman, the Awami League (AL) won 160 seats out of 162 seats in Pakistan's Eastern wing and seven women's seats who were indirectly elected. With a total of 167 seats, AL secured absolute majority in the National Assembly of 313 seats. On the other hand, Zulfikar Ali Bhutto's Pakistan People's Party (PPP) was able to win only 88 seats, including five women's seats indirectly elected and emerged as the second largest party. This loss of political power was devastating for West Pakistan's military, political and bureaucratic apparatus. On 1 March 1971, President Yahya postponed the National Assembly indefinitely. It was set to open on 3 March. This outraged the AL leaders who took to the streets demanding that West Pakistan's leaders respect the election results. However, President Yahya with his political interest of staying in power delayed the transfer of power to the legitimately elected representative Mujibur Rehman to form a government at the centre, paving the way for a deeper political crisis in the country.

After the collapse of talks between President Yahya, PPP leader Zulfikar Ali Bhutto and AL leader Mujibur Rehman to resolve the crisis peacefully, on 25 March 1971, the Pakistan Army led by Governor and Chief Martial Law Administrator of East Pakistan, Lt Gen Tikka Khan, who later became Pakistan's first Chief of Army Staff (COAS), carried out 'Operation Searchlight' to curb the Bengali nationalist movement in East Pakistan.[14] A large number of Bengalis—Muslims, Hindus, businessmen, intellectuals and students—were killed during this operation. While Mujibur Rahman was taken into custody by the Martial Law Authorities (MLAs) on the charge of 'treason' along with his principal followers, other supporters were suppressed when the arrest took place.

India was taken aback when Yahya scuttled the democratic process to deprive AL leaders of their rightful claim to form the government and resorted to a brutal suppression of the people. The Government of India expressed shock at the ghastly atrocities by Pakistan in Dhaka and conveyed sympathy for the hapless people of East Bengal.[15] However, the Pakistan Army's military operations in Dhaka continued without interruption and by 27 March when the curfew was lifted approximately 75 to 85 per cent of the population left Dhaka. The History

Division, Ministry of Defence, Government of India, in its study *Official History of the 1971 India–Pakistan War* observed that 'The massacre continued by way of indiscriminate mass killing, loot, arson and rape under a policy of annihilation. Within the next seven days, they burned down most of the populated areas in and around Dhaka'.[16]

The West Pakistani Army declared that it had restored the government's authority over the entire East Pakistan province, but it was the beginning of a bloody civil war. Massive human rights violations were reportedly perpetrated by the Pakistani Army. On 26 March, shortly after the Pakistan military crackdown, an officer of the 8th Battalion of the East Bengal Regiment (EBR) at Chittagong, Major Ziaur Rahman, in a broadcast on 'Swadhin Bangla Betar Kendra' had announced the establishment of an independent Bangladesh.[17] Mujibur Rehman, while giving a call for a general strike on 1 March after President Yahya postponed the National Assembly, had warned that 'You will see history made if the conspirators fail to come to their senses.'[18]

Following the West Pakistani Army's crackdown in East Bengal, a large number of refugees, around 10 million, fled East Bengal and entered the Indian states of Assam, Meghalaya, Tripura and West Bengal. A large number of trained Pakistani agents, along with the refugees, had also entered India, which created major economic, social, political, administrative and security problems in India.[19] In addition to this, Pakistan's friendly relations with the US and China aggravated the security concerns of India. As a result, Prime Minister Indira Gandhi, External Affairs Minister (EAM) Swaran Singh and other key members of the Cabinet went on a tour of West European countries, the US and others to inform them about the magnitude of Pakistani army's brutal crackdown in East Bengal and its implications on India. Nevertheless, Gandhi and her cabinet's sincere diplomatic efforts failed to convince the Western powers, especially the US, to use their power to persuade Pakistani military rulers to find a solution to the crisis by means of political compromise with the Bengali leaders, so that around 10 million refugees could leave India.

Meanwhile, driven out from East Bengal by the Pakistani Army, the Bengali deserters from the Pakistan military, para-military, police forces, thousands of AL and other volunteers who had taken refuge in India were steeled into the 'freedom fighters', known as the 'Mukti Bahini'. With every repressive action that the West Pakistani army took, there was birth of new freedom fighters.[20] They were the first to start hitting back at the West Pakistan army, and skirmishes continued all along the border. As the situation unfolded, India first adopted a policy of 'watch and wait', and then took a cautious stand[21] with regard to the recognition of Bangladesh, despite a strong demand for the recognition of Bangladesh by political parties and public in India. But as the condition continued to deteriorate, it got involved in the crisis. It provided political and moral support to the Bengali people, and began to train the Mukti Bahini to help them in their fight for justice and freedom. Consequently, a new and grave international crisis descended on the world stage.

United States' Perceptions and Approaches to the East Pakistan Crisis

The East Pakistan crisis came at a time when the Nixon Administration was set on a new course of developing a new power equation in Asia with US–China–Pakistan at its core. The Administration thought that the new balance of power would be more acceptable in Asia and would enable the US to continue exercising its dominating influence in the region.[22] The new balance of power initiative was based on the Administration's 'Opening to China' through Pakistan channel. In the past, Pakistan's close relations with China had caused tensions between Washington and Islamabad. But under the new initiative, the Nixon Administration took advantage of Islamabad's good relationship with Beijing to convey the Administration's interest in normalising US relations with China.[23] Pakistan became the main channel for passing messages between the US and Chinese leaders when the US–China relations were virtually non-existent. As a result, when the East Pakistan crisis came, the Nixon Administration chose to ignore West Pakistan Army's brutalities in East Bengal. They did not put pressure on President Yahya to stop killing its people and find a political solution with the AL leaders to end the crisis, because they did not want to complicate their new China initiative. In this regard, NSA Kissinger in his memoirs said that the Nixon Administration's initial policy objective was to avoid adding any complications to its China initiative.[24] The ensuing events in the South Asian region and the Administration's perceptions and approaches to the crisis should be seen from this viewpoint.

On 26 March 1971, a day after West Pakistan Army's crackdown in East Bengal, in his Memorandum to President Nixon on situation in Pakistan, Kissinger said that the West Pakistani army has sufficient strength to curb the 'East Pakistan secession movement'. He however doubted the ability of Pakistani army to sustain control in Dhaka over an extended period.[25] There were about 850 Americans, including 250 US officials and dependents, in East Pakistan when the crackdown began. The immediate goal of the Administration was to ensure their safety and evacuation. Assessing the US policy option of whether or not to involve itself in the crisis, Kissinger suggested to President Nixon the advantage of not getting involved in the crisis by stating that this would not prematurely harm US relationship with West Pakistan.[26]

The WSAG in its meeting on 26 March also reviewed the situation in Pakistan where they supported the Administration's policy of non-involvement in the crisis and recommended that the US should delay any request for recognition of an independent East Pakistani government that might be forthcoming.[27] From the very beginning, it was fully known to the Nixon Administration that the resistance movement will continue despite the arrest of the AL leaders as there was 'tremendous popular sentiment behind them'. In the same meeting, Kissinger predicted that the civil war in the East Pakistan would eventually result in 'independence fairly quickly'. However, the Administration chose not to undertake active policy to warn President Yahya against the imminent civil war. Kissinger in fact pointed out that President Nixon did not want to be accused of breaking up Pakistan. The Administration thus knew that the situation in East Pakistan was poor and it was unlikely that the Pakistan Army would be able to control it over an extended period.

In a series of cables known as Blood telegram, the US Consulate General in Dhaka raised alarm about the atrocities committed by the West Pakistan Army in East Bengal. On 28 March, the Consul General in Dhaka, Archer K. Blood reported that they were horrified witnesses to 'a reign of terror' by the Pakistani army in Dhaka.[28] On 29 March, the Consulate reported that the Pakistani army was burning houses and then shooting people when they came out. Hindus were particular focus of the campaign.[29] On 31 March, Blood reported that Pakistani army had killed about four to six thousand people since the crackdown began on 25 March, and said that Pakistani army's objective 'to hit hard and terrorize' the Bengali people had been fairly successful.[30]

US Ambassador to India, Kenneth Keating also expressed his deep shock and concern over Pakistani army's brutal repression of Bengali people with the use of US military equipment. He called for the US to promptly and publicly deplore the Pakistan Army's brutality and announce the abrogation of 'one-time exception' military supply agreement with Pakistan.[31] The US Embassy in Islamabad also expressed its sense of horror and anger at the Pakistani Army's brutal crackdown, but it suggested that it was undesirable to raise the issue to an international political level.[32] President Nixon and his NSC team paid no heed to the alarming situation and rather adopted a 'quiet diplomacy'. They never publicly spoke against the atrocities done by the West Pakistan Army. In a telephonic conversation with Kissinger, Nixon agreed with the position taken by the US Embassy in Islamabad, and said that 'I wouldn't put out a statement praising it, but we're not going to condemn it either.'[33] In another conversation, President Nixon said that the US should stay out of this crisis and do nothing as he felt there was nothing for the US to do.[34]

But key officials from his administration did not agree with him. In one of the dissent cables, the Consular Staffs in Dhaka complained that the US has failed to condemn the Pakistani army's suppression of democracy and atrocities in East Bengal.[35] Terming Pakistan army's ghastly crackdown as 'genocide', Consulate General Blood questioned the US foreign policy objectives and moral leadership at this time of crisis.[36] The Consul General Blood and his colleagues in Dhaka urged the Administration to adhere to the traditional US foreign policy and publicly condemn Pakistan's atrocities as they were unaware of the role Pakistan was playing in the secret negotiations with China.

When US Secretary of State William Rogers received this damning telegram from the Consulate in Dhaka, he informed President Nixon that the Consulate in Dhaka was in 'open rebellion'. This however did not bring any change in the Administration's policy towards the East Pakistan crisis, though President Nixon and Kissinger expressed concern that the US might get involved in the crisis. Kissinger's assessment was that if they will support the Bengali cause then the West Pakistan will turn against the US.[37] Nixon did not want Pakistan to turn against them, especially in the middle of his China initiative, which he felt would be a big mistake.

On 27 April, Pakistani Ambassador to the US, Agha Hilaly delivered a key message to the White House from the Chinese Premier Zhou En-lai green lighting a US delegation to visit China. With President Nixon's China initiative poised to take shape, the Nixon Administration was less interested in upsetting Yahya. As a result, when Kissinger sent a memo to Nixon on 28 April on the situation in East Pakistan and defining the future policy option towards Pakistan, Nixon replied, 'Don't squeeze Yahya at this time',[38] because he was arranging Kissinger's first secret visit to China. In this endeavour, Kissinger went to Beijing in July 1971 via Pakistan where Premier Zhou told him that China supports the Pakistan's position on the crisis and criticised India for the present situation. Kissinger responded to Zhou that the Nixon administration also supports Pakistan on the issue.[39] On 15 July, Nixon astonished the world by announcing Kissinger's China mission and his own upcoming visit to Beijing. Then, in a handwritten letter to President

Yahya in August 1971, Nixon personally thanked Yahya for his assistance in establishing contacts between Washington and Beijing.[40] These exchanges took place in the middle of the East Pakistan crisis while Pakistani army's killing and repression continued in the East Pakistan.

In a recent interview to *The Atlantic,* Kissinger explained that the East Pakistan crisis was essentially a popular resistance by Bengali people for achieving independence to which West Pakistan leaders responded with extreme violence. He said that by publicly condemning this violence would have destroyed the Pakistani channel which was needed to complete the opening to China.[41] The opening to China was considered essential to a potential diplomatic recasting of the Nixon Administration policy towards the Soviet Union and the pursuit of peace in Asia. In the process it forgot the basic principles of US foreign policy and supported a military dictatorship in Pakistan to pursue its objectives. However, the US Congress, intellectuals, public and media increasingly showed their alertness and sensitivity to the politics of murder being practised by the West Pakistani rulers on their own people.

India–US Dialogue on the East Pakistan Crisis

During the East Pakistan crisis, Prime Minister Indira Gandhi and her government officials met several times with President Nixon and his Administration officials where the two sides discussed issues relating to the crisis, including the Pakistan military's atrocities, the refugee problem, military aid to Pakistan, US opening to China, and necessary steps required to resolve the crisis. However, their divergent foreign policy goals, perspectives and approaches did not help in developing cooperation on the issue, instead bilateral relations strained considerably. Ambassador Keating, during his meeting with Indian Foreign Secretary T.N. Kaul on 27 March, conveyed his administration's position that the East Pakistan crisis was an internal matter of Pakistan and that it should be resolved internally.[42] However, it was no more an internal matter of Pakistan and also not a mere Indo-Pak issue. Though it was very much a problem for India as a large number of refugees were fleeing into India, thereby creating economic, social, political, administrative and security challenges, but it was now an international issue.

In May 1971, Gandhi in her letter to President Nixon spoke about the continuing Pakistan army's repression in East Bengal, pouring of refugees into the Indian states and its impact on India. She urged the US to use its 'power and prestige' to persuade Pakistan military rulers to find a political settlement.[43] Then Indian Ambassador to the US, L.K. Jha warned NSA Kissinger that the Indians might send back some refugees as guerrillas to East Pakistan, unless Pakistani military rulers take visible actions towards a political settlement. Kissinger responded that President Nixon has 'personal influence' with the Pakistanis, which he would use privately to persuade them to move towards a political settlement.[44] Nixon however did not use his 'personal influence' or US power to persuade Pakistanis to find a political settlement. During a conversation with Nixon when Kissinger said, 'the Indians are massing troops' at the East Pakistan border while the US was willing to help India in its humanitarian efforts but is opposed to any military action. Then Nixon responded angrily that the US will cut off economic aid to India if it takes military action.[45]

Kissinger, during his July 1971 visit to India, shared Washington's concerns and sympathy about the heavy economic burden placed upon India because of Bengali refugees. During his visit, he discussed the situation in East Bengal, his administration's military aid to Pakistan, and the new China policy. He explained that his administration's opening to China was not aimed against India, rather it would restore peace in the world. In fact, he assured that the US will take it seriously in case of any military action by China against India.[46] In July 1971, Acting Secretary John Irwin and Indian Ambassador Jha discussed these issues in addition to the United Nations' role in addressing the refugee crisis in India.[47] In August 1971, Gandhi in another letter to Nixon said that 'the situation has not improved'. She stated that India was not against the US maintaining 'a constructive relationship with Pakistan'. But she questioned US sincerity in working towards a political settlement of the crisis as well as the logic of US arms supply to Pakistan.[48]

Meanwhile, the number of refugees fleeing from East Pakistan reached over 7.2 million by 31 July, which significantly increased the strain on various aspects of public life in India.[49] As the situation further deteriorated and nearly 10 million refugees entered India by November 1971, Gandhi in her last effort visited several countries, essentially to persuade US, Britain and other Western powers to pressurise Pakistan to accept negotiations with Mujibur Rehman to find a political settlement of the crisis and to create conditions in which the refugees could return. But her trip was futile, as India failed to convince them to adopt an objective position on the issue.[50] In his memoirs, Nixon recalled that Gandhi's 'visit to Washington came at a critical time.' During his meeting with her in the Oval Office on 4 November, Nixon stressed that another war in South Asia was out of question. He warned consequences of war and the actions that the Chinese, the Soviet Union and the US might take if India initiates a war.[51] The next day, on 5 November, while Kissinger and Nixon were discussing Nixon's conversation with Gandhi, Kissinger said that Indians were starting a war there regardless.[52]

US' Military Aid to Pakistan

One of the major issues between India and the US during the East Pakistan crisis was the Nixon Administration's decision to resume military aid to Pakistan. The US military aid to Pakistan had commenced after Pakistan signed the Mutual Defence Assistance Pact with the US and joined the US led military blocks—SEATO and CENTO. Whenever India protested against the military aid to Pakistan on the grounds that these weapons are not going to be used against the Soviet or China but only against India, the US continued to assure that Pakistan will not use them against India. However, the 1965 India–Pakistan War proved otherwise. In fact, US arms had enabled Pakistan to wage war against India. Faced with strong criticism from the public and the US Congress after the 1965 war, US had announced suspension of the export of lethal weapons systems to both India and Pakistan. However, in October 1970, the Nixon Administration approved the sale of 20 aircraft and 300 armoured personnel carriers worth about $50 million to Pakistan under the 'one-time exception' to the US arms embargo.[53] In a statement in the US Senate on 12 October 1970, Senator William Saxbe said that between 1954 and 1965 the US had given Pakistan military aid worth nearly US$ 2 billion by way of hundreds of tanks, about 700 artillery pieces, about 20 squadrons of F-86 Sabre jets and F-104 Starfighters and other equipment.[54] Besides, the US also provided facilities for construction of airfields, military warehouses and other military infrastructure. The US military alliance policy had caused serious security implications for South Asia, particularly for India, and created mutual distrust between India and the US.

Discussing the implications of military aid to Pakistan, Ambassador Keating, during a conversation with Kissinger and NSC Staff, Harold H. Saunders on 3 June 1971, said that any additional military aid to Pakistan would have serious humanitarian implications in the region since four million refugees had already crossed over to India while the Pakistan army continued to kill Bengalis.[55] Kissinger explained to Keating that President Nixon wanted to hold up the 'one-time exception' military aid to Pakistan, but wanted to supply the military spare parts which were not applicable to the crisis. Referring to a State Department's proposed policy decision memorandum on the military supply to Pakistan, Ambassador Keating noted that this would mean ammunition.

Keating said that this military supply would 'bring terrific criticism on the President's head.' He recognised President Nixon's special friendship with Yahya, but, he said, could not understand his Pakistan policy. He suggested that certain conditions should be attached to any further economic aid to Pakistan and emphasised that necessary steps must be taken towards a political settlement of the crisis so that refugees could return to their homes.[56] President Nixon and Kissinger on 4 June discussed Ambassador Keating's approach to the crisis where they felt that Keating had effectively become an advocate for India.[57] Nixon also had doubts about Keating being able to hold the Administration's policy towards the crisis. When Nixon questioned Keating's approach, Kissinger said that he wanted the US to cut off all economic and military aid to Pakistan and support India in the situation.[58] Nixon and Kissinger however did not follow Keating's suggestions. They underlined the importance of giving more time to Pakistan since it was helping them on their China initiative.[59]

When the conflict grew into an India–Pakistan war, in a series of meetings and conversations from 4 to 16 December 1971, the Nixon Administration discussed third-party transfers of fighter aircrafts to Pakistan. In a memo, US Ambassador to UN Bush reported Kissinger's meetings with the Chinese delegation to the UN on 10 December 1971 where Kissinger encouraged China to provide military support to Pakistan and also informed that military aid to Pakistan was being provided through Jordan, Iran, Saudi Arabia and Turkey.[60] On 12 December, Alexander Haig told the Chinese Ambassador Huang Hua that his Administration was trying its best to provide fighter aircrafts to Pakistan through Saudi Arabia, Iran and Jordan. He was however disappointed when the Chinese informed him that China would not take any military action against India.[61] On 14 December, the US Department of State noted that Pakistan might have received 11 F-104 fighter aircrafts from Jordan.[62] In a cable to Kissinger on 15 December, Ambassador Farland informed that Pakistan Government had requested for additional fighter aircrafts for the survival of West Pakistan as the current F-104s and Mig-19s could not stop the Indian advance. On 16 December, the US Central Intelligence Agency (CIA) reported that Pakistan had received a squadron of F-104s from Jordan.

It also reported that India had declared a unilateral ceasefire after unconditional surrender of Pakistani troops in East Bengal.[63] In another cable, US Embassy in Iran reported that three US F-5A fighter aircrafts had arrived in Pakistan to help it fight against India.[64] These cables proved that despite the US arms embargo on Pakistan as well as on India, the Nixon Administration provided military aid to Pakistan both through third parties and also directly.[65] On India's protest against the arms supply to Pakistan, Secretary Rogers in a cable to the US Embassy in India suggested that the Embassy neither confirm nor deny the allegations that the US provided military aid to Pakistan via Iran and Jordan.[66]

India's Treaty of Peace, Friendship and Cooperation with the Soviet

India and the Soviet Union signed the Treaty of Peace, Friendship and Cooperation on 9 August 1971,[67] which stipulated immediate mutual consultations in case of an armed attack from outside on any of the two countries. It also accepted under Article IV India's non-alignment policy as an important factor in maintenance of international peace and security. The major reasons behind India's signing of the Treaty, which it had resisted in the past, were the deteriorating situation in East Pakistan; continued influx of refugees to India; President Yahya's weekly war threats to India; the Nixon Administration's unwillingness to stop military supplies to Pakistan; and, the US and China's open support to the military leader Yahya, which were creating a dangerous security situation for India.[68]

The Treaty assured India of military and diplomatic support in the event of a war with Pakistan which was seen as inevitable. At the same time, Kissinger's visit to Beijing in July 1971 gave an indication of normalisation of US–China relations with adverse effects on Soviet Union's strategic posture and global policy. The deteriorating Sino-Soviet relations also led to the strengthening of the Indo-Soviet relationship, particularly in the field of defence cooperation. India's relationship with Pakistan and China had already declined. These fast-changing strategic realities further facilitated the establishing of a new relationship of trust, confidence and awareness between India and the Soviet Union.[69] The Treaty essentially took care of India's chief apprehension regarding military pressure from the US and China coordinated with the challenge from Pakistan. It permitted India the freedom to militarily counter Pakistan. After signing the Treaty, EAM Swaran Singh on 9 August 1971 said that the Treaty would be a stabilising factor in the South Asia region as it would provide peace, security and development for India and the Soviet Union, as well as for the region as a whole. He underlined that it was not aimed against any third country.[70]

As was expected, the Nixon Administration expressed its resentment over India's signing of the Treaty with the Soviet Union, and considered it an unanticipated and disturbing event in South Asia. It said that the Treaty added dangers and difficulties to the region, and complicated US relations with India and Pakistan. The US Embassy in Moscow, after analysing the Treaty, said that the Treaty consolidated Soviet Union's position in India. At the same time, the Soviets accepted deeper involvement in the South Asian conflict.[71] In a similar vein, Kissinger in his memoirs *The White House Years* assessed that the Treaty provided India a Soviet guarantee against the Chinese intervention if India goes to war with Pakistan. It also opened the door to war in South Asia and the Soviets' involvement in it.[72]

President Nixon viewed India as a Soviet client for the rest of the East Pakistan crisis. In response to the critics of the Indo-Soviet Treaty, Prime Minister Gandhi said, it was strange that those who denounced India's non-alignment policy all along were now criticising the Treaty on the basis of India's policy. Whereas the Treaty itself clearly recognises India's non-alignment policy.[73] India's signing of the Treaty was however a big blow to the US as it saw the Treaty to be the result of deliberate collusion between Moscow and New Delhi.

Failure of Nixon Administration to Resolve the Crisis Politically

President Nixon in his *Annual Report to the US Congress* in February 1972 said that the US did not ignore or support the Pakistani military action in East Bengal.[74] Nonetheless, he and Kissinger did not take any action to stop the Pakistani army's atrocities in East Bengal and never made any public statements deploring its brutal military repression. Although Nixon in his letter to President Yahya urged to make political concessions in East Bengal, he fell short of pressing Yahya to start negotiations with AL leader Mujibur Rahman.[75] Because of his special relationship with Yahya and Yahya's role in the opening to China, Nixon did not publicly deplore Pakistan's military actions. He thought this would complicate the situation for president Yahya and embarrass him.[76] In another instance, Nixon said that the US would not measure its relationship with Pakistan on the basis of what it had done in East Bengal. By that criteria, the US would have to cut-off ties with all Communist countries because of the slaughter that took place in those countries.[77]

In a memorandum of conversation, Kissinger told Keating that President Nixon had a special friendship with Yahya and that the US cannot make policy towards Pakistan on that basis, but 'it is a fact of life.'[78] Importantly, Kissinger, during his secret meeting with Chinese Ambassador Huang Hua on 10 December, said that the US was not interested in a political settlement of the crisis and they 'will not encourage talks between Pakistan and Bangladesh'.[79] He said that the US objective was 'to protect what is left of Pakistan' from being disinterested as it has happened in the East. Thus, Nixon and Kissinger were singularly unsympathetic to the crisis.

Meanwhile, the influx of nearly 10 million refugees became too much for India to handle and posed a serious concern. The Mukti Bahini was launching guerrilla attacks to fight against Pakistani repression. Eventually tensions between

India and Pakistan were uncontrollable. All these causes were intensified by the lack of US public criticism for the root cause of the crisis—the Pakistan military rulers' disregard of the December 1970 national election results, 25 March brutal crackdown in East Bengal and the refugee crisis that followed the carnage. Besides, the lack of a political solution in East Pakistan, the Pakistan Army continued military repression and Indian support to the Mukti Bahini led to the war between India and Pakistan.

Start of the 1971 India–Pakistan War

By May 1971, the US Department of State knew that a war could take place between India and Pakistan. In a memo to President Nixon, the State Department noted three causes for the possible start of India–Pakistan war: (i) continued repression by the Pakistani army and lack of political accommodation in East Bengal, (ii) continued flow of Bengali refugees into India, and (iii) the Indian support to Bengali Guerrillas.[80] Nixon however stressed that the US would not allow India to use the Bengali refugees as a pretext for starting war. He viewed that some Indian and Pakistani interests might be served by going to war, but it was not in the US' interests as this could imperil its China initiative.[81]

Nixon in his memoirs noted that Gandhi had already made up her mind to attack Pakistan when she met him in Washington in November 1971, but she assured him that she would not.[82] Kissinger in his memoirs stated that Gandhi went to war not because of the US' failure to resolve the crisis, but because of the fear of their success.[83] It was very much clear by this time that India's dialogue with the US would not help resolve the crisis.

The India–Pakistan War began on 3 December when the PAF launched pre-emptive air strikes on north-western Indian airfields under code named 'Operation Chengiz Khan'. In response to the PAF's attacks, Prime Minister Gandhi in her address to the nation called the air strikes a 'declaration of war against India'. Then Indian troops struck back fiercely on both the Western and the Eastern fronts of Pakistan. India's attacks in the Western front were intended to ensure success in the Eastern front where Indian troops with active support from the Mukti Bahini reached Dhaka.

The US Response to the 1971 War

President Nixon was upset when the India–Pakistan war started. He wanted to avoid the war, but he had to support Pakistan as an ally. He contacted Kissinger and during their conversation Nixon said, 'Pakistan thing makes your heart sick',[84] after they warned Prime Minister Gandhi not to start the war. Nixon thought Pakistan's pre-emptive air strikes on the Indian airfields was 'a reckless act' that led India to declare war. Kissinger in his reply said that in any case Pakistan would lose half of their country whether they fight or not.[85] Then they decided to continue their military and diplomatic support to Pakistan. Nixon asked Kissinger to approach China, France and the West Asian states—Jordan, Saudi Arabia, Turkey and Iran—to send fighter aircrafts to Pakistan to help it fight against India.[86]

On 4 December, Ambassador George Bush, accused India of being responsible for the war and introduced a seven-point draft resolution (S/10416) in the United Nations Security Council (UNSC), which called upon India and Pakistan for immediate ceasefire and the withdrawal of their armed forces.[87] India expressed its 'disappointment, shock and surprise'[88] over the accusation and tabulation of the resolution. However, China supported the resolution, but it was vetoed by the Soviet Union. Then, the US along with its allies put immense pressure on the Soviets to get India to withdraw troops, but they failed. On 6 December, the day when India recognised Bangladesh Government, the US announced suspension of economic aid to India, including US$ 87.6 million worth of aid that was in the pipeline and US$ 14 million of military equipment. In fact, Kissinger said, they 'have cancelled the entire military equipment line to India', specifically 'all radar equipment for defence in the north'.[89] On 7 December, Assistant Secretary of State Joseph Sisco accused India of holding 'major responsibility for the war'.[90]

US Tilt towards Pakistan

When the India–Pakistan War was going on, the Nixon Administration tilted towards Pakistan in its public statements, supported Pakistan in the UN, supplied military equipment to Pakistan despite US embargoes, suspended economic and military aid to India, and in discussions with China encouraged Beijing to take military action against India. The 'tilt' also involved the dispatch of the US warship 7th Fleet to the Bay of Bengal to threaten the Indian activities. But the Administration publicly denied that they were following any specific anti-India policy. The NSC's Washington Special Action Group meetings however reveal that Kissinger was livid that they were not more responsive to President Nixon's desire to 'tilt' towards Pakistan.

In their efforts to 'tilt' towards Pakistan, the Nixon Administration was not just trying to express its appreciation to the Pakistani military rulers for their help in establishing contacts between Washington and Beijing, but they were also trying to impress the Chinese. The NSC staffer Harold Saunders in an interview revealed that Kissinger said on a number of occasions that Beijing would be watching how Washington treats its ally Pakistan. If Pakistan breaks up what would the Chinese think about US' reliability as an ally.[91] A few days later, syndicated columnist Jack Anderson published the minutes of WSAG meetings of 2, 4 and 6 December 1971, revealing Kissinger's statement to the WSAG relaying President Nixon's strong pressure to 'tilt' towards Pakistan. The US Congress, media and public criticized the Nixon Administration's policy 'tilt' towards Pakistan and handling of the South Asian crisis. The major factors that influenced the Administration's policymaking leading to the 'tilt' towards Pakistan were Nixon's friendship with President Yahya, the latter's role in his China initiative, and his dislike of the Indians, especially Prime Minister Gandhi.

Collusion of US–China–Pakistan Interests

The emerging US–China–Pakistan axis posed a great security threat to India because of India's already strained relations with both China and Pakistan. Pakistan already had close economic and military relations with China. Nixon's China initiative and the collusion of US–China–Pakistan interests had an impact on the India–Pakistan War. Interestingly, before his secret visit to China, Kissinger had told Ambassador Jha that if China attacks India, Washington's response would be as strong as the 1962 Indo-China War. During his visit to India in July 1971, Kissinger had assured India that in any conflict between India and China, the US will be on India's side. He also said that the US' new relationship with China was not aimed against India.[92] However, after returning from China, Kissinger told Ambassador Jha on 17 July that the US would not involve in the event of war between India and Pakistan even if China takes military action against India in support of Pakistan. Instead, Kissinger, during his secret meeting with the Chinese Ambassador to UN, Huang Hua on 10 December, encouraged Beijing to make military moves against India on its North-Eastern states and assured that the US will not stand by if the Soviets launch attacks against China. He also informed him that the US had moved a number of naval ships, the 7th Fleet, from the Western Pacific towards the Bay of Bengal to support Pakistan.[93] This clearly indicates Washington's duplicity of approach to the crisis, which was of course against India's interest and policy.

Dispatch of the 7th Fleet

When the Indian defence forces launched full-fledged attacks into the East Pakistan, the CIA director, Richard M. Helms warned President Nixon that 'East Pakistan was crumbling'.[94] Then, on 10 December, President Nixon took the decision to dispatch the US Navy's 7th Fleet into the Bay of Bengal, officially to evacuate its citizens from the East Bengal and unofficially to support Pakistan in its war efforts against India. The deployment of the 7th Fleet was however first brought up in an India–Pakistan contingency planning memo in November 1971 where the NSC Staff, Admiral Welander had indicated the approval of Joint Chiefs of Staff (JCS) for the deployment of the 7th Fleet in the South Asia crisis.[95]

Then, on 9 December, Kissinger, in his memorandum to President Nixon, mentioned about the deployment of US aircraft carrier where he suggested Nixon to direct the Chairman of the JCS to immediately dispatch the 7th Fleet to the Bay of Bengal under the pretext of evacuating US citizens.[96] This decision came at a time when Pakistan's Western front and Eastern front were crumbling under a coordinated attack by the Indian Navy and Air Force. These attacks by India and the news about the collapse of Pakistani Army at the Eastern front led the Nixon Administration to dispatch the 7th Fleet for contingency purposes.[97] Nixon wanted to save Pakistan from Indian attacks. The deployment of the Fleet was seen as a show of force by the US against India.

India's Response to the 7th Fleet

On 10 December, Indian intelligence intercepted a US message about the marching of the US warship 7th Fleet towards the war zone, Bay of Bengal. Ambassador Jha expressed India's concern over the deployment of the 7th Fleet in the region to the Nixon Administration.[98] In the meantime, based on intelligence intercept, India's MEA assessed that President Nixon had personally taken the decision to accuse India as an 'aggressor' and send the 7th Fleet. The 7th Fleet also had Nixon's blessings to attack Indian Army's communication systems and facilities.[99]

Based on these assessments, the Chief of India's Eastern Naval Command (ENC), Vice Admiral N. Krishnan asked the Indian government to give him the orders to defend the area with the support of Indian Air Force (IAF), following which Prime Minister Gandhi convened a meeting to assess the security implications of the 7th Fleet and the decision was taken to activate the Article IX of the Indo-Soviet treaty which called for immediate mutual consultations and effective measures in the event of a threat of attack to either of the two countries.[100] In response to this move, the Soviet dispatched a naval task force from Vladivostok towards the Indian Ocean and Bay of Bengal.[101]

On 13 December, Russian Ambassador to India, Nikolai Pegov dismissed the possibilities of the US or China intervening in the war by emphasising that the Russian fleet was also in the Indian Ocean. He assured India that Moscow would counteract any move by the US or China and would not allow the 7th Fleet to interfere.[102] Thus, the Soviet's dispatch of a number of nuclear armed fleets from Vladivostok prevented the US threat from materialising. Kissinger had cautioned President Nixon about this earlier by stating that given the Soviet factor, 'I must warn you, Mr. President, if our bluff is called, we'll be in trouble... we'll lose.'[103] On 11 December, he briefed Nixon about the presence of Soviet fleet in the Indian Ocean area.[104] Then they took decision to move the 7th fleet away from the area. The 7th Fleet could not come close to Chittagong or Karachi, however, the deployment of the Fleet had generated widespread anti-US feeling in India. Consequently, India–US relations deteriorated considerably.

Pakistani Army's Surrender and the End of the War

The three Indian Chiefs of Staff—Chief of the Army Staff, General S.H.F.J. Manekshaw, Chief of the Naval Staff, Admiral S.M. Nanda and Chief of the Air Staff, Air Chief Marshal P.C. Lal—were in close touch with the situation rapidly unfolding at the Eastern and Western fronts. As Pakistan's forces began to crumble under well-coordinated attacks by the Indian armed forces and the Mukti Bahini at the Eastern front, General Manekshaw, in a radio broadcast told Pakistan's troops to surrender, thereby assuring them of security and safe evacuation from East Bengal. He also told Pakistan's troops that surrendered in East Bengal would be treated with 'the dignity and respect which soldiers are entitled to'.[105] He ordered a suspension of Indian air strikes in the Dhaka area from 5 pm on 15 December until 9 am on 16 December. But he warned that unless the Pakistanis surrendered by then, he would resume his offensive with utmost vigour.[106] He then reiterated his previous assurances made in radio broadcasts, that he would guarantee the safety of all Pakistani military and paramilitary personnel who surrender and would also protect them from any reprisals.

On 14 December, Pakistan's military commander in East Pakistan, Lt Gen A.A.K. Niazi, informed the US Consulate in Dhaka that he wanted to surrender. He however delayed conveying this information because of the assurances given to him by the military leaders in West Pakistan that the US and China would take military action against India, which were evident in the secret Pakistani dispatches. In a secret signal message on 11 December, President Yahya informed Governor A.M. Malik in Dhaka that the US 7th Fleet would very soon be in position.[107]

Lt Gen Niazi was also informed that the Chinese had activated the North-East Frontier Agency (NEFA), now Arunachal Pradesh, and the Indians have not announced it for obvious reasons. He was further informed that the US had put strong pressure internationally on Russia and India.[108] Niazi continued to expect till the last day of the war that the US and China would intervene militarily to support them, but they never did. The major reason behind Beijing's decision to not attack India was that it would invite immediate retaliations from the Soviets because of the Indo-Soviet Treaty that could be tantamount to courting a disaster for Beijing. The US also chose not to attack India realising that the Soviet Fleet was already in the Indian Ocean to counteract. As a result, both the US and China finally chose not to attack India. The Treaty thus stood the test of time.

Once the Pakistani troops became clear that the US and China were not going to fight their war, the dazed and demoralised troops looked eager and relieved as they marched off to surrender areas where they would be protected by the Indian forces from reprisal by Bengali crowds.[109] The Pakistani troops surrendered on 16 December. The chief of India's Eastern Command, Lt. Gen. Jagjit Singh Aurora and Lt. Gen. Niazi signed the 'instrument of surrender' in a surrender ceremony at the Race Course, Dhaka. As a result of the surrender, around 93,000 Pakistani troops were taken as Prisoners of War (PoW) by India. The news of the surrender and unilateral ceasefire was announced by Prime Minister Gandhi in Parliament. The 13-day war came to an end without a confrontation between the Soviet Union, China and the US; and, Bangladesh was liberated from the Pakistani military rulers. It was one of the shortest wars in history, a glorious and decisive victory for India and a high point of Indian foreign policy. At the same time, it was a humiliating defeat for Pakistan in which they lost half of their country. It was an embarrassing diplomatic setback for the Nixon Administration, especially the way they managed the regional crisis. Above all, it severely damaged the India–US relations and increased the Soviet's influence in India.

Implications for India–US Relations

The role US played during the India–Pakistan War of 1971 left a deep scar on the India–US relationship. A strong and widespread feeling generated in India that the US and Indian perceptions, approaches and interests in the South Asian region did not converge. The US in particular did not bother about Indian sensibilities and core interests. The US had tried to create a military parity between India and Pakistan by providing large-scale military aid to Islamabad, which threatened peace and stability in the region. The US Administration perceived the crisis from global balance of power perspective while it was a regional issue with limited global implications.[110]

It seemed that a close relationship between the two countries would be highly improbable for a long time to come. However, once the crisis was over and Bangladesh emerged, both New Delhi and Washington tried to normalise the relationship; the US Administration's recognition of Bangladesh helped in this regard. At the hearings before the Committee on Foreign Relations, Kissinger made it clear that the new US policy aimed at improving India–US relations, which had deteriorated considerably before and during the 1971 war. He said that now 'Bangladesh exists; our objectives and those of India with respect to it, are quite parallel'.[111] With regard to the US military alliance policy and the US military aid to Pakistan, which encouraged Pakistan to wage war against India, he said that in the event of another confrontation, 'It will not be fought with American weapons'.[112]

President Nixon also said that the US would make efforts to develop 'a new relationship' with the countries of South Asia. Nixon in his *Annual Report to the US Congress* in 1973 expressed hope that India would seek a balanced relationship with the major powers. However, he said that the US will have 'a natural concern' if India's major power relations are directed against the US or its key allies which it values.[113] On the new balance of power relationship, he assured India that the US would not join in any military blocs directed against India. Referring to the new relationship the US was building with China, he further assured that Washington's good relationship with Beijing would not be at the cost of its good relationship with India. The US 'opening to China', as a result of Kissinger's secret visit to Beijing via Pakistan channel, was an important factor in the Nixon-Kissinger 'tilt' towards Pakistan during the 1971 war. Indian and American perceptions and approaches to China significantly shaped India-US relations.[114] In his Annual Report, Nixon emphasised that the US wants to build a mature and new relationship with India based on 'equality, reciprocity and mutual interest.'

On the other hand, New Delhi also thought that it was time to start a new relationship with the US. Prime Minister Gandhi in an article in *Foreign Affairs* wrote that 'We do not believe in permanent estrangement.'[115] Expressing India's readiness to start a new relationship with the US, she emphasised that Washington should respect India's foreign policy decisions and its major power status. Making a case for the need to improve India–US relations, EAM Swaran Singh in a statement in the Rajya Sabha also expressed India's willingness 'to do everything in our power to normalise and strengthen our relations with the US on the basis of recognition of the new realities and on the basis of equality, reciprocity and mutual respect'.[116]

After a decisive victory in the 1971 war, the debate over India's status as a major power in the South Asian region had also been resolved. India wanted the US to recognise this new reality. President Nixon in his 1973 Annual Report, in fact, recognised India as a major power based on reciprocity. He said that the differences of 1971 injected greater maturity and a healthy realism into the India–US relationship.[117] Thus, efforts were apparently taking place to establish normal relationship between the two countries in the aftermath of the 1971 war.

It was however with the end of the Cold War and the collapse of the Soviet Union, that the relationship between the two countries really began to develop. The US no longer viewed its relationship with India primarily through the Cold War prism. On the other hand, faced with the new geo-economic and geo-political realities, India brought a paradigm shift in its economic and foreign policies. As a result, a new relationship began to develop between the two countries where the US emerged as the extra-regional defence and security partner of India. Though problems persisted in bilateral relations relating to issues of nuclear non-proliferation, Kashmir and human rights.

The 1998 India's nuclear tests also dashed the prospects for a rapid upsurge in India–US relations as the US Administration imposed economic and military sanctions on India. However, soon the two countries began a 'strategic dialogue', which restored the mutual trust and confidence between the two countries on the matters of defence and security. The March 2000 visit by US President Bill Clinton to India marked a major turning point in the India–US relationship. Since then India–US relationship has been evolving in response to India's emergence as a regional power, emerging market, and its importance in contributing to a stable balance of power in Asia. The relationship is also evolving with a view to their shared values, interests and challenges that they face together in the 21st century. The two sides recognise each other's importance and they have been closely engaged on a wide range of bilateral and regional issues of mutual interest.[118]

Hence, India and the US have come a long way since the India–Pakistan War of 1971. In the last 50 years, India–US relationship has shifted from 'estranged democracies' to 'engaged democracies', and then from 'engaged democracies' to 'de-hyphenation' of the US' relationship with India and Pakistan,[119] and, now, transformed into a 'comprehensive global strategic partnership' based on their shared values and interests on bilateral, regional and international issues. This transformation in India–US relationship has come at a time when Chinese military assertiveness is growing in Asia and possess huge economic, political, geo-strategic and security challenges both to India and the US. Today, India–US relationship is broad-based and multi-sectoral and enjoys a strong bipartisan and popular support in both the countries. The two sides have established more than 50 bilateral dialogue mechanisms for exchange of views on issues of mutual interest. The US also recognises India as a major defence partner. Amidst all these positive transformations in India–US relationship, the ghost of 1971 war and the resultant 'trust deficit' still continues to haunt Indian consciousness somewhere, which will continue to shape India–US relationship.

NOTES

1. Chester Bowles, *Promises to Keep: My Years in Public Life, 1941-1969*, New York: Harper & Row, 1971, p. 638.
2. Norman D. Palmer, 'India as a Factor in the United States Foreign Policy', *International Studies*, Vol. 65, 1964, pp. 2–11.
3. Emeka Ohajunwa, *India-US Security Relations, 1947-1990*, Delhi: Chanakya Publications, 1992.
4. Surjit Mansingh, *India's Search for Power: Indira Gandhi's Foreign Policy 1966-1982,* New Delhi: Sage Publications, 1984.
5. John Kenneth Galbraith, *Ambassador's Journal: A Personal Account of the Kennedy Years*, Boston: Houghton Mifflin, 1969, p. 512.
6. Bowles, n. 1, p. 439.
7. Ibid., pp. 439–40.
8. After the emergence of the People's Republic of China (PRC) in 1949, there was a debate in the US about who lost China, especially after the start of the Korean War in 1950. Then the containment of China's influence in Asia became US foreign policy priority for which it was looking for a strategic partner or an ally. However, before the 1962 Sino-Indian war, India considered China a friend and not an enemy. It was one of the first countries to recognise the PRC, it supported China's entry to UN and then for a seat in UNSC, and had also signed the Panchsheel Agreement with China. See Mansingh, n. 4, and Jawaharlal Nehru, *India's Foreign Policy: Selected Speeches, September 1946 to April 1961,* Delhi: Publication Division, Ministry of Information and Broadcasting, Government of India, 1961.
9. Selig S. Harrison (ed.), *India and the United States*, New York: MacMillan, 1961, p. 63.
10. US Congress, *Congressional Record*, Senate, 85th Congress, End Session, Vol. 104, 25 March 1958, p. 5248.
11. Henry Kissinger, *The White House Years,* New Delhi: Vikas Publishing House Pvt. Ltd., 1979, p. 849.
12. Baldev Raj Nayar, 'America and India: The Roots of Conflict', in K.P. Misra (ed.), *Foreign Policy of India: A Book of Readings*, New Delhi: Thomson Press, 1977, p. 276.
13. Dennis Kux, *India and the United States: Estranged Democracies,* Washington DC: National Defence University Press, 1993.
14. The Hamoodur Rahman Commission (HRC) report squarely blames three men—President Yahya Khan, PPP leader Z.A. Bhutto, and AL leader S.M. Rehman—principally responsible for the East Pakistan crisis, loss of 1971 war with India, and the half of Jinnah's Pakistan. The HRC was set up by then Pakistan president Z.A. Bhutto on 26 December 1971 under Chief Justice Hamoodur Rahman as Chairman to inquire into the Pakistani debacle in the 1971. For details, see the text of *Hamoodur Rahman Commission (HRC) Supplementary Report*, Government of Pakistan, Pakistan, 1974.

15. Ministry of Defence, *Official History of the 1971 India-Pakistan War,* Chapter-IV, History Division, Ministry of Defence, Government of India, published on 12 October 2006, pp. 107–27.
16. Ibid., Chapter-II, p. 73.
17. Ibid., Chapter-III, p. 93.
18. Ibid.
19. Ibid., Chapter-VII, pp. 274–75.
20. As the situation in East Pakistan continued to deteriorate, the strength and operational capability of the Mukti Bahini forces also kept increasing. As a result, the overall strength of the Mukti Bahini reached to over one lakh by 30 November 1971. See Ibid., Chapter-VI, pp. 203–04.
21. Srinath Raghavan in his book '1971' points out that India was very ambivalent in its approach towards the crisis in the beginning and even doubted the capability of Bengali freedom fighters to handle the situation. See Srinath Raghavan, *1971: A Global History of the Creation of Bangladesh,* Massachusetts: Harvard University Press, 2013.
22. Hedley Bull, 'The New Balance of Power in Asia and the Pacific', *Foreign Affairs,* Vol. 49, No. 4, July 1971, pp. 669–81; and, V.P. Dutt, *India's Foreign Policy,* New Delhi: Vikas Publishing House Pvt. Ltd., 1993, p. 100.
23. Kux, n. 13, p. 280.
24. Kissinger, n. 11, p. 848.
25. Louis J. Smith (ed.), *Foreign Relations of the United States, 1969–1976, Volume XI, South Asia Crisis, 1971,* Washington: United States Government Printing Office, 2005, p. 22.
26. Ibid., pp. 22–23.
27. Ibid., p. 24.
28. US Department of State, *Foreign Relations of the US, 1969–1976, Volume E-7, Documents on South Asia, 1969–1972,* Document 125, 'Telegram 959 from the US Consulate General in Dacca to the Department of State', 28 March 1971.
29. US Department of State, *Foreign Relations of the US, 1969–1976, Volume E-7, Documents on South Asia, 1969–1972,* Document 126, 'Telegram 978 from the Consulate General in Dacca to the Department of State', 29 March 1971.
30. Telegram 1007 from US Consulate in Dacca to the Department of State, 'Extent of Casualties in Dacca', 31 March 1971, Record Group 59, Subject Numeric File 1970-73, Pol and Def, Box 2530, *The National Security Archive,* at https://nsarchive2.gwu.edu/NSAEBB/NSAEBB79/
31. Telegram 4494 from US Embassy in New Delhi to the Department of State, 'Selective Genocide', 29 March 1971, Record Group 59, Subject Numeric File 1970-73, Pol and Def, Box 2530, *The National Security Archive,* at https://nsarchive2.gwu.edu/
32. US Department of State, *Foreign Relations of the US, 1969–1976, Volume E-7, Documents on South Asia, 1969–1972,* Document 128, 'Telegram 2954 from the Embassy in Pakistan to the Department of State', 31 March 1971.
33. n. 25, pp. 35–36.
34. Ibid., p. 37.
35. Ibid., p. 45.
36. Ibid.
37. Ibid., p. 65.
38. Ibid., p. 98.
39. Ibid., 245.
40. Richard Nixon, 'Hand-written Letter from President Nixon to President Yahya', The White House, Washington DC, 7 August 1971, Record Group 59 PPC S/P, *Directors Files* (Winston Lord), Box 330, *The National Security Archive,* at https://nsarchive2.gwu.edu/

41. Prakhar Gupta, 'Henry Kissinger Reveals Why the US Supported Pakistan in 1971', *The Atlantic*, 17 November 2016.
42. n. 25, p. 32.
43. Ibid., pp. 117–19.
44. Ibid., pp. 129–30.
45. Ibid., p. 140.
46. Ibid., p. 234.
47. US Department of State Cable, 'Indo-Pakistan Situation', 15 July 1971, Nixon Presidential Materials Project (NPMP), National Security Council (NSC) Files, Indo-Pak War, Box 578, *The National Security Archive,* at https://nsarchive2.gwu.edu/
48. n. 25, pp. 349–51.
49. Since the crackdown began in 25 March, the number of East Pakistan refugees reaching India reached to over 9.5 million by 31 October 1971, and the community-wise breakup of the refugees was: Hindus 82.3 per cent, Muslims 17 per cent, and Budhists, Christians, etc. 7 per cent. The majority, 82.3 per cent, were Hindus because of the targeted killing by the Pakistani army. See *Official History of the 1971 India-Pakistan War,* Chapter-III, n. 15, pp. 194–95.
50. Text of the Letter dated 15 December 1971 from Prime Minister Indira Gandhi to President Richard Nixon on Event in Bangladesh, Ministry of External Affairs (MEA), Government of India (GOI), *Foreign Affairs Record,* 1971, pp. 393–94.
51. Richard Nixon, *RM: The Memoirs of Richard Nixon,* London: Sidgwick & Jackson Ltd., 1978, pp. 525–26.
52. n. 25, p. 499; and, US Department of State, *Foreign Relations of the US, 1969–1976, Volume E–7, Documents on South Asia, 1969–1972*, Document 150.
53. The Nixon Administration also reaffirmed the intention to continue the 1967 policy of 'one-time exception'. See Kux, n. 13, p. 284; and, Kissinger, n. 11, p. 849.
54. Vinod Gupta, *Anderson Papers: A Study of Nixon's Blackmail of India,* Delhi: An ISSD Publication, 1972, p. 65.
55. n. 25, p. 164.
56. Ibid., p. 165.
57. Ibid., p. 167.
58. US Department of State, *Foreign Relations of the US, 1969–1976, Volume E–7, Documents on South Asia, 1969–1972,* Document 136.
59. n. 25, p. 167.
60. 'Event Summary by George H.W. Bush', 10 December 1971, George Bush Presidential Library, George H.W. Bush Collection, Series: *United Nations File,* 1971-1972, Box 4, *The National Security Archive,* at https://nsarchive2.gwu.edu/; and, also see Ibid., pp.751–63.
61. n. 25, p. 783; and also see Memorandum of Conversation between Deputy NSA Alexander Haig, Senior NSC Staff Winston Lord and Chinese Ambassador to UN Huang Hua, 12 December 1971, Record Group 59, PPC S/P, *Directors Files* (Winston Lord), Box 330.
62. 'Situation in India-Pakistan as of 0700 hours (EST), 14 December 1971', India-Pakistan Working Group Situation Report #41, NPMP, *NSC Files,* Indo-Pak War, Box 573.
63. 'India-Pakistan Situation Report as of 1600 (EST), 16 December 1971', Intelligence Memorandum, CIA, NPMP, MDR# 4. And, 'The Tilt: The US and the South Asian Crisis of 1971', *National Security Archive,* Electronic Briefing Book No. 79, 16 December 2002.
64. 'Telegram 7391 from US Embassy in Tehran to the Department of State', 29 December 1971, 'F-5 Aircraft to Pakistan', NPMP, *NSC Files,* Indo-Pak War, Box 575.
65. In a NSC memo on 7 December, NSC Staff Harold H. Saunders observed that 'by law', the US 'cannot authorize' any military equipment transfers to Pakistan either directly or any third party unless the Administration was willing to change the policy.

66. Telegram 230056 from Department of State to the US Embassy in New Delhi, 23 December 1971, 'Supply of Third Country US Arms to Pakistan', NPMP, *NSC Files*, Indo-Pak War, Box 575.
67. Before signing the Treaty with the Soviet Union, India assessed whether the Treaty would adversely affect India's long cherished non-alignment foreign policy objectives. It found that the Treaty would not conflict with the basic tenets of non-alignment policy, on the contrary it would strengthen it. See the text of Treaty of Peace, Friendship and Cooperation between the Republic of India and the Union of Soviet Socialist Republic, signed between EAM Swaran Singh and Russian Foreign Minister, A.A. Gromyco in New Delhi on 9 August 1971.
68. n. 15, pp. 142–47.
69. See text of the Statement by EAM Swaran Singh in the Rajya Sabha on 19 July 1971, MEA, GOI, *Foreign Affairs Record*, 1971, pp. 137–38; and, also Kux, n. 13, pp. 289–312.
70. EAM Swaran Singh further emphasised that 'It strengthens our policy of non-alignment ... and will become an effective instrument for the safeguarding of our national interests'. See Statement by EAM Sardar Swaran Singh in Parliament on the Indo-USSR Treaty of Peace, Friendship and Cooperation on 9 August 1971, MEA, GOI, *Foreign Affairs Record*, Vol. 17, No. 8, 1971, p. 159.
71. n. 25, pp. 313–15.
72. Kissinger, n. 11, p. 767.
73. Indira Gandhi, 'India and the World', *Foreign Affairs*, Vol. 51, No. 1, October 1972, p. 74.
74. Richard Nixon, *Third Annual Report to the Congress on United States Foreign Policy*, President Richard Nixon, the White House, Washington DC, 9 February 1972 available at http://www.presidency.ussb.edu/
75. n. 25, pp. 483–85.
76. Ibid., p. 115; and, also see n. 63, *National Security Archive*, 16 December 2002.
77. n. 25, p. 325.
78. Ibid., p. 164.
79. Ibid., p. 761.
80. Ibid., p. 147.
81. Ibid., p. 324.
82. Nixon, n. 51, p. 531.
83. Kissinger, n. 11, p. 880.
84. n. 25, p. 594.
85. Ibid.
86. 'Role of Big Powers in Indo-Pak War of 1971', by *ANI*, 16 December 2015, available at https://www.india.com/news/india/role-of-big-powers-in-indo-pak-war-of-1971-788574/
87. n. 15, p. 711.
88. n. 25, p. 657.
89. Ibid., p. 752.
90. Kux, n.13, p.302.
91. Ibid., p. 306.
92. Memorandum of Conversation between Dr Sarabhai, Dr Haksar, Dr Kissinger, Mr Winston Lord on 7 July 1971, NPMP, *NSC Files*, Pres/HAK Memcons, Box 1025.
93. n. 25, p. 754.
94. Ibid., p. 712.
95. Ibid., p. 518; and, Rakesh Krishnan Simha, 'Gunboat Diplomacy: Revisiting the Enterprise Incident', *Russia Beyond*, 14 December 2016.
96. n. 25, p. 727.
97. Simha, n. 95, 14 December 2016.

98. n. 25, pp. 816–17.
99. Josy Joseph, 'US Forces had Orders to Target Indian Army in 1971', *The Times of India,* 6 November 2011; and, also see Simha, n. 95, 14 December 2016.
100. See the text of Treaty of Peace, Friendship and Cooperation between the Republic of India and the Union of Soviet Socialist Republic, signed between EAM Swaran Singh and Russian Foreign Minister, A.A. Gromyco in New Delhi on 9 August 1971.
101. Simha, n. 95.
102. Ibid., and, also see Raghavendra Mishra, 'Revisiting the 1971 "USS Enterprise Incident": Rhetoric, Reality and Pointers for the Contemporary Era', *Journal of Defence Studies*, Vol. 9, No. 2, April–June 2015, p. 61.
103. US Department of State, *Foreign Relations, 1969–1976, Volume E–7, Documents on South Asia, 1969–1972,* Document 165, 'Conversation among President Nixon, NSA Kissinger and Attorney General Mitchell', 8 December 1971.
104. n. 25, p. 766.
105. Charles Mohr, 'Dacca Captured', *The New York Times,* 17 December 1971.
106. Charles Mohr, 'Attacks Suspended', *The New York Times,* 16 December 1971.
107. *The HRC Supplementary Report*, n. 14, p. 114.
108. Ibid.
109. Sydney H. Schanberg, '2 Men at a Table', *The New York Times,* 17 December 1971.
110. Dutt, n. 22, pp. 94–111; and, Kux, n. 13, pp. 306–12.
111. Cited in Sagar Ahluwalia and Raj Gill, *Henry Kissinger: The Miracle Man*, New Delhi: Young Asia Publication, 1974, p. 115.
112. Ibid., p. 116.
113. Nixon said reflecting his concern over the special Indian relations with the Soviet Union in light of the Indo-Soviet Union Treaty of Friendship. See Richard Nixon, *Fourth Annual Report to the Congress on United States Foreign Policy,* President Richard Nixon, the White House, Washington DC, 3 May 1973 available at http://www.presidency.ussb.edu/
114. Tanvi Madan, *Fateful Triangle: How China Shaped US-India Relations during the Cold War,* Gurgaon, India: Penguin Random House, 2020.
115. Gandhi, n.73, p. 75.
116. *Parliamentary Debates,* Rajya Sabha, Vol. 82, No. 1–14, 1972, columns 224–25.
117. Nixon, n. 113.
118. Rudra Chaudhuri, *Forged in Crisis: India and the United States since 1947,* New Delhi: Oxford University Press, 2014.
119. Saroj Bishoyi, 'De-Hyphenating of India-Pakistan Relations: United States Strategic Engagements with India and Pakistan', in Sanjay Kumar, Dhirendra Dwivedi and Mohammad Samir Hussain, *India-Pakistan Relations: Issues and Challenges,* New Delhi: G.B. Books in association with ARIDSS, 2016, pp. 127–44.

14

Shaping the World Opinion

Media, War Reporting and Radio Broadcasting during the 1971 War of Liberation

Smruti S. Pattanaik

Media plays a momentous role in shaping public opinion, especially in times of crisis. In the 1971 war of liberation, the media—international media, including Indian media, and other small journals managed by those fighting for the liberation of Bangladesh—contributed in shaping public opinion against the military regime in Pakistan. Indeed, both the print and the radio played a very significant role. Unlike the present, there was no social media in 1971 and information on developments within East Pakistan was difficult to come by, especially in the context of Yahya Khan's military regime which intimidated the media outlets, forcing the closure of many. Thus, apart from the state-owned agencies, only those media outlets were allowed to operate whose function was to provide information supporting the government's position and policies. When the Pakistani state made all efforts to enforce information blackout, it was some courageous journalists who took the risk to break the news of military repression against the Bengalis to the world. Unfortunately, in the initial days of Operation Searchlight, the international community refused to take note of the brutality of Pakistan Army operations in East Pakistan.

The Western print media also played a significant role, many a time going against their own government's position on the crisis, in bringing the developments in East Pakistan to the attention of the international community and emphasising that the brutality inflicted on unarmed Bengali people and the genocide committed by the state cannot be treated as internal affairs or sovereign decision of the Pakistani state. Prior to Operation Searchlight, on 25 March 1971, the journalists were confined to Intercontinental Hotel, next to Dhaka University where the army action unfolded. The journalists staying in the hotel were not given any information of the massacre and they were confined to their rooms, with soldiers from the Pakistan Army keeping a watch on them. They were, thus, completely cut off from the events in Dhaka.[1] Yet, the 'genocide' captured the headlines in the Western press. Saddiq Salik, the Public Relations Officer of Pakistan Army, blamed the officials responsible for expelling the foreign press from Dhaka for the adverse reports in the foreign media, which made the world believe that several millions perished. Further, it forced them to base their stories on what he described was 'the fantasy of Indian propagandists and whims of opinionated tourists'.[2] These journalists were finally bundled out of East Pakistan in army trucks and taken to the airport, after being thoroughly checked to see whether they possessed any photos or films of the atrocities unleased by the Pakistan Army. They were flown out of Dhaka and left via Karachi; and some of them later returned to cover the war from India.

Pakistan lost its case even before the war began as the media exposed army action and killings through photographs and news reports. Hasan Zaheer, a civil servant who was posted in East Pakistan, stated: 'The mindless handling of the world's powerful media was only slightly less catastrophic than the army action itself. They did not forget or forgive this treatment and Pakistan's case suffered immensely in the world opinion-making forums for the next nine months.'[3] It was also surprising that the state did not admit to the massive killings. Even if Pakistan had not expelled and prevented the foreign media from reporting, it is rather unlikely that it would have got a favourable press on what happened on the night of 25 March. In this context, the print media and broadcasting played an important role in shaping public opinion, turning the tide against Pakistan.

Western governments, mainly the United States (US), remained hostile to the war of liberation. They framed the political crisis in East Pakistan as a sovereign decision of an independent country and took a view that these developments were an internal matter of Pakistan, to be resolved by the country as deemed appropriate. This reaction, in part, can be attributed to the fact that the US was beholden to Pakistan for facilitating a diplomatic opening with China that subsequently paved way for President Nixon's visit and Sino-US rapprochement. Further, the US had been backing Yahya Khan for a negotiated political settlement with Sheikh Mujibur Rahman. As the military option to resolve the political crisis weighed on and Operation Searchlight was ordered, the US administration demonstrated its support to the military regime in Pakistan both militarily, by supplying ammunition, and diplomatically, through statements in support of Pakistan and by pressurising India to refrain from intervening militarily. The US diplomats stationed in Dacca[4] and Delhi were sending notes describing how Yahya Khan had decided on a military solution to the political crisis in East Pakistan. Surprisingly, the US Embassy in Islamabad denied these reports that were being despatched from Delhi and Dhaka.[5]

As the US remained "profoundly grateful" to President Yahya Khan for facilitating US's rapprochement with China, the US administration made tireless efforts to support Yahya Khan to reach a political settlement, however it did not realise how much the two wings of Pakistan had drifted apart, with Bangladesh notionally emerging with the announcement of independence on 26 March. Henry Kissinger wrote: 'For us to gang up on Pakistan—as our media and Congress were so insistently demanding—would accelerate the danger; it would give India an even stronger justification to attack. It would jeopardize the China initiative.'[6] As the US media started publishing on the atrocities committed by the Pakistan Army on the night of 25 March and the US administration attempted to turn the adverse public opinion towards Pakistan's military regime, the war broke out. The Nixon administration was keen that India gets the blame for the war. In fact, Kissinger assured Nixon that he had taken steps to ensure that the major US newspapers, especially 'on front page of *The New York Times* and *The Washington Post*', would put a headline that 'India is largely to blame for the outbreak of hostilities and it lists all the things the Indians have rejected.'[7]

Print Media and War Reporting

The 25 March military operation unfolded mainly in the Dhaka University campus and adjoining areas. The mayhem and bloodletting began with well-coordinated planned attacks on student dormitories, minority halls and targeted those who sympathised with the Awami League. The Pakistan Army took precaution to keep the developments under wraps. This army action was justified in a White Paper published by Pakistan in August 1971, which argued: 'President Yahya Khan ordered the army into action [on 25 March] to fore-stall the plot, put down the insurrection, and thwart the treasonous secessionists.'[8] In a radio broadcast on 26 March, Yahya blamed Mujib for 'obstinacy, obduracy, and absolute refusal to talk sense'[9] and said that he ordered the army action in East Pakistan to 'fully restore the authority of the Government'.[10]

Though the news of the regime's inability to reach an understanding with Mujib and the consequent breakdown in negotiations was known, the people of West Pakistan were neither informed nor aware of the aforementioned developments in East Pakistan. Indeed, the extent of atrocities unleashed by the Pakistani Army was unknown at that point of time. The government had built up public opinion in the western wing that portrayed the developments in East Pakistan and the demand of Awami League—mainly by its leader, Sheikh Mujibur Rahman—as a grave threat to the unity of Pakistan. The fact that Mujib's party had won the majority of seats in the National Assembly in the 1970 election was disregarded by the critics of Mujib in the western wing. The military regime referred to him as a separatist and an agent of the 'enemy'.

In this context, the Agartala conspiracy case, in which Mujib was accused of conspiring against Pakistan in collusion with India, came in handy for the ruling elites to project Mujib as a conspirator.[11] This case was however, withdrawn unconditionally and Mujib was released by Ayub's regime in 1969 due to massive demonstration. Pakistan's government was able to portray the army action in East Pakistan as indispensable and necessary to clean Pakistan from 'miscreants' who wanted to divide Pakistan with the help of India. This was acceptable to the majority of West Pakistanis who, having been fed with anti-India propaganda, believed that protests in East Pakistan for democratic rights were an Indian mechanisation for the separation of East Pakistan.[12] In any case, such characterisation of demands of Bengalis was not new. On 24 March 1948, Mohammad Ali Jinnah had rejected the Bengali's demand to recognise Bangla as one of the national languages, saying: 'the state language of Pakistan is going to be Urdu and no other language. Anyone who tries to mislead (you) is merely the enemy of Pakistan.'[13]

Interestingly, the newspapers in West Pakistan, including well-respected newspapers like the *Dawn*, *Nawa-i-Waqt* and *Jung*, preferred to tow the government line on East Pakistan crisis. They were rather more aggressive in their approach to the crisis, especially in supporting the army action, than government-controlled Radio Pakistan, Pakistan Television and Associated Press of Pakistan. All of them did not mention domestic political aspects of the East Pakistan crisis but alluded to the 'Hindu and Jewish conspiracy' that required a wholehearted support to the army action.[14]

The Western governments and Muslim countries were unsympathetic to the cause of the Bengalis. It became a challenge to generate support for the movement for Bangladesh's liberation. The adage, 'A picture is worth a thousand words', slowly brought the atrocities to light as famous Indian photographer Raghu Rai captured the suffering of the people in his photographs. As the refugees poured in, stories of killing and atrocities, including pictures of suffering masses, were flashed across the world. According to an analyst: 'The coverage of the civilian crisis was thus framed around images of women, children, and refugees.'[15] This was indeed powerful in conveying the message to the world in a nutshell. All these stories, even though selected by photographers and journalists, helped shape the public opinion.[16]

Many journalists who filmed the exodus started sending these pictures to the newspapers they were accredited to. Anthony Mascarenhas, a Pakistani reporter, who was part of the guided tour arranged by the Pakistan Army that wanted to give the journalists a glimpse into the army's effort to save the motherland, did a story on the army massacre in East Pakistan, titled 'Genocide', which was published in 13 June 1971 edition of *The Sunday Times*.[17] The article shook the world and exposed Pakistan's lie as well as pretentious American arguments that what was happening in East Pakistan was the internal affair of that country. Other journalists who were part of the same group in the army-guided tour filed stories for their respective newspapers describing the army action in glowing terms, including how the army was being welcomed by the people in East Pakistan. One of the advertisements in the *Morning News* published from East Pakistan read, 'History was made in September 1965, history repeats itself, the nation stands pledged to live up to its glory', even as Pakistan was facing a huge military defeat.[18]

It needs to be emphasised here that the Bengali media sympathised with Mujib and gave wholehearted publicity to his efforts to secure the democratic rights of Bengalis. Despite the adverse situation in East Pakistan, some of them managed to publish their newspapers, but soon had to close them down. The first attack, on 25 March night, was on *The People*, a vocal media outlet against the Pakistan regime, which was burnt down. This was followed by attacks on *Dainik Ittefaq* and *Sangbad* the next day. Offices of *Dainik Pakistan*, *Dainik Purbodesh*, *Morning News* and *Pakistan Observer* were also attacked; and periodicals like *Swaraj* and *Banglar Bani* were closed down.[19] Pakistan government also made it clear that there would be no news which would have an impact on Pakistan's unity and there should be no criticism of the Pakistani military. The government instructed the controlled media in East Pakistan to refrain from using 'so called' before

Mukti Bahini, or Mukti Fauz,[20] and asked them not to use these terms glorifying the 'miscreants' but to use 'rebel' and 'Indian agent'. Words like 'Bangladesh' and 'Joy Bangla' were banned. Some of the media owners also fled the country as government put restrictions and imposed Act 77 of the martial law. For instance, newspapers like *Ganobani*, *Dainik Ittefaq* and *Dainik Sambad*, as also Eastern New Agency, were banned, while the Jamaat Islami mouthpiece, *Dainik Sangram*, was allowed to be published. Taking into account the Jamaat's support to the military regime, it portrayed Tikka Khan as the protector of Islam and Pakistan.

The government took control of the print media, radio and television in East Pakistan. These were used for propaganda by the Pakistani military government.[21] However, the Bengali officials who continued with the state media outlets subtly sabotaged the content of broadcast. According to Salik, when the Pakistan government thought of reactivating the radio station to use it to announce martial law proclamations and instructed the Bengali officials in charge of broadcast to play instrumental music in between announcements, they played dirges. Also, when asked to play devotional songs that emphasised the religious bond between the people of the two wings, they played 'row the boat to the safety of shores'—the boat symbolising Awami League's election symbol; and when asked to underline the importance of creation of Pakistan, they played Maulana Mohammad Ali Johar's powerful play on the 'virtues of independence'.[22] Further, to keep the Indian journalists away from reporting on East Pakistan, two Indian Bengali journalists, Dipak Bandyopathyay and Surojit Ghosh, who had crossed over to Comilla for gathering news were brutally tortured and killed by the Pakistan Army to set an example of the dangers of adverse reporting.[23]

In India, the vernacular media in Bengal 'was bordering on indifference', as described by veteran journalist Manas Ghosh who followed the war and wrote the first article in *The Statesman* on the unfolding political situation in East Pakistan prior to the 1970 election. According to him, 'Bengalis were comparatively in the periphery both in the Indian political mainstream and in the media', which he attributed to the dominance of Hindu migrants from West Pakistan.[24] Thus, the enormity of the situation in East Pakistan was either ignored or given very little space in the press. Moreover, as political situation unfolded, even Bengali media treated it as an internal affair of Pakistan and remained obsessed with developments in West Pakistan. In fact, some of the reports of Indian journalists were seen with scepticism as many were not ready to accept the brutality that Pakistan Army unleashed on the Bengalis. For example, the killing of young Bengali officers and other non-combatant officers in Chittagong and Comilla, reported by Indian journalist S. Handa, was declared as 'cock-and-bull stories' by apologists of Pakistan regime and sceptics in India.[25]

The oath-taking ceremony of the Bangladesh government-in-exile which is popularly known as Mujibnagar government took place in Baidyanathtola in Meherpur district on 9 April 1971. It was given full publicity by the print media, which announced the formation of the Government of Bangladesh. People like Barrister Amirul Islam invited journalists from Calcutta Press Club to attend the swearing-in ceremony of the Mujibnagar government and made arrangements for their travel so that this big news could be given wider publicity. Around 50 foreign journalists witnessed the birth of the new nation and the inauguration of its government.[26]

After this, several newspapers from Calcutta, like *Amrit Bazar Patrika*, *Daily Anand Bazar Patrika*, *Hindustan Times*, *The Statesman*, *Hindustan Standard*, *Frontier*, *Yugantar*, *Kalantar*, *Agartala Dainik Sambad* and *Saptahik Samachar*, both published from Tripura, began publishing stories on the liberation war. *Yugantar* was especially very critical of India's inability to take action against Pakistan.[27] In the initial days of refugee crisis, these newspapers carried appeals to create a favourable world opinion as well as build pressure on the Indian government to recognise Bangladesh.[28]

Reports in the Indian Urdu media on the developments in East Pakistan was divided. However, a section of Indian Muslims saw this as an attempt to break up Pakistan and did not support the Bengalis.[29] As the external environment remained hostile to the Bengali's struggle for liberation, keeping the morale of the fighters high was an important consideration. In this context, the print media and the radio—both All India Radio (AIR) and Swadhin Bangla Betar Kendro (SBBK)—played an important role by not only bringing the news but also making the effort to keep the morale high. In fact, media became the only source to keep one updated on the war front. Notwithstanding the reason for mass exodus, Pakistan also claimed that India was using its radio station to provide publicity to Pakistani atrocities to encourage outflow of refugees.

Though 10 million refugees fled to India, another 65 million remained trapped inside East Pakistan. For them, to know what was happening on the war front and inside Bangladesh was difficult as the government propaganda machine was not providing correct information; and most of the information was suppressed and controlled as part of information warfare.

Broadcasting Triumph and Tribulations of Bengali Freedom fighters

Media and broadcasting remained a vital line of communication between the refugees, Mukti Bahini and the Bengalis who were still trapped in East Pakistan. It also helped in shaping public opinion in India in favour of the refugees. It would indeed have been difficult to sustain the liberation war without drawing on the empathy of Indians. The Government of India used this medium to the fullest; and the effectiveness of broadcast was already evident on 25 March itself. The first announcement of independence was made on 26 March 1971, though Mujib had hinted at independence in his 7 March speech. Mujib sent the message of independence to be transmitted across Bangladesh, which read:

> From today Bangladesh is independent. I call upon the people of Bangladesh wherever you may be and with whatever you have, to resist the army of occupation to the last. Your fight must go on until the last soldier of the Pakistan occupation army is expelled from the soil of Bangladesh and final victory is achieved.[30]

Freedom fighters also used the media to essentially seek the support of international community for the Bengalis in their efforts to liberate Bangladesh.[31]

SBBK: Voice of Mujibnagar Government

In the 1971 war, the radio played an important role and its reach was pervasive compared to the print media. Distributing newspapers that carried stories against the government was considered risky and hence, radio transmission remained an important mode of communication. The declaration of independence was made from the 10 KW transmitter of the Kalurghat radio station in Chittagong, whose transmitter was shifted to Shalbagan, Bagafa–Belunia Forest, Agartala (Tripura), after the Pakistan Air Force bombed the station on 30 March.[32] On 25 May, it was shifted to Kolkata and came to be known as Swadhin Banglar Betar Kendro or SBBK. The Government of India allotted a transmitter to the station on 2 May 1971 as part of a broader strategy to reach out to those trapped within Bangladesh, and to give wider publicity to the developments within that country. Swadhin Bangla Betar Kendra was set up in the 57/8 Ballygunj circular road in Calcutta to provide a voice to the Mujibnagar government. Technical help to set up the radio station was provided by Akashvani Calcutta (now Kolkata) station. Prime Minister Tajuddin Ahmad, who was also the information minister of the Mujibnagar government, took a lead role in the establishment of SBBK after discussions with Indira Gandhi in Delhi.[33] Finally, it became Radio Bangladesh on 6 December after India officially recognised Bangladesh.

Both SBBK and AIR followed their own programme. The SBBK functioned as a broadcasting corporation for the Mujibnagar government. Moreover, the Mukti Bahini, who needed the support of the people within East Pakistan, used SBBK to counter Pakistan's propaganda by keeping the people informed about the progress in the battlefield. It was important as many pro-Pakistani elements had started spreading rumours about how Pakistan was gaining an upper hand in the liberation war. Ali Usman Qasmi, in a study of two newspapers of East Pakistan, *Morning News* and *Pakistan Observer*, between 23 November 1971 and 30 December 1971, found that 'these newspapers projected an image of Pakistan as being in complete control of the situation. Both newspapers, till the very end of the war, kept on reporting on the advance of Pakistan's military and the huge losses incurred by the Indian military.'[34] Such propaganda also had a negative impact on those who were fighting for liberation and it was important to boost their morale. In addition, the SBBK was used by some elements within the Mujibnagar government who attempted to project the objectives of the liberation war as either it could result in the release of Mujib or independence.[35] Such propaganda had a negative impact on those who were fighting for liberation and those who expected a victory.

The Bengalis in East Pakistan also tuned in to AIR which, according to Salik, was trying to persuade the Bengalis to 'save their life and honour'.[36] Radio Pakistan's bulletin that emphasised that 'normalcy' was soon returning lost credibility as this 'normalcy' bulletin was accompanied by 'search and sweep operations' that targeted Bengali households.[37] The Bengalis who chose to stay in East Pakistan were eager to know the future of those who had already fled to India and the progress of *muktijuddho* (war of liberation), as their future hinged on the success of the freedom fighters. Hence, AIR and SBBK remained the only source of reliable news on the developments on the war front.

The transistors were widely available and most of the times, a single transistor catered to many people who keenly listened to the broadcast. Indeed, for those who remained inside Bangladesh, AIR remained the main source of information on details on the war front, as well as learning about the reaction of the international community.[38] The AIR news bulletins were both in English and Bengali, and included Bengali songs evoking pride in Bengali identity, its language, culture and river—all of which generated emotions among the people. In addition, the radio became the source of news for many in India as it was easily accessible, which is evident in the speech by Pranab Mukherjee, former President of India:

> ...it was the Free Bangladesh Radio and All India Radio that gave us reports of the heroic struggle of our brothers and sisters in Bangladesh. These bulletins were keenly followed by us in India—as the minds and hearts of all Indians were with the people of Bangladesh.[39]

Meanwhile, as mentioned earlier, the SBBK provided a voice to the Mujibnagar government; played a significant role in motivating freedom fighters through the broadcast of inspirational songs and satire; and kept the hopes of liberation alive by highlighting battlefield victories in its news bulletin.[40] It thus ensured that the people in East Pakistan did not get disheartened or lose hope, contrary to the Pakistani propaganda on radio, television and newspapers. As a newsreader of this radio station said, 'Without this radio, the people of the country would have died of the strain. It was the main tool for us in the psychological warfare.'[41] Journalist Manas Ghosh, who extensively covered the liberation war, also noted that it was the broadcasts by AIR and SBBK that motivated the peasants and youths to fight for the liberation of Bangladesh.[42]

The day-to-day activities of SBBK were supervised by Abdul Mannan, Member of the Legislative Assembly. Mannan was also the editor of *Joy Bangla*, published in Bangla language, which became the mouthpiece of the Mujibnagar government. An English weekly, *Bangladesh*, too was brought out by the Mujibnagar government.[43] The information ministry was structured to print posters, produce films, along with deciding the content for information and broadcasting, and also the radio station. Interestingly, it was a Border Security Force (BSF) personnel who, every day without fail, picked up the tape from SBBK for broadcast from a transmitter that was located elsewhere and these broadcasts were aired as part of SBBK.[44] Not surprisingly, programme producer of SBBK Shahjahan Farouk described the SBBK as 'second front' of the liberation war.[45]

The SBBK had numerous programmes, including: news bulletins; 'Kathika' (stories) (inspiring people to take up arms); and satires, such as 'Jallader Durbar' (The Hang man's court) by Kalyan Mitra, depicting Yahya Khan's military regime, and 'Chorompotra' (ultimatum) by M.R. Akhtar Mukul, who changed his voice and acted in this show caricaturing important people of the Pakistani military regime.[46] There were programmes for the freedom fighters, 'Agnishikha' (the flame) and 'Rakta Sakshar' (written in blood); 'Bajra Kantha' (thunderous voice) that broadcasted Mujib's speeches; and several motivational songs, like 'Jagarani' (awakening) and 'Oikatan' (patriotic songs). Many artists who worked in this radio station took pseudo names and were called 'sobdo sainik' (word warriors) of the liberation war. They played an important role in keeping the morale of the fighting force high and in assuring the Bengalis of impending victory as the war progressed. It was important to bring to the knowledge of the world the atrocities committed by the Pakistani forces, by the Bengalis themselves, through the SBBK.

While Radio East Pakistan had a programme called the 'Whole Truth' on the developments in East Pakistan, the SBBK had a programme called the 'Naked Truth' to counter the Pakistani propaganda.[47] It was in SBBK's Ballygunge studio that songs, like 'Purbo Digante, Suryo Utheche' (On the Eastern Sky, a New Sun has Arisen), 'Shono Ekti Mujjiberer Theke' (Hear from One Mujib), 'Mora Ekti Phool ke Bachabo Bole Juddho Kori' (We Fight to Save one Flower) and 'Ek Sagor Rokter Binimoye'(in exchange of an ocean of blood), were played to inspire the liberation war. They were written and composed by Govinda Haldar and recorded in the SBBK.[48] The SBBK had the rule that no foreign artist/lyricist or composer can perform for it, so as to give the broadcasting centre the stature of being independent. Haldar's lyrics were accepted and broadcasted without any attribution. Apart from using other available sources for its report on the war front, SBBK picked up news from AIR and transmitted it. In spite of restrictions on Indian artists to participate in SBBK programme, AIR and SBBK had some lyricists and composers—like Govinda Haldar, Salil Chowdhury and Shyamol Gupta—who were common to the programmes on both the radios. Similarly, Kazi Sabyasachi and Sandhya Mukherjee were exceptions who contributed to both AIR and SBBK.[49]

While SBBK kept the morale high by inspiring freedom fighters with patriotic songs, AIR mobilised Indian public opinion to support the efforts of the Indian government for the refugees, as well as to create empathy for them. This was important because it was felt that the pressure on limited resources due to the refugee crisis may create a hostile environment for them. Most importantly, many had not forgotten the horror of the Partition. The government was also careful about the information on refugees, majority of whom were Hindus, so as to prevent any communal backlash.

AIR and the War of Liberation

The AIR, especially the Calcutta station, played songs that inspired the soldiers. These songs were about the glory of Bengal and the struggle of Bengalis for their legitimate rights.[50] Samar Guha, speaking in the Lok Sabha on 26 March 1971, said: 'The Dacca Betar Kendra has been forcibly closed. The All-India Radio is the only source of information from the people of Bengal. The All India Radio should broadcast the news.'[51] The Mujibnagar government also thought it important to use the AIR for psychological operations as it had a 1,000 kilowatt (kW) transmitter. According to Richard Sisson and Leo Rose, the AIR:

> described battle field victories of the Pro-Awami League forces against the Pakistan Army in glowing terms. While these reports were greatly exaggerated, they did have the immediate effect of persuading some East Pakistanis that victory was near and there was no need to seek refuge in India—some political activists were persuaded of this until it was too late. The Indians may have wanted to encourage East Pakistani resistance, but they did not desire a flood of refugees from province.[52]

Upen Tarafdar produced 'Sambad Bichitra', which mainly contained stories of Pakistan atrocities, sometimes told by the victims themselves, which was transmitted by AIR during the liberation war period. These eyewitness accounts helped in countering the Pakistani propaganda.[53] As he recollected:

> Sometime in March of 1971, a Bangladeshi youth, somehow managed to cross over to India, and was waiting outside the *Akashvani Bhavan* in Kolkata to meet me. The young man brought a cassette with him which contained only scenes of fear... [of those] who were killed and tortured.... It was around the time we realised we have to play our role as newsmen.[54]

Angshuman Roy, singer and composer, sang the famous song written by Gauri Prasanna Majumdar:

> *Shono ekti Mujiborer theke lokkho Mujiborer konto*
> *Swarer dhwani protidwani akashe batashe ute roni*
> *Bangladesh amar Bangladesh.*
>
> *Shei sobujer bukchhera metho pothe*
> *Abar je jabo phire,*
> *Amar harano Banglake abarto phire pabo*
> *Shilpe kabye kothay pabe haire emon sonar khoni.*
> *Shono ekti Mujiboere theke....*[55]

This song, broadcast on 13 April 1971 from Akashvani Calcutta, was extremely inspiring for the Bengali freedom fighters. Lyricist Gauri Prasanna Majumdar also wrote 'Banglar Hindu', 'Banglar Bouddho', 'Banglar Christian' and 'Banglar Musalman', emphasising the unity of all religions in this struggle. Similarly, Pranabesh Sen's 'Sambad Parikrama' contributed to the war of liberation. Acknowledging the services of AIR, in 2012 Bangladesh government awarded it with "Bangladesh Freedom Honour" for its contribution towards the liberation war.

How the radio influenced the liberation war was also recorded by several people who were trapped inside East Pakistan. A freedom fighter, Major Shamsul Arefin (Retd)—who had joined the Pakistan Army in 1969 and later deserted it to join the liberation war—elaborating on the role of AIR said:

> we heard the Indian broadcast on 26th March morning about the independence declaration. On 27th it was clear from the announcement that there is a revolt in the Defence forces. Regular update broadcasted by AIR reached every corner of Bangladesh. It was little difficult for people living in the government controlled area to get any information on the progress of war since Pakistan army declared these as propaganda by the Indian government and there was a ban on broadcasting of the AIR news. But people continued to listen to it carefully because at that point of time it was not clear who is a friend and who is an enemy. Sometime news broadcast was jammed by the authorities.[56]

Another freedom fighter, Shamsher Mobin Chowdhury, who revolted in Chittagong against the Pakistan Army, recollected:

> I first heard AIR (Akash Bani, Kolkata) in Chittagong on the morning of 26th March, 1971. It was in Bangla and was in the form of a 'Breaking news' kind of announcement saying, I paraphrase, 'Civil war has broken out in East Bengal. There are reports of many deaths in different parts of East Bengal in the hands of the Pakistan Army. Bengali elements in the Army in East Bengal have revolted against the Pakistan government'. This broadcast was repeated throughout the day. For those of us who had mutinied on the night of 25th March, this was a great thing, mainly because we realized that the news of the outbreak of the liberation war (at that time we called it War of Independence) has now reached the outside world.

He further said:

> The role of AIR, especially Akash Bani Kolkata, during our War of Liberation was indeed most helpful in furthering our cause as it reached out to the entirety of our population. It also worked as an effective counter to the false propaganda that Radio Pakistan was sending out. Deb Dulal Bandapadhya of Akash Bani Kolkata became a household name in Bangladesh. Akash Bani's role also greatly complimented the very effective role that Shadhin Bangla Betar Kendro based in Calcutta was playing during that very critical period. A programme called 'Chorom Potro' hosted by MR Akhtar Mukul from Shadhin Bangla Betar was not just effective, it was also greatly inspirational. Since I was already a prisoner of war in the hands of the Pakistani Army by then, I myself did not have the opportunity to listen to any of this but I heard the details of all this from family and friends after our

> liberation. Everybody was full of praise for the role of Akash Bani Kolkata and Shadhin Bangla Betar. The broadcasts from both Akash Bani Kolkata and Shadhin Bangla betar reached almost every home not just in Dhaka but all over Bangladesh. Pakistan may have controlled the radio stations but that was the age of transistors, which the Pakistanis could not block. I heard that almost every home would be tuned into Akash Bani and Shadhin Bangla Betar, especially in the evenings with the curtains drawn and in low volume so as not to be heard outside. All in all, the Akash Bani Kolkata and Shadhin Bangla Betar played a massive role in keeping the spirits of the people up even when there was death and destruction all around.[57]

Ambassador Humayun Kabir recollected the role radio played in the liberation war:

> Those who were indeed preparing and pioneering the struggle towards a climax have always been listening to Air India news coverage since the elections of 1970. So for me, AIR was a familiar stuff to me and my family well before the military crackdown on 25 March 1971. Yes, I did hear about India's first silence and then the reaction of PM Indira Gandhi sometime on 26/27 March. Well, in a deep way AIR influenced and helped mobilize the people toward the war effort. What was striking was that people trusted AIR in Bangladesh and the Indian media campaign indeed got a willing audience who were already motivated and engaged in a variety of ways to intensifying the fight against the Pakistani forces with a view to achieving our Independence. Some names became popular in almost every household in Bangladesh, such as Debdulal Banerjee from Kolkata station, Nilima Sanyal and Iva Nag from Delhi station, just to mention a few. Yes, AIR could be heard in Dhaka, but people used to listen to AIR very secretly.[58]

Another freedom fighter recollected:

> the news about the Pak Army crackdown was aired in the AIR very soon after the night of 25th March. For most of the Bangladeshis, AIR was the most important source of information about the political developments and all the events relating to the War till 16 December 1971. No Bangali listened to Radio Pakistan. In fact, AIR Calcutta and BBC were the most tuned in stations during the tumultuous days of March 1971 and the months following. And that was so because of the reliability of the news broadcasted by AIR.

Nobody could control either, and the bloody Pakistanis could not. The role of AIR and SBBK was indeed significant in the war. This was corroborated by another author who wrote that people eagerly waited to listen to Debdulal Bandopadhyay's 'Songbad Parikroma'.[59]

However, apart from AIR, Zaheer argues that there was a clandestine transmitter near the mouth of river Hooghly, which 'beamed to East Pakistan daily accounts of the achievements of the freedom fighters.'[60] There was another programme by Pallab Sengupta, 'Camera re Chokkhe' (through the eyes of camera), on AIR. He interpreted pictures published in newspapers or available through the freedom fighters and described 'in words with all minute details so that innumerable listeners of A.I.R would become more aware of the devastating situation in Bangladesh.'[61]

Ultimately, the surrender ceremony of 16 December 1971 was widely covered by the media.

Conclusion

The liberation war remains a unique event, when majority of population of Pakistan seceded from the minority population to establish an independent country of Bangladesh. The nine-month struggle was preceded by the fight of Bengalis for recognition of their language and culture; their aspiration for democratic rule; and their rejection of communal politics based on separate electorate in the Constituent Assembly of Pakistan and increasing Islamisation of the state to emphasise religious unity as the sole binding force between the people of Pakistan as Muslims. On 16 December 1971, the independent state of Bangladesh emerged. The message for the Pakistan Army to surrender was broadcast from AIR by General Sam Manekshaw, signalling the end of the war and a new beginning for the state of Bangladesh. The yearning for democracy, non-discriminatory citizenship and cultural and linguistic basis of the state found manifestation in the first Constitution of Bangladesh that was promulgated in 1973.

In international relations, media plays a significant role in shaping world opinion on developments of international import that otherwise would have escaped attention. Reports on events in many parts of the world, the suffering of people because of conflict and suppression and exploitation of people by the state, all influence public opinion and have an impact on the international standing of the state. Therefore, in 1971, it was not surprising that soon after the military crackdown, the military regime of Yahya Khan went after the foreign reporters and clamped down on newspapers and journalists. However, in the context of the war, the media played a significant role in building public opinion against what was happening inside East Pakistan. The job was not easy, especially when the government did not allow access to the journalists, and there were powerful actors, like the US and China, that supported the Pakistani military regime by supplying weapons. The state-run newspapers and Pakistan radio emerged as channels that were used as propaganda machinery for the military regime. Countering the propaganda, providing people with news on the war front, as well as keeping the freedom fighters morale high were all important contributions of media. Without media reports on developments in East Pakistan, which moulded the public opinion in favour of Bengalis' struggle, the liberation war would have been difficult to win.

NOTES

1. Imam Ahmed and Sakhawat Liton, *Genocide They Wrote*, Daily Star Books, 2016, p. 65.
2. Saddiq Salik, *Witness to Surrender*, Dhaka: University Press Limited, 2001, p. 90.
3. Hasan Zaheer, *The Separation of East Pakistan: The Rise and Realisation of Bengali Muslim Nationalism*, Dhaka: University Press Limited, 2001, p. 169.
4. See the telegram sent by Archer Blood, US Consul General in Dacca, available at https://nsarchive2.gwu.edu/NSAEBB/NSAEBB79/BEBB8.pdf, accessed 29 March 2022
5. Gary J. Bass, *The Blood Telegram: Nixon, Kissinger, and a Forgotten Genocide*, Delhi: Random House India, 2013, p. 55.
6. Henry Kissinger, *The White House Years*, New Delhi: Vikas Publishing House, 1979, p. 862.
7. 'Transcript of Telephone Conversation between President Nixon and His Assistant for National Security Affairs (Kissinger)', 5 December 1971, available at https://history.state.gov/historicaldocuments/frus1969-76v11/d228, accessed on 27 March 2022.
8. Harry W. Blair, 'Sheikh Mujib and Deja Vu in East Bengal: The Tragedies of March 25', *Economic and Political Weekly*, Vol. 6, No. 5, 1971, p. 2555.
9. Zaheer, *The Separation of East Pakistan*, n. 3, p. 164.
10. Government of Pakistan, *White Paper on the Crisis in East Pakistan*, 5 August 1971, p. 40.
11. Ibid., p. 45. The Government of Pakistan accused that Mujib's involvement in the conspiracy dated back to 1964, even though it was unearthed in 1967.
12. According to Hasan Zaheer, the Indian connection in East Pakistan was not so fatal to the political leaders as it was in the West. See Zaheer, *The Separation of East Pakistan*, n. 3, p. 99. Also see Anam Zakaria, *1971: A People's History from Bangladesh, Pakistan and India*, Penguin, 2019, pp. 316–17.
13. Refer to 'Address by Muhammad Ali Jinnah, Governor General of Pakistan, in Dacca, East Pakistan', 21 March 1948, available at http://www.columbia.edu/itc/mealac/pritchett/00islamlinks/txt_jinnah_dacca_1948.html, accessed on 10 March 2022. During his speech at the Dacca University convocation on 24 March 1948, Jinnah said to the students:

    Does it not strike you rather odd that certain sections of the Indian press to whom the very name of Pakistan is anathema, should in the matter of language controversy set themselves up as the champion of what they call your just rights? Is it not significant that the very persons who in the past have betrayed the Mussalmans or fought against Pakistan, which is after all merely the embodiment of your fundamental right of self-determination, should now suddenly pose as the saviors of your just right and incite you to defy the Government on the question of language? I must warn you to beware of these fifth columnists.

    Available at http://www.jinnahofpakistan.com/2010/04/students-role-in-nation-building-24th.html, accessed on 10 March 2022.

14. Zaheer, *The Separation of East Pakistan*, n. 3, pp. 325–26.
15. Sheram Mokhtar, 'Reading War Photographs: The 1971 India–Pakistan War in the Anglo-American Press', *Visual Communication*, Vol. 19, No. 1, 2020, p. 133, available at https://journals.sagepub.com/doi/pdf/10.1177/1470357219838602, accessed on 1 February 2022.
16. For how the stories are framed in the media, see Naeem Mohaiemen, 'Accelerated Media and the 1971 Civil War in Bangladesh', *Economic and Political Weekly*, Vol. 43, No. 4, 2008, pp. 36–40.
17. Mark Dummett, 'Bangladesh War: The Article that Changed History', *BBC*, 16 December 2011, available at https://www.bbc.com/news/world-asia-16207201, accessed on 17 February 2022.
18. Ali Usman Qasmi, 'Believing in One's Own Propaganda: Newspapers of Dhaka and the War of 1971', *The Express Tribune*, 14 December 2015, available at https://tribune.com.pk/article/30831/believing-in-ones-own-propaganda-newspapers-of-dhaka-and-the-war-of-1971, accessed on 17 February 2022.
19. Helal Uddin Ahmed, 'The Role of Press during Liberation War', *The Financial Express*, 25 March 2020, available at https://thefinancialexpress.com.bd/special-issues/independence-national-day/the-role-of-press-during-liberation-war-1585147416, accessed on 12 March 2022. According to Ahmed, several newspapers managed by journalists from Bangladesh were published during the period of liberation war, such as: *Joy Bangla, Banglar Bani, Desh Bangla, Biplobi Bangladesh, Notun Bangla, Dabanal, Sangrami Bangla, Shashwata Bangla, Muktijuddha, Obhijan, Saptahik Bangla, Bangabani, Durjoy Bangla, Janmabhumi, Jagrata Bangla, Ekota, Amod, Banglar Mukh, Swadhin Bangladesh, Biplobi Andolan, Chabook, Ora Durjoy Ora Durbar, Swadhinata, Bajrakantha, Janata, Protinidhi, Mayer Dak, Kalantar, Kafela, Kaler Pata, Dak Diye Jai, Banglar Katha, Jatrik, Swadesh, Rudrabeena, Darpan, Swaraj, Hatiar, Amar Desh, Ranangan, Swadhin Bangla, Agradoot, Bangladesh, The People, The Nation, Rashtradoot, Mukto Bangla, Sonar Bangla, Mukti, Protinidhi, Swandip Thekey Dhaleshwari, Bangladesh Sangbad, Protirodh, Swadhikar* and *Grenade*.
20. According to Subrata Roy Chowdhury, 'the change of nomenclature from Urdu word "Fauj" to the Bengali word "Bahini" two months after its birth was indicative of the expansion of a purely land based guerrilla army....' See Subrata Roy Chowdhury, *The Genesis of Bangladesh: A Study in International Legal Norms and Permissive Conscience*, Bombay: Asia Publishing House, 1972, p. 156.
21. Abu Mohammad Delwar Hossain, *Sambadpatre Dhaka r Muktijoddo*, Dhaka: Pragati Press and Publication, 2017, p. 43.
22. For details, see Salik, n. 2, p. 94.
23. Ibid., p. 61.
24. Manas Ghosh, *Bangladesh War: Report from Ground Zero*, Delhi: Niyogi Books, 2021, pp. 32–33.
25. Ibid., pp. 63–65.
26. Subrata Roy Chowdhury, n. 20, p. 152.
27. For an interesting take on political cartoons in print media, see Urvi Mukhopadhyay, 'Waging War through Humour: Political Cartoons and the War of 1971 as Depicted in Calcutta-based Print Media', *Strategic Analysis*, Vol. 45, No. 6, 2021, p. 610.
28. Hossain, *Sambadpotre Dhaka r Muktijoddo*, n. 21, pp. 57–58.
29. 'Muslim Press in India and the Bangladesh Crisis', originally published in *Quest* (Bombay), No. 94, March–April 1975, available at http://www.columbia.edu/itc/mealac/pritchett/00litlinks/naim/ambiguities/14muslimpress.html, accessed on 15 March 2022.

30. 'Proclamation of Independence', available at https://en.banglapedia.org/index.php/Proclamation_of_Independence, accessed on 31 March 2022.
31. David Ludden, 'The Politics of Independence in Bangladesh', *Economic and Political Weekly*, Vol. 46, No. 35, 2011, p. 85.
32. Available at http://en.banglapedia.org/index.php?title=Swadhin_Bangla_Betar_Kendra.
33. Interview with Amirul Islam, p. 119.
34. Qasmi, 'Believing in One's Own Propaganda', n. 18.
35. Kissinger, *The White House Years*, n. 6, pp. 869–72.
36. Salik, n. 2, p. 95.
37. Ibid.
38. See Vivekananda Ray, 'Akashvani o Bangladesher Janmo', in Abu Sayeed (ed.), *Muktijuddhe Radio*, Swapno 71 (Muktijuddho bishesok traimasik, 10th Edition, pp. 340–46.
39. 'Acceptance and Banquet Speech by the President of India, Shri Pranab Mukherjee on Receipt of Bangladesh "Liberation War Honour"', 4 March 2013, available at http://pranabmukherjee.nic.in/sp040313_01.html.
40. For details, see the article by Belal Mohammad, who played an important role in SBBK, 'Let Me Tell it Once Again', *The Daily Star*, 10 April 2015, available at https://www.thedailystar.net/op-ed/let-me-tell-it-once-again-73963.
41. Afrose Jahan Chaity, 'Swadhin Bangla Betar Aided Psychological Warfare in 1971', *Dhaka Tribune*, 6 March 2018, available at https://www.dhakatribune.com/opinion/special/2018/03/06/swadhin-bangla-betar-aided-psychological-warfare-1971.
42. Ghosh, *Bangladesh War: Report from Ground Zero*, n. 24, p. 124.
43. Ahmed, 'The Role of Press during Liberation War', n. 19.
44. Nasreen Ahmad, 'My Days at the *Swadhin Bangla Betar Kendro*: The Radio Broadcasting Centre during Bangladesh Liberation War in 1971', *Strategic Analysis*, Vol. 45, No. 6, 2021, p. 500.
45. Interview with Shahjahan Farouk, in Afsan Choudhury (ed.), *Mujibnagar: Kathamo o Karjyobiboran*',(Mujibnagar: Structure and its work) Kathaprakash, Dhaka, 2021, p. 167.
46. Joking about Yahya Khan and others, according to Mukul, was one way of breaking the personality of stakeholders of the military regime and encouraging the fighters not to be scared of them. See interview with Akhtar Mukul, in Afsan Choudhury (ed.), n. 45, pp. 162, 165.
47. See Aly Zakir, 'Muktijuddhe Radio', in Abu Sayeed (ed.), Muktijuddho Besayak Traimashik, *Swapno 71*, Mukto ashor, 10th issue, May–July 2019, p. 196.
48. '50 Years on, B'desh Remembers Kolkata Radio Station that gave them Hope during Liberation War', *The New Indian Express*, 25 May 2021, available at https://www.newindianexpress.com/world/2021/may/25/50-years-on-bdesh-remembers-kolkata-radio-station-that-gave-them-hope-during-liberation-war-2307457.html, accessed on 31 March 2022.
49. Bhavesh Das, 'Ekattorer Muktijuddho: Dui betarer Moitri' (71 Liberation War and Friendship between Two Broadcasting Corporations), *Monthly Bulletin*, Vol. LI, No. 3, March 2022, p. 39, available at https://www.asiaticsocietykolkata.org/uploads/Bulletin%20March%202022.pdf, accessed on 12 May 2022.
50. Navine Murshid, 'India's Role in Bangladesh's War of Independence: Humanitarianism or Self-interest?', *Economic and Political Weekly*, Vol. 46, No. 52, 2011, p. 56.
51. Discussion on 'Developments in East Bengal', 26 March 1971, available at https://eparlib.nic.in/bitstream/123456789/770/1/lsd_05_01_26-03-1971.pdf, accessed on 12 January 2022.
52. Richard Sisson and Leo E. Rose, *War and Secession: Pakistan, India, and the Creation of Bangladesh*,

Berkeley: University of California Press, 1990, p. 147.

53. See the interview with Upen Tarafdar, available at https://www.youtube.com/watch?v=Z7Fxope KogE, accessed on 15 May 2022
54. 'Remembering the "Genocide" in Bangladesh', *The Hindu*, 27 March 2017, available at https: //www.thehindu.com/news/national/remembering-the-genocide-in-bangladesh/ article17668798.ece.
55. Available at https://lyrics71.net/lyrics/shono-ekti-mujiborer-theke/, accessed on 10 March 2022.
56. ASM Shamsul Arefin, email interview, 16 July 2020.
57. Shamsher Mobin Chowdhury, email interview, 16 July 2020.
58. Ambassador Humayun Kabir, email interview, 17 July 2020.
59. Hossain, *Sambadpotre Dhaka r Muktijoddo* (Liberation War as depicted in the Newspapers), n. 28, p. 55.
60. Zaheer, *The Separation of East Pakistan*, n. 3, p. 276.
61. Pallab Sengupta, 'Liberation of Bangladesh: Some Personal Reminiscences from Kolkata', *Monthly Bulletin*, Vol. LI, No. 3, March 2022, p. 14, available at https://www.asiaticsociety kolkata.org/uploads/Bulletin%20March%202022.pdf, accessed on 10 May 2022.

SECTION III

In Retrospect

15

Did Pakistan Learn from its Bangladesh Experience?

Ashok Behuria

Pakistan's brush with its own history is at best problematic, and at worst both self-defeating and self-destructive. Perhaps, every multi-ethnic and multi-national country does have to grapple with the very issues that Pakistan has had to deal with—inter-ethnic accommodation, power-sharing, majoritarian politics, minority-ism, etc.—during the last 74 years of its sovereign existence; however, the urgency shown by the state to crush any show of resistance at any level, with the massive might of the state, driven by an acute sense of paranoia, is unique to Pakistan, with the result that it has suffered a bloody vivisection (secession of East Pakistan) followed by chronic inter-ethnic tensions. This is despite the fervent use of Islam as a common denominator of national identity and perpetuation of fear and hatred of India as a unifier.

All this begs closer analysis of the case of Bangladesh—the difficult process of constitution-making, the demand for a separate state, the reaction of the state, formation of a new state, the lessons learnt, if any, from this experience, and the shape of politics in Pakistan in its aftermath. In this chapter, an attempt is also being made to study the narratives the state has spawned, to come to terms with what many would call, a humiliating division. In the absence of an honest admission of failure of its policies, the temptation to externalise the origin of the problem (meddling by India) has inhibited the process of development of a transformative political framework that could have helped Pakistan deal with disintegrationist threats in better ways.

History

The original federal idea of Pakistan was mooted in the Lahore Resolution of the Muslim League, on 23 March 1940. The second article of the resolution stated:

> ...it is the considered view of this Session of the All India Muslim League that no constitutional plan would be workable in this country or acceptable to Muslims unless it is designed on the *following basic principle*, namely that geographically contiguous units are demarcated into regions which should be so constituted, with such territorial readjustments as may be necessary, that the areas in which the Muslims are numerically in a majority as in the North-Western and Eastern Zones of India, *should be grouped to constitute "Independent States" in which the constituent units shall be autonomous and sovereign.*[1]

The operative part italicised in the above excerpt talked about 'states' rather than 'state' and held that these 'units' or 'states' would be 'autonomous and sovereign'. In the resolution, it was also mentioned that 'the scheme of federation embodied in the Government of India Act, 1935, is totally unsuited to, and unworkable in the peculiar conditions of this country and is altogether unacceptable to Muslim India'. Therefore, implicit in the resolution was endorsement of the idea of a very loose federation. However, the 'truncated' Pakistan, as Jinnah called it, that finally came into being on 14 August 1947 with two different non-contiguous parts/units separated by 1,000 miles veered towards a centralised system of governance. Now that Pakistan had become a reality, there was an ideological about-turn in the views of Jinnah and his companions. Jinnah, the undisputed leader, seemed to disfavour the idea of a loose federation. The office of the Governor General that he held till his death accumulated all executive powers and emitted a strong centralising flavour that also impeded the process of accommodation and understanding that would have ideally propelled the efforts at constitution making.

In case of India, 299 members of the Indian Constituent Assembly debating over different issues for 2 years, 11 months and 17 days finalised a constitution which survives to this day with amendments. In comparison, the constituent assembly of Pakistan moved haltingly and took inordinately long time to settle the basic issue of power sharing between the two units of Pakistan. In western

Pakistan, which is Pakistan today, there were four provinces (Punjab, Sindh, Balochistan and the then North Western Frontier Province or better known in its acronymic form NWFP), while on the eastern side, there was East Bengal (which was later called East Pakistan).

East Bengal Denied Natural Advantage

As per the 1951 census in Pakistan, East Bengal had more population (41.93 million or 58 per cent) than all the provinces put together in the West Pakistan (33.704 million or 42 per cent).[2] Therefore, in any representative assembly, East Bengal was entitled to more seats which would have tilted the power balance in its favour. However, this was not acceptable to the Pakistani leaders, who came either from various parts of India or provinces on the west. The other important issue was language. The top leadership led by Jinnah held that Urdu should be the national language. The views of top leadership in the discussions[3] over these issues in the Constituent Assembly smacked of arrogance and condescension. In comparison, the views of the Muslim members from East Bengal were remarkably faint and feeble, whereas the Hindu members from East Bengal were quite vocal over the issue of Bengali language. On 25 February 1948, it was Dhirendra Nath Dutta who proposed as an amendment to the rules of procedure that in addition to Urdu and English, 'Bengalee' should be accepted as the language of discussion in the assembly. He argued passionately addressing his speech to Jinnah in the chair:

> ...I do so not in a spirit of narrow Provincialism, but, Sir, in the spirit that this motion receives the fullest considerations at the hands of the members present. I know, Sir, that Bengalee is a Provincial language, but, so far [as] our State is concerned, it is the language of the majority of the people of the State....Out of six crores and ninety lakhs of people inhabiting this State, 4 crores and 40 lakhs of people speak the Bengalee language...... I consider that Bengalee language is a lingua franca of our State......Hindustani, Hindi or Urdu has been given an honoured place in the sister Dominion [India] because the majority of the people of the Indian Dominion speak that language. So, we are to consider that in our State it is found that the majority of the people of the State do speak the Bengalee language, then Bengalee should have an honoured place even in the Central Government.

Dutta was backed by Prem Hari Barma, who said that it was 'not the intention of the amendment altogether to oust English or Urdu, but to have Bengalee also as the *lingua franca* of the State'. What Liaqat Ali Khan said in response to this is worth reproducing in detail, here:

> He [Mr Dutta] should realise that Pakistan has been created because of the demand of a hundred million Muslims in this sub-continent and the language of a hundred million Muslims is Urdu and, therefore, it is wrong for him now to try and create the situation that as the majority of the people of Pakistan belongs to one part of Pakistan, therefore, the language which is spoken there should become the State language of Pakistan. Pakistan is a Muslim State and it must have as its *lingua franca* the language of the Muslim nation. My Honourable friend is displeased that Urdu should replace English.... Sir, [he] never minded it, never pressed for Bengalee as long as English was the State language. I never heard in the Central Assembly for years and years any voice raised by the people of Bengal that Bengalee should be the State language.... [Moreover] we must have a State language-the language which would be used between the different parts of Pakistan for inter-provincial communications.... Urdu can be the only language which can keep the people of East Bengal or Eastern Zone and the people of Western Zone joined together. It is necessary for a nation to have one language and that language can only be Urdu and no other language.... As a matter of fact, when the notice of that amendment was given, I thought that the object was an innocent one. The object to include Bengalee was that in case there are some people who are not proficient in English or Urdu might express their views in that language, but I find now that the object is not such an innocent one as I thought it was, *The object of this amendment is to create a rift between the people of Pakistan*, ...to take away from the Mussalmans that unifying force that brings them together.... My honourable friend may go on questioning for the rest of his life. He has done that. Was it not necessary for the people of Bengal—Bengalee speaking people—to have remained united? No, because it was to be a State where Mussalmans were in a majority. Therefore, Bengal must be divided. There was no question of Bengalee language or Bengali culture taken into consideration at that time.

Liaqat even went further to kill the amendment considering the issue 'most vital' and 'a question of life and death' for Pakistan:

> It is really *the most vital question, a question of life and death for the Muslim nation* not only for Pakistan but throughout this whole sub-continent and I most strongly oppose the amendment which has been moved. I hope the House will not lend its support to such a kind of amendment, if ever it comes forward in future.

It was interesting to observe that while Raja Ghaznafar Ali from the western part brought in the issue of other languages being spoken in Pakistan and asked as to what would happen if there was a demand to accommodate them as well, Khwaja Nazimuddin, a Bengalee Muslim from East Bengal was found tamely accepting the proposition that Urdu alone could act as a link language and the 'majority principle' would not apply to language of the state citing the case of India, where, he averred, Hindi was not spoken by the majority. It was also noticeable that there was a marked communal divide over the issue and the motion was supported by mostly the Hindu members of the assembly (i.e., Bhupendra Kumar Datta, Prem Hari Barma, Siris Chandra Chattopadhyaya), while those who opposed the motion were all Muslims, i.e., Abdur Rab Khan Nishtar and Alhaj Muhammed Hashim Gazder. Finally, the motion was defeated marking, quite early in the day, the inability of the top leadership to foresee the shape of things to come. In fact, barely a month later, on 21 March 1948, during his trip to East Bengal, Jinnah made an announcement that only Urdu can be the national language, which went down poorly among the population there.

Ten days earlier, on 11 March 1948, the students of East Bengal had observed a general strike to protest non-recognition of Bengalee as the official language; however, their voices went unheard. Jinnah's spirited defence of Urdu as the national language on 24 March in the Curzon Hall in Dhaka and later reiteration of the stance on radio on 28 March only aggravated the situation further. As Jinnah's successor, Khwaja Nazimuddin, from then East Bengal, stuck to the same position. Gradually, the step-motherly attitude of the Pakistan government towards East Bengal galvanised the Bengali population into action. As the popular movement in favour of Bengalee language gathered momentum, the state adopted a repressive policy *vis-à-vis* the protesting students and on 21 February 1952, a number of students were killed in police firing leading to further protests across East Bengal.

Language Issue Comes Up Again

In April 1952, the issue of Bengalee language came up again and this time round, there were some Muslim voices from East Bengal (A.K. Fazlul Huq) and west part of Pakistan (Sardar Shaukat Hayat Khan, Asadullah Khan Jan) who backed the motion brought in by Raja Kumar Chakravarty. Predictably, the Hindu members (like Bhabesh Chandra Nandy, Sris Chandra Chattopadhyaya, Dhirendra Nat Datta, Bhupendra Datta, Birat Chandra Mandal) supported grant of official status to Bengali language. However, with a 41-12, voting a motion was moved which said that 'there being no immediate necessity of taking a decision thereon be it resolved that the Question be decided by this Assembly when it comes up before it in due course'. It was clear that the Bengali Muslim leaders like Nurul Amin, Nur Muhammad looked at the issue as if it was a communal issue because it was being backed by Hindu Bengalis from East Bengal. There were references to Dr Shyama Prasad Mukherji inciting youth from East Bengal to raise the issue and there was a debate over whether Bengali language was closer to Sanskrit or had an evolution of its own, backed by Muslim rulers of Bengal, with heavy borrowings from Urdu and Persian language.

In the meantime, the apathy shown by the top leadership inevitably led to an autonomist political assertion in the politics of East Bengal as a native coalition of Awami Muslim League, the Krishak Praja Party, the Ganatantrik Dal (Democratic Party) and Nizam-e-Islam led by popular Bengali leaders—A.K. Fazlul Huq, Huseyn Shaheed Suhrawardy and Maulana Bhashani—trounced Muslim League in the March 1954 provincial elections. The United Front demanded autonomy in decision making in East Bengal in all subjects, except in defence and foreign policy, and the recognition of Bengali as an official language.

East Bengal Hardens Stance on Language

As the situation in East Bengal continued to simmer, the leaders of Pakistan continued with their efforts to deny Bengalis as much political importance as they deserved and equalise representation from both parts of Pakistan in the face of numerical disadvantage that western part had *vis-à-vis* the east. The Bogra formula which proposed more seats in the lower house for East Bengal (165 out of 300) also brought in an upper house (50 seats) with co-equal powers where East Bengal was offered equal representation with the other four provinces. This was resented by politicians in East Bengal.

On 24 October 1953, Fazlul Huq read out the resolution passed by people of East Bengal to the constitutional proposal presented by then prime minister, Muhammad Ali Bogra on 7 October 1953, which invoked Lahore resolution and expressed its dismay that the proposal '[gave] no indication of East Bengal's universal demand for complete zonal autonomy on the basis of the historic Lahore Resolution of 1940', expressed its displeasure over equating of East Bengal with smaller units like Balochistan and Karachi in the proposed upper house and favoured the idea of 'a unicameral Federal Legislature directly elected by the people having two specified reserve subjects, namely Defence and Foreign Affairs'. Huq went on to appeal in favour of complete autonomy and asked the assembly to 'leave East Pakistan to work out its own destiny'. Saner voices like Khan Abdul Ghaffar Khan urged the assembly to heed the appeals being made by the representatives from East Bengal. On 8 April 1854, taking the floor after March 1954 election in which the League was wiped out in East Bengal, he said:

> The Bengalis are our elder brothers—Bengal is the largest province, and its people constitute the majority of the people of Pakistan. If we ignore Bengal now, it will be tantamount to ignoring the majority of Pakistan, which will be against all accepted democratic practice. The newly elected representatives want the dissolution of this House and its replacement by a newly elected House, which should frame Pakistan's constitution. Bengal has given its verdict against the Muslim League and I believe, if fresh elections were to be ordered in the other provinces of Pakistan now, the verdict would not be in favour of the League. In these circumstances, if the voice of Bengal is not heeded or attended to, frustration would be wide-spread in the country. Unfortunately, conditions in our country are such that any further discontent and dissatisfaction will ruin us. It is therefore necessary to hold talks with the new representatives of Bengal and come to a compromise with them.

As expected, his voice was ridiculed and rejected, and he was branded as an 'enemy of Pakistan'. In May 1953, the United Front government in East Bengal was dismissed and the legislature suspended. Later, the then Governor General, Ghulam Muhammad dissolved the Constituent Assembly through an executive proclamation on 24 October saying that 'the Constituent Assembly as at present constituted has lost the confidence of the people and can no longer function'. The Prime Minister was, however, asked to run the administration, with a new Cabinet, until the elections. Maulvi Tamizuddin, President of the dissolved Assembly, challenged the order in the Sindh High Court, which quashed the decision. However, the government appealed in the Federal Court, where the then Chief Justice Muhammad Munir, upheld the decision and Tamizuddin lost the case.

The Second Constituent Assembly Delivers the Equaliser

The second constituent assembly of Pakistan was constituted through an order of the Governor General in May 1955. It comprised of 80 members, with the membership equally divided between the two wings of Pakistan and the members were chosen by an electoral college composed of the members of the provincial assemblies.

In September 1955, the then Governor General, Ghulam Ahmed brought in the one-unit scheme to merge the four provinces and the tribal areas in the west and called it West Pakistan, while East Bengal was renamed as East Pakistan. Ahead of it, the East Bengal provincial assembly was reinstated. The new Constituent Assembly endorsed the one-unit formula. The draft of the Constitution was introduced in this Assembly on 9 January 1956 and passed on

29 February 1956. Governor General Ghulam Muhammad assented to it on 2 March 1956 and it was enforced from 23 March 1956, the sixteenth anniversary of passing of the historic Pakistan Resolution. The representatives from East Bengal including Hussain Shaheed Shurawardy were not happy with the constitution. Mahmud Ali expressed it through a popular saying in Bengali: *Parbater mushik prosab* (the mountain has produced a mouse) and said categorically:

> As one reads through the pages of the Constitution before us, it becomes evident that it is nothing but a deception. The hopes and aspirations of the people are belied.....the hopes and aspirations that actuated the hundred million people in the sub-continent of India to struggle for the achievement of Pakistan, have been sadly belied. There have been delays in the past for which the Constituent Assembly entrusted with the responsibility had to go. Today we are going to give the country a Constitution. It is in no respect better than the one proposed by the former Constituent Assembly. If their proposals were unacceptable to the people, the present ones are still more so. Then, Sir, what for were all these delays and what for are all this hurry? *Is it not in the interest of adjustment between the members of the oligarchy that has been ruling over us sometimes in disguise and at some other times in the open?*

This constitution at least recognised Bengali as one of the languages of the State, provided for parliamentary form of government and a unicameral legislature. However, the sense of disenchantment of the people of East Pakistan continued, who still felt that 'an oligarchy' had rooted itself deeply within the power hierarchy, impervious to their demands of equal and equated share in the statecraft.

Within two and a half years, the constitution was abrogated and martial law was declared by Ayub Khan. It was now his turn to engineer yet another constitution through a self-appointed constitution commission (on 17 February 1960). The constitution came up in March 1962 and it endorsed a federal state with a presidential form of government. Unicameral legislatures at the centre and in the provinces were mere lame-duck ones while all executive power was vested in the office of the president.

Into the 1960s and the 1971 Experience

In the 1960s, Pakistan had to pass through the war of 1965 with India, which was planned under the nose of inconclusive and initiated the decline of Ayub Khan. The early 1960s witnessed growing political assertion in East Pakistan under Awami League with a new popular leader, Sheikh Mujibur Rahman, who felt the pulse of the people well and evolved his famous 'Six Points' in February 1966, where the spirit of the Lahore declaration was invoked to establish a true federation, where the constituent units would be autonomous with absolute power to tax and collect revenue while the federal government will only deal with defence and foreign affairs. It went even further to propose two different freely convertible currencies for the two wings and a separate military and paramilitary forces for East Pakistan with the Naval headquarters to be based in East Pakistan. Mujib's stance pitted him against many fellow Awami Leaguers in rest of Pakistan. Ayub was furious and Mujib was branded as a separatist and secessionist. The ill-advised step that Ayub government took in January 1968, to lodge a fictitious case of conspiracy against Mujib (allegedly aided by India) and some in-service and ex-servicemen, known infamously as the Agartala conspiracy case, contributed to Mujib's stature as the voice of Bengali people of East Pakistan. When the case fell through and Mujib was released unconditionally in February 1969, he was given a hero's welcome with a new title, 'Bangabandhu' (friend of Bangla), at Paltan ground in Dhaka. There was a popular unrest in East Pakistan following this release. In the political turmoil that ensued, Ayub had to resign and go. Gen Yahya Khan took over the administration on 25 March 1969 and imposed martial law. Through a Legal Framework Order (LFO), Yahya Khan held the first ever oft-claimed only-free-and-fair elections in Pakistan on 7 December 1970, based on adult franchise and the seats were allocated to both the wings strictly on the basis of population, disregarding the earlier logic of parity and one-unit.

The new elected assembly had 313 members¯169 from East Pakistan and 144 from West Pakistan including 13 seats reserved for women (six from West and seven from East Pakistan). The Awami League secured 160 out of 169 seats in East Pakistan and even without the seven reserved women seats was in a comfortable position to form government at the centre. However, this was not acceptable to the West Pakistan leadership. Zulfikar Ali Bhutto's Pakistan Peoples' Party (PPP) had secured 81 out of 144 seats, which was about half of the strength of Awami League.

The West Pakistan leadership was found unwilling to accept the fact of Awami League's victory and procrastinated unnecessarily, which acted like pouring *ghee* on fire. Bhutto was rushed to Dhaka on 27 January 1971 with a large delegation of 15 leaders to negotiate with Mujib on his six points. Mujib was predictably inflexible, and Bhutto was neither authorised by Yahya nor in a mood himself to concede on matters relating to taxation, external trade, foreign aid as well as over the issue of military and paramilitary forces for the Eastern wing. The talks were destined to fail. When Yahya announced the inaugural session of the newly elected Assembly to be held in Dhaka on 3 March 1971, Bhutto refused to allow elected members of his party to attend it and in fact, reportedly threatened to break the legs of anyone from his party who would dare to attend.[4]

On 1 March 1971, Yahya chose to postpone the date, which was not received well in East Pakistan. As street protests intensified in East Pakistan and Mujib hardened his stance, Yahya Khan announced that the inaugural session would be held on 23 March, to which Mujib said that he would consider it only if martial rule was lifted and power transferred to the elected government. Seeing the situation worsening fast, Yahya did attempt to work out a deal with Mujib and flew down to Dhaka on 15 March and stayed there for about 10 days commiserating with Mujib and Awami League leaders over the six points. After initial hesitation, Bhutto also joined the discussions on 21 March but to no avail. Mujib took strong objections to the military killing his brethren in East Pakistan even when the talks were on and declared 23 March as a public holiday. In the meantime, the leadership of West Pakistan, both military and political, decided to bring in excessive force to deal with the situation. The main ruse was that the armed goons of Awami League, advocating independence, had started attacking pro-Pakistan forces in East Pakistan, and in the face of such armed secessionist threat, there was no alternative to military action.

As Yahya Khan flew out of Dhaka on 25 March in the evening, the military was ordered to carry out indiscriminate action in an apparent bid to silence the voice of the Bengalis by force. By all accounts, the intervening night of 25–26 March was the bloodiest one. Soon after Yahya's plane touched down in Karachi, the Pakistan army unleashed a reign of terror, which has been written about by journalists, diplomats and scholars as a clear instance of Pakistan's desperate and foolish attempt to keep the country together. What happened afterwards is well-known—large-scale migration of people from East Pakistan to India fleeing genocide unleashed by the Pakistan army; Pakistan's attack on India's western front forcing India to join what was otherwise a bloody civil war; and finally surrender of the Pakistani forces on 16 December 1971, which is remembered with a sense of humiliation in Pakistan as *Sukoot-e-Dhaka* or fall of Dhaka, even today.

Narratives in Pakistan

If one analyses the narrative that has been spawned by successive governments, there is a clear effort to suppress the facts that explain the situation leading to the demand for separation in East Bengal. It is most visible in the history textbooks that officially depict the entire issue. For example, the Class V textbook developed by Sindh Text Book Board makes an introductory mention of the 1971 experience in a cursory manner:

> In 1971, the people of East Pakistan protested against the Government and started a civil war for a separate country. Pakistani troops tried to stop them but India militarily intervened in the civil war. A new country Bangladesh came into being on 16 Dec 1971.[5]

The History textbook designed by Punjab Text Book Board is even more economical with truth: 'In December 1971, East Pakistan was separated due to conspiracy of India and became a new country named Bangladesh'.[6]

The Pakistan Studies textbook developed by the Punjab Curriculum and The Textbook Board for Class VII[7] re-emphasises India's role:

> The results of the elections made it clear that the Awami League could form government in the center. West Pakistan's political leadership and bureaucracy were concerned because the manifesto on which the Awami League had won was unacceptable to the political leadership of West Pakistan. Therefore, the transfer of powers to the new government was delayed, resulting in a wave of concern in east Pakistan. General Yahya Khan held talks with the head of Awami League, Sheikh Mujibur Rahman, but these did not succeed. Thereafter, a civil war situation developed in east Pakistan. Bengalis chanted slogan of independent state with the help of pro-Indian organization Mukti Bahini. Pakistan armed forces had to intervene to crush the revolt. Thus, bloody riots began in east Pakistan. (p. 53)

It goes on to say:

> ...Under these circumstances, on March 15, 1971 Zulfikar Ali Bhutto, General Yahya Khan and Sheikh Mujibur Rahman met in Dhaka to restore peace. The negotiations ended without any results. Due to the tense situation, millions of Bengalis began migrating to India. India officially announced to help the Bengalis. Indian army provided weapons to the rebels and started training them which worsened the situation between Pakistan and India. General Yahya Khan send more troops to east Pakistan, with the result that Pakistan army gained control of most of the areas. Given the situation, India attacked East Pakistan with its armed forces. The Pakistan army in East Pakistan contained the Indian forces for two weeks. When they ran out of supplies and no more aid could reach from West Pakistan, India succeeded in its nefarious designs. Thus, on December 16, 1971, East Pakistan got separated and became an independent country by the name of Bangladesh. (p. 54)

This narrative is followed by outlining of the causes of 'the secession of East

Pakistan'. Nine causes are discussed out of which the four main ones are related to Hindus and India. Even while discussing the issue of geographical distance of one thousand miles between the two wings of Pakistan, it is mentioned that India was there between the two 'engaged in its efforts to undermine Pakistan's integrity ever since the partition of the subcontinent in 1947'. The second important cause was that the Hindus dominated trade and government jobs in east Pakistan and they 'were stirring up separation sentiments under hidden motives'. Among the causes was also the role of the Hindu teachers who controlled the education sector entirely and 'poisoned the Bengalis against Pakistan and aroused their sentiments'. After this there is a brief mention of the problem of representation and a quiet admission that although the Bengalis 'accepted representation on the basis of equality in the constitutions of 1956 and 1962, yet they did not get their legitimate rights which led to frustration in them' (p. 55). However, the issue of interference by India that 'provided training to Mukti Bahini workers and encouraged the separatists' worsening the situation further is brought out towards the end ahead of Mujib's six-point formula and election of 1970 as possible reasons for formation of Bangladesh. All in all, there is an attempt to inject a negative idea about India into the minds of the students, at an impressionable age by implying that the situation could have been salvaged had India not interfered and that the Pakistan state was not to be blamed too much for the entire episode. Such narratives have enabled a mindset that is reflexively anti-India.

Report of the Hamood-ur-Rahman Commission: Soft on Army Action

At the level of the state, the blame for the 1971 debacle was never conclusively put on any particular institution or event, if one goes by the reports of the Hamood-ur-Rahman Commission that was set up 10 days after the surrender of the Pakistan army at the hands of India, to enquire into:

> the circumstances in which the Commander, Eastern command, surrendered and the members of the Armed Forces of Pakistan under his command laid down their arms and a ceasefire was ordered along the borders of West Pakistan and India and along the ceasefire line in the State of Jammu and Kashmir.

The first and second reports of the commission held that the defeat was the cumulative impact of moral, political, international and military factors. The second report which was leaked to the media maintained that

> ...due to corruption arising out of the performance of Martial Law duties, lust for wine and women and greed for lands and houses, a large number of

> senior Army Officers, particularly those occupying the highest positions, had not only lost the will to fight but also the professional competence necessary for taking the vital and critical decisions.[8]

It also held that 'extensive and prolonged involvement of the Pakistan Army in Martial Law duties and civil administration had a disastrous effect on its professional and moral standards'. Distilling from the views expressed by various officers from the army, navy and air force, the commission drew this conclusion that

> the foundation of this defeat was laid way back in 1958 when the Armed Forces took over the country.... While learning the art of politics in this newly assigned role to themselves, they gradually abandoned their primary function of the art of soldiering, they also started amassing wealth and usurping status for themselves.

Interestingly, the report, while investigating into allegations of excesses seemed to imply that these actions were in response to 'harrowing tales of ... atrocities ... narrated by the large number of West Pakistanis and Biharis committed on them by the Bengali insurgents'. It cited the book by a renowned journalist of high-standing, Mr Qutubuddin Aziz, who took pains to marshal the evidence in a publication called *Blood and Tears*[9] and held that

> ....[the] tales of wholesale slaughter of families of West Pakistani officers and personnel of several units had also reached the soldiers who were after all only human and reacted violently in the process of restoring the authority of the Central Government.

There is a quiet admission that 'indiscriminate killing and looting could only serve the cause of the enemies of Pakistan' and 'in the harshness, [Pakistan] lost the support of the silent majority of the people of East Pakistan'. It was also pointed out that there was deep hatred against the Bengalis within the armed forces of Pakistan and there were orders to eliminate Hindus. The commission found Gen Tikka Khan more responsible and sensitive to human rights issues than Gen A.A.K. Niazi and held that 'the words and personal actions of Lt. Gen. Niazi were calculated to encourage the killings and rape'.

In sum, the report spent a great deal of its energy and attention rubbishing Mujib's allegations about widespread rapes and wanton killings including targeting of intellectuals. It held that the claims were exaggerated while the action of the Pakistan military was a natural reaction to the existing circumstances in East Pakistan. Nevertheless, the Commission recommended that 'irrespective..of the magnitude of the atrocities...it's necessary for the Government of Pakistan to take effective action to punish those who were responsible for the commission of these alleged excesses and atrocities'. It also considered it imperative,

> ...to book these senior army commanders who have brought disgrace and defeat to Pakistan by their professional incompetence, culpable negligence and wilful neglect in the performance of their duties, and physical and moral cowardice in abandoning the fight when they had the capability and resources to resist the enemy.

Dwelling on the political background, the commission held that no effort was made between May and September 1971 to initiate a political dialogue and this led to popular disaffection, which was leveraged well by India to mount training programmes for the Mukti Bahini and conduct guerrilla raids into Pakistan territory. Yahya Khan's refusal to negotiate with both Mujib and Kamal Hussain, both under Pakistani custody, drew criticism from the Commission in this connection. Lastly, the Commission took exception to Gen Niazi's decision to surrender when he could have held out for at least two more weeks and if he 'had done so and lost his life in the process, he would have made history and would have been remembered by the coming generations as a great hero and a martyr, but the events show that he had already lost the will to fight' after the fall of his major fortresses at Jessore and Brahmanbaria on 7 December 1971 and the 'question of creating history, therefore, was never in his mind'. The Commission also sought public trial of Yahya Khan and Gen Niazi for their moral degeneration.

Post 1971 Pakistan: Lessons Learnt?

It is useful to ask here whether the ruling elite of Pakistan, the feudal–military combine or the 'miltablishment' a term popularised by Najam Sethi, a perceptive observer of civil–military relations in Pakistan, learnt any lessons from such a debacle. Subsequent developments in Pakistan suggest that the inertia of political lassitude and quest for accumulating power continued with most rulers of Pakistan. Zulfikar Ali Bhutto, the populist, who had raised a political storm *vis-à-vis* Ayub Khan and reaped a good political harvest in West Pakistan, after assuming power from Yahya Khan, as perhaps the first and last civilian martial law administrator of Pakistan on 20 December 1971, made an effort to frame a new constitution for the country. At long last, the first session of the National Assembly was held on 14 April 1972 at the State Bank Building, Islamabad. All 144 Members from West Pakistan and two from erstwhile East Pakistan (Noor-ul-Amin and Raja Tridev Roy from Chittagong) participated in the session and an Interim Constitution was adopted on 17 April 1972. It provided for a Presidential form of Government and the Assembly was given an extended life till 14 August 1973, within which the new constitution was to be finalised. A 25-member Constitution Committee was formed on 17 April 1972 to prepare the first draft. The Committee presented its report on 31 December 1972, and it was passed by the Assembly in its session on 10 April 1973, not without controversy. It was signed by the President on 12 April 1973 and promulgated on 14 August 1973, the day, Bhutto was sworn in as the Prime Minister and Fazal Illahi Choudhary as the President of Pakistan.

The debates in the Assembly on what form the new constitution should take were very interesting. Predictably, the issue of parliamentary form of government and federalism were debated. The opposition parties, especially the National Awami Party (NAP) which formed government in then NWFP and Balochistan and JUI were courted by Bhutto to ease the process of constitution-making. However, the Baloch and Pakhtun members continued with their demands of provincial autonomy and a decentralised form of governance which was not taken well by Bhutto and his followers, who were gravitating towards a centralised power structure under the façade of a federal form of government. Mir. Ghous Bakhsh Khan Bazanjo (also written as Bizenjo) thundered in the house:

> ...a Constitution, a Government, a system or any 'Ism' are all meant for the human beings and for their well-being and prosperity. The people of a country are not meant for any Constitution or any 'Ism'. Therefore, we had expected that after such a bitter experience that we had had in East Pakistan, there would be presented a Constitution, which would promote unity, solidarity, love and affection in the country and would guarantee the integrity and solidarity of the people. It is clear that this can only happen when the people of different parts of Pakistan are given responsibility and proper and lawful share in the affairs of the country in this Constitution. Howsoever we may like to hide and make efforts to conceal the facts by simulation, it is an open secret that Pakistan is a multi-national state. In this country, different languages are spoken, there are different civilizations and various people have different thoughts and views regarding their affairs. We have always tried to conceal the facts; sometimes we did it in the name of religion and sometimes we tried to stifle the voice of the people by branding them as enemies of Pakistan. But it is a fact that so long as we do not give due rights and place to the people having different ways of life, we would not be able to lay the foundations of a united and integrated Pakistan. This can only come about when Pakistan becomes a federal parliamentary state in the true sense. And in that federation, different federating units are given their due rights There is no doubt that the word 'Federation' has been used in the

> Constitution, but when we read the Constitution, we find neither federal nor parliamentary system in it.[10]

Bizenjo went on to argue that the States/provinces should be allowed to retain the revenue generated from their soil and particularly referred to sui gas and earnings from fishing along the coastlines of Balochistan and raised his objections to the interim constitution allocating such sources of income to the centre. He forcefully argued:

> The total allocation for Baluchistan in the annual budget comes to Rs. 8 crore, whereas the Centre is getting Rs. twelve and half crore from Sui gas only. Then, why are we told that our Province is a deficit one? Baluchistan earns foreign exchange worth Rs. 350 crore from fish and the Income from minerals is in addition to it. I would submit Sir, that our main sources of income should be returned to us.[11] (p. 375)

Abdul Hayee Baluch spoke of Wali Khan also brought out the ruse that the NAP-ruled provinces had with the centre and talked about the need for recognising the multi-national character of Pakistan:

> I think it is necessary that this House should recognise this basic fact and *as the State is a multi-national State of different nationalities*, so their languages and culture must be given due status and their due share and that only could be done by providing them as the national languages—all these four languages as the national languages of Pakistan and the official languages of their respective provinces and Urdu should be the State language or official language of the whole State.

Mian Mahmud Ali Kasuri, a PPP parliamentarian (with NAP background and father of Khurshid Mahmud Kasuri) tried to impress upon the members the dangers of ignoring the minorities and criminalise them and stop projecting Pakistan as a project of few Punjabis alone:

> Every Baluchi is a 'ghaddar', every Pathan is a 'ghaddar' and if you go to Sind, to Punjab, you will find people who say that Sindhis want Sind Desh. Apparently, only a few people in Punjab are the custodians of Pakistan.[12]

The constitution that finally emerged out of the debates provided for a parliamentary form of government with a federal form exemplified by a bicameral legislature. The lower house had 10 seats reserved for minorities who were to be elected through the system of separate electorate. In the run-up to the adoption of the constitution on 10 April 1973, Bhutto displayed the very same dictatorial leanings that characterised his predecessors in uniform. Bhutto was hell-bent on manufacturing a consensus by hook or by crook to back the constitution, which was being framed. In February 1972, shortly before the whole exercise began, Bhutto took charge of the National Press Trust, the official media, to disseminate the official narrative and control the press. He used his authority to harass political leaders opposed to his policies and some of them died under mysterious circumstances; others were intimidated, threatened and taken into custody. On the eve of finalisation of the constitution, the Governors of the two NAP-led governments in Balochistan and NWFP were on 15 February 1973, in reaction to which the NAP government of the NWFP resigned. The governors of Punjab and Sindh were ordered to ensure that all the members would be present to back the constitution in the assembly.[13] Interestingly, five opposition parties who boycotted the debates on constituent making in the assembly were suddenly seen to be engaged by members of the ruling party on 9 April 1973 and made to accept all the provisions of the new constitution! That the opposition was largely ignored during the process of constitution making can be gleaned from the following facts. The appeals of the NAP for recognising the multi-ethnic/multi-national character of the state and basing the constitution on a non-majoritarian outlook guaranteeing equality of all four major ethno-national groups fell in deaf ears. The NAP's boycotted the proceedings at a time when the assembly had approved only one-third of the provisions of the draft constitution. Only one out of about 400 amendments proposed by the opposition was accepted. The remaining two-thirds was adopted in the absence of opposition members. About 1,600 amendments moved by the opposition members were allowed to lapse. It was strange to find the opposition finally coming to the assembly on the final day backing the constitution, which could not have been possible without 'the threat of prosecution on treason charges'.[14]

Be that as it may, the 1973 constitution lasts to this day even if it had been either amended to suit the needs of the military rulers or kept under suspension during the rule by two military dictators—Zia-ul-Haq and Pervez Musharraf.

As has been pointed out by numerous observers, Bhutto was also very authoritarian in his approach and repeated the mistakes of his predecessors by not allowing the opposition to play its role and using the army and machinery of the state against his political opponents. Even if he recognised federalism as a major objective of the 1973 constitution, he was not too willing to allow the provincial governments to assume any degree of autonomy. Like the military dictators preceding him, he was extremely obstreperous in his dealings with his detractors and did not brook any opposition to his point of view. Bhutto started by striking an agreement with both the NAP and Jamat-ul-Ulema-i-Islam (JUI), however, he refused to pay any attention to their genuine appeals during the process of constitution-making, especially for cultural autonomy. For example, the issue of the Baloch government rooting for Roman instead of Arabic script and endorsing education in mother tongue riled many in the central government.

Soon afterwards, the Baloch versus Punjabi issue was raised by the centre and on a trumped-up charge that the Baloch leaders were in league with external forces and were planning sedition against the state, the Balochistan government was dismissed in February 1973. The political turmoil gave a fresh lease of life to Baloch insurgency. The army was soon sent in, and with the help of Iranian as well as American helicopter gunships the resistance was put to rest. According to some estimates, there was armed engagement between more than 80,000 Pakistani troops and some 55,000 Baloch guerrillas. And the casualty was high—about 3,000 Pakistan troops and 5,300 Baloch guerrillas.[15] In 1976, federal government initiated the Hyderabad Conspiracy case against 55 persons from NWFP now Khyber Pakhtun Khwa (KPK) and Balochistan. The political atmosphere was thus vitiated again on the same issue of language and provincial autonomy soon after secession of East Pakistan and formation of Bangladesh.

Interestingly, Zia-ul-Haq, the military dictator who usurped power from Bhutto took full advantage of the situation and reversed the steps taken by Bhutto against Baloch and Pakhtun nationalists. When Musharraf came to power in 1999, he continued with the policy of Bhutto *vis-à-vis* the Baloch insurgents, which was to use excessive force to crush the rebellion. The killing of veteran Baloch leader Nawab Akbar Khan Bugti in July 2006 when the cave in which he was present collapsed due to massive bombing by the Pakistan military. The insurgency has continued despite the use of disproportionate force and, in fact, intensified to such an extent that like in the case of Bangladesh, even palliative political measures like *Aghaz-e-Haqooq-e-Balochistan*[16] offered by civilian administration in 2009 was not acceptable to the people of Balochistan, many of whom are demanding independence rather than autonomy.

In fact, Nawab Bugti's case was a classic one. As a young man educated at Oxford, he had voted in favour of accession to Pakistan in the Shahi Jirga held in 1947 and he had a chequered political career that saw him participating openly in the political processes and becoming the 6th chief minister and 4th governor of Balochistan. Even then, the praetorian reflexes of the Pakistani state turned him into a hardcore rebel, unwilling to compromise. The pre-Bangladesh syndrome of holding Pakistan together by force rather than carefully crafted political consensus continues to haunt the power-scape in Pakistan.

Federal Relations Today

Coming to the issue of federal relations, the political class showed some maturity after the signing of the charter of democracy in 2004. After Pakistan reverted to democracy, the two main political parties (Pakistan Muslim League-Nawaz and Pakistan Peoples' Party or PPP) have, despite intense political competition between them, have hung together on issues that threaten to undermine civilian power. The passing of 18th amendment in April 2010 that removed all extra-constitutional undemocratic and praetorian insertions into the 1973 constitution and restored the system of the parliamentary democracy could not have been possible without both parties coming together on this important issue.

The third political force in the shape of Imran Khan's Pakistan Tehrik-e-Insaf (PTI) has also so far not reversed some of the federal provisions in the 18th amendment despite the displeasure of the deep state. The argument of the military has been that these provisions impede the process of national integration by allowing provinces to defy the centre and pose a critical challenge to national security. These provisions, in a way, come in the way of the deep state bringing in security measures intended to perpetuate its hold on power at the cost of the civilian dispensation. The amendment among other things has tilted the balance of federal power sharing in favour of the states at least in theory. In practice, however, while the federal government largely determines the federal dynamics, the deep state or 'miltablishment' influences the way the federal relations are carried out on the ground.

A close analysis of the federal situation in Pakistan reveals that 'the military's dominant role [has] serious implications for the multi-ethnic federation as well, undermining provincial rights and autonomy guaranteed through the 18th amendment'.[17] The miltablishment has even held 18th amendment more dangerous than the 'Six Points' of Mujibur Rahman that led to secession of East Pakistan.[18] In a situation, where a hybrid civil–military system is at work, it requires a perennial struggle for states to safeguard the rights and privileges granted to them through the constitution.

Conclusion: Has Pakistan Learnt its Lessons?

In the last five decades, Pakistan has passed through several political upheavals during which it has gravitated towards what Pakistani observers have called a hybrid political system where power is shared by both civilian and military elites with the balance titled in favour of the latter. The memories of Bangladesh continue to haunt the military elite which has, therefore, viewed demands for ethnic/

linguistic autonomy and provincial rights with extreme suspicion. While the civilian governments have sought to plug ethnic grievances through political packages like *Aghaz-e-Haqooq-e-Balochistan*, the primary way of handling ethnic assertions has been through use of brute force or raw military power. Through the regimes of Zia and Musharraf, it has been noticed that the military has increasingly arrogated unto itself extra-constitutional powers to deal with such issues which, on the face of it, threaten Pakistan's integrity and existence. To some extent, the military has been more innovative in its radical counter-insurgency measures. It has used force to manage popular rebellion rather than supporting the civilian government's efforts to seek out political alternatives to strengthen the practice of genuine federalism and inter-ethnic harmony. The military has used local political dynamic, tapped into intra-ethnic fault-lines and used Islam against secular militant forces like Baloch insurgents and Pashtun Tahfuz Movement (PTM) to manage the situation. Use of brute military power against both the Baloch rebels and pacifist Pakhtuns along the border has aggravated the situation rather than settling it.

In the process, Pakistan seems to be held together by force rather than will of the people (especially that of the ethnic minorities). The shadow of civil–military competition for power has also hampered the process of natural evolution of political impulses that bind a multi-ethnic (or multi-national) country like Pakistan together.

If Pakistan's military has learnt anything from its 1971 experience, it is to continue to instil fear into the minds of minority ethnic groups and the provinces where they held sway to ensure that no further secession becomes possible ever, upsetting the efforts of the political class to manage ethnic disaffections with empathy through political measures. The fear of secession, often manufactured by the deep state and its collaborators in the political space, continues to perpetuate the same authoritarian and centralising mindset/reflexes that had led to the fall of Dhaka.

NOTES

1. Syed Sharifuddin Pirzada (ed.), *Foundations of Pakistan Vol-2: All India Muslim League Documents 1906-1947*, Karachi: National Publishing House, 1969, p. 341.
2. Census of Pakistan, 1951, Population according to religion, Table 6, Census Bulletin No. 2, Office of the Census Commissioner, Government of Pakistan, Ministry of Interior, October 1951, p. 1.
3. The quotes used in the entire paper from the discussions in the Constituent Assembly of Pakistan have been excerpted from the documents accessed from the website of the National Assembly of Pakistan available at http://www.na.gov.pk/, accessed on 8 September 2021.

4. As mentioned in Hamood-ur-Rahman Commission report, according to many deponents that the commission debriefed by the Commission, it could also have been the machination of Gen Yahya Khan and his henchmen who pressurised political parties based in West Pakistan not to participate in the inaugural session. There was a fear that if the session was allowed to take place it would have legitimised Awami League's inevitable assumption of power, which was not acceptable to the West Pakistan leadership. See the second report produced by the Commission leaked to media: "Tragic Events of 1971: Hamoodur Rahman Commission Report". Excerpts of the Report was published in the weekly magazine *India Today* and reproduced by *Dawn* and later by *Daily Star*, available at https://www.thedailystar.net/sites/default/files/upload-2014/freedomintheair/pdf/Hamoodur%20Rahman%20Commission%20Report_Dawn%20(1).pdf
5. *Social Studies for Class V*, Sindh Textbook Board, Jamshoro, 2018, p. 70.
6. Malik Muhammad Sharif (ed.), *Social Studies for Class V*, Punjab Curriculum and Textbook Board, Lahore, 2018, p. 33.
7. *Pakistan Studies* for Class IX, Punjab Curriculum and Textbook Board, Lahore, 2020–21.
8. 'Tragic Events of 1971: Hamoodur Rahman Commission Report', n. 4, p. 5.
9. Qutubuddin Aziz, *Blood and Tears*, Publications Division of the United Press of Pakistan Ltd., Karachi, 1974.
10. *National Assembly of Pakistan Debates*, *Official Report*, Monday, 17 April 1973, Printing Corporation of Pakistan Press, Karachi, 1972, pp. 326–28.
11. Ibid., p. 375.
12. Assembly Debates, National Assembly of Pakistan (Constitution Making), Friday, 2 March 1973, p. 595.
13. For details, see Rahat Zubair Malik, 'Parliamentary System and Framing of the 1973 Constitution: Contest between Government and Opposition inside the National Assembly', *Pakistan Perspectives*, Vol. 25, No. 1, January–June 2020, pp. 29–47.
14. See an impartial analytical piece titled 'Constitutional History of Pakistan', available at https://constitutionnet.org/country/pakistan [The International Institute for Democracy and Electoral Assistance (International IDEA), an intergovernmental organization that supports sustainable democracy worldwide.]
15. Gulshan Majeed and Rehana Saeed Hashmi, 'Baloch Resistance during Zulfiqar Ali Bhutto's Era: Causes and Consequences', *South Asian Studies*, Vol. 29, No. 1, January–July 2014, pp. 321–31, available at http://pu.edu.pk/images/journal/csas/PDF/24%20Ghulshan%20Majeed_29_1.pdf
16. For an analysis of the package, see 'The Aghaz-e-Haqooq-e-Balochistan Package–An Analysis', PILDAT, 1 December 2009, available at https://pildat.org/parliamentary-development1/the-aghaz-e-haqooq-e-balochistan-package-an-analysis; and also 'Aghaz-e-Huqooq-e-Balochistan Package: Speakers Bemoan Slow Implementation', *Dawn*, 30 June 2011, available at https://www.dawn.com/news/640595/aghaz-e-huqooq-e-balochistan-package-speakers-bemoan-slow-implementation, accessed on 1 November 2021.
17. See a perceptive essay by a young researcher, Salman Rafi Sheikh, 'Military Creep: Pakistan's Federal System is being Undermined by Militarisation", *Himal*, Kathmandu, 4 Aug 2021, available at https://www.himalmag.com/military-creep-pakistan-2021/. Also see Fatima Khan, 'Why the 18th Amendment has become a cause for irritation for the Pakistani Army', *The Print*, 12 June 2020, available at https://theprint.in/opinion/why-the-18th-amendment-has-become-a-cause-for-irritation-for-the-pakistani-army/440126/, accessed on 1 November 2021.
18. Suhail Warraich, 'The Bajwa Doctrine: From Chauvinism to Realism', *The News*, 19 March 2018.

16

Mistakes on Repeat Mode

Pakistan's Civil–Military Debacle

Karnika Jain

The grim landscape of the political affairs in post-partition Pakistan impelled the institution of military to take the leading role in national politics instead of emergence of a democratic civilian state. The Pakistan Army has been playing a significant role in the governance of Pakistan since its inception. In the path of new state building, the absence of strong governance and democratic leaders led to the grappling of political power by the military rule, as no other alternative was left. Ever since independence, the military has continued to influence and display its presence directly or indirectly in the policymaking process of the country. From the beginning, the military presented itself as the guardian of the state and penetrated into the political system to an extent of influencing almost all political decisions.

To understand the civil–military relations of Pakistan, one must revisit the historical foundation of the country on which it was created. The outburst of the strong sense of religious identity resulted in the division of British India into two states in 1947. The animosity between Hindus and Muslims resulted in the brutal fragmentation of the Indian subcontinent into a separate state for Muslim majority population (Pakistan) and for a Hindu majority (India). Unlike India, which adopted democratic foundation, Pakistan embraced the opposite. The country was ruled by bureaucrats along with the military as a junior partner till the late

1950s.[1] While the Indian military chose to abide by the principle of civilian supremacy, the Pakistan military gradually expanded its role in the political decision-making apart from defence and security matters. Inadequacy of political culture, weak administrative infrastructure and internal aggression within communities made military the powerful elite. In addition, Pakistan's internal contradictions and geographical distance between its two parts (West and East Pakistan) separated by more than 1,000 miles of Indian territory in the middle made the task of nation building a troublesome exercise.[2] Law and order disruptions combined with Pakistan's external threat perception of India justified military to assume power in the domestic politics. The tendency of civilian authorities to rely in particular on military for nation-building increased after the death of Prime Minister Liaquat Ali Khan in 1951. Clearly, the civil bureaucracy misinterpreted the intentions of the military to influence the path of national politics and control the state completely.

The year 1958 witnessed major transformations as the military brazenly intruded and assumed primary position in the politics, economics and society of the state. The absence of a stable political environment in the country made space for military rule to intervene not just in 1958 but also in 1969, 1977 and 1999. The military assumed its right to rule while blaming parliamentary system and government mismanagement. The independence of East Pakistan in 1971 is a prime example of Pakistan's inapt civil–military relations that elevated the feeling of alienation and frustration to such an extent that the state which was integrated on Islamic solidarity got bifurcated into two countries. Therefore, the very military establishment created to protect the nationality and polity became itself a cause for the division of the unified state. Unfortunately, even after 50 years, the only lesson Pakistan seems to have learnt is that military strength is necessary to prevent itself from losing another battle. In pursuance of promoting a flawed unified national identity, it persists on the strategy to dominate other ethno-nationalist identities. The country continues to follow the path of greater centralisation and military intervention in politics. The contended Baloch identity is an apparent example of the dominance of the military and a culture of undemocratic politics. The military's atrocities, brutal ethnic suppression and extrajudicial killings against the Baloch people reflect the complexities of civil–military relations in Pakistan. Thus, lack of comprehensive political leadership and unregulated control of military over civilians offer an interesting case study.

In this context, the objective of the paper is to assess the evolution of civil–military relations during the initial years of Pakistan till the time imbalance in the institutions led to the spilt of the country. Using a multi-dimensional approach from the economics, political, cultural and societal background, the paper delves into the analysis of the predominant role of the military. It examines the factors that have contributed towards making the institution of military respected widely within the country. Further, the paper attempts to offer a brief theoretical background on the understanding of civil–military relations. Lastly, the paper looks into the case study of Balochistan in which it is observed that the country hasn't learnt from the partition of 1971 and still chooses to confront the crisis within the civil-military relations. Altogether, the findings aim to highlight how an inclination towards the military rule has impacted the state-building process. The study has taken the period up to 1971 as these years (1947–71) laid the foundation of military supremacy over civilian institutions. Also, 1971 witnessed a watershed change as the imbalanced relations between the East Pakistanis and military rule altered the political landscape of South Asia by causing circumstances that gave birth to a new nation-state of Bangladesh.

Theoretical Understanding

This section deals with the theoretical framework of civil–military relations and analyses factors (internal political crisis, regional security dynamics and military's strategic interest) that formed the subsequent civil–military relations in Pakistan.

As the name suggests, the term civil–military relations is an interaction between the military and civilian institutions of the state. It encompasses a whole range of different typologies of the control and regulation of the military by the civilian governments. The subject is quite complicated as the imbalance between the negotiated parties (political civilian authorities and military) could result in tensions and change the course of domestic and foreign affairs of the nation-state. Huntington has argued that there are subjective and objective types of civil-military relations.[3] He advances objective civilian control, which believes in sheer separation between the functioning of the military, state and the bureaucracy; permitting military to have an independent autonomous space.[4] He believes professionalism and absenteeism from politics would enhance capabilities of military as an institution and lead it to better focus on external enemies. However, in these types of set-up, the overt threat or fear of the military to use coercive power to displace civilian rule is always hanging upon states. James Madison argues that "the means of defence against foreign danger have always been the instruments of tyranny at home".[5] It could be assessed as internal insecurity that opens avenues for greater involvement of the military in societal affairs. Therefore, political pluralism remains necessary to check and curb the power of military frequently.

Military intrusion is mostly perceived as associated with countries characterised by weak political leadership and ineptness of the institutional structure to resolve internal conflicts.[6] In these states, the inability of political institutions and civilian system to manage state affairs gives way for military intervention. Similarly, Keith Hopkins links the military intervention with weak political institutions. He explains that "where social and political institutions are weak, and the levels of social mobilisation and professionalisation of politicians are low, a gesture of self-interested or public-spirited despair" might trigger coups.[7] Huntington also argues that "institutional decay has become a common phenomenon of the modernising countries. Coups d'état and military interventions in politics are one index of low levels of political institutionalisation: they occur where political institutions lack autonomy and coherence".[8] Pakistan represents one of the countries that confronted the blight of political crisis, ultimately leading to the supremacy of military over civilian institutions. The factors that led the military to dominate civilian institutions and be a power bloc are:

Internal Political Crisis

One of the major reasons for military to emerge as a dominant institution was the internal political conditions of the country. Some factors like the legitimacy crisis, absence of effective leadership and weak democratic practices discredited civilian regime and provided tremendous power to military to dominate over civil institutions. For example, the failure of Muslim League to transform itself from a nationalist movement to a nationalist party or the death of prominent political leaders resulted in the political degeneration and contributed to the military intervening in non-military affairs. In addition, at the time of independence, the Pakistan Army was one of the most established institutions in the country. Its roots can be traced back to the British Indian Army that had the experience of extensive training and skills. It was no surprise that the army started colonising its own country in the name of safeguarding it from internal instability and external threat.

Pakistan represents a unique case study of continuous reliance of civilian institutions on military to restore law and order situation and address the religious-sectarian divide. In other words, the military curbed the insurgencies to "preserve national integrity".[9] The first time the army was called upon to oversee civilian functions and perform non-military action was in the 1950s in the wake of anti-Ahmadi riots in Punjab. It exemplifies how the army is perceived to be a defender of Islam and how its actions involving violence are considered legitimate. Till present, being the strongest of all the state institutions, military doesn't hesitate in imposing martial law at the cost of democracy when a political rule seems to be weakening. Hasan Askari Rizvi, a prominent analyst, writes: 'Pakistan can be described as a praetorian state where the military has acquired the capability, will, and sufficient experience to dominate the core political institutions and processes. As the political forces are disparate and weak, the military's disposition has a strong impact on the course of political change, including the transfer of power from one set of the elite to another'.[10]

Another main reason for military's strong presence appeared to be the regional security dynamics, marked by Pakistan's insecurity syndrome from India, which affected its domestic and foreign policies. Protecting the state from external and internal threat made army's position as an institution even stronger in the country, in turn, aggravating the imbalance in institutional establishments. The external threat to sovereignty made civilian government rely on the military to manage the affairs. It was no surprise that the military did not face any opposition when it overtly displaced civilian governments in 1958, 1969, 1977 or 1999. Stephen P. Cohen defines the role of Pakistan's army: "There are armies which guard their nation's borders, there are armies that are concerned with protecting their own position in society, and there are armies that defend a cause or an idea. The Pakistan Army does all three."[11]

Military's Strategic Interest

The extent of military dominance over civilian institutions also needs to be evaluated from the point of view of military's ulterior motives. It posits its coercive power in politics under the veil of corporate economic interests that suppresses all the other ethnicities and classes that come in its way of governance. The onset of diminishing political power incites insecurity related to benefits, leisure and income within soldiers, for which the survival of the state is necessary; hence it leads to military intervention.[12] The same rationale also explains the skewed allocation of resources towards military rather than the requirements for development purpose of the state. This led to overall growth in the organisational capacity of military while the civilian institutions continued to remain weak. Hence, political autonomy has been directly proportional to fulfilling their financial interests.

Likewise, prominent Pakistani historian Ayesha Jalal finds the army manipulative and speculates that the military's deliberate strategies to hold multiple roles and in turn projecting the state as weak, is for their ulterior motives. Jalal further argues that the alignment of Pakistani Army with Britain and the US was also done to acquire warfare strategies and become more influential in comparison to national political forces and civil institutions.[13] The defence treaties like South East Asia Treaty Organisation (SEATO) and Central Treaty Organisation (CENTO) strengthened the influence of military in domestic politics of the country. Thus, the connections developed at the international level assisted the institution in acquiring training, skills and new equipment, which naturally presented the image of the military institution as superior to other institutions of the state. Ejaz Hussain describes Pakistan as a "praetorian state which structurally inherited the pre-partition 'praetorian oligarchy'. This praetorian oligarchy constructed 'Hindu India' as enemy to pursue politico-economic interests. The military, a part of praetorian oligarchy, emerges as a powerful political actor due to its coercive power. It seeks political power to pursue economic objectives independently".[14]

Given the history of Pakistan, the rule over state has fluctuated between the civilian party in power and the military. This resulting disequilibrium between civil institutions and military system has often been seen in post-colonial societies, especially in South Asian countries, where it has been difficult for them to build nation-state and consequently military has pervaded in the political spheres. Although India and Pakistan inherited almost the same British parliamentary political system, political institutions and civil bureaucracy, Pakistan represents how weak democracies combined with military's corporate interest could eventually lead to the military taking a primary position in the civilian matters of the country. Hence, it could be best understood that many internal factors (political crisis, inherent colonial politics, ideological conflict, strategies doctrines, India's insecurity syndrome, etc.) have shaped the civil-military relations of Pakistan.

Civil–Military Relations During 1947–1971

Political Disenfranchisement

Pakistan is a country that proves the ineffectiveness of secular forces and political leadership to counterbalance the military and practice democracy. The reasons for the subordinate position of political institutions to military institutions lie in Pakistan's structural and domestic dynamics. After the death of charismatic Jinnah (the then Governor-General and President of the Constituent Assembly) and later assassination of his lieutenant and the country's first Prime Minister Liaquat Ali Khan in 1951, the country was in shambles with no political leader to lead and strengthen democratic forces.[15] The new emerging state faced the leadership crisis needed to legitimise institutions to practice and implement democratic principles. In this fragile state, bureaucratic-military interest made inroads into power politics to such an extent that it altered the very foundation of parliamentary system on which it began.

It wasn't shocking, though, because even when the country was under parliamentary governance, it saw the shift of power between seven prime ministers between 1950–58.[16] Not a single general election could be conducted during 11 years of the so-called parliamentary system (1947–58), and provincial elections were termed as 'a farce, mockery and a fraud upon the electorate'.[17] Political chaos, internal uncertainty and unstable leadership were the reasons that led to the partial involvement of army during those years. For instance, Ayub Khan's noteworthy role in restoring orders during the "persistent clashes with the tribal and parliamentary forces on the North West Frontier" was one of his involvements in decision making.[18]

Because of the legitimacy crisis and ineffective leadership, factors like linguistic challenge, delay in constitution making and ethnic imbalance paved the military regime to come in power. After independence, it took nine years for Pakistan to produce its first constitution in 1956. The issue of power-sharing at the inter-regional and inter-institutional levels, the country's geographical outline and the presence of diverse ethnic identities hobbled the process of the constitution making. One of the many challenges in framing the constitution was to produce a document that would satisfy both secularists and sectarians. Ulemas wanted the constitution that would not provide full citizenship rights to non-Muslims, including no rights for them to have voice in law-making or to uphold public offices. This was not accepted by the Pakistani intelligentsia that believed in providing equal rights irrespective of religion or creed.[19] Another major reason for the delay laid in the representation between both the wings in the federal legislature.[20]

In 1954, after grappling with the problem of constitution making, when the constituent assembly nearly completed the draft, the then head of the state Governor-General Ghulam Mohammad Ali dissolved the constituent assembly itself.[21] The amendments compelled the Governor General to act only on the advice of his ministers. Indeed, the country's present state of affairs would have been different if the executive authorities did not constantly control and supervise the actions of the legislature. More so, the sad state of judiciary and inability to perform its role independently resulted in the state power to be more in the hands of executive. In this case, Mohammad Ali's action was backed by the federal judiciary, in particular by Chief Justice Munir, who declared that the constituent assembly was not a sovereign body.[22] Hence, the dynamics of institutional power and nine years of constitutional deliberations could not restore the politics needed for stable governance.

In the case of East Pakistan, the impact of militarised politics and its abusive strategies on Eastern wing widened the cultural, economic and political divide between the two parts of the country. At the time of independence, territorially, East Pakistan constituted 54 per cent of the total population of Pakistan, which meant majority over West Pakistan and other ethnic groups.[23] However, despite being in the majority, the Bengalis of East Pakistan were continuously suppressed and denied rights within the state bureaucracy and in army recruitment. For instance, the army with Punjabi majority always beheld the Bengalis as pseudo Pakistani citizens.[24] The privileged groups of West Pakistan—Punjabi and Muhajir political elites—ensured that East Pakistan did not benefit from the populous advantage to dominate the politics of the new state.[25] Equally significant was the economic discrimination. During 1947-1971, the per capita income gap between East and West widened by 400 per cent, from 50 rupees to 200 rupees.[26] These disparities were deliberately used to establish the domination over Bengalis.

The Challenge of Bengali Language

Following the independence, the language resentment was the first challenge for Pakistan's leaders and emerged as the first threat to the unity of the state. The Punjab-based praetorian oligarchy foresaw a threat in majority Bengalis due to their demand for a constitution and general election. To subdue this challenge, Jinnah declared Urdu a national language in March 1948, in East Bengal, ignoring the fact that people of East Pakistan cherished Bengali as their language.[27] As stated by Michel Foucault, a profound French postmodernist philosopher, "Power is everywhere; not because it embraces everything, but because it comes from everywhere".[28] Language oppression was also a tool of maintaining power supremacy by West Pakistan over East Pakistan citizens as it implied not only cultural suppression but also economic deprivation. Consequently, it resulted in the eruption of protest in East Pakistan, especially by students, as language barrier meant fewer employment opportunities via competitive entrance exams, which would imply an inferior life for Bengalis.[29] This enduring five-year-long Bangla Language Movement to instate Bengali as an official language took a horrifying turn when the police exterminated innocent students during a bloody battle on 21 February 1952.[30] Though later in May 1954, Bengali was declared as one of the state languages, but the incident forever marked the bitterness and hatred against the army and police. Therefore, the language movement altered the political scenario of Pakistan permanently, later to be turned into a large-scale Bengali nationalism and separatist movement.

Ethnic Imbalance

Pakistan was formed on the unifying factor of Islamic religion, but soon after its independence, several ethnic and regional factions emerged, demanding recognition for their separate identities. In the process of keeping the state intact, the state blatantly disregarded ethnic heterogeneity and started deploying the principle of 'one nation (Pakistan), one language (Urdu) and one people (Muslims)'.[31] Islam became the driving force in the nation building and a tool to manipulate and perpetuate power by West Pakistani elites. The country could not create a common national-identity and whenever ethnic groups asserted their identities, the army was called to suppress insurgencies to protect national integrity.[32] It was ironic that the nation which was created on the basis of religion started using it negatively to integrate the country. It was these schemes and attitudes of bureaucratic and military elites that again led to the rise of the sentiments of colonisation among Bengalis. West Pakistanis never treated the Muslims of East Pakistan with equal respect and honour. There was a belief that the Islamic values practiced in Bengal was "contaminated" because of its continued proximity to Hindu culture.[33] West Pakistan considered themselves superior to East Pakistan citizens and elites often labelled Bengalis as "black bastards".[34]

Even the military composition and recruitment was infested with biases and discrimination against other ethnic identities. Historically, Punjabis comprised around 71–75 per cent of military's strength, Pushtoon around 15–21 per cent, Mohajir and Sindhis about 3–5 per cent and Baluch about 0.3 per cent.[35] The military institution continued to remain dominated by Punjabis and Pathans. Islam was the criteria of recruiting people in the army. For instance, Zia's idea of a professional army as he mentioned was "the professional soldier in a Muslim army, pursuing the goals of a Muslim state, cannot become 'professional' if in all his activities he does not take on 'the colour of Allah'".[36] Undoubtedly, such ethnic homogeneity is considered a threat to democracy and one of the causes of civil-military debacle in Pakistan. Also, other material benefits enabled the penetration of military into the civilian sectors. For example, during the Zia regime (1977–88), 10 per cent quota of civil jobs was reserved for military personnel.[37] This resulted in the expansion of military influence in the society and to what Finer describes as the "military colonisation of other institutions".[38]

In the East Pakistan context, the British had considered Bengalis a non-martial race and hence, at the time of independence, the representation of Eastern wing's soldiers amounted to only a per cent of the total strength of Pakistan's armed forces.[39] Following the independence, the trend didn't unfold the way the Bengalis expected it. As per the statistics, of the total government administrative jobs, Bengalis represented only 15 per cent, whereas in army, their representation was even lower, accounting for 10 per cent.[40] Hence, the failure of political leadership to assess and understand the significance of ethnic identity and diversity of East Bengal resulted in the increased political role of the military in post-colonial Pakistan. The institution started being perceived as a guardian and ultimate arbiter but, at the same time, they manipulated social, economic and political policies for their own objectives.

Ayub Khan's Regime (October 1958–March 1969)

Unfortunately, until the time the 1956 Constitution was framed, it was too late as the politics had already worsened and caused the imbalance between civil and military institutions. Within two years of the adoption of the constitution, the country witnessed its first military coup by pro-American Major General Ayub Khan. The year 1958 proved to be the watershed moment as the army took complete control over the state; abrogated the constitution and imposed martial law. Political parties were banned to participate in the 1962 elections and politicians of East Pakistan were imposed under the ideas of West wing.[41] Policies during Ayub era exacerbated the issue of exclusion and non-participation. Bengalis were hardly given any equal participation in the decision-making process.

Apart from political suppression, economically too, they were deprived. His economic strategies were well appreciated and the period of his reign was considered 'decade of development'.[42] However, these developments came at the cost of socio-economic exploitation of the majority people of the country. The decade of his rule had sown the seeds of inherent conflicts and income divide between the two wings of Pakistan. His policies were sheer biased towards West Pakistan, affecting the Bengalis to greatest possible extent. In 1968, the Chief Economist of the Planning Commission stated that "only twenty families control 66 per cent of the entire industrial capital, 80 per cent of the banking and 97 per cent of insurance capital".[43] East Pakistan was economically deprived, despite being the exporter of two-third of the total export of the country. It was evident with its inadequate share in the distribution of foreign aid resources and development funds.[44] One of the major reasons for these disparities was the direct control of the central government over provincial revenue; it was entirely subservient to the centre.

Eastern wing was appalled at these arrangements as it felt West Pakistan was colonising them. Soon after the 1965 war between India and Pakistan, Sheikh Mujibur Rahman proposed the six-point programme[45] in 1966 to attain substantial autonomy for the East Wing and establish Pakistan as a federal state in true spirit. It was an attempt to demand economic progress for the Bengalis. Certainly, it was a demand to put to an end the prolonged abusive strategies against East Pakistan and so it was rejected by West Pakistan leaders. Instead of negotiating with Mujib, the Ayub Khan government preferred to use 'the language of weapons', which turned to be a fatal mistake during that period.[46] But even a graver mistake was committed by involving Mujib in the 'Agartala Conspiracy Case'. The government framed and arrested Mujibur Rahman along with 34 other Bengali army personnel and government officers on charges of conspiracy with the Indian government against Pakistan, to form a separate country, Bangladesh, in Agartala (Tripura).[47] However, the failure to assess Mujib's popularity and the successive widespread mass movement compelled the government to withdraw the case and release Mujib along with other officers. It is believed that these events turned out to be the victory component for Mujib in the elections of 1970.

General Yahya Khan's Regime (1969–71)

Following the resignation by Ayub Khan, General Yahya Khan governed the second military regime. He tried to rectify the problems created by Ayub Khan's government and brought in various socio-economic and political reforms. But the soured relations between the two parts of Pakistan coupled with political crisis could not curb the disintegration of Pakistan.

He announced free and fair elections to be held on the basis of one man, one vote.[48] However, by December, when the elections were held, one more event fractured the trust of Bengalis over West Pakistan military and bureaucracy. The 1970 Bhola cylone hit the East Pakistan along with India's West Bengal in November 1970 and it is believed that the government mishandled the natural calamity by delaying sending in adequate relief materials and assistance.[49] This was highly criticised by East Pakistani leaders. Tensions further arose between both the wings in December 1970 elections; the West Pakistan ruling generals suffered a devastating blow as the Awami League led by Sheikh Mujibur Rahman gained a landslide victory and won the national elections. Awami League won 167 seats in East Pakistan; whereas Bhutto's Pakistan Peoples Party (PPP) won 81 seats in Punjab and Sind in West Pakistan.[50] The West Pakistan ruling generals were not happy with the Awami League's victory in the National Assembly, as it clearly meant that they could frame a separate constitution as well as it would induce the shifting of power from military rule to civilian government. Because none of the parties in the election could win seats in the other's region, political negotiations started between Bhutto, Mujib and Yahya Khan. Two reasons during this time deepened the trust deficit between the Awami League and Pakistani leaders. First was the fear of possible partnership between military and Bhutto's PPP, which might not be willing to transfer power to Awami League. Second was the hijack of an Indian Airlines flight to Lahore by two Kashmiris, who released the passengers ultimately but destroyed the aircraft. These actions were highly condemned by Mujibur Rahman and held Pakistan military responsible for the destruction.[51]

As the negotiations could not produce a consensus, the army under Yahya Khan kicked in brutal 'Operation Searchlight' to suppress the freedom movement of Bengalis, which commenced the Bangladesh Liberation War and expanded into the 1971 Indo-Pak War. During the operation, the army committed widespread atrocities against the unarmed people: homeless street people were killed; students, teachers and non-teaching staff were shot at; unarmed civilians comprising women and children were killed.[52] The sole objective behind this operation was to reduce the number of people in the nationalist freedom struggle so that the Army could gain control over East Pakistan province. During the period of war, it is estimated that the Pakistan army approximately killed three million Bengalis, particularly targeting Hindus, academicians and freedom fighters.[53] Moreover, to produce loyal off springs of their race, the obnoxious strategy of rape was used and around 200,000–400,000 Bengali women were raped by the Pakistani Army.[54] Eventually India intervened in the war and by 16 December, East Pakistan got liberated from Pakistan. The prolonged unrest between both the wings came to an end with the creation of Bangladesh in 1971. It can, thus, be argued that the army failed to recognise that the Bengali identity and ethnicity was not a secessionist movement from the beginning; it was a political turmoil which got intensified by the imbalanced military structure of the state.

The next section deals with the case study of Balochistan by showing how despite the partition of Pakistan in 1971, the state continues to choose to confront the crisis within the civil–military domain.

The Case of Balochistan: Imbalanced Military Crisis

Unfortunately, even after the tragic divide of Pakistan, the country could not escape being a praetorian state. The complicated pattern of civil–military relation has suppressed the interests of other units (previously East Pakistan) and presently Balochistan. The nature of Pakistani state has always been oppressive towards the ethno-nationalities, a practice continued till present. Pakistani establishment views ethnic heterogeneity, demand for provincial autonomy and cultural pluralism as a threat to its national unity. Balochistan is the most persecuted province in Pakistan, which has witnessed innumerable violation of human rights since 1948. The first military operation began with the forceful invasion of the district of Kalat in April 1948. Since then, the province has been fighting for its independence and to protect human rights. The invasion was followed by another two military operations where Balochistan's resentment against one unit scheme was suppressed in 1958 and Pakistan army attacked Balochistan to fight against left wing nationalists in 1962.[55]

Balochistan covers the largest percentage of Pakistan's territory (approx. 44 per cent), with mere less than 5 per cent of Pakistan's total population.[56] According to the 2017 census, Pakistan's population accounts for 207,774,520 as compared to Balochistan's only 12,344,408.[57] The most resource-rich province with 40 per cent of Pakistan's energy needs and 36 per cent of its gas production is least developed with 46.6 per cent of households having no electricity.[58] The country has systematically militarised the entire province while depriving the community from its own natural resources. It has been observed that despite the discovery of natural gas at Sui in 1952, 70 per cent population of the province remains deprived of access to these resources.[59]

Post-1971, when Zulfiqar Ali Bhutto rose to power, he raised hopes of civilian supremacy in the country. But, this could not materialise as the fourth brutal military operation was launched in Balochistan that continued for five years from 1973 to 1977. The centre sent some 80,000 troops, backed by combat helicopters, to crush the Baloch movement, followed by the ban on National Awami Party (NAP) and the arrest of Baloch prominent leaders.[60] Since the local police had to seek help from the army in Balochistan to handle political crisis, it gave a chance to the army to again prove its supremacy over civilian establishments.

Even the composition of Pakistan Army has not changed in its homogeneity of Punjabi domination and in exclusion of other ethnicities. Balochs are still underrepresented and it is confirmed by the fact that "ex-servicemen from Balochistan for the period from 1995 to 2003 numbered 3,753 men only while the numbers for the North Punjab and the NWFP for the same period were 1,335,339 and 229,856, respectively".[61] True democracy is the one that always upholds ethnic heterogeneity and provides an atmosphere that allows minorities to flourish. No wonder, Pakistan does not fall under this category, as despite the presence of democratic government, the domestic politics of the state has always strategically and structurally favoured certain communities only.

However, it is interesting to note that the situation of Baloch opposition was still manageable under Pakistan's government during that period, Baloch nationalists remained open to compromise. The reason behind this was the serious attempts by civilian leadership to address the grievances of the Baloch people. One of them included the 18th amendment to the constitution, which granted greater autonomy to smaller provinces like Balochistan. Also, throughout the democratic decade of the 1990s, nationalist parties such as Balochistan National Party (BNP) and Jamhoori Watan Party (JWP) emerged as prominent political forces.[62] Baloch leaders were also represented in the main political parties, PPP and Pakistan Muslim League Nawaz (PML-N).[63] Although this period witnessed differences between the central government and Baloch nationalists, the relations did not turn into conflict. It was only because of the military's oppressive tactics in Balochistan that the tensions aggravated and relations degenerated.

Revival of Military Crackdown

Today, Balochistan is witnessing its fifth military operation that started during Pervez Musharraf's time. During the Musharraf period, Baloch nationalists showed reluctance and disagreement with the gradual expansion of military coup in the province. But, what deteriorated the situation markedly was the rape of a female doctor, Shazia Khalid, by army personnel. Later, the government's decision to release the accused triggered the masses, followed by huge protests, which eventually led to the idea of separatism.[64] The tension rose further in 2006 with the killing of a senior political leader and Baloch tribal leader, Nawab Akbar Khan Bugti, along with 35 of his followers by the Pakistan military.[65] Ever since the assassination, Pakistani security forces have been blamed for innumerable human rights violations, inclusive of extrajudicial killings, torture, enforced disappearances, and excessive use of force against protestors.[66] Since 2010, "around 400 (and by some accounts over 500) bullet-riddled bodies with marks of brutal torture have been found 'dumped' on the roadsides in Balochistan".[67] Moreover, as per the government data, by 2016, some 936 "kill and dump cases" were recorded. However, the independent human rights body, Voice for Baloch Missing Persons (VBMP) recorded more than 1200 such cases.[68] Evidently, since the early 2000s, there is a prominent increase in the atrocities by Pakistan's military over Baloch civilians. The province is in a dire situation by the state-sponsored forced disappearances and killings.

Worryingly, the problems have got magnified with Pakistan opening its gates to China for the China-Pakistan Economic Corridor (CPEC). Balochi people fear that they would be pushed out of their own province and be more alienated. In addition, Pakistan Army is facing flank for forceful evacuations of people in the areas of Gilgit-Baltistan and Balochistan so that land can be made available for CPEC.[69] As per one report, in October 2019, some 28 military operations were conducted in the province that have resulted in forced disappearance of some 30 people and deaths of 25 others.[70] These killings and enforced disappearances include activists, journalists, human rights defenders, students and intellectuals who raised voices against the atrocities committed by security forces. According to Amnesty International, at the end of 2019, UN Working Group on Enforced or Involuntary Disappearances (WGEID) had 731 unresolved allegations of enforced disappearances from Pakistan Amnesty.[71] Certainly, the country has failed in securing the lives of its citizens. The case of deaths and abduction in military raids has also been reported in the times of COVID-19 induced lockdown. According to the Hakkpan organisation, a Baloch human rights organisation, in April 2020, 16 Baloch were killed and as many as 73 people were picked by the military forces, including students, women, children and infants. Though, later 28 of them were released.[72]

Unfortunately, the education sector is also under surveillance, as stated by Dil Murad Baloch, the information secretary of Baloch National Movement. Frontier Corps has been accused of breaching the privacy of hundreds of Baloch students by recording their candid videos with the help of hidden cameras to later blackmail students.[73] Thus, Balochistan's deteriorating human rights situation at present reflects the imbalance of the civil-military relations in Pakistan. The military has emerged as the ultimate arbiter in the politics and the state. Several reasons such as political intrigues, cultural suppression, economic marginalisation, social incoherence, dispossession and brutal attacks have generated antagonism amongst the civilians against the state.

Conclusion

The long years of presence in the state and society has strongly secured the military its place in civilian institutions in Pakistan. It's been 50 years since Bangladesh (then East Pakistan) separated from Pakistan, yet the army has not been restrained from playing its multiple roles. Several factors have contributed to the military's persistent dominance in the state; first, the absence of stable civilian government at the central and provincial levels pushed civilian institutions to repeatedly rely on the military to maintain law and order, and national security. These actions escalated the significance of military in the polity. Also, the judiciary failed miserably in protecting the rights and enforcement of the constitution against imposed martial laws. Pakistan represents the case that if it had effective governance, organisational capacity, sparing supervision of military actions and a strong well-organised infrastructure, the country could have been saved from the current crisis within civil-military affairs.

The re-application of colonial tactics by military bureaucratic elites over other ethnic groups raises concerns regarding the shrinking role of political institutions in the state. Hence, the country still hasn't learned lessons from its past; Pakistan needs to understand that the military has to be more vital in protecting the state from external enemies; for internal matters, the institution needs to support political system governed by parliamentary and democratic forces. The sooner it realises this, the better it would be for Balochistan and the entire country.

NOTES

1. H. Alavi, 'Authoritarianism and Legitimation of State Power in Pakistan', in S. K. Mitra (ed.), *Post-colonial State of Asia: Dialectics of Politics and Government,* New York: Harvester Wheatsheaf, 1990.
2. G. Mustafa and A. Nawaz, 'The Separation of East Pakistan: Socio-Economic Factors', *Asian Journal of Multidisciplinary Studies,* Vol. 2, No. 1, 2014, pp. 45–51.
3. S.P. Huntington, *The Soldier & the State – The Theory & Politics Politics of Civil–Military Relations,* Harvard University Press, 1957.
4. Ibid.
5. Yale Law School, 'Madison Debates', *Lillian Goldman Law Library,* 29 June 2008, available at https://avalon.law.yale.edu/18th_century/debates_629.asp, accessed on 13 August 2021.
6. V. Kukreja, 'Civil-Military Relations in Developing Countries', *India Quarterly,* Vol. 45, No. 2/3, 1989, pp. 154–192.
7. Kotera M. Bhimaya, 'Civil-Military Relations: A Compartive Study of India and Pakistan', RAND Graduate School, 1997, available at https://www.rand.org/content/dam/rand/pubs/rgs_dissertations/2006/RGSD136.pdf, accessed on 22 August 2021.
8. S.P. Huntington, 'Political Development and Political Decay', *World Politics,* Vol. 17, No. 3, 1965, pp. 386–430.
9. A. Hussain, 'Ethnicity, National Identity and Praetorianism: The Case of Pakistan', *Asian Survey,* Vol. 16, No. 10, 1976, pp. 918–930.
10. H.A. Rizvi, 'Pakistan: Civil-military Relations in a Praetorian State', in R. May and V. Selochan (eds), *The Military and Democracy in Asia and the Pacific,* ANU Press, 2004, pp. 88–100.
11. S.P. Cohen, 'Pakistan: Army, Society, and Security', *Asian Affairs,* Vol. 10, No. 2, 1983, pp. 1–26.
12. A. Siddiqa, *Military Inc. Inside Pakistan's Military Economy,* Oxford University Press, 2007.
13. A. Jalal, *The State of Martial Rule,* Lahore: Vanguard Books Pvt Ltd., 1991.

14. E. Hussain, 'Pakistan: Civil-Military Relations in a Post-Colonial State', *PCD Journal,* Vol. IV, No. 1, 2012, pp. 113–146.
15. Rizvi, 'Pakistan: Civil-Military Relations in a Praetorian State', n. 10.
16. F. Aguilar, R. Bell, N. Black, S. Falk, S. Rogers and A. Peritz, 'An Introduction to Pakistan's Military', *Harvard Kennedy School,* 2011, available at https://www.belfercenter.org/sites/default/files/legacy/files/Pakistan-Military-final-B.pdf, accessed on 10 August 2021.
17. G.W. Choudhury, 'Bangladesh: Why it Happened', *International Affairs,* Vol. 48, No. 2, 1972, pp. 242–249.
18. L. Ziring, *The Ayub Khan Era: Politics in Pakistan, 1958-1969,* The Syracuse, 1971.
19. G.W. Choudhury, 'Constitution-Making Dilemmas in Pakistan', *The Western Political Quarterly,* Vol. 8, No. 4, 1955, pp. 589–600.
20. Ibid.
21. A. Jalal, 'The Politics of a Constitutional Crisis: Pakistan, April 1953-May 1955', in D. A. Low (ed.), *Constitutional Heads and Political Crisis,* Hampshire: Macmillan Press, 1988, pp. 57–66.
22. Ibid.
23. H. Alavi, 'Bangladesh and the Crisis of Pakistan 1971', *Mainstream Weekly,* 27 March 2021, available at http://mainstreamweekly.net/article10302.html, accessed on 1 August 2021.
24. J. Meher, 'Dynamics of Pakistan's Disintegration: The Case of East Pakistan 1947-1971', *India Quarterly,* Vol. 71, No. 4, 2015, pp. 300–317.
25. C.C. Fair, *Fighting to the End,* New York: Oxford University Press, 2014.
26. M.N. Asadullah, 'Educational Disparity in East and West Pakistan, 1947-71: Was East Pakistan Discriminated Against?', *The Bangladesh Development Studies,* Vol. XXXIII, No. 3, 2010, pp. 1–46.
27. Hussain, 'Pakistan: Civil-Military Relations in a Post-Colonial State', n. 14.
28. M. Foucault, *The History of Sexuality,* (Vol. I). (R. Hurley, Trans.) New York: Pantheon Books, 1978.
29. S. Maron, 'The Problem of East Pakistan', *Pacific Affairs,* Vol. 28, No. 2, 1995, pp. 132–144.
30. Meher, 'Dynamics of Pakistan's Disintegration: The Case of East Pakistan 1947-1971', n. 24.
31. V. Kukreja, *Contemporary Pakistan: Political Processes, Conflicts and Crises,* New Delhi: Sage, 2003.
32. Hussain, 'Ethnicity, National Identity and Praetorianism: The Case of Pakistan', n. 9.
33. Fair, *Fighting to the End,* n. 25.
34. Ibid.
35. A. Siddiqa, 'Pakistan Military-Ethnic Balanced in the Armed Forced and Problems of Federalism', A paper commission for the Conference on Diversity organized in Kathmandu, 2011.
36. Smruti S. Pattanaik, 'Civil-Military Coordination and Defence Decision-Making in Pakistan', *Strategic Analysis,* Vol. XXIV, No. 5, 2000.
37. Rizvi, 'Pakistan: Civil-Military Relations in a Praetorian State', n. 10.
38. Ibid.
39. Kukreja, *Contemporary Pakistan: Political Processes, Conflicts and Crises,* n. 31.
40. J. Coates, 'Bangladesh-the Struggle for Cultural Independence', *Index on Censorship,* Vol. 1, No.1, 1972, pp. 17–35.
41. EFSAS, '1971 Liberation war, birth of Bangladesh and comparison with present day Pakistan', *European Foundation for South Asian Studies (EFSAS),* April 2017, available at https://www.efsas.org/publications/research-dossiers/1971-liberation-war,-birth-of-bangladesh-

and-comparison-with-present-day-pakistan/, accessed on 12 August 2021.
42. Kukreja, *Contemporary Pakistan: Political Processes, Conflicts and Crises,* n. 31.
43. A.H. Rizvi, *The Military and Politics in Pakistan 1947-1997,* Lahore: Sang-e-Meel Publications, 2013.
44. International Commission of Jurists, 'The Events in East Pakistan, 1971', *International Commission of Jurists,* 1 June 1972, available at https://www.icj. org/ wp- content/ uploads/ 1972/06/Bangladesh-events-East-Pakistan-1971-thematic-report-1972-eng.pdf, accessed on 5 August 2021.
45. The Six-Point demands included: "1. Pakistan would have a federal structure of government based on the spirit of the Lahore Resolution of 1940, with a parliament elected on the basis of a universal adult franchise; 2. The central government would have authority only in defense and foreign affairs and all other subjects would be handled by the federating units of the state of Pakistan; 3. There would be two freely convertible currencies for the two wings of Pakistan or two separate reserve banks for the two regions of the country; 4. The power of taxation and revenue collection would be vested in the federating units; 5. There would be two separate accounts for foreign exchange reserves for the two wings of Pakistan; 6. East Pakistan would have a separate militia or paramilitary force as a measure of its security" (Bangladesh Awami League, 'Six-Point Demands: Roadmap For Bangladesh's Emancipation', *Bangladesh Awami League,* 1 June 2021, available at https://www.albd.org/articles/news/31111/Six-Point-Demands:-Roadmap-For-Bangladesh%E2%80%99s-Emancipation, accessed on 18 August 2021).
46. Choudhury, 'Bangladesh: Why it Happened', n. 17.
47. EFSAS, '1971 Liberation war, birth of Bangladesh and comparison with present day Pakistan', n. 41.
48. L. Ziring, 'Militarism in Pakistan: The Yahya Khan Interregnum', *Asian Affairs,* Vol. 1, No. 6, 1974, pp. 402–420.
49. R. Naeem, 'Fifty Years of the Cyclone That Triggered a Civil War and Created Bangladesh', *The Wire,*11 November 2020, available at https://thewire.in/history/cyclone-bhola-mujibur-rahman- bangladesh-liberation-yahya-khan-pakistan, accessed on 3 August 2021.
50. Ziring, 'Militarism in Pakistan: The Yahya Khan Interregnum', n. 48.
51. H.A. Rizvi, *Military, State, and Society in Pakistan,* Macmillan Press Ltd., 2000.
52. Meher, 'Dynamics of Pakistan's Disintegration: The Case of East Pakistan 1947-1971', n. 24.
53. S. Bose, 'The question of genocide and the quest for justice in the 1971 war', *Journal of Genocide Research,* Vol. 13, No. 4, 2011, pp. 393–419.
54. A. Roychowdhury, 'Birth of Bangladesh: When raped women and war babies paid the price of a new nation', *The Indian Express,* 19 December 2016, available at https://indianexpress.com/article/research/birth-of-bangladesh-when-raped-women-and-war-babies-paid-the-price-of-a-new-nation-victory-day-4430420/, accessed on 17 August 2021.
55. A. Khan, 'Renewed Ethnonationalist Insurgency in Balochistan, Pakistan: The Militarized State and Continuing Economic Deprivation', *Asian Survey,* Vol. 49, No. 6, 2009, pp. 1071–1091.
56. Zeus Hans Mendez, 'Repression and Revolt in Balochistan', *Journal of Indo-Pacific Affairs,* Fall 2020, pp. 43–61.
57. 'Province Wise Provincial Results of Census-2017', Pakistan Census, 2017, available at https://www.pbs.gov.pk/sites/default/files/PAKISTAN%20TEHSIL%20WISE%20FOR %20WEB%20CENSUS_2017.pdf, accessed on 3 October 2021.
58. Haqqani Husain, 'Injustices in Balochistan Need the World's Attention', *The Wire,* 24 September

2017, available at https://thewire.in/external-affairs/balochistans-injustices-need-worlds-attention, accessed on 3 October 2021.

59. Yogesh Gattani, "The Resilience of Baloch Insurgencies: Understanding the Fifth Period', *E-International Relations*, 2 February 2021, available at https://www.e-ir.info/2021/02/02/the-resilience-of-baloch-insurgencies-understanding-the-fifth-period/, accessed on 3 October 2021.
60. Imtiaz Ali, 'The Balochistan Problem' *Pakistan Horizon*, Vol. 58, No.2, 2005, pp. 41–62.
61. Gattani, 'The Resilience of Baloch Insurgencies: Understanding the Fifth Period', n. 59.
62. International Crisis Group, 'Pakistan: The Worsening Conflict in Balochistan', *International Crisis Group*, 14 September 2006, available at https://d2071andvip0wj.cloudfront.net/119-pakistan-the-worsening-conflict-in-balochistan.pdf, accessed on 21 November 2021.
63. Ibid.
64. E. Hussain and A. Khan, 'Civil-Military Relations in Pakistan: The Case of Balochistan', *Asian Studies, Jahangirnagar University of Journal of Government and Politics*, No. 33, 2014, pp. 11–24.
65. 'Pakistan: Security Forces 'Disappear' Opponents in Balochistan' *Human Rights Watch*, 28 July 2011, available at https://www.hrw.org/news/2011/07/28/pakistan-security-forces-disappear-opponents-balochistan, accessed on 10 October 2021.
66. Ibid.
67. Sushant Sareen, 'Balochistan Forgotten War, Forsaken People', *Vivekananda International Foundation*, September 2017, available at https://www.vifindia.org/sites/default/files/Balochistan-Forgotten-War-Forsaken-People.pdf, accessed on 4 October 2021.
68. Ibid.
69. 'Protests against military operations and Chinese intervention in Balochistan', *ANI*, 23 August 2017, available at https://www.aninews.in/news/world/business/protests-against-military-operations-and-chinese-intervention-in-balochistan/, accessed on 4 October 2021.
70. 'Pak army continues its barbarism in Balochistan; 28 operations conducted, 25 bodies found: Dil Murad Baloch', ANI, 9 November 2019, available at https://www.aninews.in/news/world/asia/pak-army-continues-its-barbarism-in-balochistan-28-operations-conducted-25-bodies-found-dil-murad-baloch20191108195502/, accessed on 9 October 2021.
71. 'Pakistan: The disappeared of Balochistan', *Amnesty International*, 12 November 2020, available at https://www.amnesty.org/en/wp-content/uploads/2021/05/ASA3333342020ENGLISH.pdf, accessed on 4 October 2021.
72. 'Balochistan: 16 killed, 45 abducted in April as military raids increased', *Human Rights Council of Balochistan (Hakkpaan)*, 8 May 2020, available at https://hrcbalochistan.com/balochistan-16-killed-45-abducted-in-april-as-military-raids-increased/, accessed on 9 October 2021.
73. 'Pak army continues its barbarism in Balochistan; 28 operations conducted, 25 bodies found: Dil Murad Baloch', n. 70.

17

50 Years after 1971

State Narratives, People and Politics in the Subcontinent

Shruti Pandalai

On 13 June 1971, an article by Pakistani journalist Anthony Mascarenhas in *The Sunday Times* decisively changed the history of South Asia. Many in the Western press reported that it not just helped turn the tide of 'world opinion against Pakistan and encouraged India to play a decisive role' but also may have 'effectively helped end the war'.[1] Harold Evans, editor of *The Sunday Times*, recalled in his memoirs that this was not Mascarenhas' intention, but he was 'just a very good reporter doing an honest job'.[2] He added that Indian Prime Minister (PM) Indira Gandhi stated that Mascarenhas' account 'had shocked her so deeply' that it had 'set her on a campaign of personal diplomacy in the European capitals and Moscow to prepare the ground for India's armed intervention.'[3]

Mascarenhas, then assistant editor with the *Morning News* in Karachi, ironically was considered an 'establishment journalist' and was one of the eight Pakistani reporters allowed by the military government to visit East Pakistan in April 1971. The Pakistan Army, after expelling foreign journalists, wanted to dispel the narrative that it was crushing the 'insurrection in East Pakistan'. They took the journalists, including Mascarenhas, on a 10-day tour, expecting them to write what was told to them, especially about the violence against non-Bengalis. Reportedly, seven of them toed the line and wrote what was expected of them. However, Mascarenhas, scarred by the violence he witnessed and knowing that the story he wanted to write would never pass the military censors, pretended to visit his sick sister in London. He gave up his home and job in Pakistan, arranged for his family to leave the country and flew to the United Kingdom (UK) to write his account for *The Sunday Times* in London. While Mascarenhas emphasised his shock at the killings of non-Bengalis as the Pakistani military wanted him to do,[4] what he described in greater detail was how much more scarred he was by the 'systematic killing spree' carried out by the army against the Bengalis. He wrote:

> The real toll, I was told everywhere in East Bengal, may have been as high as 1,00,000; for thousands of non-Bengalis have vanished without a trace. The Government of Pakistan has let the world know about that first horror. What it has suppressed is the second and worse horror which followed when its own army took over the killing. West Pakistani officials privately calculate that altogether both sides have killed 2,50,000 people, not counting those who have died of famine and disease.... 'We are determined to cleanse East Pakistan once and for all of the threat of secession, even if it means killing of two million people and ruling the province as a colony for 30 years,' I was repeatedly told by senior military and civil officers in Dacca and Comilla. The West Pakistan army in East Bengal is doing exactly that with a terrifying thoroughness.... THIS IS GENOCIDE conducted with amazing casualness.[5]

The first-hand account of what Mascarenhas called 'a genocide' changed the course of history and galvanised people into action, forever changing South Asian geopolitics. Historians have written at length of how the Indians, Pakistanis and Bangladeshis tried to frame their cause, generate support and mobilise international opinion to legitimise their respective policies.[6] They all felt that '[w]inning this contest for world opinion...was at least as important as winning the conflict on the ground.'[7] Motivations were varied:[8] for India, the imploding refugee crisis on its borders, an opportunity to trounce the 'two-nation theory' that used religion as a justification for the partition of a Hindu India and a Muslim Pakistan in 1947, as well as a clear shot to tilt the military balance in its favour in the subcontinent were drivers. For Pakistan, it was an internal quarrel rising out of East Pakistan's attachment to a 'Hindu language and culture' that was stoked by India to unsettle Pakistan and break its unity. For Bangladesh, it was West Pakistan's arrogance and 'second class treatment' of its East Pakistani brothers. Thus, in the larger geopolitical backdrop of the Cold War, 1971 became an India–Pakistan war where, as some argue, 'Bangladesh's independence is incidental'.[9]

While the 1971 war will remain etched in the collective memory of the Indian subcontinent for years to come, it has also created nationalistic narratives in Pakistan, Bangladesh and India. Some of these have endured through generations—

and in some cases, have been reconstructed for the young in these nations—for all actors want to be seen on the right side of history. This chapter seeks to explore the motivations behind these narratives; how they were framed and shaped behind the scenes; and their impact on the current state of geopolitics.

The Contest for 'Legitimate Narratives'

Bias is natural when nations narrate their own histories and the 1971 war is no different. Yet, it is the contest of 'whose story wins', which drives the protagonists of the 1971 crisis to convince domestic and external audiences that their motivations and actions were legitimate. Consequently, historical lenses from each of these nations—Bangladesh, India and Pakistan—are, to an extent, coloured. However, downright denial in some quarters has over time exacerbated differences between the nations.

Syed Badrul Ahsan, Bangladeshi journalist and biographer of Sheikh Mujibur Rahman (Mujib), the founding father of Bangladesh, poignantly captures this:

> In a visit to the Pakistan parliament a few years ago, this reviewer was shown what was given out as a wall of democracy along the corridor of the upper house of the country's legislature. Four pillars were painted black, as symbols of darkness caused by the four martial laws Pakistan had fallen victim to. Apart from the four pillars, the wall sought to depict Pakistan's history beginning with the adoption of the Lahore Resolution in March 1940. A quote from Dhirendranath Dutta in defence of the Bengali language is emblazoned on the wall, without of course any mention of his brutal murder by the Pakistan army in 1971. The reference to the 1970 general elections does not mention the results of the vote. The narrative moves straight to 1971, to note that Pakistan's first elected government took office in that year. No mention is made of the political crisis of March 1971 and atrocities committed by the soldiers, no reference is there of how or why East Pakistan went out of the federation; nothing is there to suggest that a guerrilla war had forced the army into capitulation in December 1971.[10]

Today, bilateral ties between Pakistan and Bangladesh still bear the strain of this denial. It has been a long-standing demand in Bangladesh, by both political parties and civil society, to mark the atrocities committed by the Pakistani Army on civilians in the then East Pakistan during the liberation war in 1971. On 11 March 2017, the Bangladesh Parliament passed a resolution calling on the government to observe 25 March as the 'Genocide Day'. With Bangladesh proceeding to prosecute alleged war criminals who collaborated with the Pakistani Army in 1971 and working to get international recognition for the genocide in a move to heal its internal scars and appease public sentiment, polarising narratives continue to impact ties. Pakistan's refusal to apologise has done little to bring closure to many bereaved families who continue to bear the burden of 1971's tragic memories.

In fact, this denial finds mention in a 1972 report by the International Commission of Jurists (ICJ): 'The Indian Government and the provisional Government of Bangladesh agreed to cooperate fully with the Commission, but unfortunately the former Pakistan Government refused their cooperation, contending that the subject of the enquiry was a purely internal matter.'[11] However, it is this passage in the report that captures the genesis of the problem interestingly:

> The name of Pakistan, first thought of in 1930, is composed of letters from Islamic provinces or countries, Punjab, Afghania (the old North West Frontier region of India), Kashmir, Iran, Sind, Turkharistan, Afghanistan and Baluchistan. It may have been ominous for the future of Pakistan, but Bengal was not one of the regions which lent its letters to the name.[12]

This exclusion rings loud in the feeling of neglect that accounts of East Pakistanis often echo as the primary reason they wished to liberate from West Pakistan.

For Bangladesh: Unwanted in Pakistan, the Bengalis Struggle for a Homeland

The two-nation theory which led to the creation of India and Pakistan (East and West) centred on religious identity of their people had given hope to the Muslims of Bengal that they would finally achieve a better standard of life. Unfortunately, the Government of West Pakistan proved even more discriminatory towards the people of East Pakistan compared to the Hindu landlords in pre-Partition India. Whether it was social, political or economic, the Muslims of East Pakistan often described their treatment as 'second class' citizens in their new nation.

Most historians trace the struggle for Bengali rights to when Pakistan gained independence as a country with two unconnected wings known as West Pakistan (today's Pakistan) and East Pakistan (today's Bangladesh). The refusal to accept Bengali as a state language of Pakistan in the early years after the Partition; stark economic disparity between the two territories; the hegemony of the West Pakistani ruling elite over Pakistan; martial laws; and a demeaning attitude towards Bengali culture and the Bengali population soured relations between the two parts. As a Bangladeshi columnist reminisced:

> There was a famous poster designed by Bangabandhu [Sheikh Mujibur Rahman], which posed the question 'Shonar Bangla shoshan keno?' (Why is the Golden Bengal a crematorium?). The answers to the question were there in terms of discrimination of the West Pakistani elites against the Bengali people.[13]

Further, as documented by historians, economically East Pakistan contributed to the profits of the West Pakistani government, but did not receive adequate investments for its development.[14] It is inferred that the President, General Muhammad Ayub Khan, did not undertake any measures to economically uplift East Pakistan and continued the exploitative structures adopted by the British, resulting in stark disparities between East and West Pakistan in terms of international trade, inter-wing trade, foreign exchange earnings, aid flow and developmental expenditure.[15] Despite a larger population size in East Pakistan, the majority of the national budget (75 per cent) was spent on West Pakistan. The indifference is substantiated when seen through the figures of per capita income of that period, which was 32 per cent higher for West Pakistan during 1959–60 and 61 per cent higher during 1969–70.[16] Most of the industries of the eastern wing were owned by West Pakistanis, who were the beneficiaries of financial support from the central government. Consequently, traditional Bengali small-scale and cottage industries were wasted away. While East Pakistan provided over half of the country's exports, West Pakistan gained most of her imports.

Under the Ayub regime, the disparities only amplified. It is claimed that the economic neglect stemmed from Ayub's personal disdain for East Pakistan, despite a majority of his early military career being spent there.[17] Describing Bengalis as a 'burden for West Pakistan', Ayub spoke of East Pakistan as 'a mill stone around our neck', with the Bengalis making constant effort to 'grab whatever they could'. He also thought less of the East Pakistani economic issues and demands for more political authority because he believed that 'the Bengalis did not want to work but only wanted solutions to their political issues'.[18] Historians believe that while Ayub tried in the end to bridge the economic disparity between the two wings, it was too late: 'his rule, through the exclusion of East Pakistan from a share in political authority and its economic subservience to West wing, only contributed to the rise of the movement for regional autonomy in the eastern province.'[19]

The education sector also saw discrimination in terms of investment and quality of education. Since enrollment of students was low, it reflected again in the central services, with the majority of the administrative service officers being from West Pakistan and very few from East Pakistan. In the armed forces too, a majority of senior positions were occupied by West Pakistanis. It has been argued that one of the reasons Mujib drew up the Six-Point Demand (known as the Six-Point Movement or Charter of Freedom) was because during the 1965 Indo-Pak War, East Pakistan was left with limited military defence. In fact, the western wing is said to have had 25 times higher military personnel compared to that in the eastern wing.

Cultural discrimination, which led to political disparity, was also identified as a driver for the liberation of East Pakistan. From early on, the Pakistan government made it clear that Urdu would be the official language of the state, even though the Bengali-speaking East Pakistanis accounted for more than 50 per cent of the country's population. Feeling that this policy was an attempt to subvert their culture, the people of East Pakistan founded the Bengali Language Movement in 1948, to protest the removal of Bengali script from currency and stamps. The next four years saw protests and picketing by students worried about diminishing career prospects with the rejection of Bengali, which eventually led to the arrest of the leaders of the language movement. Again, in February 1952, the request was rejected by PM Khwaja Nazimuddin, himself an East Pakistani, leading to widespread agitation which continued until the Constituent Assembly's decision in 1956 to accept both Bengali and Urdu as state languages. The incident not just broke trust between East and West Pakistan but also resulted in East Pakistanis feeling increasingly marginalised and without a voice in their own nation. It is also said to have given a push to the need to imagine a stronger Bengali identity, which trumped its Muslim identity.

Pakistani writers have published extensively about why this fault line of identity and prejudice triggered the demand for liberation in East Pakistan.[20] President Ayub had often suggested that 'most Bengali beliefs are only barely punctuated by Islam because Bengalis are essentially Hindu'.[21] He also wrote in his diary:

> Without meaning any unkindness, the fact of the matter is that a large majority of the Muslims in East Pakistan have an animist base which is a thick layer of Hinduism and top crust of Islam which is pierced by Hinduism from time to time.[22]

According to Hafsa Khawaja:

> By conflating Bengalis with Hinduism, Ayub and other military officials casted them as disloyal and unfaithful citizens. As early as 1967, a law minister branded Bengalis as 'traitors and enemies of the country', a judgement Ayub agreed with. As he wrote in his diaries, 'This is the sort of language in which they should be spoken to.'[23]

Ironically, many writers and historians also highlight that there was nothing inevitable about the build-up for the demand of liberation of Bangladesh. A columnist in Pakistan's *Express Tribune* has written:

> In those impressionable years that I spent in the then East Pakistan, I do not recall any discernible secessionist vibes or any demand for an outright break from Pakistan. The basic discourse was that as Bengalis were in majority, they had every right to design the future political landscape so that their essential rights could be secured. The prevalent system was equated with internal colonialism wherein East Pakistan was the periphery to serve the interest of the core, the western part of the country, and policies in all the key fields were designed and executed towards that end.[24]

In fact, most writers are in agreement that the Bengali leadership was wedded to the idea of Pakistan and expected flexibility in the early years after the Partition to accommodate East Pakistan's aspirations.[25] Renowned Bengali leader, Hussein Shaheed Suhrawardy—Sheikh Mujibur Rahman's mentor—in his early years for the struggle of Pakistan, was wedded to the same idea. He had rallied Bengali sentiment for consensus on the 1956 Constitution, wherein the Bengali leadership 'accepted the principle of parity in political and economic fields and conceded their majority'.[26] Mujb, despite his reservations on what he saw as an 'outrageous claim of 98 per cent autonomy to their province', backed Suhrawardy.[27] However, Ayub's promulgation of martial law and abrogation of the constitution in 1958 following 10 years of authoritarian rule ensured that any expectation of emancipation of East Pakistan fizzled out. Nevertheless, as Srinath Raghavan points out: 'like many Bengali Muslim politicians of his generation, Mujib hoped both to preserve the unity of Pakistan under a federal structure and to make a bid for national leadership by leveraging the Bengalis' potential electoral majority.'[28]

So, under Ayub, and later his successor, Yahya Khan, the widening chasm of economic, social and cultural disparity between the two wings only grew, fuelling regional aspirations for more autonomy. From 1966 till 1970, despite being jailed many times, including for allegedly conspiring with India to undermine the unity of Pakistan—the so-called Agartala conspiracy case—Mujib became the undisputed Bengali leader and was able to garner political support for his six-point programme. The agenda spelt a more federal structure, with only defence and foreign affairs remaining with the centre. It became an election plank in the 1970 general election, gathering widespread support from the eastern wing; however, it was rejected by the political power in the western wing.

The subsequent mishandling and apathy of West Pakistan towards the devastation in East Pakistan after the 1970 Bhola cyclone finally broke the camel's back. Sydney Schanber, a *New York Times* journalist, described the outlook of the Pakistani government, including their failure to tackle the cyclone:

> Whether deliberately callous or not, the Pakistan government's cyclone relief effort was certainly slow and careless of appearances. There was an effort to imply that the Bengali political leaders were crying wolf and overstating the devastation...Declassified US State Department cables show that even Henry Kissinger, no friend to Bangladesh and a good friend to Pakistan's military ruler General Yahya Khan, found it difficult to excuse this failure to the general's other champion, President Richard Nixon. The Pakistani authorities may have been callous, but since they were also staging the first direct elections in this huge country, their inaction defies explanation.[29]

Most books documenting the liberation of Bangladesh portray the callousness exhibited by Yahya: surveying the cyclone damage from the air; nursing a hangover with a few beers; and in the few instances that his boots did get muddy, touring with a gold-topped cane.[30] Yahya was on his way back from China and stopped over in Dhaka, reportedly 'celebrating his freshly won commitment from Beijing for increased military assistance' and concluding 'that the extent of the calamity had been blown out of all proportion'.[31] Meanwhile, the Bengali leadership led by Mujib described the devastation as a 'holocaust' and the government's response as 'criminal negligence'.[32] It was now determined in its demand that the six-point programme would be a non-negotiable public compact. These series of events solidified the view that '[a] complex political problem was subjected to an administrative and later on to a military solution which spelt disaster for the country.'[33]

Finally, despite the Awami League sweeping the polls in 1970, the mandate was rejected by the West Pakistan establishment because it did not want an East Pakistani political party heading the federal government. Arguably, the military leadership had expected that the electorate would return a fractured verdict since they had spent considerable resources to deride the Awami League. Moreover, they had banked their hopes on a divided national assembly, which would make the mandate of constitution making within the 120-day period impossible and ensure a fresh call for elections. Apparently, Yahya was planning for a Turkish type of 'military–civilian (i.e., concealed) regime', which would preserve the military's political position and corporate interests. According to Syed Badrul Hasan, a senior General from Yahya's coterie had gone to the extent of telling his soldiers on a trip to Dhaka in 1970: 'Don't worry...we will not allow those black bastards to rule over us.'[34]

With the adverse reaction to the poll results, the civil disobedience movement spiralled in East Pakistan and the military leadership responded with massive force, targeting the Awami League and its supporters. Luckily for Yahya, West Pakistan-based Pakistan People's Party (PPP), led by Zulfikar Ali Bhutto, had come second in the elections and despite a constitutional loss, it was not willing to accept an Awami League government. According to Yahya, Bhutto advised him in the summer of 1970 to not worry about the elections: 'Yahya the soldier and Bhutto the politician will make a very good team and can together run the country.'[35] Bhutto, while inviting Mujib to form a hybrid government, was deploying other strategies. He tried to build a consensus among the West Pakistani parties against the six-point programme and for the inclusion of his party in the future government. Simultaneously, he also sought to raise doubts about the Awami League's commitment to a united Pakistan, thereby undermining its credibility in West Pakistan.[36]

On the other flank, the Awami League was watching with concern the military build-up in East Pakistan and was worried about the Bhutto–Yahya combine postponing the convening of the national assembly. Mujib was trying to rein in the radical factions of the Awami League from demanding outright independence as he was worried about a military crackdown; also, the lack of diplomatic recognition of a new state globally would severely damage their struggle. Adding to his worries was the lukewarm response to his outreach to the United States (US) Embassy in Dhaka, where he had expressed that 'he wanted very much to work out with Yahya some political settlement that would avoid bloodshed, satisfy Bengali aspirations, and preserve some vestige of link with Pakistan.'[37] The Consul General, Archer Blood, 'politely indicated that the United States wished Pakistan to stay united and that it was loath to involve itself in Pakistan's internal affairs'. His restraint barely masked Nixon and Kissinger's completely different geopolitical priorities of using Islamabad to forge peace with China.

By February 1971, East Pakistan was on the boil and despite the advice of two East Pakistani officials on his team, Yahya was adamant about postponing the convening of the national assembly. After Yahya announced the postponement on 1 March 1971, East Pakistan saw spontaneous protests break out in outrage and life came to a standstill. Yahya, while publicly blaming Mujib for the impasse and defending the strict martial measures as 'duty of the Pakistan army', sent a message to Dhaka behind the scenes telling Mujib not to take a hasty decision and assuring him that a compromise will be reached. Yahya was trying to control the damage that a declaration of independence by Mujib would trigger domestically and internationally. The military was not yet ready for a full operation in East Pakistan and a declaration of independence would not just grab international attention but also invite intervention.[38]

However, with the negotiations going nowhere, Mujib, on 7 March at the Race Course grounds where thousands had gathered, threw down the gauntlet in a rousing speech which went down in the annals of history. In a fiery oration, he hit out the west wing for continuing to obstruct the transfer of power and pledged to lead the struggle for emancipation, which he punctuated was 'a struggle for independence'.[39] Meanwhile, Yahya and his military was getting increasingly dissatisfied with the direction of the talks. Irked by the perseverance of Mujib and the Awami League in sticking to their demands, Yahya told Tikka Khan, Pakistan's Chief or Army Staff (later labelled the Butcher of Bengal): 'The bastard is not behaving. You get ready.'[40]

Historians believe that West Pakistan had made up its mind to subdue the East Pakistan movement. So, on 24 March, even as Bhutto, leaders from smaller West Pakistan parties and Yahya were in Dhaka for talks to finalise the interim constitution with the Awami leadership, the military was readying itself for war.[41] Astoundingly, Yahya had ordered his officers to launch the operation after his exit from Dhaka and time it to coincide with his arrival in Karachi. It was too late by the time Mujib and his supporters got a whiff of the impending military action and at 11:30 p.m. on 25 March 1971, Operation Searchlight began. According to media estimates, the military killed at least 7,000 Bengali civilians—both Hindus and Muslims—in a single night.[42] On 26 March, Sheikh Mujibur Rahman was arrested and taken to West Pakistan, but before his arrest, he declared that East Pakistan was to become Bangladesh, an independent sovereign country. Thus commenced the violent and bloody struggle for the liberation of Bangladesh.

For Pakistan: The Betrayal by East Pakistan, India the Instigator and Denial of History

Naturally, Pakistan's narrative on the 1971 war continues to retell the conflict as one of East Pakistan's secession, where Bengalis, while dealt with unfairly by some accounts, betrayed the idea of Pakistan as the homeland for the Muslims of South Asia. The official portrayal always blames India for instigating Bengali separatism and for using the movement to break up Pakistan. However, it is what they omit that is more interesting: Operation Searchlight, as also the infighting and distrust within the Pakistani establishment that led to many blunders escalating to the bloody birth of Bangladesh.

Pakistani writer Anam Zakaria's book on people's narratives from the subcontinent is revealing as to how the Pakistani state has resorted to 'selective forgetting' of what happened in 1971.[43] Perceived as a humiliating defeat, the war is brushed over in textbooks and there is little acknowledgement of the military oppression and resulting atrocities in East Pakistan. Zakaria says, 'Growing up, East Pakistan was rarely discussed and the creation of Bangladesh always seemed sudden and illegitimate.'[44] Arguing that the 'Pakistani narrative towards Bangladesh has been far too simplistic and myopic', she describes the official version of history as one where, 'in a Muslim brotherly nation, one wing went astray' because of India's meddling in Islamabad's internal affairs. So, the 1971 war and the creation of Bangladesh are presented as a loss. There is resentment against the Hindus and pro-India Bengalis/'Indian-funded' Bengalis, all painted as 'the demons responsible for Pakistan's break-up'.[45]

Zakaria also brings out repeatedly how, both in popular imagination and in the classrooms in Pakistan, the narrative focuses solely on blaming India's vicious efforts to destabilise Pakistan after 1947 because it could not stomach the defeat of partition. She traces narratives speaking of India finding fertile ground in East Pakistan which was dominated by 'Hindu Culture', and had it not been for "India's treacherous manipulation Pakistan would still be one".'[46] She also highlights the irony that she grew up believing East Pakistan had a Hindu majority, for her teachers and others had 'failed to mention that East Pakistan had a Muslim-majority population', for '[a]fter all, isn't that what the two-nation theory—which serves as Pakistan's raison d'être today—had proposed? That Hindus and Muslims were two separate nations, incapable of coexisting?'[47]

Zakaria outlines that Grade 9 and 10 textbooks in Pakistan, endorsed by the country's Federal Textbook Board, have a section titled, 'The Fall of East Pakistan', detailing the reasons for growing resentment amongst the Bengalis, with India's role in the breaking away of East Pakistan given maximum space. When 1971 is addressed, she says, it is generally brought up to focus upon the killings of non-Bengalis before the war, presented as a justification for military action. Ironically, there is no mention of Operation Searchlight, which the Bangladeshi's have labelled as a genocide. There is also little reflection on Pakistan's own policies, such as the economic, social and cultural deprivation of East Pakistan, that triggered the civil disobedience movement. Statist narratives found in media, like *Dawn*'s edition of 7 May 1971, are reproduced to liken Mujib's demand for autonomy and attempts used to achieve it as 'conspiracy' and 'force using Nazi style tactics'.[48]

In fact, Zakaria argues that even today, the Pakistani narrative makes some exaggerated claims, such as India-influenced Hindu teachers manipulating students and breeding secessionist sentiments in East Pakistan.[49] The historical narrative thus limits itself to 'the weeks prior to 25 March, particularly emphasising the violent behaviour of East Pakistanis, and then fast forwards to August 1971, when India signed the Indo-Soviet Treaty of Friendship and Cooperation and received Soviet backing to crush Pakistani forces in East Pakistan. Pakistan is then painted as a victim, forced to 'fight against two enemies, an enemy from within and an aggressor from without'.[50] Zakaria describes the prevalence of these narratives in a cross-section of society—bureaucracy, media, armed forces personnel—as well as entrenched in the minds of the public. She calls 1971 an awkward moment in history, where the defeat to India 'is too humiliating to delve into'. Yet, in what is testament to the extent of the prevailing denial of the state narrative are these words: '...had the army operation (Op Searchlight) and the resulting deaths been discussed in any detail, which they are not, they too would be justified in the book as a reaction to such barbaric behaviour on the part of the Bengalis.'[51]

Zakaria's assertions ring loud when we look back into history. The day after launching Operation Searchlight, Yahya Khan addressed the people of Pakistan in a radio broadcast. After outlining his version of talks with the Awami League, he claimed that Mujibur Rahman's "obstinacy, obduracy and absolute refusal to talk sense" could mean only one thing: the man and his party were enemies of Pakistan and they wanted East Pakistan to break away completely from the country.[52] Not only did Yahya ban the Awami League, he also promised that Mujib and his party's crime will not go unpunished, while of course assuring (ironically) to 'transfer power to the elected representatives of the people'. Bhutto too was quick to tell the press, 'By the Grace of Almighty God, Pakistan has at last been saved.'

Denial continued to remain entrenched in Pakistan's state response even after the creation of Bangladesh. Bangladeshi writers have spoken of the time after the defeat and surrender of Pakistan Army in Dhaka, when the new government, led by Bhutto, 'kept up the fiction of "East Pakistan" in all its pronouncements regarding Bangladesh'.[53] There was no official acknowledgement by Pakistan and newly sovereign Bangladesh's government was referred to as the 'Dhaka authorities'. 'The imaginary province of "East Pakistan" also found a place in the constitution enacted in Pakistan in 1973.'[54] It was only by 22 February 1974, when it was compelled to accord diplomatic recognition to Bangladesh to ensure Mujib's presence at the Islamic summit in Lahore, that Islamabad came to terms with the new realities in the subcontinent.

However, what Pakistan's statist narratives also hide is the deep mistrust within the establishment that held them back from reading the tea leaves. Accounts from aides[55] of the military establishment of that time reveal that up to November 1971, President Yahya Khan was hopeful that he would pull things off, fix East Pakistan, avoid a war and settle scores with Pakistani political opponents, partly because sycophants surrounding him told him so.[56]

While Yahya made no scruples about his dislike for Mujib, he was also no fan of Bhutto. For him, Bhutto, though young and bright, was also 'power crazy and fascist at heart'.[57] He felt that a direct showdown with the Awami League could avoided by using the PPP. So, while assuring Mujib that he had no objections to the six points, Yahya put the onus on the Awami League to carry all West Pakistani leaders with him. Mujib went to the extent of assuring Yahya that the military leader would be the next 'elected President of Pakistan', to which Yahya had slyly said he was a 'mere soldier' who would prefer to 'return to the barracks of his house'.[58] Pronouncing discussions with Mujib satisfactory in public initially, he often referred to the latter as the future PM of Pakistan. However, privately, Yahya was absolutely dismissive of Mujib's offer and seemed to think of it as a ceremonial office a la 'Queen Elizabeth of Pakistan'.[59] He wanted to ensure an active presidency that would preserve the military's institutional interests and deny primacy to the Awami League. Yet, as a memoir reveals, one evening the 'spirited' President picked up two balloons after a party and kicked them in the air and said, 'here goes Bhutto, and here goes Mujib'.[60]

Other memoirs by insiders also shed light on the peculiar power plays between Yahya and Bhutto that led to disastrous blunders for Pakistan in hindsight. For example, after successive military setbacks, Yahya's administration declared an emergency and set up an emergency council around the 20th of November. A last-minute civilian government was put together with Nurul Amin as the PM and Bhutto as the Deputy PM-cum-Foreign Minister. In a bid to buff up military support, Bhutto was asked to lead a delegation to China, accompanied by Yahya's confidants, Lieutenant General Gul Hassan and Air Marshal Rahim Khan. Yahya sent the aides to keep an eye on Bhutto, though officially they were ordered to discuss the military situation with their Chinese counterparts. While China assured full support, Premier Zhou Enlai and Foreign Minister Chen Ye advised the Pakistanis to delay the war till the spring of 1972, when the Himalayas would be more amenable for military intervention. According to insiders,[61] it was here that Bhutto hatched a conspiracy to mislead Yahya. It is alleged that Bhutto led Yahya to believe that the Chinese Special forces would intervene even during the winters, which in turn emboldened Yahya to launch the pre-emptive strikes on India on 3 December 1971.

There are many such accounts which burn a hole in the story Pakistan tells itself and the world, but they are beyond the scope of this chapter. However, a telling example of Pakistan's attempt at narrative setting can be found in Yahya's efforts to put himself on the right side of history in 1971. While Cold War dynamics played out with the US supporting Pakistan militarily, but not morally, and China too choosing to help from behind the scenes, global politics and media pressure forced Yahya to undertake a disastrous public relations exercise. The first line of effort manifested itself in the shape of a documentary film, *Great Betrayal.*

Brigadier A.R. Sidiqqi—Director of the Inter-Services Public Relations directorate during 1971—says in his book that the movie tried to portray the excesses perpetrated by the Bengalis and the Mukti Bahini guerrillas on West Pakistani civilians and soldiers. However, he also captures the scepticism of Yahya when he saw the film and the callous banter with his coterie on masking of the brutal violence against their own in East Pakistan:[62]

> A preview (of the film) was arranged for the president, with Generals Hamid Khan, Gul Hassan, and myself, together with Roedad Khan (a former senior Pakistani civil servant), Aslam Azhar (Chairman and Managing Director of PTV under Ayub) and few others. Yahya sat through the first half of the 35-minute documentary quite excited, throwing in a good word or two every now and again. Thereafter, he went silent. As the film ended, he gave Roedad Khan (civil servant) quite a quizzical glance that caused him to cup his chin and wet his lips nervously. 'Good work on the whole,' said Yahya, 'but are you sure that all the ruined buildings and destruction you have shown in the movie are not the result of the army action?'
>
> 'No sir, we did ensure that. You know, sir, you can't miss the difference between army-targeted damage and that wrought by miscreants.

Yahya asked about the skulls shown in the film, allegedly only some 60–70:

> Tell me Roedad, how you can tell one skull from another. I am damned if I could tell the difference between a Punjabi and a Bengali skull?' Roedad wet his lips with his tongue and looked at Aslam Azhar for an answer. Speaking English with a native fluency, Aslam Azhar responded, 'We did the best we could to distinguish between the two.'...
>
> Continuing the narration, 'Okay, okay', cutting Azhar short, Yahya looked at Generals Hamid and Gul. They both laughed. Gul looked at me, 'What can I say sir, but this is hardly the time to bring the dead back to life. Let bygones, be bygones.'

> Turning to Roedad, Yahaya [*sic*] said, 'Well I'd hate to have such a lot of good work go down the drain. Consider showing it to a limited selective audience, only if you must.' That brought the discussion to a close.

Simply put, Brigadier Siddiqui's exposition tells us why denial became central to the Pakistani state's response, given that even Yahya Khan himself couldn't buy his own propaganda!

The second line of effort was undertaken in August 1971 when West Pakistan published a white paper which, by Pakistani accounts, was another report to demonise the Mukti Bahini and their actions against the Biharis.[63] The report according to them was 'inordinately delayed' and 'gave a disappointingly sketchy account of the massacres of the non-Bengalis by the Awami Leaguers and other rebels'.[64] So, attempts by Yahya's government to purify the army from any genocidal actions and crimes failed to persuade not just the global audience but domestic constituencies too.

For India: A Refugee Crisis and a Moral Victory amidst Great Power Competition

Recently, Foreign Secretary Harsh V. Shringla said that '1971 was as much a moral and political victory as it was a decisive military victory for India.'[65] It is evident from the accounts of historians,[66] as well as semi-official narratives,[67] that for New Delhi, the liberation of East Pakistan and creation of Bangladesh was not as inevitable as often portrayed.

When the Awami League swept the elections, India welcomed the results, but some within the government did raise doubts about the stability of Pakistan. The dominant perception was that an Awami League government would be ideal for many of India's concerns—such as, normalisation of relationship with Pakistan by reducing tensions on the Kashmir issue; re-establishing trade links with East Pakistan disrupted by the 1965 war; and reducing migration of Hindus to India from East Pakistan—due to their secular credentials and the possibility that a government formed by them would not support anti-India insurgent groups operating out of East Pakistan.[68] Concurrently, there was also an expectation that Mujib and Bhutto had common interest in working together to keep the military out.[69]

From January 1971, R.N. Kao, the Chief of India's Research and Analysis Wing (R&AW), had been preparing intelligence assessments on the situation in the east wing. He had also been contacted by the Awami League, which conveyed Mujib's interests in securing arms and logical support for the movement. It was

Kao who cautioned the Indian leadership that a long liberation struggle would mean a greater possibility of control of the movement landing in 'the hands of extremists and pro-China communists in Bangladesh', which would thereby be antithetical to Indian interests.[70] He made the case for India ensuring all possible support to the liberation movement.

By early March, PM Indira Gandhi, now in her second term with a strong majority, was critically weighing her options. New Delhi's initial expectation that 'negotiations would be resumed after a brief show of military might'[71] dwindled after Mujib's speech on 7 March. India was confronting two dilemmas: one, what should be the nature of military action by India; and two, the implication of diplomatic recognition of independent Bangladesh. By 27 March, after the brutal crackdown by Yahya Khan, spontaneous protests broke out all over India in support of the people of East Pakistan. Demonstrations by political parties in the capital and student protests in Calcutta, combined with outrage in media editorials, had incensed the public sentiment, adding pressure on the government to act.[72] Indira Gandhi was criticised for inaction after Foreign Minister Swaran Singh's statement in the Parliament, which was described as tepid across press in English, Hindi, Urdu, Bengali and other languages all around the country.[73] Despite the government's measured approach to the crisis and appeals in the Parliament to proceed with caution and not make this a matter of public discussion, outrage was mounting. The PM, not wanting to give the opposition an opportunity to revive itself after their electoral defeat, moved a resolution in the Parliament on 31 March, strongly criticising the military action, demanding an end to the violence 'which amounts to genocide' and promising 'whole hearted sympathy and support' for the people of East Bengal.[74]

P.N. Haskar, PM's top aide:

> wrote to a confidant that 'our entire country is seething with a feeling of revulsion' at the Pakistan army's actions. The government had to 'reckon with it and deal with it, giving it some constructive direction. Prime Minister has been able to withstand the demand echoing from all the Legislatures in our land and from all our people to accord recognition to East Bangla Desh as a separate entity.'[75]

Further, according to Haskar, there were demands that the Indian leadership give 'the people of Bangla Desh...the necessary wherewithal with which to fight the bestiality of West Pakistan army. Many of the respected leaders of the people of East Pakistan have sent us appeals for help. We are in a terrible dilemma.'[76]

While India was debating the kind of support and military action to be taken, it was being overwhelmed by the deluge of refugees pouring in from across the border. The diplomatic missives coming from Islamabad suggested that liberal and secular values in Bengali culture had become 'an unacceptable threat to Pakistan's Islamic ideology and to its existence' and the crackdown was aimed at changing the composition of East Pakistan.[77] Records suggest that the flow of refugees, which was negligible in March, had multiplied manifold in April. By May 1971, 'the average daily influx of refugees was a staggering 102,000,72 with around seventy-one refugees entering India every minute.'[78] Though India set up refugee camps in West Bengal, chief ministers of border states in the North-East warned the PM of depleted funds, ethnic tensions rising among the locals and refugees becoming a new security threat. Foreign Minister Swaran Singh told Indian envoys, 'In India we have tried to cover that up, lest it may inflame communal feelings but we have no hesitation in stating the figure to foreigners.' The composition of the refugees was also a red flag because of the possibility that the Hindus might seek to stay on in India rather than return to their homes in East Pakistan. So, India's strategic calculus had to factor many wrestling tensions.

Meanwhile, Mujib was in custody and the Awami League leadership in exile, led by PM Tajuddin, faced internal rebellions from time to time, making New Delhi wary of their expectations from India. Many strategic thinkers in government and outside, including K. Subramanyam, Director of the Institute of Defence Studies and Analyses (IDSA), were of a view that it would be cheaper to wage war to solve the Bangladesh problem than look after millions of refugees indefinitely. Subramanyam also argued that early military intervention for the cause of the genocide would have to be accepted as fait accompli by external powers and would constrain China from opening up a new front against India.[79] Taking all aspects into consideration, the Indian government took a considered call on postponing military intervention till later when conditions favoured Indian Army's operational victory. Until then, India exercised the military option of providing support to the Bengali guerrilla fighters—the Mukti Fauz or the Mukti Bahini—who were first trained by the Border Security Force (BSF), and then by Indian military, in camps close to the border.

Despite pressure, the PM's advisors, including Haksar, argued that:

> India should not recognize Bangladesh, which would 'raise false hopes that recognition would be followed by direct intervention of the Armed Forces of India to sustain and support such a Government.' For a meeting with opposition lawmakers, Haksar briefed Gandhi to say, 'We cannot, at the present stage, contemplate armed intervention at all...[A]ll the sympathy

> and support which the Bangladesh has been able to evoke in the world will be drowned in Indo-Pak conflict. The main thing, therefore, is not a formal recognition, but to do whatever lies within our power to sustain the struggle.'[80]

The turning point, according to historians, was PM Gandhi's visit to Assam, Tripura and West Bengal on 15–16 May. P.N. Dhar, a close aide of the PM, is quoted recalling that Indira Gandhi 'was so overwhelmed by the scale of human misery that she could hardly speak.'[81] At the end of their visits, she told Dhar, 'The world must know what is happening here and do something about it. In any case, we cannot let Pakistan continue this holocaust.'[82]

India's plans had to ensure international credibility and legitimacy for offensive action. Hence, the government set out political aims where political and diplomatic offensive would go hand in hand with military preparations. The leadership set out to put forth a strategic narrative as follows:[83]

1. The East Pakistan crisis could only be resolved through a political process by accepting the electoral mandate of the Pakistani parliamentary elections. To start the process, Mujibur Rahman must be released immediately. Pakistan must immediately cease military operations in East Pakistan and the troops must return to the barracks.
2. Via the United Nations (UN) and other diplomatic channels, the international community must involve itself in resolving the crisis in East Pakistan through peaceful means. The burden of looking after the refugees cannot rest on India alone. The UN must take immediate and adequate relief efforts to assist the refugees in India and ensure their speedy return to their homes.
3. Building national public opinion in the country for the likely expansion of formal and active support for the East Pakistani liberation struggle was necessary. Simultaneously, a well-planned diplomatic initiative had to be undertaken to make the world aware of the plight of the Bangladeshis and the constraints of India.

So, led by the PM, India launched an outreach around the world, in various capitals, highlighting the plight of the people of East Bengal. Beginning with a speech in the Parliament on 24 May 1971, the above-mentioned was communicated to not just the domestic and international constituencies but also the Government of Pakistan.[84] New Delhi was focused on countering Pakistan's claim that the crisis was an internal matter that had exacerbated at India's instigation. In fact, India made more than 40 interventions at the international level within a span of four months.[85] In addition, New Delhi hosted a spate of international conferences to draw global attention to the situation and the last of these was held in September 1971, where 150 representatives from 24 countries participated. World opinion makers, including leaders and media organisations, were engaged widely and multiple times. India continued to strongly support the democratic credentials of Sheikh Mujibur Rahman and the Awami League and was able to convince many in the international community to support the cause of the people of Bangladesh.[86] Foreign Minister Swaran Singh told Indian diplomats: 'We are in the right and we have always to say that our cause is just...Plug this once, twice, thrice, four times. Start from the lower rung(,) go up to the highest levels.'[87] Additionally, several leaders of the opposition visited various countries, at the request of PM Gandhi, to convey India's constraints and the socio-economic issues overwhelming Delhi due to the refugee crisis.[88]

The shadow of great power rivalry did dampen India's efforts, with global politics choosing to turn a blind eye to the carnage in East Pakistan. It has been widely documented as to how President Nixon and his Secretary of State, Henry Kissinger, decided 'not to squeeze Yahya' on the violence unleashed by Pakistan's military junta in East Pakistan because Islamabad was facilitating a historic opening to China for Washington. Declassified documents and tapes have also recorded Nixon's bias against all things Indian,[89] including PM Indira Gandhi[90] whose many appeals were ignored by Washington in favour of the grand bargain with Islamabad over Beijing. More fundamentally, the Nixon administration was very clear from the beginning of avoiding another complication in the subcontinent; instead, it wanted to exploit the breakdown in Sino-Soviet relations to pursue a US–China rapprochement. Kissinger defends this decision in his memoirs:

> There was no doubt about the strong-arm tactics of the Pakistani military. But Pakistan was our sole channel to China; once it was closed off it would take months to make alternative arrangements.... To some of our critics our silence over Pakistan—the reason for which we could not explain—became another symptom of the general moral insensitivity of their government.[91]

Kissinger's weak defence has been discredited systematically in Gary J. Bass's book, which documents the impact of a telegram dispatched by Archer Blood, the then American Consul General to Dhaka, expressing discontent with the White House's indifference to Yahya's brutality against Bengalis using American weapons. Referred to as 'The Blood Telegram', the note indicts Nixon and Kissinger for choosing to not use their leverage over Pakistan and being responsible for an event that stands as one of the worst moments of moral blindness in the US foreign policy'. The telegram called the US leadership out for 'moral bankruptcy, ironically at a time when the USSR sent President Yahya a message defending democracy'.[92] This led to an open rebellion within the state department, which 'outfoxed Nixon and Kissinger, quietly using its bureaucratic power to jam the shipment of U.S. weaponry to Pakistan.'[93] Enraged by this rebellion in ranks, Nixon and Kissinger fired Blood and the US Ambassador to New Delhi, Kenneth Keating, labelling them as India sympathisers and vowed to stay the hell out of there.' Talking about why Nixon and he could not manage the crisis, Kissinger writes in his memoirs: 'we ran up against three obstacles: the policy of India, our own public debate, and the indiscipline of our bureaucracy.'[94] Bass describes how the Americans reacted with horror over the butchery in East Pakistan, which was widely reported by newspapers and broadcast networks. Politicians in Congress, led by Edward Kennedy and emboldened by public outrage, seized the opportunity to pin the White House down. Pressure from the Congress and bureaucratic manoeuvring by the state department led Kissinger to complain to Nixon, 'We are the ones who have been operating against our public opinion, against our bureaucracy, at the very edge of legality.'[95]

In July of 1971, when Kissinger visited both India and Pakistan as a cover for his trip to China, the meetings ended up heightening suspicions between Washington and New Delhi. Kissinger was convinced that 'India was bent on a showdown with Pakistan', while the Indians were frustrated with the US not cutting aid to Pakistan. Kissinger had assured Indira Gandhi that 'the US would take a grave view of a Chinese attack on India', but when news broke of his China visit a week later, New Delhi felt deceived, perhaps with good reason. Indeed, when Kissinger met Chinese Premier Zhou Enlai, he was told: '"Please tell President Yahya that if India commits aggression, we will support Pakistan." Referring to India aggression against Pakistan, he also outlined what the US government position should be, adding, "You are also against that."' Moreover, Kissinger told Nixon, 'hell, if we could reestablish relations with Communist China, we can always get the India back whenever we want to later—a year or two from now.'[96]

When, in August 1971, the Soviet Union and India signed the Indo-Soviet Treaty of Peace, Friendship and Cooperation, the US saw it as a guarantor for support in case of an Indo-Pak war, which could see the possibility of Sino-Pak collusion and assertive action by the US. Thus began the evolution of a regional conflict escalating into one with global political overtones, unwittingly simplified by many as another proxy war in the larger context of the Cold War playing out between the US and the Soviet Union. In September, Russian Premier Alexei Kosygin, describing Pakistan's policies in East Pakistan as 'indefensible', authorised 1 billion dollars in economic and military aid to India.[97] From India's perspective, when war became a distinct possibility, the Soviet airlifting of military equipment to India in late October proved critical. Similarly, in the crucial hours of the battle, the Soviet Union imposed its veto power in the United Nations Security Council (UNSC) a couple of times to give India time for a swift military operation. So, for New Delhi, despite Soviet neutrality in the beginning, at the nth hour, the Indo-Soviet Treaty proved to be the main political and diplomatic influence for India during the 1971 war.

Meanwhile, for the US, all moral concerns were trumped by the Nixon administration's single-minded focus on China. When PM Gandhi visited Washington in November 1971 to urge the US administration to act, President Nixon assured her that he would work with Pakistani President Yahya Khan to find a political solution. However, privately, the US was clear that a political settlement was impossible; but Nixon can be credited for preventing the execution of Mujib in August and September of 1971. By December, when the prospect of an Indo-Pak war became imminent, Kissinger and Nixon reportedly encouraged China to take military action. They had agreed to transfer military planes to the Chinese and told them that 'if you are ever going to move this is the time'.[98] Knowing that such indiscreetness would make the Chinese suspicious, Kissinger told them that if the People's Republic 'were to consider the situation on the Indian subcontinent a threat to security, and if it took measures to protect its security, the U.S. would oppose efforts of others to interfere with the People's Republic'.[99] China did not take the bait, fearing that even limited coercive actions against India would invite an immediate backlash from Moscow. After Russia's rapid military escalation to Chinese provocations in their 1969 border crisis, Chairman Mao Zedong was weary. Soviet Defence Minister Andrei Grechko had plainly told Indian representatives, 'for China to "invite a conflict" after the conclusion of the Indo-Soviet Treaty would be tantamount to "courting a disaster".'[100]

China also found ways to play mind games with India. It has been recounted that in the May Day celebration in Beijing in 1970, Mao Zedong had given the impression to India's charge d'affaires, Brajesh Mishra, that China was interested in improving relations with India.[101] In July 1971, PM Indira Gandhi wrote to Chinese PM Zhou Enlai explaining India's concerns on the situation in East Pakistan. On 25 October 1971, two-thirds of the member states of the UN General

Assembly, including India, voted to replace the Republic of China with communist China in the UN, including the UNSC. Ironically, this brought communist China into the UN and UNSC debates on East Pakistan, on the side of Pakistan.

So far, India had invested all its political capital at the diplomatic front on two levels. Bilaterally, India had engaged primarily with the four great powers (France, the UK, the Soviet Union and the US), as part of the larger international community, to prevail on Pakistan to reach a 'political settlement' in East Pakistan and mitigate the burden of 10 million refugees in India pushed out by Islamabad's genocidal campaign. Multilaterally, India had coordinated with three of the great powers (France, the UK and the Soviet Union), from 4 December 1971 onwards, to prevail on the UNSC to prioritise such a political settlement while making a case for a ceasefire to India's military campaign launched in response to Pakistan's declaration of war on India. While PM Gandhi's personal campaign to lobby the Western powers to manage the East Pakistan crisis had provided crucial breakthroughs for India, New Delhi was disheartened by the wait and watch approach of the international community, including the UN. It has been observed by Indian diplomats[102] that while UN Secretary General U. Thant had provided the UNSC with detailed reports regarding the humanitarian crisis in East Pakistan, he did not play a proactive role in advising the UNSC to resolve the crisis. Further, the UN response remained limited due to disagreement among the great powers during the Cold War.

India did not officially recognise Bangladesh until 6 December, despite pressure from the opposition parties and the Bangladeshi government-in-exile. As part of this policy, the military was asked not to move troops for early deployment in the western sector so that India was not seen as an aggressor. The military deployment was, thus, not completed until November 1971. However, on 3 December 1971, Pakistan launched a pre-emptive air strike from West Pakistan against Indian airfields. Though the air strike did little lasting damage to India, the attack was enough for PM Gandhi to declare war against Pakistan. While India's official narrative maintains that it was unwittingly drawn into the war, it was the months of preparation preceding the war that led to India's decisive victory, forcing Pakistan to surrender in less than 14 days. During the war, members of the Nixon administration continued to take diplomatic steps against India, publicly referring to India as the 'major aggressor' and supporting resolutions in the UN that called for an immediate ceasefire. The Soviet Union, however, blocked any decisive action being considered by the UNSC. Interestingly, France and England, both generally natural allies of the US, chose to join the Soviet Union in abstaining from voting on a UN resolution calling for an immediate ceasefire, reflecting a win for Indian diplomacy for the cause of Bangladesh.

With the fall of Dhaka, India's Army Chief, General Sam Manekshaw, broadcasted repeatedly calls for surrender, emphasising that Pakistan's prisoners of war (POWs) would be treated honourably under the Geneva Conventions. According to historians, many Indian officials felt that Pakistani troops would probably fare better if they surrendered to Indian soldiers rather than to the Mukti Bahini. Bass quotes Haskar ordering Indian diplomats to drive home to Bangladeshi leaders the need for mercy:

> they should say that they have been victims of such bloodshed and would not wish to spill any blood and deal with their opponents with humanity as a civilised State. Bangladesh is emerging as a State in the family of nations. Their representatives have everything to gain by appearing dignified, calm, and self-possessed.[103]

After reading the warning from the UN official in Dacca, Haksar instructed General Manekshaw, the defence ministry and other outlets to declare 'that Indian Armed Forces will not resort to the barbarism of Pakistan Armed Forces, that everybody who peacefully surrenders will be treated with respect and his life safeguarded.'[104]

Finally, narratives in India often question if PM Gandhi squandered an opportunity to resolve the Kashmir question when she agreed to release all 93,000 Pakistani POWs, as per the Shimla Agreement. As one of Indira Gandhi's confidantes disclosed: 'her biggest worry after the surrender of Pakistan in 1971 was the safety of Mujibur Rahman. The release of Pakistani POWs was the price Zulfiqar Ali Bhutto (and the ISI) extracted for the safe return of the Bangladeshi leader.'[105] In fact, new memoirs reveal that Pakistan delayed asking for POWs to keep the Indians from using them as a bargaining chip for settling Kashmir. However, in the Indian narrative, this was never the mandate. New Delhi understood that attacking West Pakistan would diminish the international support India had for dealing with the refugee crisis and would leave India dependent on the Soviet Union for military assistance in the event of any Chinese or American involvement. Gandhi was not willing to squander India's political capital or its reputation as a leader in the non-aligned movement.

On 27 December 1971, *Time* magazine stated: 'Islamabad was the principal looser in the outcome of war. But there were two others as well. One was the UN and the other was Washington, who appeared wholeheartedly committed to the Pakistan dictator.'[106] Many outside observers were convinced that Bangladesh would become an Indian 'protectorate', and those same observers were quite surprised that all Indian forces had left Bangladesh well before Independence Day on 26 March 1972.

1971: The First Global Media War, Power of Public Diplomacy[107]

The 1971 war, in many ways, was a key marker of media influence, which played out in the wider canvas of globalisation and the rise of humanitarianism as a transnational cause in the 1970s, right after the Vietnam war. For the West especially, the genocide played out in the frames of race and became the centrepiece for 9 p.m. news. The British Broadcasting Corporation (BBC) and the Columbia Broadcasting System (CBS) camerapersons were in the region, capturing scenes of the tragedy. Television cameras entered into refugee camps; documentary filmmakers trailed US Senator Edward Kennedy on his fact-finding mission; guerilla activism for the cause of Bangladesh rose in the West; and several crusading journalists burst into the spotlight.

Reporters covering the conflict included Sydney Schanberg (*The New York Times*; won Pulitzer for his 1971 reporting); Tad Szulc (*The New York Times*); John Chancellor (*NBC News*); and Jack Anderson (*The Washington Post*; won Pulitzer for his reporting on Nixon's handling of the crisis). The coverage by Anderson, dubbed 'The Anderson Papers', brought out the disconnect between public White House statements and secret meetings after the war broke out between India and Pakistan. While Nixon informed leaders of Congressional groups that the administration planned to be 'even handed in the dispute', secret memos obtained by Anderson proved the opposite. Kissinger, in these conversations, confirmed the tilt towards Pakistan and was quoted as trying to find ways to arm Pakistan despite an embargo. Worse was the revelation that Nixon had secretly ordered the nuclear-operated *USS Enterprise* into the Bay of Bengal to confront Indian forces. A tense standoff between the *Enterprise* and a Russian frigate, which could have escalated into another Cuba-style nuclear standoff, was revealed by Anderson who lambasted Nixon over his handling of the Bangladesh crisis: 'Now you don't like to say the President lied, but there is no other word for it. The President lied. It was an outrageous lie. It was deliberate and it was in violation of the US constitution.'[108] Historians say these public battles saw the emergence of the crusading American journalist and hero figure.

'The Concert for Bangladesh' was another major turning point in the development of Western awareness for Bangladesh's plight. It was organised by musicians George Harrison and Ravi Shankar (Indian sitar maestro) in New York in August 1971, and raised global awareness as well as funds for Bangladeshi refugees. By invoking the name of 'Bangladesh' instead of 'East Pakistan' or 'East Bengal', Ravi Shankar and George Harrison openly declared their political sympathies. By the time the concert had finished, Bangladesh had captured global public's attention. High profile performers such as Ringo Starr, Bob Dylan and Eric Clapton participated ensuring public attention towards Bangladesh's plight. The impact of the event was unparalleled. It made print and television headlines and the record of the concert performance became a top seller. In fact historians recount how the original cover of the album, which featured the photograph of an emaciated child sitting in front of an empty plate, became an iconic image of Bangladesh.[109] The notes accompanying the album held the Pakistan Army responsible for 'a deliberate reign of terror' and for perpetrating 'undoubtedly the greatest atrocity since Hitler's extermination of the Jews'.[110] Meanwhile, the Pakistan government warned all its embassies and missions that the concert album 'contains hostile propaganda against Pakistan' and that they should work their contacts 'to have this excluded from broadcasts'.[111]

Consequently, Bangladesh used public diplomacy[112] to influence the world opinion to get more support. The newspaper industry suffered a tremendous blow during the Bangladesh Liberation War as the Pakistani Army burnt down the offices and presses of three of its leading daily newspapers, *Dainik Ittefaq*, *The People* and *Sangbad*, all of which were published from Dhaka. Thus, radio emerged as a powerful voice for the people of Bangladesh and *Swadhin Bangla Betar Kendro*—a radio station—became the symbol of this resistance. By broadcasting the independence declaration, patriotic wartime songs and propaganda campaigns, it raised the morale of the population, serving a pivotal role in Bangladesh's struggle for independence. Public diplomacy was also effectively used by the East Pakistanis who were students in different universities abroad. Nobel laureate and Grameen Bank founder Muhammad Yunus was one of them. He mentioned in his memoirs that he garnered support for the Bangladesh cause through an interview with a local television channel in Tennessee in the US, also emphasising the important role played by the Indian Embassy as a facilitator and ally in Bangladesh's struggle for independence.[113]

Within weeks of the military crackdown, Britain emerged as the focal point for efforts to rally international public opinion on behalf of Bangladesh. The Bangladeshi diaspora, along with humanitarian organisations, played a critical role in publicising the cause of Bangladesh and in mobilising political opinion against Pakistan's government. Action Bangladesh was created by young, international and active Britons to raise funds for victims of war. Similarly, Oxfam provided relief and aid during the crisis in Bangladesh. Interestingly, Oxfam's campaign climaxed with the publication of an unusual document, titled 'Testimony of Sixty', which contained short statements and articles by 50 prominent public figures, including Mother Teresa and Senator Edward Kennedy.

In the interim, India made coordinated efforts to make the world media aware of the plight of refugees from Bangladesh and its compulsions. Further, as pointed out by Ambassador Shivshankar Menon, former Indian Foreign Secretary and National Security Advisor, the now routine 4 p.m. daily briefing by the Ministry of External Affairs spokesperson actually began in 1971. 'The use of publicity to get public opinion on our side, using television to spread pictures, made it impossible for the other governments such as UK and France to support the US and Pakistan in consortium meetings,' he said, calling 1971 'the first media war on global scale'.[114]

A recent book also revealed how the despatches written for All India Radio by distinguished broadcaster and commentator, U.L. Baruah, then Director of the External Services Division, were responsible for conveying India's perception of those extraordinary events to audiences outside India—especially in Pakistan.[115] The despatches were broadcast on All India Radio's services in Urdu, Punjabi, Sindhi, Pushto and Bengali, and provided a fascinating peek into the battle of narratives that unfolded alongside the battles on the ground. Aired from May to July 1971, Baruah's despatches sought to puncture wide censorship and disinformation by the Pakistani military regime. A recurrent theme in these broadcasts was undermining the regime's claim that the crisis had been stoked by India or that Bangladeshi fighters were Indian personnel or agents. Clearly, India's cause found support—the report by Pakistan's Hamidoor Commission on the 1971 crisis revealed that 'Indian propaganda had been so successful' that all efforts by the Pakistani military regime to defuse the situation in East Pakistan had left the world unimpressed.[116]

Conclusion: Nations, Memories and Subcontinental Politics

The 1971 war redefined subcontinental geographies, ideologies and politics, irrespective of which national prism it is viewed from. In the India–Pakistan relationship itself, it manifested in the nuclearisation of both the countries; Islamabad's sponsorship of cross-border terrorism; a proxy war over many decades in Kashmir; conflicts over Siachen Glacier and Kargil; and unabated friction over the Line of Control. Spilling over into the subcontinent, the war has had significant impact on regional and global geopolitics, even if the great power politics of the time seem transposed today.

1. **'The hesitations of history'**: When PM Modi spoke of India–US strategic partnership overcoming 'hesitations of history,'[117] he was referring to the legacy of 1971 which ingrained in India a distrust of the US, which, despite a complete rehaul in the relationship today, continues to linger and colour public imagination from time to time. Even today, older generations of strategists who caution against the intensification of US–India relationship often point to the docking of *USS Enterprise* in the Bay of Bengal during 1971 as a reminder of its duplicity. Nixon and Kissinger, at the height of the Indo-Pak conflict, authorised the move of Task Force 74 from the 7th Fleet into the Bay of Bengal, to show China and Pakistan that the US stood by its allies. In their memoirs, they justified the move as an action to thwart India's plans to attack West Pakistan after its victory in the East. This was untrue as it has been well established that PM Gandhi had no such plans, knowing that international support for handling the refugee crisis was more crucial for India. The incident did not do anything to change the outcome of the war, but risked a nuclear clash with the Soviet Union and damaged US–India relations for years. Even today, for example, the public debate over India's purchase of S-400 missile systems from Russia and threat of US sanctions, despite the strengthening of ties, often seems an overhang of this incident. This is despite the redefining of China–Russia strategic relationship as well as the growth in Russia–Pakistan relationship.
2. **'Hyphenation/de-hyphenation of India–Pakistan'**: In many ways, the relationship of US with Pakistan and how it is viewed in New Delhi also bears the burden of 1971. The de-hyphenation of India and Pakistan from the strategic calculus of the US is credited with the transformation in the relationship today, but it took over a decade to materialise. For the US, 'de-hyphenation' translated into compartmentalisation of its relationship with India and Pakistan as distinct strands of policy. This would break past US approach of obsessive focus on the state of the Indo-Pak bilateral or its role in the relationship. Historical records going back to 1963 show attempts by the then Kennedy administration to prepare a guidance document on the partition of Kashmir and play the role of a moderator between India and Pakistan, which was decisively rejected by PM Nehru. India's consistent stand on Kashmir being a

bilateral issue and refusal to be clubbed with Pakistan in the US' South Asia policy has been a prickly issue in the ties. Back in 2009, weeks before the Obama administration appointed Richard Holbrooke as the Special Representative to Pakistan and Afghanistan, New Delhi sent an unequivocal message to the US that any move to include India, and by consequence Kashmir, in his brief would be 'unacceptable'.[118] Today, after the US exit from Afghanistan, Washington's assistance to bolster Taliban-run Afghanistan and Pakistan has raised concerns in New Delhi, with many arguing that to appease Pakistan, the Americans are, like in the past, chary of letting India play a bigger role in Afghanistan despite New Delhi being one of the biggest sponsors of development in Kabul.[119]

3. **'The strengthening of the China–Pakistan axis':** While Pakistan played an instrumental role in the rapprochement of US–China ties in 1971 at the cost of Indian interests, the China–Pakistan nexus had been growing from strength to strength from the 1950s. New Delhi has accused Pakistan of illegally ceding 5,180 sq km of disputed territory, known as the Shaksgam Valley, in the 'so-called Sino-Pak 1963 boundary agreement'.[120] The agreement laid the foundation of the Karakoram Highway, which was built jointly by the Chinese and Pakistani engineers in the 1970s. Pakistan, thus, not only compromised India's traditional frontier along the Kunlun range to the north-west of the Karakoram Pass but also enabled China to build a claim line eastwards along the Karakoram range in Ladakh. This collusion allowed China to claim the whole of Aksai Chin, in which it had no historical presence. The China–Pakistan Economic Corridor, which passes through Pakistan-occupied Kashmir and Gilgit-Baltistan under the Belt and Road project, is opposed by India on the same principle. The collusion has not just created a permanent threat for India having to confront a two-front war, it has extended to cover many other issues, including: China's support to Pakistan on the Kashmir dispute; thwarting India's attempts to isolate Pakistan on the issue of state-sponsored terrorism at the UNSC; clandestine development of Pakistan's nuclear programme; joint exercises developing interoperability in military relationship; and use of Pakistan to secure Chinese interests in the Afghan conundrum. China has also made it increasingly clear that it does not see India's rise as being in its interest. Thus, for China, 'Pakistan is a counterweight, or at least a stone tied to the ankle of India.'[121]
4. **'Victorious India, a net security provider for South Asia':** The victory

in the Indo-Pak War of 1971 gave a powerful boost to India's belief in its abilities and shifted the balance of power in its favour in the subcontinent. India continued to develop its military capabilities, including investing in nuclear weapons, believing it would compel China and Pakistan to change their hostile attitude towards India. The 1971 war emboldened New Delhi to signal its willingness to do whatever it would take to secure its periphery. India acted in its national interest, whenever necessary, to impose or thwart changes in its neighbourhood, with interventions in Mauritius, Maldives, Seychelles and Sri Lanka. It also continued to build and exercise significant political influence in Nepal, Bhutan and even Afghanistan. However, New Delhi's relationship with the subcontinent has had to face several roadblocks due to scarcity of resources as well as mismanagement of expectations. Today, with the subcontinent and the Indian Ocean Region becoming a theatre of geopolitical rivalry given Chinese interests and inroads, India is trying to reimagine its relationship with the neighbourhood beyond the proverbial sphere of influence, which many South Asian neighbours argue is not New Delhi's entitlement. As strategists have pointed out, 'India's task in the neighbourhood is more prosaic—that of managing the messy regional reality and striving for steady improvement in the regional dynamic',[122] which is easier said than done.

5. **'The burden of Southeast Asian Association for Regional Cooperation (SAARC), shadow wars with China':** For Pakistan, 1971 is a humiliating defeat where India wrangled a vivisection of its borders, extracting its revenge for the Partition. Islamabad has never been willing to accept New Delhi's claims to primacy in South Asia, and has constantly sought to internationalise its disputes with India. The disparity in economic and strategic weight has had the worst impact on South Asian regionalism. The main regional forum, the SAARC, has not had its annual summit since 2014, apart from a virtual meeting during the pandemic which Pakistan sat out of. The forum is held hostage by the acrimonious relationship. As a result, regional economic integration has suffered and brought no gains to people in the subcontinent. With China's economic wooing of the subcontinent, India has now to contend with the so-called 'China card' and considerable weight of Beijing's influence in its own backyard.

1971: A Subcontinent Remembers, Scars yet to Heal

Fifty years after the war, while India remembers the war as one of its most decisive military victories, in Bangladesh, the struggle to reconcile competing domestic political perspectives about 1971 continues. Experts suggest there are deep differences in the interpretation of the nation's history, the nature of its ideology and preferred ties with India and Pakistan. Delhi, it is argued, will be unwise to underestimate the depth of these domestic contestations or to take the relationship with Bangladesh for granted.

Since 2009, PM Sheikh Hasina has made war crime trials for those who collaborated with Pakistan one of her top priorities, setting a national war crimes court that has targeted Bangladeshi Islamist leaders. The horrors of 1971 are still a living memory for many Bangladeshis—and for many, a defining national trauma. Despite overtures to improve relations between Pakistan and Bangladesh, experts have warned that Pakistan must issue an apology for atrocities committed during liberation war for there to be any real progress. Pakistan, however, continues to remain in denial and has ensured its younger generations remember this as a war where India was the aggressor who instigated a brutal partition of their nation.

What Zakaria has written in her book about Dhaka's efforts to reclaim the liberation struggle as a people's movement needs to be understood sensitively:

> ...many of them (monuments) erected only recently as part of the effort to reteach and relearn history, stand to remind Bangladeshis that the liberation war was a people's war. Repeatedly, in my interactions with people, I was told that though India had helped gain freedom, it was not the reason the country was free. It was the people's effort, their struggles and their sacrifices that had made Bangladesh. There was resentment against Indians and Pakistanis treating the war as a bilateral issue, as if it was a fight between them, as if India had secured freedom or broken Pakistan—depending on one's perspective. Bangladeshis wanted to reclaim the war as a people's movement, as the people's liberation.[123]

It is not just the subcontinental scars that need healing, closure is yet to come for the complicated narratives of rape, killing and carnage suffered by women at the height of the 1971 war. Historians note that when the Pakistan Army surrendered in December 1971, the Indian Army and Mukti Bahini rescued many Bengali 'comfort' women from army barracks, but the scale of horrifying experiences of rape and resultant pregnancies was immense.[124] The new government of Sheikh Mujibur Rahman declared the title of 'birangona' (the valiant woman/war heroine) to reintegrate all victims of sexual violence into society, but it largely did not work. These women were ostracised and the burden of silence denied them justice. It is only in 2018 that five hardline Islamists were sentenced to death by a special Bangladeshi tribunal for committing crimes against humanity, including 'using rape as a weapon' when 'siding with the Pakistani troops in carrying out the genocide during the Liberation War in 1971'.[125] Within Bangladesh, there is a yearning that while these survivors are still alive, Bangladesh must honour their testimonies and have these crimes prosecuted in the war crimes tribunal.

Bangladesh's relationship with its past will have to be reconciled if the subcontinent really wants to move forward.

NOTES

1. Mark Dummett, 'Bangladesh War: The Article that Changed History', *BBC*, 16 December 2011, available at https://www.bbc.com/news/world-asia-16207201, accessed on 10 October 2021.
2. Ibid.
3. Ibid.
4. He wrote:

   The West Pakistani soldiers are not the only ones who have been killing in East Bengal, of course. On the night of March 25—and this I was allowed to report by the Pakistani censor—the Bengali troops and paramilitary units stationed in East Pakistan mutinied and attacked non-Bengalis with atrocious savagery. Thousands of families of unfortunate Muslims, many of them refugees from Bihar who chose Pakistan at the time of the partition riots in 1947 were mercilessly wiped out. Women were raped, or had their breasts torn out with specially fashioned knives. Children did not escape the horror: the lucky ones were killed with their parents; but many thousands of others must go through what life remains for them with eyes gouged out and limbs roughly amputated. More than 20,000 bodies of non-Bengalis have been found in the main towns, such as Chittagong, Khulna and Jessore.

   Excerpt accessed from *The Daily Star*'s republishing of the 1971 article by Anthony Mascarenhas, available at https://www.thedailystar.net/supplements/victory-day-special-2017/genocide-1505440, accessed on 10 October 2021.
5. Ibid.
6. For more, see Anam Zakaria, *1971: A People's History from Bangladesh, Pakistan and India*, Penguin Random House 2019; Srinath Raghavan, *1971: A Global History of the Creation of Bangladesh*, Cambridge, MA: Harvard University Press, 2013; and Gary J. Bass, *The Blood Telegram: Nixon, Kissinger and a Forgotten Genocide*, London: Hurst & Co., 2014.
7. Raghavan, n. 6, p. 10.
8. For more, see Anam Zakaria, *1971: A People's History from Bangladesh, Pakistan and India*, Penguin Random House, 2019; Srinath Raghavan, p. 10, *1971: A Global History of the Creation of Bangladesh*, Cambridge, MA: Harvard University Press, 2013; and Gary J. Bass, *The Blood Telegram: Nixon, Kissinger and a Forgotten Genocide*, London: Hurst & Co., 2014.
9. Urvashi Butalia, '"1971" Review: Twists in a Common History', *The Hindu*, 16 May 2020, available at https://www.thehindu.com/books/books-reviews/1971-review-twists-in-a-common-history/article31582248.ece, accessed on 20 October 2021.

10. Syed Badrul Ahsan, 'Narratives of a War across Frontiers', *Dhaka Tribune*, 8 February 2020, available at https://www.dhakatribune.com/magazine/arts-letters/2020/02/08/narratives-of-a-war-across-frontiers, accessed on 21 October 2021.
11. *The Events in East Pakistan 1971: A Legal Study*, Geneva: Secretariat of the International Commission of Jurists, 1972, available at https://www.icj.org/wp-content/uploads/1972/06/Bangladesh-events-East-Pakistan-1971-thematic-report-1972-eng.pdf, accessed on 21 October 2021.
12. Ibid.
13. M.M. Akash, 'Fulfilling the Promises of Liberation War: Pitfalls and Progress', *The Financial Express*, 15 December 2020, available at https://today.thefinancialexpress.com.bd/print/fulfilling-the-promises-of-liberation-war-pitfalls-and-progress-1608038570, accessed on 21 October 2021.
14. Ayyaz Gull, 'Development of Underdevelopment: The Case of East Pakistan 1947–1969', *Journal of the Punjab University Historical Society*, Vol. 28, No. 1, 2015, pp. 1–12.
15. Ibid.
16. G.W. Choudhury, *The Last Days of United Pakistan*, p. 15, cited in Ibid., p. 10.
17. Ibid. Gull has quoted an excerpt: 'Once Bhutto said, "above all, he (Ayub Khan) bore an intense prejudice against East Pakistan"', Ibid., note 48.
18. Ibid., p. 10.
19. Hamid Yousaf, *Pakistan in Search of Democracy 1947–77*, p. 91, cited in Ibid., p. 10.
20. Murtaza Haider, 'What they Never tell us about Ayub Khan's Regime', *Dawn*, 1 November 2016, available at https://www.dawn.com/news/1293604, accessed on 22 December 2021; and Hafsa Khawaja, 'The Caricatured Bengali & the Pakistan Army', *Jamhoor*, 19 December 2021, available at https://www.jamhoor.org/read/the-caricatured-bengali-amp-the-pakistan-army, accessed on 22 December 2021.
21. Khawaja, 'The Caricatured Bengali & the Pakistan Army', n. 20, accessed on 22 December 2021.
22. Ibid.
23. Ibid.
24. Tariq Mahmud, 'Grim December', *The Express Tribune*, 15 December 2016, available at https://tribune.com.pk/story/1264508/grim-december, accessed on 22 December 2021.
25. Ibid. Also see Raghavan, *1971: A Global History of the Creation of Bangladesh*, n. 6.
26. Mahmud, 'Grim December', n. 24.
27. Raghavan, *1971: A Global History of the Creation of Bangladesh*, n. 6, p. 21.
28. Ibid.
29. Naomi Hossain, 'The Perfect Storm and the Final Famine', *Himal Southasian*, 24 July 2015, available at https://www.himalmag.com/the-perfect-storm-and-the-final-famine/, accessed on 21 December 2021.
30. Ibid., also see Raghavan, *1971: A Global History of the Creation of Bangladesh*, n. 6, pp. 32–33.
31. Raghavan, *1971: A Global History of the Creation of Bangladesh*, n. 6, pp. 32–33.
32. Ibid.
33. Mahmud, 'Grim December', n. 24.
34. Syed Badrul Ahsan, '1971: Yahya, Bhutto and the fall of Pakistan', *Dhaka Tribune*, 16 December 2021, available at https://www.dhakatribune.com/bangladesh/2022/01/05/1971-yahya-bhutto-and-the-fall-of-pakistan, accessed on 22 October 2021.
35. Raghavan, *1971: A Global History of the Creation of Bangladesh*, n. 6, p. 36.
36. Ibid., p. 39.
37. 'Telegram 697: From the Consulate General in Dacca to the Department of State, Dacca,

March 10, 1971', in *Foreign Relations of the United States, 1969of Statehe. E-7: Documents on South Asia, 1969969of,* available at https://history.state.gov/historicaldocuments/frus1969-76ve07/d124, accessed on 22 October 2021.
38. Raghavan, *1971: A Global History of the Creation of Bangladesh*, n. 6, pp. 44–45.
39. Ibid., p. 45.
40. Ibid.
41. Syed Badrul Ahsan, 'March 1971: A State Collapses, a Republic Rises', *Dhaka Tribune*, 26 March 2021, available at https://www.dhakatribune.com/bangladesh/2021/03/26/march-1971-a-state-collapses-a-republic-rises, accessed on 22 December 2021.
42. Anthony Mascarenhas, 'Genocide', *The Daily Star*, 16 December 2017, available at https://www.thedailystar.net/supplements/victory-day-special-2017/genocide-1505440, accessed on 10 October 2021.
43. Zakaria, *1971: A People's History from Bangladesh, Pakistan and India*, n. 6, p. 66.
44. Ibid., p. 30.
45. Ibid., p. 28.
46. Ibid.
47. Ibid., p. 31.
48. Ibid., p. 39.
49. Ibid., p. 33. Zakaria states:
Firstly, by accentuating the existence of the Hindu population, with little focus on the number of Muslims in the region, children learn to 'otherize' East Pakistan; to treat it as alien, as a part that was never truly Pakistan. And then to project all Bengali Hindus as being pro-India is to swiftly cast away East Pakistanis as treacherous traitors, working behind Pakistan's back and in the interests of its enemy. It is no wonder that the popular perception in the country is that the break-up of East and West Pakistan happened because of India. Pakistan's own role is minimized. The language movement, the economic disparity, the social discrimination and other injustices meted out to the Bengalis, which will be discussed during the course of this book, may receive attention but only in the shadow of the 'India factor'. In fact, the language movement, which was one of the most significant causes of tension and conflict between the two wings is presented as the last reason for the growing resentment in East Pakistan in the textbook chapter. It is stated, almost as an afterthought.
50. Ibid., p. 34.
51. Ibid., p. 35.
52. Raghavan, *1971: A Global History of the Creation of Bangladesh*, n. 6, p. 51.
53. Syed Badrul Ahsan, 'Pakistan...Fifty Years after 1971', *Daily Sun*, 28 March 2021, available at https://www.daily-sun.com/printversion/details/543807/Pakistan—.-.-.-Fifty-Years-after-1971, accessed on 23 December 2021.
54. Ibid.
55. See the analysis of Ambassador Sami Khanus book, *Three Presidents and an Aide*, by Ashwani Sharma, 'Indo-Pak War 1971: An Insider's View of a Blundering Pakistan', *Financial Express*, 16 December 2021, available at https://www.financialexpress.com/defence/indo-pak-war-1971-an-insiders-view-of-a-blundering-pakistan/2381353/, accessed on 22 December 2021.
56. Ibid.
57. Raghavan, *1971: A Global History of the Creation of Bangladesh*, n. 6, p. 36.
58. Ibid., p. 38.
59. Ibid.
60. Sharma, 'Indo-Pak War 1971: An Insider's View of a Blundering Pakistan', n. 55.
61. See the analysis of Ambassador Sami Khanus book, *Three Presidents and an Aide*, by Ashwani

Sharma, 'Indo-Pak War 1971: An Insider's View of a Blundering Pakistan', *Financial Express*, 16 December 2021, available at https://www.financialexpress.com/defence/indo-pak-war-1971-an-insiders-view-of-a-blundering-pakistan/2381353/, accessed on 22 December 2021.

62. Zarak Khan Mehsud, 'The Forgotten Attempts to Whitewash 1971 Atrocities', *The Friday Times*, 5 September 2021, available at https://www.thefridaytimes.com/the-forgotten-attempts-to-whitewash-1971-atrocities/; also see Brigadier A.R. Siddiqi (Retd), *General Agha Mohammad Yahya Khan: The Rise & Fall of a Soldier, 1947–1971*, Karachi: Oxford University Press, 2021.
63. Mehsud, 'The Forgotten Attempts to Whitewash 1971 Atrocities', n. 62.
64. Ibid.
65. 'Foreign Secretary's Remarks at the Swarnim Vijay Varsh Conclave: 2021 on "Humanitarian, Political and Diplomatic Facets of the 1971 War"', 23 October 2021, available at https://mea.gov.in/Speeches-Statements.htm?dtl/34412/Foreign_Secretarys_Remarks_at_the_Swarnim_Vijay_Varsh_Conclave_2021_on_Humanitarian_Political_and_Diplomatic_ Facets_of_the_1971_War, accessed on 23 January 2022.
66. See Raghavan, *1971: A Global History of the Creation of Bangladesh*, n. 6, pp. 56–79; and Bass, *The Blood Telegram*, n. 6, pp. 283–321.
67. S.N. Prasad and U.P. Thapliyal, *The India–Pakistan War of 1971: A History*, New Delhi: Natraj Publishers, 2014, available at https://www.bharat-rakshak.com/archives/OfficialHistory/1971War/1971Chapter04.pdf, accessed on 23 January 2022.
68. See Raghavan, *1971: A Global History of the Creation of Bangladesh*, n. 6, pp. 56–57.
69. Ibid.
70. Ibid., p. 58.
71. Bass, *The Blood Telegram*, n. 6, p. 284.
72. Raghavan, *1971: A Global History of the Creation of Bangladesh*, n. 6, pp. 60–61.
73. Bass, *The Blood Telegram*, n. 6, p. 286.
74. Raghavan, *1971: A Global History of the Creation of Bangladesh*, n. 6, pp. 60–61.
75. Bass, *The Blood Telegram*, n. 6, p. 292.
76. Ibid.
77. Ibid., p. 289.
78. See Raghavan, *1971: A Global History of the Creation of Bangladesh*, n. 6, p. 74.
79. Ibid., pp. 69–70.
80. Bass, *The Blood Telegram*, n. 6, p. 321.
81. Raghavan, *1971: A Global History of the Creation of Bangladesh*, n. 6, p. 77.
82. Ibid.
83. For analysis, see Ibid., pp. 56–79; Bass, *The Blood Telegram*, n. 6, pp. 283–321; and 'Politico-Military Strategy for the 1971 Indo-Pak War: A Perspective', *Indian Defence Review*, 15 October 2021, available at http://www.indiandefencereview.com/news/politico-military-strategy-for-the-1971-indo-pak-war-a-perspective/, accessed on 23 January 2022.
84. Same as note 65.
85. 'Foreign Secretary's Remarks at the Swarnim Vijay Varsh Conclave: 2021 on "Humanitarian, Political and Diplomatic Facets of the 1971 War"', n. 65.
86. Ibid.
87. Bass, *The Blood Telegram*, n. 6, p. 423.
88. Prasad and Thapliyal, *The India-Pakistan War of 1971*, n. 67.
89. See the following excerpt from Bass, *The Blood Telegram*, p. 56:
Nixon was baffled and annoyed by Americans' popular sympathies for India, which he repeatedly described as a psychological disorder. He scorned a 'phobia' among some Americans that 'everything that India does is good, and everything Pakistan does is bad,' and once told the

military leader of Pakistan, 'There is a psychosis in this country about India.' The Americans who most liked India tended to be the ones that Nixon could not stand. India was widely seen as a State Department favorite, irritating the president. He recoiled from the country's mystical fascination to the hippie counterculture, which he despised. Henry Kissinger thought that Nixon saw Democratic 'obsequiousness toward India as a prime example of liberal soft headedness.'

90. Bass speaks of a mutual loathing between Nixon and Gandhi: 'He once said that "her father was just as bad as she is".' Ibid., p. 59.
91. 'Henry Kissinger's Book Titled White House Years Elicits Eager Anticipation', *India Today*, 22 January 2015, available at https://www.indiatoday.in/magazine/cover-story/story/19791015-indo-pak-crisis-why-america-tilted-towards-pakistan-822445-2014-02-22, accessed on 23 January 2022.
92. Foreign Relations of The United States, 1969–1976, Volume XI, South Asia Crisis, 1971, Telegram From the Consulate General in Dacca to the Department of State, Dacca, 6 April 1971, 0730Z, available at https://history.state.gov/historicaldocuments/frus1969-76v11/d19, accessed on 23 January 2022.
93. Bass, *The Blood Telegram*, n. 6, p. 35.
94. 'Henry Kissinger's Book Titled White House Years Elicits Eager Anticipation', n. 91.
95. Bass, *The Blood Telegram*, n. 6, p. 33.
96. See Ankit Agarwal, 'The United States and the Indo-Pakistani War of 1971: A Critical Inquiry', *Indian Journal of Asian Affairs*, Vols 27–28, Nos 1–2, 2014–15, pp. 21–42.
97. Ibid.
98. Ibid.
99. Zorawar Daulet Singh, 'Calling the U.S.'s Bluff in 1971', *The Hindu*, 19 December 2019, available at https://www.thehindu.com/opinion/op-ed/calling-the-uss-bluff-in-1971/article30341831.ece, accessed on 25 January 2022.
100. Ibid.
101. AG. Noorani, 'Brajesh Mishra & Mao's smile', *Frontline*, 16 March 2018, available at https://frontline.thehindu.com/books/brajesh-mishra-amp-maos-smile/article10085029.ece, accessed on 25 January 2022.
102. Asoke Mukerji, 'A Diplomatic Narrative of the 1971 War', *The Wire*, 18 December 2021, available at https://thewire.in/diplomacy/a-diplomatic-narrative-of-the-1971-war.
103. Bass, *The Blood Telegram*, n. 6, p. 810.
104. Bass, *The Blood Telegram*, n. 6, p. 478.
105. Sashanka S. Banerjee, 'The True Story of India's Decision to Release 93,000 Pakistani POWs After 1971 War', *The Wire*, 16 December 2021, available at https://thewire.in/history/the-untold-story-behind-indira-gandhis-decision-to-release-93000-pakistani-pows-after-the-bangladesh-war, accessed on 25 January 2022.
106. Amitabha Bhattacharya, 'Where Pakistan lost out to India in 1971', *The Statesman*, 28 April 2022, available at https://www.thestatesman.com/opinion/pakistan-lost-india-1971-1503065232.html, accessed on 22 June 2022.
107. This section has been culled out from the chapter in Raghavan, *1971: A Global History of the Creation of Bangladesh*, n. 6, pp. 131–54; and Naeem Mohaiemen, 'Accelerated Media and the 1971 Civil War in Bangladesh', *Economic and Political Weekly*, Vol. 43, No. 4, 2008, pp. 36–40.
108. Naeem Mohaiemen, 'Accelerated Media and the 1971 Civil War in Bangladesh', *Economic and Political Weekly*, Vol. 43, No. 4, 2008, p. 37.
109. Raghavan, *1971: A Global History of the Creation of Bangladesh*, n. 6, p. 145.

110. Ibid.
111. Ibid.
112. Anuttama Banerji, 'Bangladesh's Freedom wasn't All about Indian Military. Public Diplomacy Played a Huge Role', *The Print*, 26 March 2021, available at https://theprint.in/opinion/bangladeshs-freedom-wasnt-all-about-indian-military-public-diplomacy-played-a-huge-role/627354/, accessed on 25 January 2022.
113. Ibid.
114. 'Revisiting India's Role in the Bangladesh Liberation War', Centre for Social and Economic Progress (CSEP), 9 December 2021, available at https://csep.org/wp-content/uploads/2021/11/Revisiting-Indias-Role-in-the-Bangladesh-Liberation-War.pdf, accessed on 25 January 2022.
115. Syed Akbaruddin, 'How the AIR Commentaries Shaped Public Opinion during the Bangladesh War of Independence', *The Indian Express*, 29 August 2021, available at https://indianexpress.com/article/books-and-literature/how-the-air-commentaries-shaped-public-opinion-during-the-bangladesh-war-of-independence-7475776/, accessed on 25 January 2022.
116. 'Tragic events of 1971: Hamoodur Rahman Commission Report Excerpts of the Hamoodur Rahman Commission Report', published in Indian weekly magazine *India Today* and reproduced by Pakistan's *Dawn* newspaper. This commission of Inquiry was appointed by the President of Pakistan. See https://www.thedailystar.net/sites/default/files/upload-2014/freedomintheair/pdf/Hamoodur%20Rahman%20Commission%20Report_Dawn%20(1).pdf, accessed on 25 January 2022.
117. 'Modi says India, U.S. have overcome "the hesitations of history"', *pbs.org*, 8 June 2016, available at https://www.pbs.org/newshour/politics/watch-live-indian-pm-burnishes-his-standing-with-address-to-congress-at-11-a-m-et, accessed on 25 January 2022.
118. Mukund Padmanabhan, 'How India kept Kashmir out of U.S. Af-Pak Envoy's Brief', *The Hindu*, 21 May 2011, available at https://www.thehindu.com/news/the-india-cables/how-india-kept-kashmir-out-of-us-afpak-envoys-brief/article2035576.ece, accessed on 25 January 2022.
119. Sushant Sareen, 'The Strategic Disconnect between India and US has been Revealed by Afghanistan', 8 September 2021, available at https://www.news18.com/news/opinion/the-strategic-disconnect-between-india-and-us-has-been-revealed-by-afghanistan-4179290.html, accessed on 25 January 2022.
120. Ministry of Home Affairs, 'Border Disputes with Neighbouring Countries', available at https://mea.gov.in/Images/attach/ans22.pdf, accessed on 25 January 2022.
121. 'China's Rising Support for Pakistan, and their Collusion, may affect our Interests: Says Former NSA Shiv Shankar Menon', *The Times of India*, 25 April 2021, available at https://timesofindia.indiatimes.com/home/sunday-times/all-that-matters/chinas-rising-support-for-pakistan-and-their-collusion-may-affect-our-interests-says-former-nsa-shiv-shankar-menon/articleshowprint/82234601.cms?val=3728, accessed on 25 January 2022.
122. C. Raja Mohan, 'India and South Asia: The Elusive Sphere of Influence', ISAS Insights, 6 January 2022, available at https://www.isas.nus.edu.sg/papers/india-and-south-asia-the-elusive-sphere-of-influence/, accessed on 25 January 2022.
123. Zakaria, *1971: A People's History from Bangladesh, Pakistan and India*, n. 6, p. 57.
124. Mallarika Sinha Roy, 'The Women of 1971, on Either Side of the Bengal Border', *The Wire*, 19 February 2019, available at https://thewire.in/women/1971-bengal-violence-women-naxalbari, accessed 25 January 2022.
125. See https://www.ndtv.com/world-news/5-men-awarded-death-sentence-in-bangladesh-for-1971-war-crimes-1899698, accessed on 25 January 2022.

Index

*